MW01252765

The International Monetary Fund and Latin America

The
International Monetary Fund
and Latin America

THE ARGENTINE PUZZLE IN CONTEXT

CLAUDIA KEDAR

TEMPLE UNIVERSITY PRESS
Philadelphia

GUELPH HUMBER LIBRARY
205 Humber College Blvd
Toronto, ON   M9W 5L7

TEMPLE UNIVERSITY PRESS
Philadelphia, Pennsylvania 19122
www.temple.edu/tempress

Copyright © 2013 by Temple University
All rights reserved
Published 2013

Library of Congress Cataloging-in-Publication Data

Kedar, Claudia, 1968–
    The International Monetary Fund and Latin America : the Argentine puzzle in context /
Claudia Kedar.
        p.   cm.
    Includes bibliographical references and index.
    ISBN 978-1-4399-0909-6 (cloth : alk. paper)
    ISBN 978-1-4399-0911-9 (e-book)
    1. International Monetary Fund—Argentina.   2. Financial crises—Argentina—History.
3. Debts, External—Argentina.   4. Argentina—Foreign economic relations.   5. Argentina—
Economic policy.   I. Title.

    HC175.K43 2013
    332.1'520982—dc23   2012017782

♾ The paper used in this publication meets the requirements of the American National Standard
for Information Sciences—Permanence of Paper for Printed Library Materials, ANSI Z39.48-1992

Printed in the United States of America

2 4 6 8 9 7 5 3 1

For Sandy, with all my love

Contents

Acknowledgments

This book is the result of many years of exploring and analyzing the International Monetary Fund (IMF), one of the most central and polemical players in the current global economy. During those years, I have been fortunate to receive invaluable feedback, counsel, and support from friends and colleagues in Israel (my country of residence), Argentina (my country of origin), and the United States (the country in which the IMF is located and in which I spent some of my postdoctoral years at the University of Michigan). I owe a huge debt of gratitude to all of them.

Because several parts of this book are a significantly revised and expanded version of my doctoral dissertation at the Graduate School of Historical Studies, Tel-Aviv University, much of my intellectual debt is to my main supervisor, Raanan Rein, who helped me deepen my understanding of Argentina's history. Over the years, Raanan has always been ready to give me needed guidance, not only about my research, but also about the best way to become a scholar.

I am grateful to two friends and outstanding historians, Jeffrey Lesser and James N. Green. Jeff is among the first people I contact every time I face an "academic" dilemma. I deeply appreciate his understanding and optimism, his willingness to answer in detail my (too) numerous questions, and his readiness to read my work. My dear friend Jim generously invested precious time in listening to me and reading my manuscript from cover to cover. He always came back to me with challenging questions, criticism, and recommendations. Jim's friendship and support has been crucial in the completion of this book. I am highly indebted to Arie Kacowicz, my mentor and friend at the Hebrew University of Jerusalem. During the past few years, Arie has provided me with smart and realistic advice and has helped me to feel at home at the university. Most important, he encouraged me to embark on a socialization process through which I became more familiar with questions, concepts, and theories from the area of international relations. I have no doubt that the analytical framework of this book, which is based on the idea of the "routine of dependency," reflects the impact that process had on my way of understanding asymmetrical relations, especially those between the IMF and its Latin American member states.

Many friends and colleagues have given me extremely helpful suggestions, as well as intellectual, moral, and emotional support, through many months of writing this book. Howard Stein convinced me to expand the focus of my work and manuscript from "just" IMF–Argentina relations to IMF–Latin American relations. He raised this brilliant idea as I began to teach in the World History Program at the Hebrew University, which made an idea that might have sounded crazy to me not long ago—that is, shifting from the national to the regional level or, perhaps, from a micro- to a macro-history—suddenly seem logical and wise. I am particularly grateful to Eduardo Elena, Ruth Fine, Moshe Hirsch, Leonardo Leiderman, Patty Mullally, Ron Robin, Richard Turits, and Yfaat Weiss, who in different ways and at different times all supported this project. Vera S. Candiani, Ronald H. Chilcote, Mark Healey, and Peter Smith read previous and partial versions of the manuscript. Their insights and suggestions had helped me shape and improve the structure and scope of the book. Orit Friedland did a wonderful job of translating and editing parts of the manuscript. I am also grateful to the members of the Centro de Estudios Económicos de la Empresa y el Desarrollo, University of Buenos Aires—particularly to Raúl García Heras. Of course, I am solely responsible for any remaining flaws.

I thank the following institutions for hosting and supporting me at different stages of my research and writing: the Sverdlin Institute for Latin American History and Culture, Tel-Aviv University; the Center for Latin American and Caribbean Studies, University of Michigan; and the Leonard Davis Institute for International Relations, Department of International Relations, and Department of Romance and Latin American Studies, the Hebrew University of Jerusalem. The Lady Davis Postdoctoral Fellowship I was awarded in the 2010–2011 academic years allowed me to dedicate time to the manuscript and fund one more research trip to Washington, DC. The Sverdlin Institute and the Faculty of the Humanities at the Hebrew University of Jerusalem generously helped finance the translation and editing of the manuscript.

I also extend warm thanks to the staff of the IMF Archives, especially to Premela Isaac and Jean Marcouyeux, who assisted me both professionally and generously. Thanks also to the staff of the Archives and Library of the Banco Central de la República Argentina and of the Library of the Universidad Torcuato Di Tella in Buenos Aires. I thank the staff of the Instituto Gino Germani at the University of Buenos Aires for giving me access to their incredible and comprehensive Oral History Project.

I am grateful for the help and professionalism of the staff of Temple University Press and especially to its director and my editor, Alex Holzman. I acknowledge the three anonymous readers provided by the press for their thoughtful insights and recommendations. There are rumors that publishing a book can be a nightmare, but working with Temple University Press has been a pleasure. I feel that I have learned a lot about what it means to turn a raw manuscript into a book.

I thank my parents, Frida and Aníbal Niemetz, and my brother Guillermo for their interest and support and for making me purchase, back in 2002, the Spanish version of Joseph Stiglitz's *Globalization and Its Discontent*. Who could have imagined that Stiglitz's book—which was sold in every bookstore and newsstand in Buenos Aires—would lead me to write a book of my own on the IMF? I am highly indebted to my in-laws, Ruthie and Paul Kedar, for their amazing intellectual curiosity and for their ongoing support and encouragement.

Finally, I dedicate this book to Sandy (Alexandre) Kedar, love of my life and father of our wonderful children Michal and Yoav, the youngest experts on the IMF on earth. I have no words to express how fortunate and grateful I am to have Sandy (another IMF expert by now) by my side and with me. Sandy's love and unconditional and permanent support have indeed made this book possible.

Introduction

To understand what happened in Argentina we need to look to the economic reforms that nearly all Latin America undertook in the '80s. Countries emerging from years of poverty and dictatorship were told that democracy and the markets would bring unprecedented prosperity. And in some countries, such as Mexico, the rich few have benefited. More broadly, though, economic performance has been dismal, with growth little more than half of what it was in the 1950s, '60s and '70s. Disillusionment with "reform"—neo-liberal style—has set in. Argentina's experience is being read: This is what happens to the A-plus student of the IMF. The disaster comes not from not listening to the IMF, but rather from listening [to it].[1]

The Argentine crisis of 2001 inevitably raises the question of how a country that until the 1930s was expected to join the list of the richest countries in the world ended up suffering such economic deterioration. Although Argentina may have made its own economic mistakes over the years, we must also look at the international economy in general, and at the International Monetary Fund (IMF), in particular to understand what went wrong. In effect, the crisis in 2001 took place as an already heavily indebted Argentina was following the IMF's advice to the letter. But Argentina was not the only country that experienced economic stagnation or worse while implementing painful austerity measures promoted by the IMF. Other Latin American countries also suffered a considerable decline in growth in the 1990s. Indeed, the acute recession that began in 2001 triggered what experts from the United Nations Economic Commission for Latin America and the Caribbean (ECLAC) termed the "lost half decade" for Latin America, a period characterized by declining growth rates, increasing poverty, and social inequality.[2]

Although most of the problems discussed here are common to many countries in the region, this book focuses mainly on Argentina's experience as the most comprehensive prism for understanding IMF–Latin American relations. As Joseph Stiglitz rightly indicates, no other country in the region tried harder to endear itself to the IMF; no other country was so applauded by the IMF; and no other economy experienced so traumatic a crisis as Argentina. But Argentina is a good case in point for political reasons, as well. Since the IMF's foundation in 1944, the various forms of regime that have existed in Argentina—including dictatorships and democracies, some populist, others conservative, liberal, reformist, or developmentalist—have prevailed in all of Latin America. The history of the relations between the IMF and the shifting Argentine administrations serves to illustrate (1) how every twist and turn in Latin American politics has (or has not) affected the IMF's modus operandi in the region; and (2) the countries' willingness to approach or confront the IMF, to continue to interact with it almost daily, or to interrupt interactions with this influential institution. To this mix must be added an ambivalent and often tense relationship with the United States as the strongest member state in the IMF since its establishment and the only one with de facto veto power. Argentina is thus an even more illuminating case than Brazil or Mexico, whose ties to Washington have been friendlier and significantly more stable.

To understand Latin America's lost half decade at the turn of the twenty-first century, it is not enough to look back at the "lost decade" of the 1980s. To appreciate fully not only *what* happened to one of the most promising economies of the region but, more important, *how* it happened, we must begin at the seminal historical moment in which the IMF and the World Bank were created: the Bretton Woods Conference of 1944 and the surprisingly neglected formative period of the IMF from the 1940s to the 1970s. The early and contemporary history of IMF–Latin American relations offers a window onto the formal and informal processes and patterns that were well under way in the 1980s and 1990s, when countries in the region fairly unanimously embarked on a series of neoliberal reforms promoted by the IMF and inspired by the Washington Consensus—the set of ten policies that the U.S. government, the IMF, and the World Bank believed were necessary elements of "first-stage policy reform" that developing countries should adopt to increase economic growth.

To weave together the story told in this book, I conducted extensive historical research in archives on three continents, including complete series of IMF documents that I had the fortune to be among the first researchers to access. The focus of this book is the relationship between the IMF and its "chronic" borrowers, a topic that to date has been dominated by social scientists. In contrast with the existing literature, which focuses almost exclusively on recent events, this book covers the full history of the relations between the parties. My goal in this study is to build a much needed bridge among history, international relations, political economy, and political science, with the historical narrative and empirical data at its center.

The Analytical Framework:
The Routine of Dependency

This book, which proposes an atypical and revisionist approach to understanding the IMF–Latin American relationship, illustrates unequivocally that the strictly economic aspects of the partnership (loans, stabilization and adjustment programs) are merely the tip of the iceberg. Developing under the surface is a multifaceted array of routine and almost ritual interactions that continues even when the countries are subject to no loan agreements with the IMF. These interactions include detailed weekly reports dispatched to the IMF's headquarters from the central banks of the borrowing countries; trips to Washington made by presidents and ministers; periodic IMF missions to Latin America; and, in some instances, the fixed presence of IMF officials in national central banks and ministries of economy. A large corpus of letters, memoranda, reports, and resolutions deposited at the U.S. National Archives and Records Administration, the British National Archives, the Archives of the Central Bank of Argentina, and the Argentine Ministry of Economy, along with recently declassified collections held in the IMF Archives in Washington, DC, reveals the inner workings of this mutual, though asymmetrical, relationship. I refer to this unexplored yet fundamental facet of the relationship between the IMF and Latin America—which constitutes a core component of the IMF's relations with each and every borrowing country, whether it is in Latin America, Africa, Asia, Eastern Europe, or, now, Europe (i.e., Greece)—as a "routine of dependency." This routine exists at varying levels over time and emerges as an integral component of the IMF's and the borrower's economic and political life.

I recognize that "dependency" may be a loaded term for some Latin Americanists. My concept of the routine of dependency represents an attempt to reflect the countless cyclical interactions that have been taking place routinely—day by day, year after year—between the IMF and a borrower country such as Argentina. The term "routine of dependency" seemed to be a natural fit for the concept of economic and finance ministers', central bank presidents', and their unstable and in some cases undertrained staffs' expending great time and effort to maintain routine interaction with highly qualified representatives of a solid, stable institution that has as one of its main goals an engagement in these complex interactions and mechanisms. Clearly, lender–borrower and creditor–debtor relations are not merely asymmetrical. They are power relations. They are dependency relations between economically, politically, and often professionally unequal parties that nevertheless are equally active and equally accountable for their actions. In effect, even poor countries can alter or interrupt the routine of dependency—a concept that has little in common with the determinism and pessimism of dependency theory.

That said, this book may serve as an invitation to rethink dependency theory, to reframe center–periphery relations in ways that are more in line with the current globalized economy. In that economy, multilateral institutions such as the IMF and the World Bank play the role that until recently was filled by only the most developed countries, and nations can considerably improve their economic positions (as have the so-called BRIC countries—Brazil, Russia, India and China).

In contrast with many scholarly works in which the IMF's borrowing states are presented as manipulable, passive victims of the IMF's neoliberal policies— or, alternatively, scholarly works in which the IMF is described as a scapegoat used by corrupt elites, interest groups, and governments to justify the questionable results of unpopular economic programs—this work emphasizes the political, economic, and bureaucratic motivations and constraints of all parties involved. Hence, it devotes attention to the rapid strengthening and evolution of the IMF, to the high level of political and economic instability in Latin America, and to the impact of the United States on what appear to be not only bilateral relations between the IMF and each of its borrowers but also a triangular IMF–Latin American–United States relationship.

In line with the emergent literature on the IMF as an organization that is controlled not only by its most powerful member states but also by a highly professional and homogeneous staff of economists—such as the groundbreaking works by Sarah Babb and Jeffrey Chwieroth[3]—this book advocates the need to better understand the far-reaching impact of the formal and informal interactions between members of the IMF staff and officials of the debtor countries. According to the findings that I present, the massive presence of IMF economists in borrowing member states has led to a process of socialization and internalization of common working norms and ideas, especially on the part of the borrowers. In this manner, and through the creation of professional and personal ties (or what the international relations literature usually refers to as an "epistemic community"), some of the most prominent officials in economic and finance ministries and at central banks provide the conditions for the IMF's growing and mutually condoned influence and intervention in the local sphere. Moreover, the IMF appears to be one of the few long-term constants in Latin American nations that have experienced economic, social, political, and institutional turmoil.

The conflictive IMF–Latin American relationship has attracted the attention of numerous economists and political scientists. Most of them have focused their attention on the loan agreements signed from the 1990s onward.[4] This interest in loans is understandable: Latin America has experienced serious debt crises in more than just the past few decades; in fact, the region's struggle to repay foreign debt is as old as the independent nations themselves. During the independence wars of the early nineteenth century, leaders in Latin America signed loan agreements with foreign creditors that were necessary to achieve political independence but that also engendered premature economic dependence. In 1824, the newly independent nations of Argentina, Mexico, and Peru, following similar steps taken by Colombia and Chile two years earlier, contracted their first loans with the British Barings Brothers Bank. Because most Latin American countries were already familiar with debt crises and defaults when the IMF launched its activities in the region, the signing of conditional loan accords was highly controversial among politicians, economists, and the public.

Few books have been published on the history of relations between the IMF and countries in Latin America. One by Jon V. Kofas focuses on the Colombian and Chilean cases, and one by Thomas Scheetz focuses on Peruvian–IMF relations.[5] Only three books have included the formative period of the ties between Argentina and the IMF: the first by Luigi Manzetti; the second, by Raúl García Heras; and the third, by Noemí Brenta (the last two in Spanish).[6] While significantly different from one another in scope and nature, these three books emphasize the Argentine perspective and focus on specific periods of the IMF's involvement in that nation.

In contrast to conventional approaches in the literature, this book presents the origins and evolution of Argentine–IMF ties as an example whose relevance transcends national boundaries. As historical evidence demonstrates, Argentina is one of many Latin American nations whose relationship with the IMF has been shaped, on one hand, by norms, policies, ideas, and practices designed by this multilateral organization, and on the other hand, by economic ills common to most Latin American nations (e.g., unfavorable terms of trade and balance-of-payments problems), similar economic strategies (e.g., import-substitution industrialization adopted in the 1930s, populist and expansionist policies of the 1940s and 1950s, and neoliberal models from the 1970s on), and pernicious, widespread political instability.

Irrefutably, the routine of dependency that is described here by systematically following the Argentine case reflects the IMF's patterns of interaction with other borrowers. This assertion derives not only from the notion that most Latin American debtors have experienced similar political and economic processes, but also from the fact that the working mechanisms that characterize Argentina's ties with the IMF are part and parcel of the institution's functioning. Indeed, IMF missions to member states all proceed the same way: a number of IMF economists serve as permanent residents in borrowing countries; the IMF Executive Board approves all loan arrangements; and all stand-by arrangements (SBAs) follow the same guidelines and include a clause that defines uniform monitoring processes. Indeed, Stiglitz gave a telling account of one of his missions as a senior World Bank official to conduct negotiations with a borrowing country. When all of the parties involved began to read the draft of the SBA the IMF had produced, they noticed that the name inserted in the document for the borrowing nation was that of another country, from another continent. This technical error, as Stiglitz noted, suggests that the IMF's agreements are based on a single template; in this instance, the technocrats had failed to cut and paste the name of the borrowing country into all of the relevant clauses.[7]

Certainly, the mechanisms that I gather under the umbrella of the routine of dependency are generally conducted by the same individuals. Thus, for instance, the head of the IMF's Western Hemisphere Department is responsible for relations with all countries in the region, and he and his staff negotiate with delegates from all of the Latin American nations. Jorge del Canto, who headed the Western Hemisphere Department from 1957 until 1977, was deeply involved in the IMF's interactions not only with Argentina but also with Brazil, Chile, and other neighboring nations. That is, the same members of the IMF bureaucratic apparatus perform the same routine actions time and again, based on the same instructions, rules, economic premises, and goals. There is little room to maneuver or innovate, and there is no time to tailor a different pattern of interaction to each of the 188 IMF member states. As the Argentine Claudio Loser, who led the Western Hemisphere Department from 1994 to 2002, noted, "I have always compared the IMF with three other structures that, like the IMF, are characterized by great cohesion and vertical discipline: the old Communist Party (I am not joking), the Vatican, and the military. Everything is pleasant, very structured. There is lot of tension, lots of work and satisfactions. But there is very little freedom of action."[8]

Outline of the Book

Since the real scope and meaning of the routine of dependency, both as an analytical tool and as a very concrete behind-the-scenes mechanism, can be better understood when we look at it over the long term, this book covers an expansive period of time. It opens with the planning of the Bretton Woods Conference in 1942 and ends with the repayment of debts to the IMF by several Latin American nations in 2005, making a final reference to more recent events.

While the chapters are structured around the relations between the IMF and Argentina as a window onto the inner workings of a phenomenon that is common to other countries, examples from other Latin American borrowers support critical events and insights. Indeed, as this book demonstrates, Latin American nations experience not only simultaneous cycles of populism, neoliberalism, or dictatorship but also simultaneous efforts to strengthen or weaken their interaction with the IMF. For instance, while the dictatorships of the 1970s in Argentina, Brazil, and Chile were friendly to the IMF, the current leftist (or "neopopulist") administrations of a large number of nations (including Argentina, Bolivia, Ecuador, Uruguay, and Venezuela) have adopted powerful anti-IMF stands. In other words, changing relationships with the IMF have reflected widespread trends in the region.

In keeping with the historical nature of this book, the chapters are organized chronologically, allowing the reader to follow the inception, entrenchment, and institutionalization of the routine of dependency year by year, step by step, loan by loan, and interaction by interaction. As my analysis reveals, the routine of dependency has not been exempt from friction and disagreements or from periods of decreased intensity. Interestingly, in most cases in which the work routine was altered, diminished interaction was initiated by Argentina. In effect, the IMF has been (sometimes overly) tolerant of and flexible toward Argentina and has made considerable efforts to keep the wheels of the routine of dependency in motion—efforts that are explicable, since the routine of dependency secures not only the IMF's permanent intervention on the local, regional, and global scenes but also the engagement, relevance, and influence of its staff.

Chapter 1 discusses the planning of the IMF and World Bank during World War II and emphasizes the marginal role that the United States and Britain assigned to Latin America in the design and management of both institutions. The U.S. decision to invite the Allied nations—including all of the Latin American countries except Argentina—to the Bretton Woods Conference illustrates that alignment with Washington has always been a precondition to gaining access to the alleged fruits of multilateralism. Through its analysis of the differential voting system of the IMF and World Bank, Chapter 1 explains the weak formal position that Latin American member states have held within the IMF, as the allocation of quotas confirms.

Chapter 2 covers the thus far neglected negotiations between Argentina and the Bretton Woods institutions during 1946–1955, or the first Perón era. It demonstrates that, contrary to the monolithic approach in the historiography, which describes the nationalist leader Juan D. Perón as the archenemy of the IMF and of U.S. hegemony in Latin America, Perón made significant and continual efforts to gain membership for Argentina in the Bretton Woods institutions. In addition, studying the relationship between Perón and the IMF provides an alternative platform for challenging broadly accepted premises about how the United States shapes the IMF's policies and decisions. Contrary to the usual assumptions made by scholars who adopt principal-agent theories or state-centered approaches, analysis of the Argentine case indicates that the IMF and the U.S. administration do not always have the same interests and goals: While the IMF was willing to expand the number of its member states by opening its doors to Peronist Argentina, for example, the United States was reluctant to approve the move. It is interesting to note that, at the time, the IMF had established a strong collaborative relationship with Getúlio Vargas, the populist but remarkably pro-United States president of Brazil. Chapter 2 ends with the overthrow of Perón in September 1955 and the acceptance of post-Peronist and dictatorial Argentina into the IMF and World Bank. Argentina's inclusion among the Bretton Woods institutions in 1956 is represented as an opportunity to increase Latin America's representation and influence within the management of both organizations.

Chapter 3 describes and defines the routine of dependency. The first loan agreement Argentina signed with the IMF, in 1958, and the subsequent implementation of a belt-tightening stabilization program become a window onto the broad range of monitoring activities stipulated in the loan agreements signed by borrowers in Latin America and elsewhere from the 1950s on. Chapter 3 maintains that these monitoring procedures paved the way for a long series of interactions between Argentine and IMF technocrats and high-ranking officials. These interactions, which took place with few local nuances in most of the IMF's borrowing countries, soon became fertile ground for the development of a socialization process through which local representatives and institutions internalized the standards, working norms, precepts, and ideas of the IMF, thus creating an epistemic community. As historical documents indicate, the socialization process was not just a byproduct of the lender–borrower relationship. It was also a central component of the new multilateralism and a reflection of the need or desire of key economists and politicians in Argentina and other countries to transform their governments into active players on the new multilateral economic scene.

Chapter 4 explores the political ups and downs that affected the routine of dependency from 1962 to 1972, one of the most unstable and turbulent decades in contemporary Argentine political history. The chapter shows that the routine of dependency was not always immune to the political crises that erupted in Argentina. Indeed, at times Argentina promoted what I call "temporary episodes of detachment" from the IMF. These episodes did not cause complete interruptions in the routine of dependency, but they did lead to decreases in its intensity—decreases that the IMF attempted to prevent. Chapter 4 focuses on, among other issues, the intriguing case of President Arturo Illia (1963–1966), whom numerous critics called (in my view, unfairly) a political "turtle." Illia, the leader of the Radical Cívic Union, was the first Argentine president to actively and deliberately interrupt the routine of dependency and resist the pressures exerted by the international financial community. Illia's autonomist position vis-à-vis the IMF has since been adopted by only two Peronist presidents: Néstor Kirchner in 2005 and now Cristina Fernández de Kirchner. At the beginning of his presidency, Raúl Alfonsín (1983–1989) intended to follow a similar autonomist path, but in the wake of a serious economic downturn, he finally signed a new loan agreement with the IMF.

Chapter 5 focuses on two stormy chapters of Argentina's history: the Peronism of the 1970s and the military dictatorship led by General Jorge Rafael Videla, which began with the coup of March 1976 and ended in 1983. An examination of the relations between late Peronist Argentina and the IMF sheds new light on the debates, doubts, and conflicts that interactions with the IMF triggered within the ruling party and government. In addition, it highlights the IMF's willingness to compromise in approving new loan agreements even when it seemed unlikely that the borrowing country would be able to repay its debts and fulfill the conditions of the loan. The IMF's flexibility toward Argentina represents a broader institutional attempt to keep the routine of dependency intact. As Chapter 5 illustrates, the dictatorial regimes in Argentina, along with those in Brazil and Chile, were eager to rehabilitate and further entrench themselves in their relationships with the IMF, which lent international legitimacy to illegitimate governments. The perceived honeymoon between the IMF and José Alfredo Martínez de Hoz, the economic minister during the cruelest dictatorship in Argentine history, is a symbol of the ideological alliance between two parties that supported the liberalization of Argentina's economy. The alliance between that neoliberal government and the IMF was not unique; the close ties between Augusto Pinochet's regime in Chile and the IMF is another case in point.

Chapter 6 examines the relationship between the IMF and its Latin American member states in the aftermath of the debt crisis that erupted in 1982 and during the lost decade—a period characterized by economic stagnation and inflation, on one hand, and by democratization around the region, on the other. Chapter 6 pays particular attention to the application of heterodox programs under President Raúl Alfonsín, as well as under his counterparts in Brazil and Peru. Then it turns to the double tenure of Carlos Saúl Menem (1989–1999), the poster child for neoliberalism, and the brief and in some ways tragic presidency of Fernando de la Rúa (1999–2001). The chapter concludes with Néstor Kirchner's term (2003–2007) and with the repayment of IMF loans by several debtors in 2005, signaling a shift in Latin America's relations with the IMF.

Finally, this book makes an empirical assessment of several key questions often raised by social scientists (and by citizens of debtor countries). One set of questions explores the true meaning of the economic neutrality that is the source of such pride for the IMF: Does the IMF really remain economically neutral in its dealings with its member states in general, and with its potentially unstable Latin American debtors in particular? How and why did essentially different Latin American regimes establish and promote their intense routine of dependency with the IMF? The other set of questions relates to the nature of the IMF itself; as the Argentine case reveals, there is considerable tension between two interrelated and complementary facets of the institution. On one hand, the IMF is a multilateral organization that is highly influenced by its strongest shareholders—in particular, the United States—leaving its decisions subject to political considerations. On the other hand, because the IMF is a well-established bureaucracy comprising a professional team of hundreds of economists who hold doctorates from the most renowned (and, for the most part, U.S.) universities that, over the years, has established its own goals, beliefs, norms, and interests, it is expected to act according to strict economic criteria. As this book demonstrates, the tensions between the two faces of the IMF coin are not always resolved in the same manner. How are they resolved? To find answers to these and other intriguing questions about IMF–borrower relations, we must put aside old truisms and dichotomies that were never tested empirically and follow the historical documents to the heart of the routine of dependency.

1

Multilateralism from the Margins

*Latin America and the
Founding of the IMF, 1942–1945*

In July 1944, as the battles of World War II continued to rage, representatives of forty-five countries met in Bretton Woods, New Hampshire, to forge a permanent mechanism of economic coordination among countries and avert a new crisis in the postwar era. The conference, almost exclusively a U.S. initiative and supported by a declining Britain, established the foundations for two international organizations: the IMF and the International Bank for Reconstruction and Development, better known as the World Bank. Although the United States invited all Latin American countries except Argentina to participate in the Bretton Woods Conference, the role they played in the new economic order was secondary.

This chapter focuses on the Bretton Woods Conference, described in the historiography as the cornerstone of the "new economic order." However significant the planning and establishment of the IMF is for understanding the relationship that evolved between the institution and its Latin American members, there has been no empirical examination of its early and formative stages, largely because the Bretton Woods Conference Collections in the IMF Archives have been closed to the public until very recently. The lack of empirical research on the IMF's formative years also seems to reflect the misleading assumption that the loan agreements signed with the IMF are the most crucial, if not the only component of the IMF's mission and activity vis-à-vis its clients. Consequently, almost nothing has been published on the IMF's involvement in the region before 1954, the year in which the IMF signed its first stand-by arrangement

Parts of this chapter appeared in my article "The Beginning of a Controversial Relationship: The IMF, the World Bank, and Argentina, 1943–1946," *Canadian Journal of Latin American and Caribbean Studies* 35, no. 69 (2010): 201–230.

with a Latin American nation (Peru).[1] This partial and fragmented analysis of
IMF–Latin American relations leaves important political questions unanswered,
including those related to the relatively minor involvement of Latin America in
the conference in 1944, as well as questions surrounding Argentina's incorporation into the IMF and the World Bank in September 1956, twelve years after the
institutions were established and ten years after all of the other countries in the
region had joined them.

This chapter analyzes the planning and early outcomes of the Bretton
Woods Conference from different though complementary angles. First, I examine what motivated the United States and Britain to embark on such an ambitious undertaking. Second, I look at the Bretton Woods Conference through the
eyes of the Latin American countries that were officially invited to send delegates to this international gathering. Third, and equally illuminating, I examine
the events from Argentina's unique perspective as the only Latin American
country to have been excluded from the foundational events of the IMF and
World Bank. That exclusion was predictable, I argue, and aimed not only to
block Argentina's access to the supposed benefits of the new multilateralism
but also to convey the unambiguous message that alignment with Washington's
policies was a precondition for financial assistance.

The creation of multilateral economic organizations committed to providing loans to their member states created great expectations among Latin American republics. Countries in the region had for some time been pressing for the
establishment of international institutions capable of backing their new development priorities. In 1933, Latin American nations proposed the formation of
an inter-American bank that could provide credit lines and mobilize capital to
improve the conditions of many countries negotiating foreign loans.[2] Moreover,
the economic impact of the World War I, the Great Depression, and World War
II caused serious disruptions to Latin America's traditional international markets and increased the conviction that an outward-looking structure had failed
to increase the region's autonomy. It was precisely this disillusionment with old
economic strategies that led to the promotion and diversification of industrialization and to the adoption of inward-looking models of development.[3] But
economic development demanded massive investments that local creditors and
investors were unable to fully provide, consequently increasing the need for
foreign financiers. At the same time, Latin American nations expected that the
Bretton Woods institutions would turn into a more convenient and less controversial option to exclusive reliance on U.S. capital.[4] For these reasons, Latin
American republics were strongly motivated to back the foundation of multilateral institutions in which they expected to have a say.

Latin America's optimism was further fueled by the fact that Harry Dexter
White, one of the main designers of the new institutions, had been deeply
involved with U.S. lending programs to Latin America in the late 1930s and

early 1940s, as well as with a draft proposal for an inter-American bank, which he had elaborated in close consultation with Latin American nations in the early 1940s.[5] In other words, the personal and intensive involvement of White in the planning process increased the hopes that the new institutions, and especially the proposed development bank, would be strongly committed to projects in peripheral countries.

Optimism quickly evaporated. As I show in the chapters that follow, the sums provided by the IMF and World Bank were never enough to counter the region's dependence on U.S. government and private capital. The main promoters of the new world order, as might be expected during wartime, gave much higher priority to Europe than to Latin America both at the conference in 1944 and in the management of the new institutions. In this respect, two different perceptions were at stake at Bretton Woods: Latin America, as well as China and India, insisted on a development focus in the Bretton Woods vision; Western Europe, by contrast, advocated reconstruction.[6]

The U.S. decision to exclude Argentina, a leading Latin American economy at the time, from the emerging multilateral economic system contributes to our understanding of some of the mechanisms through which the United States used the withholding of IMF and World Bank membership (or funds, in the case of member states) to exert pressure on countries that did not support its policies. In effect, this chapter demonstrates that Argentina's ongoing exclusion from the Bretton Woods institutions in their formative years should be understood as a consequence of its decision to remain neutral during the war and as a result of a long-standing and reciprocal enmity between Washington and Buenos Aires—a political enmity that was influenced by the fact that the two countries' economies were competitive.

The New World Order in the Making: Planning the Bretton Woods Conference

Since the Great Depression, the United States had been dedicating increasing efforts to creating a mechanism to coordinate world economic activity. The more prominent initiatives in this arena were the Tripartite Monetary Agreement of September 1936, the Atlantic Charter of August 1941, and the Mutual Aid Agreement of February 1942.[7]

These efforts notwithstanding, before the Bretton Woods Conference was held in 1944, the main protagonists in international economic initiatives were the liberal capitalist countries of Europe, with Great Britain, France, Belgium, the Netherlands, and Switzerland the first to become involved. Although the United States played a role in many of those initiatives, its participation was mostly technical. Despite the vulnerability of Latin American countries to external economic shocks, neither the United States nor Europe had invited them to take part in any of the agreements signed before 1944. Latin American countries also could expect no significant improvement in their status vis-à-vis Europe and the United States in terms of participating in future international economic enterprises. When the United States entered the war in late 1941, it decided it could no longer afford to help Latin America in its development efforts, especially if those efforts (particularly in the area of industrialization) potentially hampered the U.S. economy, as Washington perceived to be the case regarding Argentina.[8]

In broad terms, the United States remained isolationist and nationalist in economic affairs until 1939. The eruption of the war, however, marked its shift to internationalism. At the core of that shift was the belief not only that the postwar world needed to be planned in advance, but also that the United States would have to play a major role in international organizations, which would be established under its leadership. According to the new policy, President Franklin D. Roosevelt charged three powerful U.S. bodies with the task of planning the postwar world: the State Department, the Department of the Treasury, and the Board of Economic Warfare.[9] It should be noted that many of the key officials involved in the project—among them, the influential Secretary of State Cordell Hull and Secretary of the Treasury Henry Morgenthau Jr.—possessed an anti-Argentine perspective.

The United States, the main promoter of the planning efforts and the only country with enough financial reserves to ensure the functioning of new international institutions, quickly recruited Britain.[10] To better understand the meaning of Britain's partnership with the United States in planning international economic institutions—and its implications for Latin America in general and for Argentina in particular—one has to consider two facts. First, a certain level of tension existed during the war between the United States and Britain, which derived partly from vigorous economic competition. Britain had been the major trading partner of Latin America until World War I. During World War II, however, import shortages of raw materials and the exigencies of war production caused British exports to the region to collapse. At the same time, World War II further consolidated U.S. military, diplomatic, cultural, and economic ties with Latin America through trade, investment, technical assistance, and cooperation in industrial development.[11] Second, the relationship between Britain and Latin America—and especially between Britain and Argentina—substantially differed from the relations between the United States and its southern neighbors.[12] Whereas the U.S. and Argentine economies were competitive, the British and Argentine economies were complementary. Moreover, while Washington expected the countries of Latin America to follow its policies and declare war on the Axis; London did not have the same expectations. British–Argentine relations provide an interesting case in point: Britain was critical of Argentina's neutrality even as its shipping benefited from the protection that neutrality provided against German U-boats operating in Atlantic waters. This was crucial because Britain imported 40 percent of its meat from Argentina.

It is worth noting that neutrality also served long-term British goals, as membership in a Pan-American alliance might lead Argentina to become a U.S. client state. Indeed, Britain aspired to safeguard its investments in Latin America in general, and in Argentina in particular, and to further develop its trade ties with the region in the postwar era. As British Foreign Secretary Anthony Eden pointed out, Latin American countries would play an increasing role "as markets for our manufactures and as sources of the supplies of raw materials."[13] Thus, the maintenance of close relations with Latin American nations, as well as the removal of "bones of contention," would pave the way to increased British exports to the region.[14] It was precisely the existence of British interests in Latin America that could make Latin America's partnership in the planning process encouraging from a regional perspective. This was particularly true for Argentina, as during the 1930s Britain gave that nation a somehow preferential economic treatment.[15]

The critical role Britain played in the creation of the Bretton Woods institutions did not lead to any improvement in Latin America's status or in Argentina's chance to join those institutions. In this sense, the evidence appears to support those scholars who portray U.S.–British tensions over Latin America in general, and Argentina in particular, during the war as secondary.[16] As far as the Bretton Woods initiative is concerned, there seems to have been firm determination to subordinate conflict to cooperation. Britain's silence regarding Latin America's marginal role in the planning process, including Argentina's exclusion from it, was a sign of this determination.

Once the British had been recruited to the project, two plans began to take shape: one initiated by the United States and one by the British. Eventually, the proposal presented as the basis for discussion at Bretton Woods would emerge as a combination of the two plans.[17] The British plan was known as the Keynes Plan, named for its author, the well-known economist John Maynard Keynes. The plan, based on the establishment of an organization called the International Currency or Clearing Union, was simple: The central banks of member and non-member states would manage their accounts within a union and coordinate the exchange rates of their various currencies. In the event of an unfavorable balance of payments, the organization would permit overdraft facilities for member countries.[18] To a great extent, Keynes expected the union to function as an international supra-central bank, serving to coordinate among the central banks of different nations.[19] The main goal of his plan was to facilitate the spread of world trade without the obstructions of barriers and discriminatory practices.[20]

At first, Keynes did not indicate which nations were potential members of the union. The original version of his proposal divided countries into three categories: the United States and Britain (the founding members); member countries; and non-member countries. All three groups were eligible to receive different levels of benefits from the organization. In the final version, dated April 1943, Keynes determined that all of the countries in the United Nations would constitute the organization's original core members, while other countries would be invited to join later, under special terms.[21]

The author of the U.S. plan was Deputy Treasury Harry Dexter White. It started to take form in 1941, and in early 1942, at Morgenthau's request, White and his advisers completed what was known as the "Suggested Plan for a United Nations Stabilization Fund and a Bank for Reconstruction of the United and Associated Nations." In contrast to Keynes, White stressed not only the importance of the monetary aspects of the undertaking, but also the need for the physical and economic rehabilitation of Europe. White's dual approach, which soon dominated the planning process, found expression in a proposal to establish two different organizations: a "stabilization fund" and a "rehabilitation bank."[22] In a draft dated April 1942, White proposed that all members of the United Nations join the Fund, subject to conditions.[23] Overall, White's plan expanded the concept of multilateralism beyond its standard meaning at the time. It not only aimed to remove barriers to world trade but also expected that members would relinquish (at least partially) their economic sovereignty.[24]

An intensive process of transforming the Keynes and the White plans into one unified proposal began in August 1942. The process was tense, as the British and U.S. governments sought to protect their own national interests.[25] In addition, divergent views posed obstacles to agreement. The most important differences were between the British wartime cabinet's search for arrangements to secure full postwar employment and economic stabilization and the U.S. State Department's unalloyed free-trade position.[26]

With the aim of endowing the plan with international legitimacy, the United States first looked to gain the backing of its major allies in the war effort. On March 1, 1943, Morgenthau sent a letter to Hull informing him that "copies of the draft proposal for a Stabilization Fund had been given to the representatives in Washington of the Governments of the United Kingdom, China and Russia several weeks ago."[27] Then, to gain legitimacy beyond the major allies, Morgenthau appended to his letter to Hull "a list of countries that seem to [the U.S. Treasury] to be the appropriate ones to receive a copy of the [U.S.] draft proposal [and send expert opinions on it]." He concluded by remarking, "You will note that France and Argentina are not included in the list."[28] The exclusion of France is understandable: The country was occupied by the Nazis at the time, and of the major allies, only Britain recognized Free France, the French government in exile. The exclusion of Argentina, as will be explained in the next section, was a direct U.S. response to the country's long-standing neutrality.

It should be emphasized that Morgenthau asked Hull whether he wanted to alter the list of consulted nations in any way, and Hull apparently made no change. Furthermore, on March 2, Morgenthau received a report from the assistant secretary of state recommending that he not send the draft to Argentina.[29] Hull's acceptance of Morgenthau's list and the letter exchange between U.S. officials is indicative not only of Washington's anti-Argentina position at the time but also of the fact that both the U.S. Treasury and the State Department condemned Argentina's neutrality. On March 4, 1943, the United States sent the draft of the White plan to thirty-five countries, including all of the countries on the South American continent except Argentina.[30]

After the consulted countries' comments were received, the United States and Britain reached an agreement. The "Joint Statement of Experts on the Establishment of an International Monetary Fund," published on April 1944, contained a relatively detailed description of what later became the IMF and the World Bank and served as the platform for the Bretton Woods Conference. This seminal document was the result of negotiations carried out almost exclusively by Britain and the United States, as "the U.K. technical experts have insisted that we [U.S. officials] do not show even a preliminary draft of the Joint Statement to the technical experts of other countries until its publication has been agreed between us."[31] This is why Latin American republics received not the full text for comment but only brief summaries prior to its official publication.[32] Nevertheless, when the document was made public, the United States invited not only the Soviet Union and China, but also Brazil, Mexico, and Cuba, to join it in making the announcement. Moreover, the United States suggested that Britain do the same while informing the Dominions.[33]

The list of Latin American invitees to join the U.S. and Britain while making the announcement is intriguing. The inclusion of the Brazil is quite reasonable: Brazil's close economic, diplomatic, and military cooperation with Washington placed it as a favored South American ally.[34] In early 1942, Brazil permitted the United States to set up air bases in its territory in return for U.S. support in developing a steel industry. Brazil severed its diplomatic ties with Germany, Japan, and Italy at the American States Conference in Rio de Janeiro in January 1942; it also provided naval units and a combat fighter squadron and sent a division of 25,000 infantry soldiers to the Italian front.[35]

The participation of Mexico, the closest neighbor of the United States, is also comprehensible. Although Mexico initially attempted to remain neutral, the sinking of two of its tankers by German submarines in May 1942 persuaded the country to join the Allies. Mexico participated in the war mainly as a supplier of labor and raw materials to the United States. Despite the history of rivalry between the two nations, which includes the Mexican-American War (1846–1848) and a bitter clash over oil in the late 1930s, World War II marked an astonishing collaboration and an advance of U.S. influence in the country, mainly in the economy. In 1942, Mexico and the United States signed a series of agreements, including one with the Export-Import Bank, in which the U.S.

government supported the development of steel and tin mills, as well as of infra-structure for railroads and communications networks in Mexico.[36]

Cuba, at the time, was governed by the U.S.-supported dictator Fulgencio Batista. With its politics and economy already subordinated to U.S. interests, Cuba joined the Allies a day after the attack on Pearl Harbor in December 1941. The U.S. Naval Station at Guantánamo Bay served as an important base for protecting Allied shipping in the Caribbean. As we shall see, conferring advantaged positions to its major allies during the war, and to several additional states, soon emerged as a permanent U.S. strategy.

Yet the joint statement was essentially an unbalanced combination of the Keynes and the White plans.[37] Notwithstanding the predominance of White's proposal, the influence of Keynes's principles could not be denied. Although the joint proposal was a U.S. victory, it initially sparked strong opposition within the United States. Several journalists and academics (some of whom simulta-neously served as senior officials of New York banks) did not hesitate to assert that "Uncle Sam" would distribute U.S. taxpayers' money throughout the world without receiving anything in return.[38]

The joint statement revealed neither the names of the countries that would become founding members of the IMF and World Bank nor the requirements for joining at a later stage.[39] During 1943 and 1944, Argentina—the only Latin American nation that had turned a deaf ear to Washington's demands and remained neutral—was singled out by the United States, with the implicit approval of Britain, to be kept outside the circle of future members of the Bret-ton Woods institutions, along with enemy countries and others that had re-mained neutral during the war. But what was the real impact of Argentina's exclusion from the planning process? And more important, what was the sig-nificance of Latin America's inclusion in the Bretton Woods initiative?

Formally, the United States and Britain defined the Bretton Woods Confer-ence as a forum for the formulation of definite proposals for an International Monetary Fund and, probably, a Bank for Reconstruction and Development. In practice, however, neither London nor Washington was interested in letting such a large group of nations significantly alter the principles that constituted the nucleus of the joint statement. What London and Washington wanted in actual-ity was the blessing of other states. To reach that goal, the United States, acting as a "reluctant superpower," tolerated several limits on the exercise of its hege-monic power.[40] For instance, after sending the White Plan to the Allies in 1943, Washington invited a limited group of countries to a preliminary drafting con-ference that took place at Atlantic City, New Jersey, in June 1944. The task of the meeting was to discuss a number of pending issues that would be much harder (and less convenient) to debate within the framework of a crowded conference.

In addition to the United States, sixteen countries were represented at Atlantic City: Australia, Belgium, Brazil, Canada, Chile, China, Cuba, Czechoslovakia, France, Greece, India, Mexico, the Netherlands, Norway, the Soviet Union, and the United Kingdom.[41] While organizing this preliminary gathering, Washington's main priority was to please China and the Soviet Union—two major war Allies but also potential rivals. Washington did not just invite the Chinese and Soviets to Atlantic City; it also created the list of invitees in close consultation with them. Initially, the United States proposed including "the four major powers plus Canada, the Netherlands and Brazil," although it believed that just the four major powers could do a much more efficient job.[42] At the same time, efforts were made to avert potentially counterproductive resentment among the Latin American nations and the British Dominions—groups that expected some kind of preferential treatment from the United States and Britain, respectively.

Washington and London held serious discussions over which and how many states to invite to Atlantic City. In the case of Latin America, they first agreed to invite Brazil and Mexico. Later, when China demanded the inclusion of the Philippines, the U.S. Treasury Department "changed [its mind] about [a] drafting committee and now says that pressure to add probably Cuba and Chile will be irresistible since there are 21 Latin American countries."[43] It is important to note that the United States invited Chile at the last minute, without enthusiasm, likely as a reward for having joined the Allies in 1943 (leaving Argentina even more isolated) and safeguarding the copper supply that was so critical to the U.S. war effort. The British had no choice but to accept the addition, because "with [its] agreement to three Commonwealth and full European representation [the United States] felt there would have to be four from Latin America."[44]

Having four Latin American countries represented at Atlantic City did not significantly alter the balance of power that, since the onset of the proposed international accord, had been adverse to the region. Each of the four participating Latin American countries sent only one representative, compared with thirty from the United States and thirty from the European countries combined.[45] As if this numerical disadvantage were not enough, White appeased the British by predicting that the representatives of Cuba and Chile would "take little part."[46] Despite their relatively weak representation, though, it seems that the Latin American delegates at Atlantic City and at Bretton Woods used their previous collaboration with White to ensure that the planned World Bank would focus not only on reconstruction (as expected by the United States and Western Europe) but also on development (as Latin America, China, India, and the countries of southeastern Europe hoped).[47]

At the end of the Atlantic City gathering, the participants took a train together to New Hampshire. The Bretton Woods Conference, which according to Roosevelt's explicit instructions was not expected significantly to amend the Anglo-American proposal, opened on July 1, 1944.[48] In addition to the United States, Britain, the Soviet Union, China, and Canada, countries related to the

British Empire; European governments in exile; Allied countries in Asia, the Middle East and Africa; and all of the Latin American countries except Argentina attended. The conference ended on July 22 with the signing of the Articles of Agreement of the IMF and of the IBRD. It is important to note that the United States (and, to a lesser extent, Britain) had the prerogative to decide not only which countries should be excluded from the conference (neutrals and Axis) but also which countries would be included, and even enjoy a relatively privileged position, in the Bretton Woods initiative. The Latin American countries were not among the privileged nations, even though they constituted one of the largest groups at the conference. As Keynes opined: "Twenty-one countries have been invited which clearly have nothing to contribute and will merely encumber the ground, namely, Colombia, Costa Rica, Dominicana [sic], Ecuador, Salvador, Guatemala, Haiti, Honduras, Liberia, Nicaragua, Panama, Paraguay, Philippines, Venezuela, Peru, Uruguay, Ethiopia, Iceland, Iran, Iraq, Luxemburg. The most monstrous monkey-house assembled for years. To these perhaps must be added: Egypt, Chile and (in present circumstances) Yugo-Slavia."[49] Keynes's hierarchical attitude was common among British and U.S. leaders.

Thus, the Latin American nations invited to the conferences in Atlantic City and Bretton Woods were by no means prominent partners in the planning of the new economic order. I will now turn specifically to discussing the exclusion of Argentina, one of the strongest economies in the region at the time. This, I argue, provides a prism through which to analyze not only the high price of nonalignment with the United States, the new hegemonic power, but also the scope and nature of postwar multilateralism. It also reveals the weak position formally assigned to those countries of Latin America that, unlike Argentina, were among the original members of the IMF and World Bank.

Argentina's Exclusion from the Bretton Woods Conference

Relations between Washington and Buenos Aires have never been simple. Tensions between the two were manifest as early as the first Inter-American Conference, held in 1889. At the time, disagreement centered on issues related to regional trade and the growing role of the United States in Latin America.[50] Efforts made by Washington that aimed to improve relations with the country's southern neighbors, including the formulation of the "Good Neighbor Policy" in 1933 and the organizing of an Inter-American Conference in Buenos Aires in 1936, did not lead to any improvement in interactions.[51]

When war erupted in Europe in September 1939, the foreign ministers of all the American nations were united in their intention to maintain neutrality. At this point, the United States viewed Latin American neutrality not only as legitimate but also as desirable.[52] Tension between Argentina and the United States intensified in 1940, however, when Ramón S. Castillo, a supporter of neutrality, replaced the President Roberto M. Ortiz, a supporter of the Allies.[53] Discord deepened after the Japanese attacked Pearl Harbor and the United States entered the war, expecting solidarity from all countries in the hemisphere. When the foreign ministers of American countries met at the Rio de Janeiro Conference in January 1942, Washington's primary aim was to pass a resolution compelling all of the participants to sever diplomatic ties with the Axis.[54] Argentina and Chile, in contrast to Brazil and other nations, decided to remain neutral.[55]

During the last quarter of 1942, several factors, including a series of Allied victories in the Pacific and North Africa and the sinking of five Chilean merchant ships by German submarines, persuaded Chilean President Juan Antonio Ríos (1942–1946) to align his country with the rest of the Western Hemisphere. Chile severed its diplomatic ties with the Axis in January 1943. Argentina's decision to remain the only neutral country in the region irritated both Hull and Morgenthau, who recommended freezing all Argentine funds in the United States.[56] While Argentina's neutrality appears to have been the more moderate possible outcome of the clash among pro-Allied, pro-U.S., pro-British, pro-Axis, pro-Franco, and neutralist groups in Argentine society, official circles, and the military, the influence of economic factors cannot be denied.[57] Indeed, Argentina maintained its neutrality largely because it depended on trade with European markets and wanted to safeguard its relations with all of the European powers, as it expected trade would resume after the war.[58] It did not take the United States long to punish Argentina: In 1943, it stopped shipping weapons, heavy machinery, and oil-drilling equipment and terminated credit and other financial instruments that could assist Argentina in building an independent economy.[59]

The crisis in Argentine–U.S. relations hit a new low after the coup on June 4, 1943, that ousted the neutralist Castillo and put General Pedro Ramírez in his place. Three factions attempted to influence Ramírez: a pro-Allies group headed by Foreign Minister Segundo Storni; a pro-Axis group headed by Colonel Enrique González; and a faction dominated by General Juan Perón and Edelmiro Farrell.[60] Instead of supporting the more moderate groups within Argentina's new regime, Hull warned Buenos Aires that the United States would provide military aid to Argentina's neighbors and impose stiffer economic sanctions, including exclusion from the planning of the postwar world.

It is worth noting that while Argentina, as a neutral country with a conflictive relationship with the United States, should have assumed that it would not be invited to take part in the creation of multilateral organizations, it nevertheless worked toward participating in that process. On April 8, 1943, four days after the draft proposals for the Bretton Woods Conference were dispatched to the Allies, U.S. Ambassador to Argentina Norman Armour reported to Hull: "Exclusion of Argentina from invitation to [international] post-war food [of

May 1943] and monetary conferences [Bretton Woods] has caused a profound impression here. . . . One of my colleagues informs me that the Finance Minister [Carlos A. Acevedo] professed pained surprise that Argentina, one of the world's greatest grain and meat producing countries, should not have been invited to the food conference."[61]

In the same vein, certain figures of Argentina's economic elite argued that the country's exclusion from the planning of the postwar international economic institutions "clearly illustrates the intention of breaking us off from all of the important discussions relating to economic and other issues. This isolation will not only have serious implications for our country; it will also have a major impact on all future decisions in world affairs, as it is unthinkable that final decisions will be made without the participation of an importing and exporting country as important as Argentina."[62] Such reactions suggest that some influential economists and government officials in Argentina did not fully internalize their country's limited power in the international arena at the time. As Carlos Escudé has emphasized, since the beginning of the twentieth century, Argentines had been influenced by a "state sponsored indoctrination" that aimed to convince them that Argentina could not be pushed to the sidelines.[63] According to Escudé, the irrational manner in which Argentina managed its relations with the United States during the war was largely a product of this indoctrination. Moreover, as David Sheinin has pointed out, through 1943 "some [in Buenos Aires] still hoped that at the end of the war, Argentina might aspire again to regional economic, strategic, and diplomatic leadership, at the expense of the Americans."[64] This arrogant and somewhat unrealistic perception is crucial to understanding why almost no one in Argentina suspected that the country would have to wait more than a decade to be accepted as a member of the IMF and the World Bank.

Growing concern over the increasingly blatant exclusion led key government officials in Argentina to take concrete steps to clarify their desire to participate in the process. On April 16, 1943, Armour sent a telegram to Hull reporting that Argentine Economic Minister Federico Pinedo and Raúl Prebisch, president of the Central Bank, "among others, have requested information on Morgenthau's Stabilization Plan."[65] Armour also asked Hull to "airmail the text if available otherwise as much information as possible." A few hours later, Armour sent a second telegram to Hull, stating, "Pinedo obtained information from the British. However will still appreciate data requested."[66] The fact that Argentina obtained information from Britain—even though it is difficult to determine the amount and type of that information—supports the notion that the relatively central role of the British in the planning process could be perceived by Argentina as a potential remedy to its exclusion.

Hull did not respond to Armour's urgent telegrams until ten days later, on April 26. His message opened with the following statement: "On March 4, 1943,

Secretary Morgenthau addressed the following letter to the Ministers of Finance of the United Nations and to countries associated with them, including all the American Republics except (repeat except) Argentina."[67] Although Hull's letter included copies of White's and Keynes's draft proposals, he clearly indicated that the documents were "for his [Armour's] information only and not for any action."[68] Hull's instruction not to transmit the requested information to the Argentine policymakers signified a new escalation in the exclusion of Argentina.

By March 1943, Britain was fully aware that the United States was excluding Argentina from the planning process.[69] Britain, which apparently was not interested in an open confrontation with the United States over Argentina, did not attempt to persuade Washington to change its mind. Moreover, Britain's abstention on this specific issue appears to have stemmed from a conscious decision to exclude Argentina if it remained neutral.[70] As a British document on the "Argentine problem" reveals: "What one deprecates is that neutrality should become a kind of classic policy with [the] Argentinean Government, just as it has been for centuries with Switzerland. Here the only possibility is to try and show that isolated neutrality may indeed be possible [for] small States, but large ones with world commitments sooner or later have to pay the price of standing on the margin."[71]

One can also hypothesize that Britain had no special interest in facilitating Argentina's incorporation into the IMF and the World Bank. Indeed, it must be noted that the predominance of the United States within the new institutions was already evident as the planning process was launched. Consequently, Britain easily could have perceived membership in the Bretton Woods institutions as a way to strengthen financial and economic ties with Washington. Therefore, it is not unreasonable to interpret Britain's lack of intervention as a legitimate strategy aimed at keeping Argentina dependent on its bilateral ties with London and far from U.S. dominance.

On January 26, 1944, Ramírez finally severed Argentina's diplomatic relations with Germany. This step, however, did not satisfy the United States; at the same time, it deprived Ramírez of military support, leaving him no choice but to resign. On February 25, General Edelmiro Farrell replaced him. Washington decided to delay its recognition of Farrell's regime and asked London to join it in exerting pressure on Argentina, which London refused to do.[72] Britain did not regard Argentina as a threat and, as mentioned, was concerned about damaging its trade relations with as prominent a trade partner as Argentina.[73]

Farrell's conciliatory gestures did little to soften the hostile position of the United States. During May–June 1944, Washington was closer than ever to freezing Argentine accounts in the United States.[74] While Washington was considering its relations with Farrell's regime, preparations for the Bretton Woods Conference reached their height. At the time, some circles in Argentina still believed that the country would be invited to the conference. For instance, a local economic journal defiantly and arrogantly stated: "The market of Argentina is undoubtedly too important . . . for us to be left out of such talks."[75]

When the United States began assembling a list of invitees to the conference, it had to simultaneously address the tension generated by its attempts to institutionalize international economic organizations, its desire to unite all of the countries in the Americas under U.S. leadership, and its anti-Argentine position. The continuing deterioration in relations with the United States, from the Argentine perspective, gave Argentina no opportunity to believe it would participate in the conference.

On May 25, 1944, at President Roosevelt's instructions, Hull sent out the invitations to the conference. The next day, the White House released the text of the official invitation to the media.[76] The United States was not only hosting the conference; it was also exclusively responsible for compiling the invitation list.[77] Because of its participation in calculating the quotas of future members of the nascent institutions (which will be discussed in the next section), the British were able to learn well in advance that Argentina would not be invited. In effect, on May 4, 1944, the British Treasury prepared a table comparing the quotas projected by Keynes and White for the initial members of the Bretton Woods institutions—a table in which Argentina did not appear.[78] On May 15, the British Foreign Office sent the United States a meticulous analysis of the proposed quotas, making not even a single note of Argentina's absence.[79] Britain's silence at this stage was not surprising; it was merely a continuation of the policy of non-intervention adopted by London during the elaboration of the draft proposals in early 1943.

Invitations were addressed to the "countries constituting the United Nations and nations associated with them in war" and to the French Committee of National Liberation in Algeria.[80] The invitation stated: "The Government of the United States . . . is confident that others have been equally gratified by this evidence of the desire of the United Nations and the Nations associated with them in this war to cooperate in meeting post-war economic problems." Washington's greeting to invitees indicates, therefore, that the declaration of war on the Axis countries and unequivocal and unconditional support of the Allies were necessary preconditions for participating in the Bretton Woods Conference. Within this context, a neutral country such as Argentina had no chance to be included, and no distinction was made between Argentina and other countries that had also maintained neutrality during the war—including Ireland, Portugal, Spain, Sweden, Switzerland, and Turkey—and that likewise were not invited to the conference.[81] Enemy states, as expected, were also excluded from the event.

The conference, attended by 730 economists, legal experts, secretaries, translators, journalists, and others, ended on July 22, 1944. The official representatives attending the event were asked to return to their home countries and work

for the ratification of the agreements in their legislatures. It was similarly determined that the endorsement process had to be completed by July 31, 1945.[82] The
institutions born at Bretton Woods started functioning approximately two years
after the end of the conference and a year after the end of the war. The joint
opening session of the Board of Governors of the IMF and the World Bank was
held in Savannah, Georgia, on March 8, 1946.

Exclusion from the Bretton Woods Conference did not mark the end of
Argentina's attempts to become part of the privileged group of original IMF and
World Bank members. In contrast, Argentina perceived the period between the
end of the conference and the launching of the new institutions' activities in
1946 as a window of opportunity for improving its fortunes. In effect, Farrell
endeavored to reverse the situation and took significant steps to enable Argentina to join the new institutions. In light of the continuing deterioration of
U.S.–Argentine relations, however, Farrell faced an especially challenging task.
Indeed, it was not until April 9, 1945, ten months after the conference had
ended and almost two weeks after Argentina declared war on the Axis powers,
that the United States recognized Farrell's government.

In January 1946, two months before the launch of the new institutions and
a few days before the general elections in Argentina, Farrell began to take steps
that, in his opinion, could pave the way to being accepted into the IMF and
World Bank. The first was the approval of a decree of adherence to the Bretton
Woods principles.[83] The decree declared that although Argentina was not a
signatory to the Bretton Woods agreements, it would not remain indifferent to
international economic developments. "Whereas [Argentina] tends to cooperate with international organizations," it stated, "it adopts the conclusions of the
monetary and financial conference held in Bretton Woods in July 1944."[84]
According to the decree, the Foreign Ministry would "take the measures necessary to enable Argentina to join the Monetary Fund and the World Bank." Even
though the decree was not made public in Argentina, it was dispatched to the
IMF.[85]

This unambiguous statement was neither the last nor the least of Farrell's
efforts to achieve his goal. In early April 1946, Argentina attempted a new strategy: The ambassador to the United States consulted the State Department to
clarify the possibility of joining the IMF and the World Bank. The U.S. official
who handled the petition reported to the IMF: "I inquired whether the communication which is being sent by Argentina was in the nature of an inquiry as
to procedure or an application for membership and [I] was told that it was an
application for membership."[86] Nonetheless, this new initiative also failed to
provide Argentina with an entry pass into the new institutions.

In early May 1946, Harry Dexter White, now the senior U.S. representative
to the IMF, announced another Argentine endeavor to the U.S. media. According to White, the authorities in Buenos Aires had attempted to further clarify

what they would have to do to join the Bretton Woods institutions.[87] These insistent efforts, however, did not improve Argentina's chances of being accepted as a full member of the IMF and the World Bank. Washington remained intransigent.

In June 1946, Farrell was replaced by General Juan D. Perón. Both Perón and his running mate, Hortensio Quijano, enjoyed wide popular support and had easily won the presidential elections of February 24, 1946. As Argentina was unable to reach a membership agreement with the Bretton Woods institutions before Perón's inauguration, it became the new administration's turn to evaluate whether Argentina was ready and able to join the IMF and the World Bank. However, as will be shown in Chapter 2, Perón also failed to end Argentina's exclusion. The country did not become a member of either the IMF or the World Bank until September 1956.

Latin America's Marginal Role in the New Multilateral Institutions

The fact that the United States, with implicit approval from Britain, blocked Argentina's entry into the group of founding members of the Bretton Woods institutions had an impact that transcends national boundaries. The exclusion of one of the most promising Latin American economies at the time surely helped to further marginalize the region not only in the planning process, but also within the management of the new institutions.

The organizational structure of the IMF and the World Bank, which had adopted the same representation model, not only clearly reflected the Anglo-American hierarchical approach but was also aimed at preserving the member states' status as non-equal partners in the new global economic order. Indeed, the Bretton Woods institutions were the first international organizations that did away with the "one country–one vote" principle and introduced differential membership. Upon joining the IMF and the World Bank, each country is allocated a quota (or shareholding). In broad terms, the quota is the amount of money that a country pays as its capital subscription when it becomes a member. The quota is intended to reflect the relative size of each national economy and is based on several figures, including national income, international trade, and international reserves. It is calculated using a complex formula agreed to at the Bretton Woods Conference. The results are then subject to political considerations. In a nutshell, the larger a country's economy is in terms of output and the larger and more variable its trade is, the larger its quota tends to be.[88]

The quota is a key factor in the establishment and development of power relations within the IMF. It determines (1) the sum that each member state pays to the IMF when it joins; (2) the amount of money that the member state will be able to borrow (or purchase) from the IMF (up to 200 percent of its quota); and (3) the member state's voting power within the management of the institutions, with higher quotas bringing greater voting power.

The implications of the distribution of quotas and voting power are extremely important. At the top of the hierarchical structure of the IMF (and the World Bank) is the Board of Governors, in which all of the member states are equally represented by their ministers of finance or economy or by the president of the central bank. But the Board of Governors, the highest decision-making body of the Fund and of the Bank, normally meets only once a year. In practice, it delegates most of its authority to the Executive Board, making that body the most powerful and influential organ in both institutions.[89]

The Executive Board is in charge of the day-to-day business of the IMF, including, among other activities, elaborating policies and approving or disapproving loan arrangements. Executive Board members select the managing director, who in turn serves as the head of the Executive Board. In effect, the board's composition is designed to preserve the unequal distribution of power that the differential quota system of the Bretton Woods institutions so carefully constructs. At the time that the IMF's activities were launched, five executive directors were to be appointed by the five countries with the largest quotas—the United States, Britain, China, France, and India—an enviable concession to the top five member states.[90] Five additional directors were to be elected (as opposed to appointed) by all of the member states except the five most powerful—and except countries on the Western Hemisphere. The last two directors were to be elected by the American countries (except the United States). In 1946, two Latin American directors were elected: Francisco Alves dos Santos Filho of Brazil and Rodrigo Gómez of Mexico.[91]

One result of this system is that the vast majority of IMF member states are not directly represented on the Executive Board. It is important to note that since the 1950s, there has been a significant increase not only in the number of executive directors, but also in the voting power and composition of those representing the five strongest members. Today there are twenty-four executive directors, and only five of them are appointed (from, in decreasing order of strength, the United States, Japan, Germany, France, and Britain). The quotas of the Latin American countries, as shown in Table 1.1, have relegated them to non-influential positions. These complex considerations shed clearer light on the dilemmas raised by the exclusion of a still economically strong Argentina. Interestingly, immediately after Argentina became a member in 1956, the IMF had no choice but to accept Latin America's demands and add a third executive director from the region.[92] Based on the size of Argentina's quota at the time, which was equal to Brazil's, the third director was Argentine (Guillermo Corominas Segura).

TABLE 1.1   Current Voting Power—The "Big Ten" and Latin America

The "Big Ten" (in decreasing order)	Votes (% of total)	Latin American member states (samples)	Votes (% of total)
United States	16.78	Brazil	1.72
Japan	6.24	Mexico	1.47
Germany	5.82	Venezuela	1.09
United Kingdom and France	4.30 each	Argentina	0.87
		Chile	0.37
China	3.82	Colombia	0.34
Italy	3.16	Ecuador	0.15
Saudi Arabia	2.81	Bolivia	0.10
Canada	2.56	Haiti	0.06
Russia	2.39		

Source: Data from IMF official website: IMF Members' Quotas and Voting Power (http://www.imf.org/external/np/sec/memdir/members.aspx), consulted on July 10, 2011.

The allocation of quotas caused a serious impasse among the architects of the Bretton Woods institutions and has been a source of permanent tension between the IMF and its members. One of the first signs of the impasse appeared in the memorandum of a meeting of several officials of the U.S. Treasury Department held at White's office on June 2, 1943. "With respect to voting," it said, "a suggestion was made that as a unit the British Empire countries appropriately have 25 percent of the votes, the United States 25 percent, Russia 10 percent, the rest of Europe 20 percent, Latin America 10 percent and Far Eastern countries 10 percent."[93] The suggested 10 percent fairly reflected Latin America's place in the international economy at the time. For example, in 1946, Latin America's share of total world exports was 13.5 percent (while Argentina's share was 25.5 percent of Latin America's total exports; Brazil's share was 21.2 percent; Cuba's and Venezuela's shares were a bit more than 11 percent each; and Mexico's share was 6.9 percent).[94] However, the memo continued, "After discussion there was general agreement that while the result of such an allocation might be satisfactory it would be best to have an objective formula."[95] The use of the alleged objective formula and the political considerations to which its results were subjected created a situation in which Latin American countries' original quotas in fact reached just $494.5 million out of the total of $8.8 billion, or hardly more than 5 percent of the total.

The centrality of the quota system is crucial to understanding the conflict that confronted the delegates from Latin America and Europe at the Bretton Woods Conference. Both regions sought to have not only larger quotas but also more representatives on the influential Executive Boards of the IMF and World Bank. Latin American delegates at the conference insisted that if they were to

TABLE 1.2 Original Distribution of Quotas (in millions of US dollars)

	Quota		Quota
Australia	200	India	400
Belgium	225	Iran	25
Bolivia	10	Iraq	8
Brazil	150	Liberia	0.5
Canada	300	Luxembourg	10
Chile	50	Mexico	90
China	550	Netherlands	275
Colombia	50	New Zealand	50
Costa Rica	5	Nicaragua	2
Cuba	50	Norway	50
Czechoslovakia	125	Panama	0.5
Denmark	*	Paraguay	2
Dominican Republic	5	Peru	25
Ecuador	5	Philippine Commonwealth	15
Egypt	45	Poland	125
El Salvador	2.5	Union of South Africa	100
Ethiopia	6	USSR	1,200
France	450	United Kingdom	1,300
Greece	40	United States	2,750
Guatemala	5	Uruguay	15
Haiti	5	Venezuela	15
Honduras	2.5	Yugoslavia	60
Iceland	1		
		TOTAL	8,800

Source: The list of original quotas appears at: Horsefield, The International Monetary Fund 1945–1965, vol. 3, 210.

* The quota of Denmark was finally determined after the Danish Government has declared its readiness to sign the Bretton Woods Agreements but before formal signature took place.

"let an international fund fix their exchange rates to help stabilize weaker European currencies, they should get something real in return."[96] They also argued that their "strong position as creditor nations resulting from the acquisition of dollars and sterling balances during the war entitle[d] them to strong representation on the executive committee."[97] The resulting distribution of quotas, as can be seen in Table 1.2, left the Latin American countries almost without power or influence.

The allocation of quotas has always been a major point of criticism for the IMF. Only when the latest revision of quotas was completed in November 2010 did Brazil become the first Latin American country ever to join the advantaged "big ten," with the rest of Latin America lagging far behind. (This change was scheduled to enter into effect during 2012.)

Conclusion

The existing literature on the foundation and formative years of the Bretton Woods institutions focuses almost exclusively on the vital role played by the United States and Britain, their main architects. This focus is of unquestionable value, as it tells us the story of the visionaries and decision makers, of those who set up the rules and provided most of the capital necessary to put the new multilateralism in motion. However, it overlooks the mostly secondary role played in the process by peripheral actors, thereby providing an incomplete portrait of this groundbreaking moment in modern economic history. When I say "peripheral actors," I refer not to three, four, or even ten underdeveloped states whose participation in the design and establishment of the Bretton Woods institutions was of relative irrelevance. Rather, I refer to the vast majority of nations that became members of the IMF and World Bank but were not part of the fortunate group of those institutions' five strongest members. This chapter thus looked at the formation of the new multilateral order not from the center but mainly from the margins, analyzing the creation and organizational structure of the Bretton Woods institutions from a Latin American perspective.

But the Latin American perspective is by no means monolithic. Like a coin, it has two indivisible sides: the side of those nineteen states that were invited by the United States to take part in the Bretton Woods Conference, and the side of Argentina—the only Latin American country excluded from it. Undoubtedly, these two sides are complementary and should be analyzed in an interrelated manner.

Empirical research reveals that Argentina's exclusion from the Bretton Woods Conference and its subsequent late incorporation into the IMF and World Bank were part of the high price the country paid not only for its wartime neutrality but also for its long-standing policy of nonalignment with the United States. In effect, I have shown that Argentina's lack of acceptance into the nascent Bretton Woods institutions stemmed from processes that were well under way before the conference convened in 1944. It has also been suggested that the kind of multilateralism the United States sought at the time left no room for a country that had been unwilling or unable to provide support at the right moment. In this sense, Argentina's efforts to join the new institutions met with an a priori and irrefutable U.S. rejection and with unambiguous British silence. This was true during the regimes of both Ramírez and Farrell.

Archival evidence demonstrates that from the beginning of the planning process, leading officials in the Argentine government made significant efforts to enable the country to join the Bretton Woods institutions. Some of these efforts were public, and most of them were confidential. What is certain is that all of them were in vain. Yet the significance of Washington's decision to exclude a somewhat rebellious nation from the list of invitees to the Bretton Woods Conference goes above and beyond the specifics of the Argentine case. By punishing a too (politically) independent Argentina through exclusion, the United States confirmed to all Latin American nations that alignment with Washington had become a precondition to gaining access to the alleged fruits of multilateralism. As will be shown in the next chapters, Argentina had to implement economic reforms in line with IMF precepts to be accepted as one of its member states; however, Latin American nations that already were members had to embrace the same economic reforms to be awarded IMF and World Bank financial assistance.

The exclusion of Argentina was detrimental not only to the country but also to the region as a whole. Had Argentina been a participant in the process, the entire region could have enjoyed somewhat higher status. In effect, when Argentina joined in 1956, the IMF and World Bank had no choice but to increase Latin American representation considerably on their Executive Boards.

The Bretton Woods Conference created the IMF and World Bank as two central pillars of the new global economic order. The United States and Britain presented these novel institutions as open, representative, and beneficial to all of their members. In practice, however, the new order—and, more specifically, the organizational structure of the Bretton Woods institutions—simultaneously represented and entrenched a balance of power that was clearly but not coercively dominated by the new hegemonic power, the United States. In this structure, Latin American countries were relegated to peripheral roles that did not always reflect their economic positions in the international arena. It is in this respect that Argentina is perhaps one of the most illuminating examples. Until the 1930s, it was expected to become one of the world's richest countries. During the war, the growth in international reserves made it a creditor country, but for political reasons, it was excluded from the Bretton Woods Conference. As will be shown in Chapter 2, it would take twelve years of exclusion and accumulation of foreign debts for Argentina to finally join the IMF and World Bank.

2

It Takes Three to Tango

Argentina, the Bretton Woods Institutions,
and the United States, 1946–1956

When I took charge of the government in 1946, the first visitor I received was the President of the International Monetary Fund, who came to invite us to join the Fund. . . . I responded cautiously that I needed to think it over and immediately assigned two trusted young experts from the government staff to investigate this dangerous monster, born as I recall in the suspect Breton Hood [*sic*] agreements. The conclusion of their report was clear and precise: In sum, we were dealing with a new putative deformed spawn of imperialism. I, who have the advantage of not being an economist, am able to explain it as it should be understood.[1]

Juan Domingo Perón, the IMF, and the World Bank: Judging by the historiography that portrays Perón as a staunch anti-imperialist, and by statements such as this one, such a relationship would seem impossible. But was it really so? As we will see, Peronist Argentina's entry into the Bretton Woods institutions was in fact desired not only by the leaders of the IMF and the World Bank but also by Perón himself. From 1946 to 1955, the years of his administration, Perón made significant and repeated attempts to reach an agreement by which Argentina could join both institutions. (Nations cannot join just one of the Bretton Woods twins.) Those efforts were translated into an almost permanent state of negotiations between the parties involved.

Some of the arguments in this chapter are also explored in my article "Chronicle of an Inconclusive Negotiation: Perón, the IMF, and the World Bank (1946–1955)," *Hispanic American Historical Review* 92, no. 4 (2012): 637–668. The article was originally written in Spanish and was translated into English by Thomas Holloway. I am grateful to *Hispanic American Historical Review* for enabling me to republish parts of the article within the framework of this book.

The thus far unknown "Peronist chapter" of the relations among Argentina, the IMF, and the World Bank provides an opportunity to reconsider a crucial historical period in which potentially contradictory processes were at work.[2] One was the formation of a new multilateral order under U.S. hegemony. The other was the emergence of nationalist, populist, and reformist currents in Latin America.[3] Specifically, the analysis of the Perón–Bretton Woods relationship offers an alternative vantage point for reconsidering different models of inclusion in and exclusion from the new world order. This case also lets us explore the impact of postwar multilateralism not only on those nations that joined the new order, but also those that, like Argentina, remained on the margins. With respect to Latin America, remaining *formally* on the margins appears not to have freed countries from the need to adopt the policies driven by the Bretton Woods institutions—policies that were at odds with the growing economic nationalism, protectionism, and interventionism in the region. Thus, while the literature argues that the IMF used conditional loans to exercise its influence on member countries, an analysis of the negotiations conducted during the Peronist decade shows that, from its formative years, the IMF promoted reforms even in the economic policies of countries that had not yet become members.

Close examination of the wide range of interactions that took place between Argentina and the Bretton Woods institutions in 1946–1956 reveals important aspects of the challenges with which Latin American nations had to deal while entering the new multilateral system. At the same time, it offers privileged lenses through which to look at the inner workings of the IMF and World Bank as their managers turned their eyes for the first time toward non-European member states. Specifically, the meetings between IMF delegates and local officials in Latin America and at the IMF's headquarters, the need to furnish the IMF with accurate financial data, the debates among several IMF departments, and the demands by Latin American nations to be given more voting power in both institutions all contribute to a better understanding of the design and establishment of the monitoring mechanisms that later became part and parcel of the borrowers' dependency on the IMF.

First, it should be clarified that in public rhetoric, the first Peronist government did not refer to the IMF and World Bank, perhaps to avoid putting the negotiations with the Bretton Woods institutions in jeopardy. The earliest criticism by Perón that I could find appears in a letter he wrote from exile in 1967 to one of his friends.[4] The passage quoted at the start of this chapter was written in 1968. In other words, Perón began to criticize the Bretton Woods institutions after almost fifteen years of exile, based on the bitter experience of the loan agreements signed between the IMF and the governments of Arturo Frondizi and Juan Carlos Onganía in 1958 and 1967, respectively. That is, Perón wrote those words after the IMF had come to play a dominant role in the world economy and the conditions attached to its loans were provoking protest, especially among the debtor nations.[5] The first Perón government, in contrast, coincided with the formative period of both institutions. By the end of December 1945, they had only thirty-five members. In those early years, the IMF and World Bank, still strongly influenced by Keynesian ideas, strove to increase the number of member countries to expand the scope of their influence and their legitimacy.[6]

Regarding the incidents Perón mentioned in 1968, suffice it to say that the IMF's managing director did not visit Latin America in 1946; nor is there any evidence to confirm that during the first meeting between the two parties, which took place in 1948, Argentina rejected the idea of joining the IMF. Furthermore, Perón was not merely loose with the facts when he claimed that Argentina had been invited to join the IMF but had rejected the invitation. Historical evidence reveals a very different reality: that Perón was, in fact, eager to join the IMF and the World Bank. This chapter thus explores the negotiations between the most prominent figures of the Argentine government and the Bretton Woods institutions carried out during the Peronist decade and immediately after Perón was overthrown. While doing so, it stresses two fundamental aspects of this relationship. One is the high level of pragmatism that has led government administrations that in some ways are very different (i.e., populist, developmentalist, liberal, democratic, or authoritarian) to aspire to receive not only loans from the IMF but, more important, its increasingly necessary seal of approval. The other is that, despite the apparent rigidity of the IMF's conditions, the institution has been relatively flexible. During its formative period, its main goal was to facilitate (rather than demand as a precondition) the transition of its members from bilateral systems of commerce and payments to a multilateral regime and from multiple exchange rate systems to the adoption of a par value system.[7]

In this chapter, I first analyze the significant contacts between the two sides from Perón's rise to power to his last months as president. I then turn to examining Argentina's entry into the Bretton Woods institutions soon after the self-proclaimed Liberating Revolution overthrew Perón on September 16, 1955.

The Unfinished Negotiation between Perón and the IMF and World Bank

Round One: Doubts and Hesitation

When Perón became president in 1946, Argentina was the only Latin American country that did not belong to the IMF and World Bank. This anomaly was just one of the unresolved issues Edelmiro Farrell passed to Perón along with the presidential sash. In reality, one of the most serious challenges the new administration faced was the prolonged crisis with the United States. Without resolving that crisis, the chances that Perón would reach a membership agreement with the Bretton Woods institutions were practically nonexistent.

Many U.S. government officials perceived Perón as incapable of easing the difficult problems in relations between the two countries. The U.S. State Department, which had been the source of the anti-Argentine policies of the U.S. Ambassador Spruille Braden, and Cordell Hull, was incapable of distinguishing between what it viewed as the fascistic positions of Farrell and Perón.[8] But Perón had more than an image problem to overcome. There were also such pressing issues as the collapse of the Argentina–Great Britain–U.S. commercial triangle. The many bilateral agreements signed by Perón failed to resolve the scarcity of dollars and capital goods from which Argentina suffered after a period of apparent abundance. In addition, the agreements Perón made with countries that had irreconcilable ideological differences—such as Britain, Franco's Spain, Latin American nations, the United States, and the Soviet Union and other states of the communist bloc—constituted a practical application of the "Third Position" that so irritated Washington and was perceived as a renewed version of Argentina's neutrality during World War II.[9] At the same time, the shortage of vital capital goods made Perón's plan for industrialization difficult to achieve and threatened the social policies that had benefited broad sectors of Argentine society.[10]

Because of the economic difficulties, and despite his pride in having paid off Argentina's foreign debt, which reflected "the national aspiration to be economically free and politically sovereign,"[11] Perón apparently concluded that the ideal of economic independence could tolerate a certain degree of pragmatism, including the eventual signing of membership agreements with the IMF and World Bank. Working with both institutions could facilitate, still relatively automatically, the funds needed to carry forward the Peronist project. But Perón also understood that it was no longer sufficient to strengthen bilateral or regional ties to overcome the isolation from which the country suffered. From 1944 on, the integration of Latin American nations into the international economic arena would not be complete without membership in the Bretton Woods institutions.

The Perón government's first contact with the new institutions took place in mid-1947. In that year, some commentators predicted that Perón would not lose time in requesting a loan from the U.S. government.[12] That prediction was not wrong, but it was inexact: Perón chose to explore short-term options that seemed less controversial and polemical than a direct loan from the U.S. Treasury. On August 27, 1947, a meeting was held in the Washington office of the economist Irving Friedman, a distinguished and influential official first of the IMF and then of the World Bank.[13] Juan Mercau, the secretary of the Argentine Embassy, also attended the meeting.[14] The two sides avoided taking a firm position regarding Argentina's membership in the Bretton Woods institutions. They did, however, discuss closely related topics. The Argentine representatives repeatedly asked about the quota Argentina would need to put up if it were to become a member and about the control of currency exchange rates.[15]

The control of exchange rates was a vital and potentially contentious issue because a considerable gap existed between what was set forth in the Bretton Woods agreement and Argentina's monetary policy. At the time, Argentina used a system of multiple exchanges rates, which was incompatible with the par value system the IMF had been promoting among its members. Argentina was by no means an isolated case, however. As of late 1946, thirteen of the forty members of the IMF, including twelve Latin American countries, still operated with a system of multiple exchange rates without the practice affecting their participation in the IMF.[16] A similar situation existed with regard to bilateralism in trade and payments, which was contrary to the multilateral system set up by the Bretton Woods agreements. But Argentina was not exceptional in that area, either.[17] The agreements allowed for a "transitional period" during which member states could slowly eliminate bilateral accords that were still in effect.[18] Through the 1940s and 1950s, bilateral trade and payment systems and multiple exchange rates were not obstacles to membership in the IMF. On the contrary: Admittance into the IMF was a way to help member countries abandon such protectionist measures, which were considered inimical to the new multilateralism.

Still, despite having talked about crucial issues, the World Bank representatives at the meeting declined to suggest concrete next steps and explained that it would be necessary for Argentina to contact the IMF. In their words, "The discussions with regard to the admission of new members were handled by Camille Gutt [the IMF's managing director,] and at most we could make merely factual comments which could not be considered authoritative and necessarily had to be taken as most informal."[19] The Argentine representatives persisted, indicating that their government aspired to membership in the IMF and World Bank and for that reason had contacted John McCloy, the influential president of the World Bank.[20] Mercau emphasized that Argentina was especially interested in joining the World Bank.[21] This was a telling comment: Interest in the World Bank, along with concern about the IMF, was common in Latin America at the time.[22] The World Bank was charged with financing infrastructure projects that the countries of the region considered fundamental for their economic development, whereas the financial and monetary reforms the IMF was promoting implied breaking with traditional protectionist and interventionist policies, which could be politically costly.[23]

A few months later, the Argentines resumed their contacts with the World Bank. In May 1948, McCloy, accompanied by other high officials of the Bank (the Cuban Luis Machado and the Chilean Víctor Moller), visited seven of the twenty Latin American countries that were already members (Brazil, Ecuador, Chile, Colombia, Peru, Uruguay, and Venezuela). The delegation did not have time to visit the other thirteen member states but did reserve part of its precious time for an official and confidential meeting in Buenos Aires. McCloy informed his staff in Washington that Argentina, "although not a member of the bank, indicated great interest. It affirmatively wanted to cooperate with the bank. . . . We didn't discuss an application to join the bank. Naturally, I didn't bring it up."[24] McCloy's use of the word "naturally" is intriguing. We should not reject the possibility that, despite McCloy's clear denial, the topic of membership was raised during the meeting. However, if the issue was ignored or dealt with only in passing, it is likely that this resulted from a decision to avoid taking any action that might facilitate an application for membership, because the United States still had economic sanctions in place against Argentina as the meeting was being held.[25] Thus, it is possible that McCloy's claimed discretion was a byproduct of the U.S. sanctions, which would have been incompatible with Argentine entry into the IMF and World Bank.

In any case, this discreet visit to the only Latin American republic that still was not a member of the World Bank was one more step in the process of mutual rapprochement, and it was initiated by Argentina. In June 1948, Argentina requested that U.S. Ambassador James Bruce convey a concise message to McCloy: "Argentina particularly wants to know about what would be her probable quota in the Fund and subscription in the Bank and what would be the cost."[26] This blunt message was transmitted via U.S. government channels even though Perón already had direct ties to McCloy, which may indicate that the intended recipient was not the World Bank but, rather, the U.S. government, whose approval was a necessary precondition for entry into the Bretton Woods institutions.

McCloy's reaction was immediate. The World Bank asked the IMF to review its calculations regarding Argentina's quota and suggested that the results be sent to the Argentine government so they could be used as the basis for negotiations.[27] The IMF also lost no time in confirming that the quota would be $160 million–$200 million—equal to that of Brazil.[28] McCloy's first visit to Buenos Aires "naturally" had been much more than a mere courtesy call.

In 1948, as contacts between the World Bank and Argentina became more substantive, relations with the IMF took a qualitative leap forward. This advance was essential: The Bretton Wood institutions took action in tandem, and the decision to accept or reject new applicants for membership necessarily followed this pattern. In November 1948, following in the footsteps of his World Bank counterpart, the Belgian economist Camille Gutt, managing director of the IMF, landed for the first time in Buenos Aires.

Gutt's visit indicated the advanced state of negotiations with Perón and at the same time reflected the IMF's efforts to expand its field of influence. Gutt's trip to Latin America resulted from—and, at the same time, consolidated— a change in the institution's modus operandi. In January 1948, the Board of Governors had decided that European countries could not have access to the resources of the IMF while they participated in the Marshall Plan.[29] Once this resolution was adopted, Gutt announced that he was leaving for a six-week tour of Brazil, Chile, Colombia, Ecuador, Peru, Mexico, Uruguay, and Argentina.[30] In other words, only after suspending activities in Europe, and as part of a process of expansion and consolidation, did the IMF turn its attention to regions that had been largely overlooked.

During his visit in November 1948, Gutt sent an urgent message to the IMF's Executive Board denying rumors that he had proposed to Miguel Miranda, president of the Argentine Central Bank, that Argentina should join the Bretton Woods institutions.[31] He continued to take that position after he returned to Washington. "I should mention that after my talk with one official," Gutt explained to the Executive Board, "a Buenos Aires paper published an account that in a two-hour interview I had entreated the official to join the Fund and he turned down the offer. All was, of course, pure invention. Not only was the length of the talk overstated by at least one hour, but during that time the idea of Argentina joining the Fund was not once mentioned."[32] If such denials were not enough, Gutt added that he had not had any expectations regarding his meeting with Perón and Miranda and that his stay in Buenos Aires had been nothing more than a technical stopover on his way to Chile. Notably, the Argentine government was also quick to deny any intention to join the IMF.[33]

This flurry of denials nevertheless raises several questions. Similar denials, it should be remembered, were made in the context of the earlier visit by World Bank President John McCloy. And as in that case, it is difficult to explain fully why the IMF's managing director decided to include Argentina on his itinerary: other Latin American countries already were IMF members and no doubt would have been gratified by his attention. Similarly, it is not logical to believe that Gutt, Perón, and Miranda were unaware of the various contacts made up to that time. Is it possible, then, to conclude that Gutt simply wanted to make a courtesy call on Perón, with no substantive agenda? Is it credible that Gutt stopped in Buenos Aires simply to rest on his way to Chile?

Despite the efforts to keep the true content of the meetings hidden, during the Peronist period both sides clearly saw the incorporation of Argentina into the Bretton Woods institutions as a real possibility. The denials by McCloy, Gutt, and the Argentine authorities did not stop the efforts to find common ground. It could be said, rather, that such denials were an indication of the doubts and suspicions that existed in both Washington and Buenos Aires. In 1948, Perón did not have sufficient reason to publicize his contacts with the IMF and World Bank, because the conditions for joining those institutions had not yet come together. The high level of caution and confidentiality of the recurring meetings may also have been due to fear on Perón's part that publicity might damage his image as firmly standing up to foreign capital. The Bretton Woods institutions, for their part, might have preferred to keep the negotiations under wraps to avoid outside pressure, especially by the U.S. government. Despite

Washington's domination of the IMF and World Bank, at least some of the officials at those institutions were interested in having Argentina join, because the influential nation's membership would help to consolidate the presence of the Bretton Woods institutions in Latin America.

After Gutt's visit, the contacts between Argentina and the IMF and World Bank continued apace. Moreover, the meetings in Buenos Aires led to a new round of discussions. In September 1949, the IMF and World Bank again studied what Argentina's quota might be. Eugene Black, the new president of the World Bank, took numerous measures intended to renew the Bank's activities and broaden its clientele. An internal memo sent to Black shows that Argentina's membership was considered imminent: "It is expected that Argentina would meet with a favorable reception from [IMF] staff and Board, even though many of its exchange practices do not meet with general approval."[34]

Determining why an agreement was not reached during this promising stage of negotiations presents a serious challenge. The available documentation does not resolve all of the questions, but it does point in several directions, not all of them mutually exclusive. Broadly, four major hypotheses can be considered. The first is that, despite Perón's apparent interest, the Bretton Woods institutions were not willing to accept Argentina as a member. The second is that the Bretton Woods institutions invited Argentina to join, but Perón rejected the offer. The third is that neither of the two sides was really interested in reaching an agreement. None of these hypotheses, however, is convincing. If there had been no more than a series of encounters with no clear objective and no result, the highest officials of both the Argentine government and the Bretton Woods institutions would not have participated as fully as they did. Along the same lines, the increase in the content and the frequency of the messages transmitted by Argentina and the repeated visits and administrative procedures carried out by the IMF and World Bank can only indicate strong intentions.

The fourth and most likely hypothesis is that all of the parties were interested in reaching an agreement, but for reasons still only partially known, they had fears or doubts about the process or simply did not consider concluding it sufficiently advantageous. It is important to emphasize that Argentina's non-participation in the IMF and World Bank during the first round of negotiations was an anomaly not only from the perspective of Argentina, but also from that of the new multilateral system. It must also be kept in mind that, in reality, not two sides but three were involved, with the U.S. government the third point in the triangular dealings. The renewal of positive relations with the United States in the postwar years was yet to be resolved, and Argentina's eventual entry into the IMF would have required Perón to reconcile his nationalist and protectionist policies with a multilateralism that promoted the opposite: openness, transparency, liberalization, and an automatic alignment with the United States. While Argentina was not the only Latin American country that faced such

40   Chapter 2

dilemmas, it is clear that the rivalry between Buenos Aires and Washington increased their magnitude. One might assume that when President Roosevelt suggested to his faithful ally Getúlio Vargas in 1943 that Brazil should begin a process of liberalization if it hoped to exercise influence in the postwar world,[35] Vargas's misgivings were not as fundamental as were Perón's three years later.

The United States, for its part, needed to come up with a way to reconcile its multilateral and regional aspirations with its anti-Argentine and anti-Perón stance. That was a difficult task, as Washington continued to impose economic sanctions on the country until 1950. The question would be whether the continued exclusion of Argentina was an impediment to or, on the contrary, an intrinsic element of postwar multilateralism. All indications are that the Bretton Woods institutions, unlike Washington, perceived Argentina's exclusion as an impediment that would be expedient to remove.

The discriminatory measures against Argentina gave rise to serious debates within the U.S. government, which was divided between those who insisted on taking a hard line against anyone who did not align with Washington and those who warned that such a policy was counterproductive.[36] Washington's vacillating policy regarding Argentina's entry into the IMF and World Bank reflected that debate. As Edward Miller, assistant secretary of state for Latin American affairs, instructed U.S. representatives in Buenos Aires, "It is even more important than ever for us to play our cards carefully in the near future and avoid any sign of weakness or eagerness. You have been doing a masterful job at this while at the same time not giving Perón any offense. It is the right policy and it is the only policy."[37] In other words, this same caution might have induced Washington to give its approval to the endless negotiations between Argentina and the Bretton Woods institutions, so long as those discussions led to neither a conclusive agreement nor open conflict.

We should not, however, discount the possibility of an inverse situation—namely, that it was Perón's determination that wavered at the last moment. For example, in May 1949, the Argentine ambassador to Washington was ordered to declare that at "a time of instability and economic readjustment it is not possible to adopt rigid standards regarding the exchange rate and to restrict liberty of action. . . . [T]his is a better position than to join these organizations and then not comply with their standards as have other countries."[38]

The pretext Argentina used was based on the concern it had already expressed about the IMF's demands, and it would seem to indicate that Perón saw the IMF as an obstacle to dealing with the World Bank. The fact that during its formative period the IMF was not yet imposing strict conditions did not mitigate Perón's concerns. In this respect, it should be emphasized that entry into the IMF required policy reforms that Peronist Argentina, for technical and political reasons, could not or did not intend to carry out.[39] Not only would joining the IMF detract from Perón's image as an anti-imperialist, but Perón would have to deal with the friction that this and other economic policies caused within his administration.[40]

In sum, even when Perón and the Bretton Woods institutions were interested in finalizing an agreement, the efforts were dashed on the rocks of doubt, fear, and resentment that lingered in both the Argentine and U.S. governments. Until 1950, the desire of Perón and some of his ministers to join the new multilateral order was foiled by fluctuating opposition that was both internal and external.

When the possibility of membership in the Bretton Woods institutions was put on hold, and with the emergence of new signs of economic exhaustion, Argentina chose to resume the old practice of negotiating long-term credits with foreign institutions, avoiding government-to-government loans as much as possible. Thus, in 1950 Argentina knocked on the doors of the Export-Import Bank, an arguably more advantageous option than the IMF.

Round Two: Renewed Efforts and Abrupt Interruptions

Interactions with the IMF and the World Bank deepened as Argentina's relations with Washington improved. Similarly, the discussions became more concrete as the barriers that aimed to limit the flow of foreign capital into Argentina, especially from the United States, continued to fall. In effect, Peronist Argentina increasingly adopted policies promoted by the IMF, to which it did not yet belong. To understand the second cycle of these negotiations, it is important to place it in that broader context.

In late 1949, Perón was considering several options that had Washington as a common reference point. On one hand, Argentina explored the possibility of joining the Bretton Woods institutions. On the other, it negotiated a loan with the Export-Import Bank. These dealings, though, were not really isolated from each other. Representatives of the IMF, World Bank, Export-Import Bank, U.S Treasury, and U.S. State Department worked together in their assessment of the Argentine situation.

The Argentine government was aware that all of the possible loans it was considering depended, in one way or another, on U.S. approval. In fact, in February 1950, when the Argentine National Economic Council (NEC) was developing its strategy for the visit by Assistant Secretary of State Edward Miller, its members assumed that Argentina's entry into the IMF and World Bank would be an integral part of the discussions with the Export-Import Bank. Based on this assumption, the NEC warned that when the time came to put up the amount of the quota, difficulties would arise. The NEC also noted the other obstacles that could emerge when Argentina joined the Bretton Woods institutions. Among them were the need to formulate a stable monetary policy, the demand that member countries abandon multiple exchange-rate systems within five years, and the requirement to obtain the IMF's approval before modifying exchange rates. While the NEC recognized that many countries had not complied with the IMF's requirements, it feared that membership would limit the Argentine government's freedom of action.[41]

Miller stayed in Argentina from February 19 to February 25, 1950. Three months later, the Export-Import Bank approved a $125 million loan to Argentina.[42] This loan, which was followed by another in 1955, gave rise to considerable discontent in the Peronist leadership, as Perón had hoped to avoid direct loans from the U.S. government. According to reports in the U.S. press, Perón tried to characterize the loan as "indirect," which in reality it was not.[43] Not only was the Export-Import Bank a U.S. government agency whose main purpose was to promote U.S. exports, but the agreement itself had been closely monitored by the State Department.[44] Moreover, the United States saw the agreement as a way to put pressure on Argentina to change its economic policy, a strategy that Washington applied broadly throughout Latin America.[45]

The loan from the Export-Import Bank was significant for several reasons. First, it made clear that using economic assistance to push for changes in borrowers' economic policies was part of the new hegemonic power's policy. Second, membership in the Bretton Woods institutions and obtaining credit from the Export-Import Bank, from the lender's perspective, facilitated those objectives. This was shown clearly in the case of Chile: In 1947, after President Gabriel González Videla refused to expel communists from his cabinet and put down labor strikes, the United States opposed an Export-Import Bank loan to that country.[46] Once countries such as Chile and Bolivia responded to such pressure and adopted anticommunist policies, however, the United States voted in favor of IMF and World Bank loans.[47] Washington, as Miller stated, expected similar changes in Argentina. Because Argentina began to adopt more liberal economic policies even without formally joining the new multilateral system, however, one might question what interest Washington would have had in agreeing to Argentina's membership, which might have been seen as a sign of weakness on the part of the United States.

As the Argentines anticipated, the U.S. government linked the negotiations with the Export-Import Bank to a renewed discussion of membership in the IMF and World Bank, as well as in other international institutions.[48] But Perón was not merely making plans to join international organizations; he had already done so. Peronist Argentina was a founding member of all of the international entities created in the postwar period, most of them as a result of U.S. initiatives. They included the United Nations, the Economic Commission for Latin America and the Caribbean (ECLAC), and the Organization of American States. The Bretton Woods institutions and the General Agreement on Tariffs and Trade (GATT) were the only exceptions.[49] It is thus clear that membership in the economic institutions represented the last hill to climb in Argentina's difficult path to full integration into world affairs.

Empirical research seems to show that after a long series of confidential talks, the Bretton Woods institutions, as well as Argentina, were willing to keep making significant efforts to negotiate, but without any explicit commitments. However, discussions went into an interval that lasted until 1954. That interval, during which Argentina continued to promote reforms that ultimately would facilitate its entry into the IMF and World Bank, was apparently propelled by the opinion that prevailed in certain circles of the State Department that a shortage of dollars would lead Argentina to a significant shift toward Washington's position. As Miller predicted in 1951, "There is going to be another sudden effort on the part of the Argentines to come to us 'to settle all our pending problems,' which, of course, means getting some fat loans from the U.S."[50]

Perón meanwhile continued to redesign his economic policies. On February 18, 1952, he announced the implementation of a new economic plan that was nothing more than a stabilization program.[51] In 1953, Perón inaugurated his second Five-Year Plan, which complemented the stabilization plan and sought to establish heavy industry in Argentina. The transition to a phase centered on efficiency and productivity brought an increase in investment. Even so, internal investment was insufficient to raise productivity and reduce the imports that had been causing problems in the Argentina government's balance of payments.

Under these circumstances, the government had no choice but to promote foreign investment. The approval of Law 14,222 on foreign capital, in August 1953, was a significant step in this process of economic opening.[52] Most important, in early 1954, Perón decided to return to the negotiating table to secure membership in the Bretton Woods institutions. To this end, he invited Eugene Black, president of the World Bank, to Buenos Aires.

Black's visit lasted three days—from March 15 to March 17, 1954—during which the Bank's delegation met repeatedly with Perón and his most influential ministers. The mood, as expressed by both hosts and guests, was "extremely pleasant and cordial."[53] The message the Argentines intended to convey focused on their sincere intention to join the World Bank, despite the "image problems" to which that move might give rise. In public statements, the Argentine officials proclaimed that they were striving to improve the country's international position, as long as the proposed actions could be based on realistic and constructive foundations that respected national sovereignty.[54]

As on earlier occasions, Argentina expressed great interest in the World Bank and serious reservations about the IMF.[55] Nonetheless, Black's impression was that Perón finally recognized that the only viable alternative was to join the IMF along with the Bank. To sweeten that bitter pill, however, Bank officials proposed a solution similar to the one Perón had adopted when he sought the

Export-Import Bank loans four years earlier: The funds the World Bank would provide to Argentina would constitute a sort of "indirect loan." It would not be necessary to register the amounts transferred on the government's accounts. Instead, they could be attributed to other entities—for example, the electric utility company.[56]

According to the report on the meeting by the World Bank delegation, Economic Minister Alfredo Gómez Morales indicated at the end of the visit that Argentina had seen entry into the World Bank and IMF as an "academic question," but that was no longer the case.[57] Meanwhile, in the last phase of the 1946–1955 period, the efforts at rapprochement with the United States yielded the hoped-for results. In practice, Argentina adapted to the new trends in international finance and trade promoted by the new hegemonic power and the institutions it had created at the same time that agreements with U.S. investors and companies were multiplying. Some notorious cases, such as the controversial contract with the Standard Oil Company of California and the new agreement with the Export-Import Bank, were concluded with the intervention of the U.S. government,[58] which began to show visible signs of rapprochement with Perón.

The meetings in Buenos Aires of 1954, which ended with Argentina's promise to do everything necessary to join the IMF and World Bank,[59] and the continually improving relations with the United States leave no doubt that Perón had decided to end Argentina's exclusion from the two multilateral economic institutions. As further evidence of this, on May 19, two days after Black left Buenos Aires, Argentine Ambassador Hipólito Paz informed Assistant Secretary of State Henry Holland that he had begun taking the necessary steps to present a request for membership in the Bretton Woods institutions and that he had scheduled a series of meetings with officials of both organizations. Holland, in turn, confirmed to Paz his willingness to assist in every possible way.[60] In 1954, neither Perón nor the U.S. government had any reason to continue to hide the contacts intended to complete Argentina's impending entry into the Bretton Woods institutions. Black's visit was the first to be reported in the Argentine press.

On September 16, 1955, the self-styled Liberating Revolution overthrew Perón. In contrast to what had occurred in the not-so-remote past, the United States was quick to extend diplomatic recognition to the government of General Eduardo Lonardi.[61] The coup d'état interrupted (though only briefly) the intensive negotiations that had been under way for almost a decade between Perón's government and the highest authorities of the IMF and World Bank. Despite this initial, and unintentional, interruption, one of the first measures adopted by the new regime, which tried to erase all traces of Peronism, was to join the Bretton Woods institutions. For the IMF, the World Bank, and especially the United States, the overthrow of Perón constituted a unique opportunity to conclude the unfinished negotiations with Argentina.

Argentina's Admission to the
Bretton Woods Institutions

The provisional presidents of the Liberating Revolution—the retired General Eduardo Lonardi (September–November 1955) and his hardline deposer, General Pedro Eugenio Aramburu (November 1955–May 1958), aspired to de-Peronize Argentina and to create a "democracy without Perón."[62] This was one the few consensual targets among the leaders of the coup, who lacked a solid ideological common denominator.[63] But the Liberating Revolution did not limit itself to the eradication of Peronism from the domestic political, economic, social, and cultural spheres. It also aspired to put its distinctive stamp on the international arena by abolishing the so-called Third Position and adopting a clearer pro-U.S. stand. It was precisely within this context that President Aramburu presented the talks with the Bretton Woods institutions not as the continuation of a long process that had begun under President Farrell and continued during the Peronist era but as a brand-new beginning.

In effect, contrary to what is usually assumed, Argentina's incorporation into the IMF and World Bank in 1956 was neither a turning point in Argentina's economic policy or an unexpected move. Rather, it was the final stage in a single and unified process that had been under way since 1946. As I will show, the three parties involved in the process that led to Argentina's admission into the Bretton Woods institutions all had very good reasons to finally make it happen. The IMF and World Bank were still fighting to expand their area of influence and legitimacy, and bringing Argentina into the fold was important to increasing and enhancing their involvement in Latin America. The United States was interested in making Argentina a friendly and aligned ally in the Southern Cone, especially in the context of the Cold War. The Liberating Revolution was both a partner in the crusade against communism and a supporter of economic liberalization and free trade.[64] Yet while all of these motivations were important in their own right, it seems that more than anything else, in the hands of Lonardi and Aramburu entry into the Bretton Woods institutions was a political and economic tool. By taking this measure, the military regime announced to both its supporters and its opponents at home and abroad that the era of populism, Third Position, and statism in Argentina was over.

Round Three: The Search for a New Economic Policy

The leaders of the Liberating Revolution aimed to consolidate an economic plan that was significantly and visibly different from the one advanced by Perón. With this goal in mind, President Lonardi invited Raúl Prebisch, the head of ECLAC, to return to Argentina as his special economic adviser.[65] In retrospect, Lonardi's choice seems pragmatically and symbolically opportune.

In Argentina, Prebisch, whom just a decade earlier Perón had humiliatingly removed from his offices at the Central Bank and the University of Buenos Aires, was strongly identified with the conservative policies of former President José Uriburu and with the interests of the local oligarchy, for which he worked in the Sociedad Rural Argentina in the 1920s and 1930s.[66] In the international sphere, Prebisch's years at ECLAC surely contributed to increasing his prestige, giving Argentina's economic team a professional and competent image that was more in line with the new standards the IMF aspired to instill in the international economic arena.

In practical terms, the provisional government charged Prebisch with the task of diagnosing Argentina's economic situation and elaborating an integral plan. His plan, which blamed Perón for all of the ills of the country's economy, consisted of three separate documents: "A Preliminary Report on the Economic Situation," "Sound Money or Run-Away Inflation," and "The Plan for Economic Rehabilitation." The first document was presented to President Lonardi on October 26, 1955. The two additional documents were put on the desk of his deposer, President Aramburu, on January 7, 1956. Although the report is identified solely with Prebisch, it was actually produced in strong collaboration with a large team of economists from Argentina, ECLAC, the IMF, and the U.S. administration,[67] thus warranting its positive reception by potential creditors and investors.

Prebisch's preliminary report focused on two acute and chronic evils—inflation and deficits in the balance of payments—along with a host of other problems, including a rundown transportation system, a power crisis, a housing shortage, low labor productivity, and a decline in agriculture. Despite the fact that the preliminary report opened with the claim, "Argentina is facing its deepest economic crisis,"[68] the situation was far from chaotic. As some scholars argue, the economy was not in crisis and was by no means the main reason behind the decision to overthrow Perón.[69]

As could and should be predicted, Prebisch recommended joining the Bretton Woods institutions.[70] Yet membership in these institutions was still highly controversial in Argentina. In effect, in 1956, as in 1946, Arturo Frondizi, the leader of the Intransigent Radical Civic Union and the next president, continued to express reluctance regarding Argentina's incorporation into the IMF.[71] Frondizi's opposition was so adamant that it raised concerns in the Argentine and U.S. administrations.[72]

Despite the controversies, Prebisch embarked on efforts to pave the way toward membership in the IMF and World Bank. Just a few days after Lonardi was ousted, Jorge del Canto, a prominent member of the IMF's Research Department who was later appointed to head the Western Hemisphere Department, informed Managing Director Ivar Rooth: "We learned to our satisfaction that the team that [Prebisch] gathered has been confirmed by the new President, and he still is quite influential in the shaping of financial policies of the New

Government. . . . I learned . . . that Prebisch is in favor of recommending that Argentina join the Fund and the Bank."[73]

Nonetheless, the IMF's enthusiasm was not enough to ensure Argentina's membership in the Bretton Woods institutions. The Liberating Revolution still had to obtain consent from the United States. In November 1955, during an official visit to Washington, César Bunge, Lonardi's economic minister, declared that "his government was eager for U.S. credits" and insisted that Argentina's ability to solve its more pressing economic problems "would depend on the amount and kind of help the United States would be willing to give."[74] Whereas Buenos Aires's message to Washington reflected a strong desire to tighten the ties between the two, the U.S. administration was still at odds over the nature and scale of support it deemed desirable to provide to Argentina, including the question of whether to approve Argentina's entry into the IMF and World Bank. Henry Holland believed that the United States should provide generous economic support to the new government.[75] As he stated in January 1956,

> The Argentine situation today gives the United States an opportunity to establish a kind of relationship with an exceedingly important American republic, . . . an opportunity to achieve a major advance in our hemispheric fight against Communism and an opportunity to establish the private enterprise system far more firmly in the entire South American continent. . . . Failure to exploit this opportunity may well mean that the present Government, which is prepared to adopt a strongly pro–United States attitude, will collapse and be supplanted by another hostile to the United States.[76]

As Holland stated, time to bring Argentina officially into the U.S. area of influence—and, consequently, into the new multilateral system—was running short. This concern prompted Washington to use the Liberating Revolution as an opportunity to reach an agreement with Argentina. Undersecretary of State Herbert Hoover nevertheless took a harder line toward Argentina than Holland did, and it was Hoover's strategy that finally prevailed. Thus, it is not surprising that at a meeting held in December 1955 with Prebisch and Argentine Finance Minister Julio Alisón García, the U.S. representatives "listened sympathetically, asked questions, agreed to further exploration of the Argentine financial problem, but left Buenos Aires without commitment except for formal signature of the already approved Export-Import Bank steel credit."[77] Although the gathering was not intended to have concrete results, the parties discussed the possibility of Argentina's joining the Bretton Woods institutions.[78]

Just two weeks after Prebisch's preliminary report was published, while Bunge was still in Washington, a summary of the document was circulated among several IMF departments.[79] A few days later, a translated version of the report was dispatched to the members of the IMF's Board of Governors and to all department heads.[80] The World Bank did not remain indifferent to the developments on the Argentine scene. It immediately engaged in a process of revising the report. Also, as early as November 1955, two high-ranking World Bank officials—J. Burke Knapp, director of Latin American operations, and Richard Demuth, an economist deeply involved in agricultural development—met with Prebisch in Buenos Aires.[81] The meeting took place at almost the same time that Holland, representatives of the Export-Import Bank, and del Canto (accompanied by several IMF economists) were conducting official visits in Buenos Aires. It is not unreasonable to assume that the presence of all of those important visitors was not a coincidence but, rather, a reflection of certainty that Argentina would soon join the international financial community.

The hopes of all of the parties involved were understandable. Not only did Argentina officially declare its intention to seek foreign loans, but in December 1955, Argentine officials confirmed to Holland that "the Government has under active consideration participation in the IBRD [World Bank] and IMF and that it will probably join these two organizations."[82] This statement, along with Prebisch's recommendations and the U.S. government's fear that the Liberating Revolution would soon be replaced by a less friendly government, seems finally to have convinced Washington to abandons its opposition to Argentina's entry into the Bretton Woods institutions.

Round Four: The IMF Ends Ten Years of Politicized Negotiations

In November 1955, even before Argentina re-entered talks with the Bretton Woods institutions, the IMF had unilaterally started to prepare to incorporate the country into its list of members. Among others things, the IMF began identifying problems that might arise if Argentina applied for membership. After ten years of negotiating with Perón, the IMF was well aware not only of the difficulties the Liberating Revolution would confront in the domestic arena but also of the changes that the IMF itself would have to make if Argentina became a member.

The IMF focused on three main problems related to admitting Argentina. The first was "the procedure and formalities Argentina would have to comply with in applying for membership in the Fund." That is, the IMF had serious doubts about Argentina's willingness and ability to provide sufficient and accurate data. The second was determining an "appropriate quota" for Argentina. And the third was "the problem Argentina's entry into the Fund would raise with respect to representation on the Executive Board of Latin American countries."[83]

With regard to the first problem, the IMF's concerns seem to have resulted from the lack of transparency during Perón's era. It is important to understand that the Articles of Agreement explicitly stipulate that the IMF "may require members to furnish it with such information as it deems necessary for its operations," including data on official domestic and international holdings, total exports and imports of merchandise, international balances of payments, international investment positions, and national income.[84] This is why the IMF's Research Department, Western Hemisphere Department, and Legal Department all recommended to Rooth that "in any discussions that may be held with Argentina concerning its membership in the Fund, the question of members' obligations in the field of statistics be clearly put at an early stage. This seems particularly necessary, as Argentina has published very little statistical information in the fields in which the Fund is most interested and, unlike other non-member countries, has shown little willingness to make data available to the Fund in the past."[85] As will be shown in the next chapters, the quality and reliability of the statistics provided by Argentina have been a constant cause of friction between the parties.

The other two interconnected problems were far more significant. Indeed, the question of Argentina's quota in the IMF had already engendered a long series of calculations and debates. In 1956, as on previous occasions, it was decided that Argentina's quota would be equal to that of Brazil—$150 million. Argentina's quota was important not only because of the IMF's desire not to disappoint a pro–United States Brazil, however; it was also important because it was strongly related to the question of Latin America's representation on the IMF's Executive Board. As mentioned earlier, the Bretton Woods institutions were the first international organizations to establish a differential system of representation, and Latin American countries had demanded more than once to increase their voting power and add another executive director on their behalf. Hence, the almost certain incorporation of Argentina, and the substantial increase in the voting power of the region that would result, opened the way for renewed debate on this issue.[86] It is in light of the complex considerations regarding the balance of power within the IMF that one can best understand the dilemmas that the acceptance of Argentina entailed. Interestingly, and to the satisfaction of the Liberating Revolution, immediately after Argentina became a member, the Argentine economist Guillermo Corominas Segura was elected as the third executive director for Latin America.[87]

Once the calculations were done, all that remained for the IMF to do was to wait for the leaders of the Liberating Revolution to apply formally for membership. This time it was clear that the U.S. administration would not object.

In early 1956, Argentina began to take the necessary formal steps to become a member of the Bretton Woods institutions. According to World Bank records from which I am still not allowed to quote directly, it was in January of that year that the IMF and World Bank were informed semiofficially that a forthcoming Argentine mission to Washington would apply for membership as part of a "package" of proposals. In March, during his visit to Washington, Prebisch told two high-ranking World Bank officials that he believed Argentina would join during 1956.

Concurrently with Prebisch's stay in Washington, Adolfo Vicchi, the Argentine ambassador in Washington, updated Holland that "he was pressing his government to join the IMF and World Bank."[88] Vicchi also emphasized that he had prepared a memorandum reassuring his government that the fear expressed by some opposition groups (especially the Radical Civic Union) that joining the IMF "would mean outside interference in internal fiscal matters" was groundless. Holland, who had openly supported Argentina's membership since 1954, responded that he "would be happy to have the U.S. delegate to the IMF available for consultation with the Ambassador's staff on any points they wished."[89]

Argentina's intentions were soon translated into actions. On April 16, Economic Minister Roberto Verrier announced that "the provisional government had decided to adhere to the Articles of Agreement of the Fund and Bank."[90] Three days later, President Aramburu issued a decree according to which Argentina committed to adopt all of the measures necessary to enter the IMF.[91] This decree, which resembled the one approved by Farrell in January 1946, underlined "the damage that could be caused to Argentina's economy if it remain[ed] isolated and outside the international organizations."[92]

With the publication of the decree, Ambassador Vicchi informed the U.S. State Department that the decision to join the IMF was well received by the Argentine public.[93] This update was a partial reflection of reality. Whereas some newspapers in Argentina, such as *La Nación,* enthusiastically supported the entry into the Bretton Woods institutions, describing it as "of transcendent importance,"[94] the decree did not silence those who warned that membership in the IMF would be detrimental to Argentina's sovereignty.[95] Unsurprisingly, Arturo Frondizi, who two years later would become the first Argentine president to sign a loan agreement with the IMF, declared, "Our position had always been opposed to the entry into the IMF and World Bank. . . . There are certain clauses in the IMF's Articles of Agreement that, without any doubt, could prevent the implementation of a monetary policy aimed at responding to the interests of the nation. . . . We believe that our country must not surrender, as others did not, its economic and monetary sovereignty."[96]

Prebisch was not alone in rejecting the criticism.[97] For instance, in an article that implicitly but unequivocally alluded to the Peronist era, one popular newspaper opined that "misleading and biased propaganda has presented the IMF as an institution that tramples the sovereignty of its member states. That was the pretext used in order to stay out of the IMF and the World Bank."[98] But most important, Finance Minister Julio Alisón García rejected the independentist and nationalist critics by declaring that the decision to join the IMF was nothing but a sovereign decision taken by Argentina to serve its own interests.[99]

On May 15, 1956, Vicchi sent an official letter to Rooth stating, "According to instructions given by the Argentine government, I hereby request that you consider the application the Argentine Republic is submitting to be accepted as a member of the organization."[100] Once the official written application was received, the IMF created a special committee to deal with Argentina's admission procedures. The committee was headed by Andre Van Campenhout, assisted by Jorge del Canto, Julio González del Solar, and Jorge Marshall, three IMF officials who had been deeply involved in the negotiations with Argentina since 1946. After 1956, they were even more active and influential on the Argentine national scene. On the same day that Argentina applied for membership, del Canto and del Solar sent a letter to Vicchi containing a detailed list of all the data the IMF required to determine Argentina's quota.[101]

Also with an eye toward joining the IMF and World Bank, and in an attempt to attract foreign investment and credits, the leaders of the Liberating Revolution promptly dispatched two economic missions abroad. Verrier headed the mission to Europe; Carlos Coll Benegas and Adalbert Krieger Vasena coordinated the mission to the United States. These young and prominent economists, it should be noted, belonged to the first generation of Argentine liberals of the postwar era. They became professionally known during the 1940s while working under Prebisch at the Central Bank. Later, Prebisch recruited them to assist him in the elaboration of his report.[102] Verrier, Coll Bengas, and Krieger Vasena were all well versed in the new trends in international trade and finance and strongly supported Argentina's incorporation into the Bretton Woods institutions. As could be expected, the missions were warmly welcomed by their hosts; however, they were unable to secure financial support.[103] In the meantime, del Canto communicated his enthusiasm to Rooth: "I would like to state for our Department that the joining [by] Argentina is considered by us one of the most important recent events of the [IMF's] history."[104]

Although some technical issues still demanded attention and the Argentines were still struggling to put the Central Bank's books in order, neither the IMF nor Argentina seems to have had any doubts about signing an agreement. Moreover, the leaders of the Liberating Revolution were by no means interested in sending out the same ambivalent and ambiguous message that Perón had conveyed during his first years in office. The IMF, for its part, was as flexible and understanding toward Argentina during this period as had been since 1946, and it would continue to show forebearance when Argentina missed deadlines or violated conditions stipulated in loan agreements. Generally, it is safe to conclude that the IMF was ready to compromise to make Argentina's membership a reality, and it was willing to remain flexible and even forgiving to maintain its close collaboration with the country.

The Argentine mission held its decisive meetings with the management of the IMF and World Bank on June 27. Two very brief summits were enough to reach agreement on all of the issues that had been debated for more than a decade.[105] Although it was portrayed as a quick procedure between friendly and professional partners by those who wanted to take credit for it, this final stage was in fact the culmination of a long process that was conducted mostly under Perón's initiative.

Finally, there is no doubt that the conclusion of the process of Argentina's admission into the IMF and World Bank was greatly facilitated by the willingness of the United States to improve its relationship with the best Argentine partner it could expect at the time. Under these circumstances, on June 29, 1956, the U.S. representatives at the IMF and the World Bank received instructions to support Argentina's membership. They were also authorized to vote for the addition of a third executive director for Latin America.[106] The membership procedures were completed smoothly and on schedule by the IMF. On August 9, the governors' votes were counted. Among the fifty-eight member countries of the Bretton Woods institutions at the time, only three (Afghanistan, Iceland, and Syria) abstained, and none voted against Argentina.[107] On August 31, Aramburu passed Law 15.970, which confirmed Argentina's official entry into the Bretton Woods institutions and the payment of a $150 million quota to each institution.[108]

Conclusion

Perón's Argentina conducted—and, on several occasions, promoted—a long series of negotiations with the Bretton Woods institutions. The ups and downs of those negotiations were not due to lack of interest; instead, they reflected how advanced the discussions had become. In fact, reconstructing those negotiations shows that the two main phases were interrupted precisely at the stage at which Argentine membership came closest to realization. While the second round was abruptly suspended by the coup d'état of 1955, it is not unreasonable to suppose that if the Liberating Revolution had not taken place, Perón would have entered history as the first Argentine president to sign an agreement with the IMF and World Bank. The speed and facility by which the new government joined the Bretton Woods institutions in 1956 suggests that the discussions conducted by Perón's government had paved the way for the final accord.

Analysis of the available documentation shows that, contrary to what is commonly put forth in the historiography, Perón's government was not only interested in joining the IMF and World Bank, but it also took increasingly substantive steps to achieve that objective. While it is true that Perón hesitated to make the decisive move during his first years in power, there is no doubt that he was very far from rejecting the option. Nevertheless, Perón, who personally conducted most of the negotiations, was not the only active player in this inconclusive relationship. If anyone had the last word and veto power, it was the United States, which controlled the final decisions taken by the Bretton Woods institutions.

The available documentation does not completely answer why these efforts did not result in the signing of an agreement among the parties. Clearly, however, an examination of the negotiations conducted during the first Perón era requires us to scrutinize old claims more carefully. Some of those claims stem from a general perception of Peronism and populism. Others, however, result from a tendency to project back to the relatively flexible IMF and World Bank of the 1940s and 1950s the more rigid positions and conditionality for which they are criticized today, sixty-five years later.

The negotiations of the first Perón era point to a combination of obstacles to Argentina's entry into the Bretton Woods institutions. While Perón might have wanted to join the World Bank, his government had neither the political will nor the necessary technical capacity to pay the price that membership, especially in the IMF, implied. That price included taking political and propaganda risks, because such an action could be seen as a betrayal of Argentine nationalist and autonomist positions. It also would have required significant changes to the country's financial system, including the institution of an exchange rate based on a single par value, reform of the banking system, and increased transparency. It should be emphasized that the IMF doubted Argentina's capacity to implement this package of reforms. Although its doubts increased with Perón's downfall, the IMF did not hesitate to accept Argentina's membership in 1956.[109] Furthermore, some of the required reforms, including the elimination of multiple exchange rates, were fully implemented only in 1958, as the first loan was being finalized.

There were also multiple obstacles on the non-Argentine side. The study of the relationship among the IMF, the World Bank, and Perón (and, later, the provisional presidents of the Liberating Revolution) shows the differences that existed in the practices and perceptions of the two institutions. It also reveals the apparent discrepancies between the Bretton Woods twins and their most powerful member, the United States. The available evidence suggests that the Bretton Woods institutions, motivated by the desire to expand and operating largely on a pragmatic basis, were more interested than Washington was in signing an agreement with Argentina.[110] The entry of this key Latin American nation, especially after activity was interrupted in Europe in 1948 by the launching of the European Recovery (Marshall) Plan, was a legitimate goal for both institutions. The U.S. government, for its part, was still debating whether ending Argentina's exclusion was appropriate. The debate involved not only old disputes (such as neutrality), but also new issues (Perón's Third Position, nationalism, anti-imperialism, and populism) and the difficulty of reversing past policies—specifically, the exclusion of Argentina from the Bretton Woods Conference.

That the Perón government gradually adopted liberalizing measures applauded in Washington would seem to suggest that the Bretton Woods institutions exercised influence not only on the policies of its member countries, but also on countries that aspired to membership. If this is the case, one cannot but suggest that Argentina's dependence on the IMF began to gestate in the years before it was admitted officially into that institution. In other words, the power to approve or deny loans was used as a tool to influence member countries (as in the case of Chile, as mentioned earlier), and the power to admit Argentina to membership in the IMF and World Bank was used in exactly the same way.

Once Argentina was admitted as a member of the IMF, the signing of the agreement brought to the surface the asymmetry that has characterized the relationship between the parties. To the fact that the IMF and the World Bank were potential lenders and Argentina was their potential borrower should be added the "professional gap." As we have seen, even before Argentina formally applied for membership, the World Bank and, especially, the IMF had begun to prepare for that possibility. That preparation was largely facilitated by the experience and professionalism that the Fund had been accumulating since 1946 through its joint work with member and non-member countries. Moreover, the fact that the same well-trained officials conducted the highly intensive talks with Argentina over the years added a new dimension to the asymmetrical relationship. Jorge del Canto is a salient example of this phenomenon. Since the launching of the IMF's activities, he had been a member of the Research Department and had been actively involved in the negotiations with Perón. Between 1956 and 1977, he served as the head of the powerful Western Hemisphere Department and exerted increasing influence on the Latin American scene.

Del Canto is an iconic example of a large group of highly professional officers who have served in the IMF for long periods of time and are therefore intimately familiar with the realities of the different countries they deal with and with the evolution of relations with member states. In other words, the IMF's power was a result not just of its material resources but also of its knowledge and experience. The negotiations in 1956 brought to the same table a group of IMF professionals and a couple of young Argentine economists who, due to the changing political scene, had been out of the public and government sphere for almost a decade. As a result, although they were assigned the task of signing a membership accord, they do not seem to have been fully aware of the details related to the negotiations that had taken place under Perón—at least, not as familiar as the IMF's economists were. Moreover, not only were these young economists only partially updated, but they represented a provisional administration that was ideologically heterogeneous and politically unstable, an unenviable position to be in when dealing with the experienced and professional IMF staff.

Following its entry into the Bretton Woods institutions in 1956, Argentina tightened its ties with the IMF and became a borrowing member dependent on the blessing of the international financial community. Since then, Argentina's Ministry of Economy and Central Bank have been governed by economists who have not only known how to convey the message that Washington has expected to hear, but who also have been entrenched in the liberal economic approach that is so closely identified with the IMF. The relationship with the IMF has had a profound impact on Argentina's political and economic life, because it has served as fertile ground for a demanding routine of dependency to grow.

3

Dependency in the Making

The First Loan Agreement and the
Consolidation of the Formal Relationship
with the IMF, 1957–1961

A rgentina joined the Bretton Woods institutions twelve years later than the other countries in the region and two years after the first IMF loan to a Latin American member state (Peru) was approved.[1] Yet the distance between Argentina's incorporation into both institutions in 1956 and the initiation of activities with the IMF was very short.

The formal relationship between the IMF and Argentina began to develop during the Liberating Revolution, the military uprising that ended Perón's regime in September 1955 and stayed in power for three years. The cautious steps taken by President Pedro Aramburu's government (November 1955–April 1958) in this area constituted a learning curve, a process of socialization,[2] and an internalization of common working norms—especially on Argentina's part.

Ironically, it was during the tenure of President Arturo Frondizi (May 1958–March 1962), the head of the Intransigent Radical Civic Union and the most fervent opponent of Argentina's entry into the multilateral system during the Peronist era, that Argentina intensified its dependence on the IMF. This chapter thus explores the paradox that Latin American leaders like Frondizi confronted while attempting to improve their countries' positions in the new economic order: In their attempt to attain economic development and independence, they actually deepened their dependence on the international community in general, and on the IMF in particular.

Through a close examination of the cyclical and continuous contacts between Argentina and the IMF when the first loan agreement was signed in 1958 and when it was renewed in 1959–1961, this chapter describes and defines what I term the "routine of dependency." In effect, the loan agreements and subsequent implementation of belt-tightening stabilization programs are used here as a window onto the broad range of monitoring activities that were explicitly stipulated in the loan agreements signed from the 1950s on, not only with Argentina, but also with other borrowers in Latin America and in other regions of the world. As we shall see, these demanding monitoring procedures were the ones that paved the road to a long series of interactions between Argentine and IMF technicians and high-ranking officials. These interactions, which vary in scope and nature and take place with a few different, local nuances in most of the IMF's borrowing countries, soon became fertile ground for the development of a socialization process through which local representatives and institutions internalized the standards, working norms, precepts, and ideas of the IMF. In this manner, they created an epistemic community of experts, if not an alliance. As the events that took place during Frondizi's tenure indicate, this influential socialization process, which is part and parcel of the routine of dependency, was not just a byproduct of the lender–borrower relationship. Rather, it was a central component of the new multilateralism and a reflection of the need or desire of certain key local economists and politicians, such as Roberto Alemann and Julio Alsogaray, to promote the opening and liberalization of Argentina's economy.

Although most of the dilemmas, conflicts, mechanisms, routines, and professional and personal ties discussed here are common to almost every Argentine regime and to other Latin American debtors that have entered into agreements with the IMF, the case of Frondizi is of particular interest. Indeed, Frondizi's close and perhaps unexpected relations with the IMF—an organization that he had steadfastly criticized on nationalist grounds—raise the question of why and how he apparently reversed his position once he took office.

First, one should keep in mind that Frondizi had been known for his developmentalist approach to addressing Argentina's challenges. Developmentalism emerged in Latin America in the 1950s not only as a theoretical tool but also as a platform to elaborate solutions to the problem of underdevelopment. Developmentalism is identified with the Economic Commission for Latin America and the Caribbean (ECLAC) and with such renowned economists as Raúl Prebisch, Victor Urquidi, Alberto Hirschman, and Rogelio Frigerio, one of Frondizi's closest allies.[3]

Developmentalism viewed the constant deterioration in the terms of trade for agricultural and mining products as the main cause of underdevelopment in countries engaged in the production and export of primary products. Massive industrialization and the expansion of energy and transportation infrastructure were defined as vital for economic development.[4] Latin American countries, however, lacked the resources and technology required to set the ambitious development project in motion. Under such circumstances, turning to foreign capital was perceived as a legitimate way to narrow the gap between the developing and the developed world. Frondizi therefore deemed passing the Law of Foreign Investment in late 1958 and accepting loans from the IMF and World

Bank two sides of the same acceptable coin. His position becomes even more intelligible in light of the fact that Latin American adherence to the Bretton Woods principles was a top priority on the U.S. agenda. Indeed, Washington expected membership in the IMF and World Bank to contribute to counter-nationalism and quasi-statism in the region.[5] In other words, the liberalizing measures Frondizi adopted attracted capital that he considered necessary for Argentina's development project and, at the same time, helped to tighten the ties with the United States, the most powerful member of the IMF and World Bank.

Frondizi's conviction that the world was on the cusp of an era of relative peace between the Soviet Union and the United States fueled his optimism regarding economic development. The decreased tension between the two superpowers was expected to redirect resources from war industry to investment. To attract foreign capital, Frondizi sought to improve Argentina's political, economic, and trade partnership with the United States and its neighbors in Latin America, on the one hand, and with the Soviet bloc, on the other.[6] In addition, Frondizi was encouraged by the support development was rapidly gaining across the continent. In 1961, in the aftermath of the Cuban Revolution and in an attempt to thwart further communist penetration into Latin America, President John F. Kennedy launched the Alliance for Progress.[7]

This chapter thus examines how broad support for Argentina's development project contributed, directly and indirectly, to the consolidation of the country's relationship with the IMF. To highlight the making and consolidation of the routine of dependency, the chapter is organized by cycles, with each cycle covering roughly a one-year period. The chronological analysis sheds light on two parallel processes: the ongoing entrenchment of the routine of dependency and the strengthening of the IMF as a key player in the international arena and as a bureaucratic and highly professional organization. At the same time, the chapter points to the gradual deterioration of Argentina's economy and institutions—a deterioration that resulted largely from Argentina's own political and economic dynamics.

The First Cycle, 1957–1958:
Argentina's Rapid Adaptation to the IMF's Norms

Joint work with the IMF was initiated during the tenure of Eduardo Lonardi, the de facto president from September to November 1955. The pressure exerted on Argentina to repay its debts to countries such as Germany and Britain,[8] the decreasing level of reserves of foreign exchange, along with the new government's determination to differentiate itself from Peronism, were among the key factors that drove cooperation with the IMF. Nevertheless, the joint working relationship began gradually.

The first contacts between the parties took place within the so-called Article IV Consultation framework, a procedure that is conducted once a year with each and every member country and consists of three phases: (1) preliminary work by the IMF at its headquarters in Washington, DC; (2) discussions in the member country with an IMF mission; and (3) analysis of the mission's report by the IMF's Board of Directors and decision making.[9] Until the early 1960s, the consultation mechanism was used mainly as a means of monitoring the actual abandonment of protectionist practices in trade and the progress made toward economic liberalization.[10] In practice, although the term "consultation" connotes reciprocity, it was a distinctly asymmetrical procedure. The IMF demanded information, supervised, and made decisions, while the member country disclosed the required data and awaited the resolution on its fate.

Yet the clarity with which the consultation mechanism was defined was not enough to prevent Argentina and the IMF from developing opposing expectations from it, in both technical and substantial terms. For instance, when Guillermo Corominas Segura, the Argentine representative on the IMF's Executive Board, asked in early March 1957 for a postponement of the first consultation, the IMF warned, "Postponement of the consultations will be misinterpreted by some as reluctance by Argentina to enter into a relationship of mutual confidence with the Fund. It is for this reason that I wish to argue that arrangements for the consultations should go forward as planned."[11]

The IMF's acerbic response subdued the Argentines, and the consultation began on time. However, soon after the arrival of the IMF mission in Buenos Aires, further discrepancies emerged. One of the most significant gaps pertained to the type and quality of information the IMF expected to receive, as opposed to the information that the Argentine Central Bank was willing and able to furnish. Therefore, as was customary in the IMF,[12] the mission gathered complementary data from other countries that maintained bilateral trade agreements with Argentina (Bolivia, Brazil, Chile, Ecuador, Paraguay, Peru, Uruguay, Finland, Israel, Japan, West Germany, Yugoslavia, and most of the members of the Paris Club).[13]

Notwithstanding the initial difficulties, the first consultation led to the first transaction between the parties—a purchase of $75 million.[14] Not only was this transaction almost automatic, but the sum approved—50 percent of Argentina's quota—was not out of the ordinary. In general, the maximum sum a member country is allowed to purchase from the IMF is 125 percent of its quota, divided into "tranches" of 25 percent each. The IMF's position with regard to purchases within the first 25 percent of the member's quota (referred to as "gold tranche") is relatively liberal. Requests to purchase beyond that sum are subject to explanation and justification. Thus, it was only toward the end of 1958, when the amounts requested by Argentina considerably increased, that the negotiations turned intense and conflictive.

The Making of the First Stand-by Arrangement

Following the first transaction, Argentina's activities with the IMF intensified. This intensification, which reached its peak with the signing of the first loan agreement in December 1958, triggered a fast diversification of the joint working routine.

The second consultation—the first step of the second cycle of joint activities—took place in mid-1958, as scheduled. This consultation was different from the previous one. First, it began during the Liberating Revolution and ended with Frondizi in office. In other words, it was a single sequence that was carried through in an orderly fashion, despite the change of governments in Argentina. Second, it reflected an increasing willingness by Argentina to adapt to the IMF's norms and procedures. For instance, in January 1958, to facilitate the preliminary preparations of the IMF mission, the Argentine Ministry of Economy dispatched a detailed report on the country's trade and payments system.[15] This time, the information was on par with IMF's specifications.

Indeed, about five months after receiving the report, and two months after Frondizi moved into the Casa Rosada in May 1958, an IMF mission set out for Argentina. It was headed by Jorge del Canto, the influential and experienced director of the Western Hemisphere Department. He was accompanied by several officials, including David Finch, John Woodly, and Eugenio Bertens, who also had been playing major roles in shaping the relationship with Argentina and other Latin American nations.

The political and technical meetings with Argentina's economic leadership took place on July 11–15, 1958. The first one was moderated by Eusebio Campos, vice-president of the Central Bank, who presented details of the exchange-rate reform proposed by Argentina. The second meeting, attended by Ricardo Lumi, secretary of the Ministry of Economy, centered on the 1958–1959 budget.[16] On the Central Bank's recommendation, the delegation met not only with representatives of the Ministry of Economy and the Central Bank, as was conventional, but also with directors of mortgage banks and of banks that served the industrial sector.[17] Such encounters undoubtedly provided a broad picture that expanded above and beyond the macroeconomic aspects on which the IMF would ordinarily focus. Thus, in the final meeting, del Canto referred to macro- and microeconomic issues, including wages in the public sector, tax increases, the price of public services provided by the state, inflation, credit policy, the banking system, and so on. Nevertheless, the topic that captured most of the attention was the planned reform of the exchange system. According to the plan, Argentina was to maintain the par value of 18 pesos per dollar, although this rate would not be applied to international transactions.[18] Despite efforts at persuasion by the Argentines, the IMF mission rejected the plan, arguing that it would lead back to the multiple exchange rate system and to protectionism in international trade, practices that the IMF was striving to eradicate.

The mission's final report was submitted on August 20. Predictably, it contained harsh criticism of Argentina's continued reliance on the bilateral trade system and of the planned exchange-rate reform.[19] The mission did not content itself with criticism, however. First, it reported to the U.S. administration that Argentina was still incapable of taking the necessary steps to restore internal and external balances.[20] In addition, it suggested a plan of its own that was based on measures such as raising taxes, curtailing government expenses, cutting wages, and encouraging investment in industry.[21] Even though Argentina was reluctant at that point to adopt the IMF's plan, it eventually relinquished its intentions to carry out the reform formulated by the Ministry of Economy.

The Argentine concession was lauded by the IMF and led to the dispatching of a new mission. Headed by Gesualdo Costanzo, a high official in the Western Hemisphere Department, the mission visited Buenos Aires during November 8–22, 1958. Its declared goal was to examine the possibility of granting a loan to Argentina. As seen below, approval of the loan was closely linked with the implementation of an economic stabilization program, which Argentina was no longer able to formulate on its own.

The Stabilization Program Elaborated by . . . Frondizi?

Before discussing Frondizi's economic plan, it is worth noting the uniqueness of IMF stabilization programs. These programs were originally designed to help member countries solve temporary (as distinct from structural) financial problems and crises in their balances of payments. If they cannot solve these problems, IMF economists believe, the borrowers will not be able to repay their debts.[22] This is why the IMF, as well as the World Bank, was pressuring Brazil, Chile, Colombia, Ecuador, Paraguay, and Peru to adopt the same programs in the mid-1950s, with almost identical austerity measures.[23]

To achieve their goals, IMF stabilization programs generally focus on four main policy areas: credit controls (domestic credit ceilings and foreign transactions); fiscal controls (devaluation, export taxes, import subsidies, cuts in public spending); exchange rate adjustments; and price and wage controls.[24] The distinctiveness of these programs is not limited to their content. It spills into their process of consolidation. In practice, when the IMF asks a member state to explain its need for a loan that exceeds 25 percent of its quota, it also asks what the local authorities intend to do to solve the problems that justify the approval of the loan. Put simply, the need for explanation and justification for sums defined by the IMF as extraordinary actually blurs the line that distinguishes between the loan negotiations and the elaboration of the stabilization program.

What was the actual scope of the IMF's involvement in formulating the stabilization program in 1958? Is "involvement" necessarily synonymous with "imposition"? Some scholars, such as Luigi Manzetti, claim that nothing in the loan agreements Frondizi signed was really imposed by the IMF.[25] My findings, by contrast, suggest that "imposition" and "choice," so prevalent in the academic literature and public debate, may not be the most accurate terms to describe the nature and complexity of the IMF's involvement. As Roberto Frenkel and Guillermo O'Donnell argue, "It is simplistic to believe that 'somebody' imposed these programs from abroad. But it is also simplistic to assert that a given government 'freely' elected a certain program that was 'later' approved by the IMF."[26] While I tend to agree with this line of reasoning, my argument is that the bureaucratic and sociological aspects of the IMF's relations with its borrowers (even more than the economic and political ones) allow the IMF to set aside the need to impose economic plans. Indeed, Argentina's active membership in the IMF led to a gradual internalization by both local politicians and economists of the principles and working norms of the Bretton Woods institutions. Once the internalization process was under way, endorsing an "IMF-style" program became nothing less than a "natural" option.

The internalization process (which brings to mind the socialization concept used by John Ikenberry and Charles Kupchan to refer to non-coercive ways by which a hegemonic nation can exercise power and secure the acquiescence of other nations[27]) is facilitated by the almost permanent interactions between the IMF and its borrowers. These interactions take place during frequent meetings, negotiations, and consultations both in Washington, DC, and in the capital cities of the borrowing nations and through the preparation, dispatching, and receipt of written reports (some of them weekly) that are in line with the IMF's instructions and requirements. By closely following the IMF's interactions with Argentina, one can certainly get a strong sense of the magnitude and intensity of the socialization and internalization processes. In effect, IMF missions have visited Argentina (as well as its neighbor countries) not once but three, four, and even six times a year, and national officials have held very similar numbers of meeting at the IMF headquarters. To this, of course, should be added the fact that, at certain times, permanent representatives of the IMF (to whom I refer later in this chapter) have been stationed for at least a year at national central banks, making the socialization process a truly permanent and routine process that affects high-ranking and low-ranking official alike.

As the case of Frondizi demonstrates, the internationalization of the IMF's norms and values occurs regardless of whether a loan agreement is in place. In effect, formal loan negotiations do not take place unless the parties reach a certain degree of concurrence in advance. For this purpose, a preliminary consultation—which in most cases is carried out separately from the annual consultation—is conducted even before the loan agreement the country seeks to renew is completed. In this specific case, the preliminary consultation took place under the auspices of Costanzo's mission in November 1958.[28]

The Argentine officials were aware that Costanzo had the mandate to determine Argentina's chances of securing a loan and were eager to collaborate with him.[29] The mission's good will was abundant. In fact, it had no reason to be otherwise: Within a few months, Argentina had made a surprising shift toward economic liberalization. Indeed, although the Fund had expressed discontent with the proposed exchange rate reform and the continuation of bilateralism back in July, it was now satisfied with the planned measures to curb inflation, the new proposed reform, and the promise to revoke the existing bilateral agreements.[30]

Despite the progress noted by the IMF, Argentina was still a long way away from launching a stabilization program. Frondizi's political weakness (deriving from his rise to power based on Peronist votes once the Peronist party was outlawed), the disputes within the ruling party, and Argentine society's difficulty in accepting an orthodox economic policy all impeded the president in his attempt to articulate his goals for the coming years.[31] Since Argentina's chances of getting a loan from the IMF were almost nonexistent without the approval of a stabilization program, the Ministry of Economy proceeded with the formulation of its final details.[32]

The program, which began to take shape following the consultation of August 1958, entered its most decisive stages in November. Toward the end of the month, Argentina begged the IMF to expedite the decision-making process.[33] Frondizi's political time was dangerously running out. Because of this urgency, Emilio del Carril, the new minister of economy, paid a visit to the United States on December 1 "to be present when the IMF discusse[d] the stabilization program," even before the program was finalized.[34]

Del Carril, though, was not content with passive attendance at the IMF debates. He held a series of meetings with the Export-Import Bank and with sixteen commercial banks in New York, hoping to secure further loans.[35] On December 4, he submitted an official request for a loan to Per Jacobsson, the influential managing director of the IMF. At the center of the request was the letter of intent, which, according to the IMF's requirements, included a detailed list of all of the measures to which the government was committing to solve Argentina's economic ills.[36]

Such measures were designed, first and foremost, to bring an end to inflation and restore the balance between internal and external price levels.[37] It is vital to understand that although a letter of intent is invariably signed only by the authorities of the borrowing country (the economic minister or the director of the central bank, and sometimes both of them), it is by no means written independently by them. On the contrary, both the letter and the loan agreement are a direct outcome of the discussions held in advance with highly professional IMF missions, which specialize in performing the preliminary reviews.[38] In this case, the letter's principles were decided on in advance with Costanzo. About a week after the request for the loan was submitted, an updated IMF report was published, that "praised Argentina's attempts to curb inflation through a stringent stabilization program."[39] It should be noted that as the IMF praised Argentina, the program remained confidential for a very simple reason: It still was not finalized.

On December 13, Frondizi held a prolonged meeting with Frigerio (who remained a close adviser even though he no longer held an official government position) and with prominent Argentine industrialists. The meeting was critical: The emerging stabilization program was expected to remove import barriers and encourage competition between domestic and foreign products; it thus raised bitterness and unrest within the national industrial sector, whose support was vital not only to the Argentine economy but also to the president's political survival.[40] Recruiting supporters for the program, both within the government and in opposition circles, proved so difficult that Frondizi arranged an additional meeting with Argentina's economic leaders "to discuss the conditions imposed by the IMF."[41]

On December 18, before Frondizi had managed to achieve a consensus, the IMF unanimously approved the first loan to Argentina, worth $75 million.[42] It is reasonable to assume that this approval was a key factor in allowing the stabilization program to be completed. On the one hand, the IMF's approval provided at least part of the legitimacy needed to launch an unpopular plan and provided a green light for foreign lenders and investors. On the other hand, and on a more pragmatic level, it provided the resources without which, according to the prevalent view in the Argentine administration, no integral development plan could ever be implemented. Indeed, the program was not published in Argentina until December 29, a few days after the fateful vote at the IMF.

The stabilization program represented a significant change in Argentina's economic policy. The agreement with the Fund was not limited to macroeconomic goals; instead, it included a list of measures directed at solving what were perceived as the most fundamental evils of Argentina's economy. For example, to reduce public-sector deficits, it stated that "the government [would] reduce by 15 percent the number of public employees by the end of 1959"; "$2 billion savings [would] be obtained by delaying the completion of public construction projects already under way and by postponing new projects"; and the operating deficits of autonomous agencies would be drastically limited in 1959.[43] One finds strikingly similar measures in agreements signed at the time with other Latin American countries—for example, the agreement signed in July 1959 by Pedro Beltrán, prime minister and finance minister under Peru's President Manuel Prado Ugarteche.[44] In any case, as could and probably should be expected, the reduction of operating deficits carried a high social price tag. In the case of the railroads in particular, and of public transportation in general, the program stipulated that tariffs would be raised by an average of 150 percent within a year and that unprofitable services would progressively be eliminated. In addition, the program set a substantial increase in electricity rates, a 200 percent increase in the price of petroleum and derivative products, and the cancellation of consumer and producer subsidies.[45] Even though the state was to maintain a certain degree of intervention in the economy, there is no doubt that most of these measures implied a departure not only from developmentalist principles, but also from the statism and protectionism that were so deeply ingrained in Argentina.

Thus, December 1958 was a major milestone in the history of the relationship between Argentina and the IMF. It was a formative phase in a process in which Argentina gradually relinquished certain components of its economic sovereignty, such as the ability to determine independently the timing of the publication of its national economic plans and, even worse, of the details of such plans. Even if we were to generalize and argue that all national economic programs are affected by external pressure, the events of late 1958 represent a substantial change. For Argentina, the beginning of interaction with the IMF meant not only increased exposure to external factors, but also the opening of a new era of direct involvement by an international organization in the formulation of national economic policy.

The Multilateralism Trap: The Approval of the First IMF Loan Agreement

The IMF's increasing involvement in Argentina did not imply the exclusion of other actors from the local scene. On the contrary, the willingness of "secondary players" (including but not limited to European countries and the United States, the Export-Import Bank, and foreign private lenders and investors) to extend loans to Argentina and other countries following an IMF loan indicates that the IMF quickly became a driving force that attracted and expedited the influx of foreign capital.

Yet it should be stressed that the IMF's powerful standing derived not necessarily from the funds that it lent to borrowers—which were relatively limited—but from the fact that its loans became an indispensable seal of approval that opened access to further funds from other lenders. According to official figures, in December 1958 Argentina received $125 million from the Export-Import Bank, $50 million from the U.S. Department of the Treasury, $25 million from the Development Loan Fund, and $54 million from eleven U.S. commercial banks.[46] In other words, of the total $329 million that found its way into Argentina, only $75 million consisted of IMF funds. Regardless of their source, the loans provided enormous relief to Argentina, at least in the short term. In late 1958, Frondizi's administration had no choice but to reinstate equilibrium in the balance of payments, increase the country's foreign currency reserves, support the Argentine Central Bank's monetary policy, and complete the liberalization and unification of the exchange market.[47]

The loan package tailored to Argentina's particular needs was not an innovation. Indeed, since its establishment, the IMF has supplied only fractions of the sums considered necessary by its member countries. In practice, what Erica Gould terms "supplementary financiers" have long been providing additional financing that has significantly increased the actual volume of assistance offered by the IMF. In the early years, and certainly during the 1950s, the main supplementary financier had been the U.S. government (both directly and through affiliated institutions such as the Export-Import Bank). Today, the supplementary financiers are mostly private creditors and multilateral organizations, who seek to have a say in the conditions imposed on borrowers in return for their financial contributions.[48]

The stabilization loans of 1958 were only part of the story, however, as Argentina made considerable efforts to increase the rate and volume of direct foreign investment. To that end, the Law of Foreign Investment (14.780) and the Complementary Law of the Encouragement of Industry (14.781) were passed in late 1958.[49] These efforts appeared to be successful. Among other things, the United States granted Argentina further credit in early 1959 for the purchase and maintenance of tractors as an expression of the State Department's support of Frondizi's regime.[50]

The capital that began to flow into Argentina in the form of loans and investments, and the unprecedented number of foreign entities involved, raises the question of how Frondizi, a leader known for his nationalistic views and his fervent anti–Bretton Woods position during the Peronist era, explained the rapid liberalization of the economy. Obviously, it could be argued that Frondizi was not the first politician to put aside some of his convictions once in office. This supposition, however, seems unconvincing, especially if we take into account that, in 1959, Frondizi expressed his fears that "foreign capital and technicians would not be enough. It is imperative that the country capitalize itself individually and collectively. . . . Otherwise, that foreign capital, instead of serving as leverage for our liberation, might become links in a chain of subordination."[51]

Frondizi thus was fully aware of the risks of relying on foreign capital. However, it might not be unreasonable to suggest that he considered loans from the IMF as belonging to a different, if not a privileged, category. To be sure, Argentina's status as a member of the multilateral institution that was providing the loans could have created a misleading impression that the funds were coming from a source that was less intrusive or dangerous than, say, foreign private lenders or powerful states that used foreign aid as a tool for political influence. After all, as was shown in chapter 2, this was part of the logic that propelled Juan D. Perón to negotiate with the Bretton Woods institutions. At the same time, it is crucial to understand that since early 1959, Frondizi had literally disappeared from the negotiating table with the IMF. Unfortunately, due to the lack of Argentine documents on this issue, it is impossible to determine whether his disappearance was the consequence of a voluntary renouncement or the result of a compromise that let pro-liberal economists set the tone in exchange for political calm.

Hypotheses aside, the approval of the stabilization program and the signing of the first SBA were not the ultimate result of a long process. Far from it: They were just the point of departure in a new phase in Argentina's intensive and demanding relationship with the IMF.

The Multifaceted Components of the Routine of Dependency

The agreement signed in December 1958 defined not only the amount of the loan and the economic goals to which Argentina had committed itself, but also the nature of the surveillance to be exercised by the IMF. In this respect, the agreement was no different from others signed in the same period with, for example, Bolivia, Brazil, Chile, Ecuador, or Peru.[52] This ostensible uniformity stemmed from the fact that in 1952, in an attempt to reach a compromise between economists who supported the automatic granting of loans and those who advocated conditionality, the IMF began to reform its lending system largely through the elaboration of a new instrument that soon became widespread: the Stand-by Arrangement (SBA).

Stand-by arrangements were approved to address a wide range of situations: to convey confidence in a certain currency, to provide supplementary resources in times of recession, to support plans designed to bring economic stability, to promote reforms in currency markets, and so on. SBAs were often signed not as solutions to problems but as ways to encourage countries to continued implementing a specific policy. In such cases, the member countries often refrained from using the funds while maintaining their right to do so in times of crisis.[53] As the Argentine case illustrates, each agreement was signed under different circumstances and was implemented for different purposes.

Stand-by arrangements are innovative in that through them, the IMF provides access to a predefined amount of money for a limited period of time and subject to conditions. The most substantial innovation, however, is that the entire sum is given not in one installment, as in an ordinary loan, but gradually, in phases, with the loan "on stand-by" between phases. Progress between phases (i.e., the ability to continue to draw funds) is conditional and contingent on the borrower's ability to meet a given number of conditions.[54] These conditions, which are in line with the key points in the letter of intent, are neither identical nor equally enforced in all cases.

In the 1950s, three kinds of SBAs were established. The simplest, which was almost unconditional, was applied, for instance, in the agreements signed with

Britain in December 1957 and 1958. A second group, which contained one or two conditions, included agreements subscribed with France and Spain in 1959. The third and most common type, which contained numerous conditions, is exemplified by the agreements signed from the mid-1950s on with Argentina, Bolivia, Brazil, Chile, Colombia, Haiti, Honduras, Mexico, Paraguay, and Peru.[55]

The phased nature of the SBAs, along with the need to evaluate whether the borrower had indeed met the stipulated conditions, led to the creation of surveillance or monitoring mechanisms. Indeed, the SBA signed with Argentina in December 1958 explicitly referred to the nature of such monitoring. Its first paragraph, that featured, with minor changes, in all SBAs,[56] determined that "Argentina and the Fund will remain in close consultation during the period the SBA is in effect. This consultation may take the form of correspondence and visits of officials of the Fund to Buenos Aires or of representatives of Argentina to Washington. In addition, Argentina will keep the Fund informed of developments in the exchange, credit, and fiscal situation through reports at intervals."[57]

The IMF thus termed its surveillance "consultation," the same word used for the review procedure that was (and still is) conducted annually with each and every member country, borrowers and creditors alike. In fact, this is yet another attempt to represent as reciprocal a procedure that is inherently asymmetric.

The nature of the consultation that follows the signing of SBAs has been notably more complex and diverse than the annual consultation. Such complexity, intensity, and subtlety are the factors that transform the surveillance mechanism into the seeds from which a relentlessly diversifying and vigorous routine of dependency begins to germinate. The surveillance is aimed at covering all aspects of the implementation (or non-implementation) of the provisions listed in the letter of intent, the SBA, and the stabilization plan. In broadly terms, it took place in two main ways: through written reports or through meetings.

The written follow-up includes weekly reports dispatched to the IMF's headquarters in the form of telegrams and letters. In effect, right after the SBA with Argentina was signed in 1958, the IMF sent to the Ministry of Economy a list of all of the items to be described in the weekly updates, such as exchange rates, Central Bank reserve levels, breakdowns of loans from other sources, and balance sheets.[58] It should be noted that as early as February 1959, the IMF was complaining (as it does today) that Argentina was providing only partial information and was firmly demanding all of the data, as agreed.[59]

For obvious reasons, monitoring through discussion has been more active, complex, and varied than that conducted through written documents. The dynamic nature of the IMF's close and personal surveillance became evident almost as soon the first SBA was signed and IMF representatives began trying to influence Argentine economic policy. In January 1959, for instance, the IMF exerted heavy pressure on Argentina to abandon its plans to fix meat prices and impose a tax on exports of meat.[60] Similarly, to take another example, "after protracted discussions" with the IMF, "Argentine officials agreed to decrease the level of advance deposits for imports to about half the sum [they had] initially proposed."[61]

In fact, IMF representatives did not refrain from interfering even when their involvement heightened tension and sharpened controversies among Argentina's economic team. A dispute over railways tariffs offers an unambiguous case in point. In the letter of intent of 1958, Argentina committed to raise its railway tariffs by an average of 150 percent within a year. While del Carril was firm in his intention to meet this commitment, the minister of transportation vehemently opposed it and eventually had no choice but to resign. The minister's departure from office did not please the IMF, however, which demanded that del Carril produce a statement promising that "regardless of the level of new railway tariffs, there will be no financing from the banking system or from the Treasury in excess of the amounts already agreed under the stand-by arrangement."[62] In an extraordinary move, del Carril dispatched the requested written statement to the IMF.

The IMF's close monitoring thus incited situations in which decisions and measures taken by Argentina were met with an immediate reaction from the Fund. Therefore, instead of subjecting every final decision to retroactive scrutiny by the IMF, Argentina often adopted a more prudent position and consulted the IMF beforehand. For instance, Argentine economic officials approached IMF delegates who were visiting Buenos Aires and asked what the Fund's opinion would be if Argentina decided to tax stocks of export commodities. The mission immediately relayed the question to Washington, received instructions, and transmitted the answer to the Argentine administration.[63]

Despite Argentina's fast adaptation, the joint working routine was by no means free of conflict. Time and again, the multifaceted character of the surveillance mechanism brought to the surface gaps in the parties' expectations and readiness to follow the terms of the agreements. For example, Bertens wrote in a confidential letter to H. Merle Cochran, deputy managing director of the IMF, that del Carril had "mentioned that in some quarters at the Fund, assurances were given to him that any changes needed for the [stabilization] program could be approved in Washington if other parts of the program are more in line with the original letter of commitment [sic] for the stand-by."[64] In practice, it appears that del Carril had cultivated a wrong impression that he could revise the list of protected import and export products based only on Argentine considerations. The IMF made it clear that it would not consent to such an independent step, and it was therefore decided that the matter would be discussed during Frondizi's visit to Washington in January 1959.[65]

Notwithstanding these and other minor or major glitches that hardly posed a threat to the routine of dependency, it could be argued that at least at this early stage, the IMF was impressed by Argentina's commitment to implement the stabilization program.[66] Argentina's compliance, however, did not lead to a decrease in the intensity of the surveillance. On the contrary: The supervision and monitoring grew. At its peak, it included unofficial meetings with senior Argentine officials, as well as the presence of a permanent IMF representative at the Central Bank of Argentina.

Permanent IMF Representation in Argentina

The time that missions and delegates were spending in member countries often was not considered sufficient by the IMF. Consequently, the Fund designed new frameworks to allow it to maintain a sustained, sometimes permanent, presence in borrowers' centers of economic power.[67] By "permanent," the IMF meant one or more of its technocrats residing in a borrowing country for at least a year to provide "technical assistance"—that is, "to help countries to strengthen their capacity in both human and institutional resources, and to design appropriate macroeconomic, financial, and structural policies."[68]

The arrival of permanent residents and missions in borrowing countries, to state the obvious, has led to a significant escalation and entrenchment of the routine of dependency. Moreover, the countless formal and informal encounters between IMF economists and Argentine officials have enabled the IMF's technocrats to easily recognize those local bureaucrats whom Jeffrey Chwieroth describes as "sympathetic interlocutors" eager to collaborate with the Fund.[69] On a more theoretical level, it could be argued that the routine of dependency facilitates, stimulates, and even guarantees the birth of what Peter Hass has termed an "epistemic community," or "a network of knowledge-based experts or groups with an authoritative claim to policy-relevant knowledge within the domain of their expertise."[70] During Frondizi's presidency, it was precisely the evolution of these small but highly respected epistemic communities that ensured the implementation of austerity measures that were unpopular not only in broad sectors of Argentine society, but within the cabinet itself.

Immediately after the first SBA was signed, Eugenio Bertens, a prestigious economist who had been involved in the negotiations with Argentina, was appointed to head a permanent delegation to Buenos Aires. When he arrived in December 1958, he stated that, if the IMF "had office space both at the Central Bank and the Minister [sic] of Economy, we [the IMF representatives] would have better access to information and day-to-day affairs."[71] Still, IMF officials ended up stationed only at the Central Bank until their mission ended in May 1960.[72] It is important to note that at the time, resident representatives were also stationed in other Latin American nations. In some cases, the IMF's permanent representatives worked with specialized government institutions, as was the case for Bruno Brovedani at the Colombian Planning Office.[73]

According to common practice, the resident representatives were funded jointly by the IMF and the national government. The former paid for air fares and salaries, while the latter covered per diem expenses for meals, transportation, and so forth for the Fund's representative.[74] Unsurprisingly, the permanent presence of IMF representatives caused tactical and substantive problems for both sides, as reported by Gesualdo Costanzo:

> Upon Mr. [Eustaquio] Méndez Delfino taking office [as the new president of the Central Bank] I was requested to use a different office, far away in a hidden corner at a different building. He [Méndez Delfino] excused himself, stating the need to avoid criticism already in the press coming from the opposition. A representative in a TV speech said that the Central Bank was receiving daily instructions from the Fund officials having quarters at the Central Bank offices, and that the Fund officials only spoke English, with the help of translators. I feel that [the IMF representative Graeme] Dorrance was not careful in avoiding seeing people and going around here.[75]

This quote reveals how local authorities attempted to navigate between domestic and external pressure, between the need or desire to strengthen ties with the IMF and the fear of the political conflicts that this could provoke in a divided—and, at the time, dangerously volatile—local sphere.

The constant presence of IMF representatives in Argentina had an impact that went far beyond what was known as "surveillance," "consultation," or "technical assistance." A few days after the stabilization program was launched, for instance, IMF representatives began to gather information and exert pressure to shape the final decisions taken on the national economic scene. In early January 1959, Bertens informed IMF headquarters that the previous night, the [Argentine] Central Bank [had] "issued all [of] the circulars related to the operations of the free market and other regulations pertaining to imports and exports. I have the opportunity to revise all of them and I am mailing a full set for our files in Washington."[76] Having dispatched the documents, Bertens awaited further instructions. When he received them, he tried to persuade the Central Bank authorities to adopt the IMF's recommendations. In one case, he reported, "I have shown [to the Central Bank officers] the cable sent from Washington about this matter [prices] and I have been able to convince the authorities that any solution different from the line suggested by the Fund should be subject to further consultations in Washington."[77] Thus, even while the IMF claimed that its financing was "intended to support a member country's own program of economic policies,"[78] Bertens's report (and those by many others) raised questions about the extent to which a debtor country was able to elaborate its "own program."[79]

In any case, their very presence in Argentina enabled IMF representatives to consolidate more convenient and less formal ways to perform their duties. Key among these was the almost natural tightening of personal ties between officials from both sides. As reported to IMF headquarters in 1959, "We have daily meetings with López and Campos which are very friendly and in which they make sure we have all the facts. Discussions at that level are adequate for all issues. Decisions are made quickly with the minimum of arguments. This is a good beginning to the comprehensive reform of the economic system and we feel sure that they are not going to slacken their efforts."[80]

To sum up, the almost uninterrupted presence of IMF representatives in the central institutions of Argentina's economy attested to the complexity of the routine of dependency. Some of the evils denounced by the IMF representatives echoed major dilemmas that originated in the very essence of the relationship between the parties. In effect, it seems that the IMF's complaints and demands about the location and size of the rooms allocated to its permanent residents at the Central Bank were in actuality a metaphor for a fundamental problem: how to determine and trace the line between areas in which the IMF was allowed (and maybe even invited) to interfere and areas to which access remained restricted or prohibited. Moreover, the tensions related to the size and location of IMF representatives' offices in national institutions could be interpreted as an allegory of the IMF's power and impact on the global system in general, and on its borrowers in particular.

Finally, IMF representatives' cultivation of both formal and informal partnerships with senior Central Bank officials not only had far-reaching implications. It also heralded a new future. The joint interests of, and ideological affinity between, the IMF and Argentina's economic leaders became another major hallmark in the evolving relationship between the parties.

There Is No Substitute for IMF Missions

The constant presence of its representatives at the Argentine Central Bank did not satisfy the IMF. The reason behind the institution's displeasure is clear: The missions that had been visiting Argentina many times a year enjoyed wide-ranging powers, while the resident representatives had no authority to make independent decisions. On the contrary, they served as a technical link to IMF headquarters. It is precisely this gap in power that made the missions a valuable tool in the IMF's hands.

Although Bertens had been doing his job well, by April 1959, preparations were being made for the arrival of a high-ranking IMF mission in Buenos Aires.[81] The timing of the visit was not random. Aware that the stabilization program had been triggering strikes and other protests in Argentina, the Fund had decided to send the mission to explain the real importance of fully implementing the economic plan as a condition for further access to it resources.[82] This constituted a serious challenge for the IMF, especially when rumors of an imminent coup became widespread in Argentina. In addition, the macroeconomic figures were rapidly worsening. Within several months, the exchange rate soared from 65 pesos to 100 pesos to the dollar. Imports plummeted and production slowed. Real wages eroded, a recession set in, and inflation set new records.[83]

The mission, led by Edgar Jones, arrived in Argentina on April 20 and left on May 9. The visitors held several summits; most of them were official, but some were not. For instance, Jones reported on an informal conversation he had with Roberto Alemann, vice-minister of economy, in which they discussed the status of the bilateral agreements that were still in force between Argentina and countries in the Soviet bloc and Latin America. As Jones reported, "We have had two discussions with the authorities here on bilateralism: the first with Mr. Alemann (Under Secretary to Del Carril), which was unofficial; the second with Mr. Del Carril and his colleagues, which was official. The first of these meetings was by far the most useful."[84]

This eloquent quote makes one wonder why the meeting with Alemann was "unofficial." It could (and probably should) have been "official." To understand Jones's comment, one must look at the issues that were discussed during the meeting. According to Bertens, Alemann used the "unofficial" gathering as an opportunity to invite the IMF to help him revoke some of the bilateral agreements to which Argentina was still a signatory.[85] Alemann's request, which contradicted the measures implemented by Frondizi's administration, suggests that the aspiration to create a strategic and ideological alliance between the parties was by no means unilateral. Indeed, Alemann's efforts indicate that some influential figures in the local leadership and in Argentina's economic elite believed that the Bretton Woods institutions could back them in promoting an economic agenda which, in certain cases, had little in common with the government's official policies.

In any case, the IMF's willingness to cooperate with a liberal economist like Alemann was very different from the cold shoulder that the institution more than once gave to del Carril, a firmer advocate of developmentalism. It also significantly differed from the IMF's reluctance to work with Frigerio, who opposed economic stabilization plans and was perceived by the IMF and the U.S. administration (as well as by the military and by right-wing groups in Argentina), if not as a communist, then at least as an obstacle to the full implementation of stabilization programs.[86]

Indeed, the political and economic worldview of the Argentine officials played a central role in their desire to strengthen—or, alternatively, to weaken—ties with the IMF. At the same time, the ideological and professional background of the Argentine economic team certainly affected the level of the IMF's affinity or enmity toward them. This phenomenon has been common not only in later periods of Argentina's history, but also in other countries in the region. In Chile and Mexico, for example, this process has been facilitated by the fact that a considerable percentage of local technocrats were trained at the same U.S. universities as their counterparts at the IMF: It was the training programs at the University of Chicago, financed by specialized agencies in the United States and the Ford Foundation, that gave rise to the so-called Chicago Boys, who played a key role in facilitating the liberalizations of the Chilean and Mexican economies.[87]

In sum, it could be said that the missions and resident representatives soon became complementary channels of political and economic influence. While this influence was a result of the IMF's determination to promote liberal economic policies, the efforts made by local economists to transform IMF representatives into active partners in the domestic sphere demonstrates that IMF's intervention was far from an exclusive consequence of external imposition. Furthermore, in certain cases (e.g., those of Roberto Alemann and Guillermo Walter Klein, or, to a smaller degree, that of Álvaro Alsogaray), it is difficult to determine which side was more eager to cooperate: Argentina or the IMF.

As we shall see, the renewal of the SBA in December 1959 derived from and simultaneously facilitated a further intensification and deepening of the relationship between the two sides.

The Second Cycle, 1959:
The IMF Loan as a Seal of Approval

The relationship between the IMF and its borrowers is cyclical. The very same activities (consultations, signing of loan agreements, launching of stabilization programs, and monitoring) are systematically repeated year after year, almost in the same order and with varying levels of intensity. At the peak, or "high point," of each cycle is the signing of a stand-by agreement, followed by a time of decreasing intensity, or a "calm phase."

The cycles are not clearly differentiated from one another. Rather, they tend to be interrelated and overlapping, especially toward their end. The relative calm that characterizes the later phases of the surveillance mechanism represents a transitional stage between cycles. This comparatively uneventful time takes place when the borrower has already drawn most of the funds at its disposal, but the stand-by period is still a few months away from completion. The transition between the cycles, however, is neither granted nor merely automatic. Very often, borrowing states have found themselves in situations in which they have had no choice but to introduce policy and personnel changes in their administration to increase the chances of renewing the stand-by. Like many countries in similar situations, Argentina, then, was still in the dark as the first cycle neared its end.

Jones's mission of April and May 1959 was the one charged with dispelling the doubts about Argentina's chances to receive a "pass" to the next cycle. Jones was skeptical about President Frondizi's ability to fully implement the stabilization program and threatened to stop the flow of funds.[88] The IMF's skepticism was largely due to the composition of the Ministry of Economy: Both the IMF and the United States held the opinion that, although Frondizi's administration was oriented toward private enterprise, it would not be possible to complete the shift in Argentina's economy "with a government which contained many counter forces and persons who were endeavoring simultaneously to go in other directions."[89]

The IMF's doubts paved the way to additional negotiations. Hence, in mid-1959, Bertens initiated a new round of talks with local authorities. Likewise, it was agreed that another mission would arrive in Buenos Aires in July.[90]

In the meantime, the Ministry of Economy and the Central Bank underwent a major upheaval as the ideological nucleus that had championed and cultivated developmentalism left office.[91] Frigerio departed in early 1959. Then, in a move that provoked a substantial shift in the Ministry of Economy, del Carril was replaced by Álvaro Alsogaray. It must be noted that the new minister could hardly staff the large number of positions vacated before he arrived. The IMF watched Alsogaray with concern and empathy as he struggled to appoint likeminded economists in both the ministry and the Central Bank.[92] Alsogaray, not surprisingly, was perceived by the United States and the international financial community as the right choice at the right time, not only because he won the support of the Argentine military (decreasing, they predicted, the threat of a military coup), but also because he objected to developmentalism and was aligned instead with the monetarist ideas underlying the stabilization program.[93]

Despite the atmosphere of change and renovation, Alsogaray did not pursue a new strategy. Instead, he carefully implemented the stabilization policies formulated by his predecessors under the IMF's guidance.[94] Concurrently, a certain calm was felt in the economy, manifested, among other factors, by a decline in the value of the dollar (from 100 pesos in May to 83 pesos in August 1959) and in the inflation rates. In addition, in 1960–1961, annual growth rates reached 8 percent.[95] Meanwhile, in light of the "facelift" that was taking place at the Ministry of Economy at the time, Argentina asked the IMF to postpone the arrival of the July mission for two weeks. Alsogaray argued that the recently appointed officials needed time to learn the issues on their agenda.[96] The IMF, perhaps as a sign of good will, accepted a two-week delay.

However, Bertens, who was still serving as a resident representative in Argentina, did not sit idly by. He met with Vance Brand, vice-president of the Export-Import Bank, who was visiting Buenos Aires at the time, and presented to him a comprehensive overview of Argentina's economic situation. Brand, in turn, protested against Argentina's inability to invest the credit he had granted to it just a few months earlier and to pursue previously agreed upon policies.[97] This meeting indicates that in 1959, the IMF was already perceived by other lending institutions not only as a reliable seal of approval, but also as a player that could supply updated information that local officials were unable or unwilling to provide. As Bertens reported: "He [Brand] stated the need for a Fund mission visit here in order to appraise the overall situation, and . . . he has emphasized the need to continue towards stabilization, and if the progress is successful it might be possible that in the financial sectors abroad some aid may be found. . . . He indicated that a good opportunity to revise in Washington the whole Argentine program would be when the Fund mission report is finished early in September."[98]

But that was not all. Bertens also met with some of the newly recruited officials at the Ministry of Economy and the Central Bank. His meetings with Guillermo Walter Klein, a new secretary at the ministry,[99] and with the recently appointed economic adviser, Roberto Alemann, are indicative of the formative and influential role played by IMF representatives at the time. As Bertens made clear:

> This meeting was very productive in terms of explaining to the Secretary of the Treasury the nature of the agreement existing between Argentina and the Fund. I gave to Mr. Klein the draft of the basic figures that the mission of last November prepared here. . . . I used this opportunity to emphasize to the Secretary of [the] Treasury the urgency to have a quite good picture for the rest of the year of the different state enterprises which the deficit has covered by transfers from the Treasury. . . . Also, I explained to the Secretary of the Treasury the urgent need to reduce the level of fiscal expenditures in order to bring into balance the fiscal budget.[100]

As Bertens's report reveals, the permanent IMF representative in effect filled the professional vacuum created when a group of developmentalist officials left the Ministry of Economy en masse. Moreover, it clearly shows that both the resident representatives and the members of the missions that arrived in Buenos Aires several times a year took part in updating and even training public officials.

This informal socialization of new bureaucrats was not limited to the lower and middle ranks. Sometimes it even included the economic minister himself. It is precisely in this context that Bertens's initial meetings with Alsogaray should be understood. When Bertens claimed that "the Minister asked me for explanations regarding the stabilization program and the main clauses of the stand-by agreement [of 1958],"[101] he probably meant to imply that Alsogaray had turned to him as a professional and trustworthy partner, in both professional and personal terms. Although it could be argued that IMF representatives intervened because of the vacuum created at the Ministry of Economy, one should not ignore the fact that the IMF was not alone in suspecting that Argentina's leadership was not fully aware of the country's actual economic situation.

As the prestigious Argentine journal *Economic Survey* stated, "We think that the real monetary situation is not known even to the government authorities."[102]

Adding insult to injury, the frequent personnel changes at the heart of Argentina's most prominent economic institutions not only provided a pretext for external influences to intervene, but they also may have damaged Argentina's international reputation. Argentina appeared acutely unstable, and many of its newly appointed officials lacked the knowledge of and experience with Argentine political and economic issues that their counterparts at the IMF were accumulating. Indeed, there was significant continuity in the IMF's personnel, including its mission members and department heads. Many of the economists recruited from the delegations to the Bretton Woods Conference of 1944, as well as those who joined the Fund in the 1950s, remained on staff until the 1980s.[103] This has considerably limited the ability of local representatives to compete with the IMF's economists in terms of expertise and sophistication.

Thus, the intensity of IMF–Argentine relations during Frondizi's tenure reveals a disturbing picture in which IMF representatives, whose economic approach was hardly compatible with the protectionism and nationalism still prevalent in broad sectors of Argentina's society, filled a professional, and even a political, vacuum created by domestic conflicts and crises. Ironically, the IMF, whose very presence had been contributing directly and indirectly to the social and political unrest in Argentina, appeared to be a major beneficiary of the country's instability. It was this instability and the need to solve Argentina's economic problems that pushed leaders from diverse ideological and political backgrounds into the open arms of the IMF.

The Wheels of the Second Cycle Begin to Turn

Although Argentina asked not to begin its meetings with the Fund before August 6,[104] a mission headed by Gesualdo Costanzo opened the annual consultation on August 5. The first summit was held with Alsogaray and several up-and-coming economists, including Méndez Delfino, Klein, Alemann, and Julio González del Solar. The minister Alsogaray sought to persuade his guests that Argentina was willing and able to adhere to the agreement of December 1958 and to the stabilization program.[105] He told the mission that the Argentine government had succeeded in "defeating the nationalistic ideas of a large part of the population of the country [and was] now in the position to reduce the burden of large investments financed directly from government resources" and that he expected "that a firm policy [would] be followed toward eliminating the Government's intervention in the economic development of the country."[106]

Despite the evident affinity between the IMF and Alsogaray—or, perhaps, precisely because of that affinity—Costanzo's visit lasted nearly a month. His report painted a mixed picture that emphasized the ongoing implementation of the stabilization program.[107] This somewhat positive evaluation facilitated the initiation of a negotiation process for a new SBA, in which Argentina expected to receive $100 million.[108]

As had occurred a year before, Argentina wished to secure supplementary loans from both government and private sources, and Alsogaray set out for the United States in October.[109] But neither his stops in Washington and New York nor the recently concluded annual consultation were enough to exempt Argentina from the need to host yet another IMF mission to determine its eligibility for further assistance. Therefore, almost concurrently with Alsogaray's departure for Washington, a new mission landed in Buenos Aires.[110]

Once in Washington, Alsogaray announced his intention to visit Europe to expand the circle of supplementary financiers. His first stop was West Germany. On November 10, the finance ministers of Argentina and West Germany jointly announced that Bonn would grant "significant credit" to Argentina.[111] Alsogaray then boarded a train to Switzerland, where he was joined by Julio González del Solar, deputy director of Argentina's Central Bank; Roberto Alemann, the economic adviser at the Argentine Embassy in Washington; and José Tinez, the economic adviser at the Argentine Embassy in Bonn.[112] The three largest Swiss banks agreed to grant "generous" (albeit undefined) credit to Argentina as part of a European fund aimed to help "stabilize the Argentine currency and liberalize its trade."[113] From Switzerland, Alsogaray proceeded to Rome, where he announced that Italy would supply 15–20 percent of the resources for a credit fund whose estimated $300 million in assets would be transferred to Argentina's Central Bank. The talks in Rome also promoted an increase in bilateral trade.[114] When he arrived in London, Alsogaray declared his intention to augment exports of meat to Britain.[115] He also met with the board of the British Baring Brothers Bank, one of Argentina's longest-standing creditors.[116]

Argentina's efforts in Europe did not overshadow the North American front, which remained paramount and constituted the inevitable starting point of any loan package. Formal talks to secure further loans opened in the United States on November 18 via a letter of intent sent by Alsogaray to Per Jacobsson.[117] On November 21, Méndez Delfino, an influential and experienced economist, visited the United States to advance negotiations with the Export-Import Bank, the World Bank, the IMF, the U.S. Treasury, and private banks that were parties to the first SBA.[118] Méndez Delfino was then scheduled to travel to Paris to secure in writing the verbal promises Alsogaray had received on his multi-country trip.[119]

During the talks in November, neither the Argentine authorities nor the foreign lenders specified exact sums. So despite the continuous media coverage of Alsogaray's travels, a heavy fog still surrounded the negotiations. It was only upon his return to Buenos Aires that Alsogaray could finally confirm that he had raised $70 million–$80 million to support the stabilization program.[120] On

November 26, he declared that the negotiations with the United States and Europe would "lead to the dismantling of the interventionist economic system,"[121] a declaration that explicitly pointed to the heart of the alliance with the IMF.

Alsogaray's optimism was encouraged not only by his extensive travels, but also by the near-doubling of Argentina's quota in the IMF on November 20, 1959, from $150 million to $280 million.[122] This was vital to Argentina, because, as mentioned, there are direct correlations among the quota level, the volume of loans, and voting power within the IMF (as within the World Bank). The significance of the move, however, should not be overestimated. Indeed, more than anything else, the increase in the quota reflected the IMF's attempts to strengthen its own international position. On December 19, 1958, the Board of Governors resolved to enlarge the IMF's resources by 50 percent, so that most of the member states—including Argentina—saw a similar raise in their quotas.[123]

Once the IMF loan was almost approved, Méndez Delfino initiated a round of talks with private U.S. banks (such as the National City Bank, Chase Manhattan, the First National Bank of Boston, and J. P. Morgan and Company), most of which had served as supplementary financiers just a year before.[124]

Finally, the Argentine economic leadership declared its excursions in Europe and the United States a resounding success. In his address to the nation on November 26, 1959, Alsogaray stated: "To the admirers of statistics I would like to say that in fourteen days we visited seven countries, met with thirteen ministers and 196 presidents of government and private banks, consulted more than fifty banks, held more than a hundred meetings and traveled 30,000 kilometers."[125] No statement could be more appropriate to recap the huge efforts invested in collecting the loans. The only thing left to do was to sign the agreement with the IMF so that all of the other agreements Alsogaray had worked so hard to obtain could be realized.

The Second Stand-by Arrangement and the Sweeping Surge of Complementary Agreements

On December 2, at a meeting attended by Roberto Alemann, González del Solar, and Méndez Delfino, the IMF's Executive Board approved a second SBA with Argentina.[126] The approval resulted not only from Alsogaray's exhausting trip but also from the enthusiastic report submitted by the mission of November 1959. Indeed, the mission's report applauded what it defined as Argentina's economic recovery and the sharp increase in private foreign investment, which had reached $163 million in the first ten months of 1959 (compared with barely $15 million in 1958).[127] It also highlighted a 30 percent increase in oil production and an impressive rise in the number of oil wells.[128]

The mission's report, it is worth noting, was severely criticized in some Argentine circles that believed it was riddled with inaccuracies and blind to the country's true, deteriorating condition.[129] The critics' comments are intriguing in that they suggest there were some who suspected that the IMF was looking at Argentina through rose-colored glasses and that the Fund might prefer over-looking the alarming symptoms of a sick Argentine economy to stopping its loans to President Frondizi. In other words, the IMF appeared ready to risk its professional prestige to maintain a working routine with an unstable borrower such as Argentina at a permanent level of intensity. After all, why would the IMF want to renounce to its intensive working routine with Argentina when that routine constituted one of its most effective means of influence?

Whether the critics were right or wrong, the report guaranteed the approval of a new SBA. The representatives on the IMF Board from Belgium, Britain, France, and the Netherlands supported the agreement. The U.S. representative, however, was more reserved, although he finally voted in favor of Argentina.[130] It should be emphasized that the U.S. position on this issue corroborates the notion that—at least, with regard to Argentina—the IMF's alignment with Wash-ington was not necessarily automatic.

The new SBA, for a total of $100 million, was in reality a direct extension of the previous agreement and was designed to ensure further progress in the implementation of the stabilization plan. Above all, it was intended to support Argentina's exchange market and facilitate increasing liberalization of its for-eign trade. In return, Argentina was required to reduce its fiscal deficit.[131]

As Alsogaray had expected, the SBA was followed by complementary loans. When the IMF officially announced the agreement, a consortium of eleven lending banks in New York proclaimed that they would also approve loans to Argentina.[132] But Alsogaray and his assistants could not yet rest on their laurels. Five days after the IMF loan was approved, Méndez Delfino was again on his way to Europe to conclude loan agreements with fifty private banks in eight countries.[133] On December 18, he signed a collective agreement with European banks for loans totaling $75 million, to be repaid within three years. Argentina would receive the initial funds in January 1960 and start repaying them by July 1961.[134] Such terms were by no means a victory for Alsogaray, though, whose original intention was to secure long-term loans.[135]

When the negotiations in Europe ended, Argentina had managed to secure loans totaling $300 million: $100 million from the IMF; $75 million from U.S. commercial banks; $75 million from European commercial banks ($5.25 mil-lion from Belgium, $17 million from Britain, $10.5 million from France, $10.5 million from Italy, $5.25 million from the Netherlands, $4 million from Sweden, $6.5 million from Switzerland, and $16 million from West Germany); and $50 million from the U.S. Treasury.[136]

Argentina was also granted development loans in 1959 that were allocated to infrastructure, industry, and agriculture. In early 1960, the Export-Import Bank lent the country $7.6 million to purchase industrial equipment made in the United States.[137] As an emblem of the increasing liberalization of Argentina's economy, the Export-Import Bank's funds were transferred, for the first time, not through the state-owned Banco Industrial Argentino (Argentine Industrial Bank) but through private banks, including local branches of U.S. banks. In October 1960, $7 million from the Development Loan Fund was added to the basket and was allocated to the expansion of the road system.[138]

While this was not the first time that Argentina had assembled a loan "package," the unprecedented variety of lenders raised several questions among U.S. and European creditors and the IMF. The key question was whether a "trustee" could be appointed to coordinate the activity of the commercial banks vis-à-vis the Central Bank of Argentina. Interestingly, and without consulting with Argentina, the lending banks suggested the IMF as the favorite candidate for that job. The IMF's Legal Department, however, was of the opinion that the IMF should undertake the task only if Argentina requested it, and only to the extent that "the Fund employs objective and predefined formulas regarding [the] withdrawal and repayment [of funds]."[139] In fact, the Managing Director Per Jacobsson appears to have been reluctant to serve as an official trustee, because he feared the role would be counterproductive and detrimental to the Fund's credibility.[140]

The very suggestion that the IMF serve as a trustee indicates that by the 1950s, the Fund was considered capable of shaping the agendas of debtor countries and of private and government lenders. Thus, Per Jacobsson was probably right to resist the temptation to turn the Fund into an official trustee or supra-supervisor. In practice, that is how the IMF was already being perceived anyway.

Each Loan and Its Own Monitoring Process

According to IMF practices, the SBA of December 1959 opened the floodgate for consecutive visits by a number of IMF missions and for intense activity by the resident representative in Buenos Aires.[141] In addition, the SBA was accompanied by a significant escalation in activities with the World Bank, the other Bretton Woods institution, which, for the first time, dispatched several delegations to Argentina. Taking into consideration Frondizi's developmentalist approach and the fact that the World Bank's top priority has always been to promote development, this escalation could imply that Argentina perceived the SBAs with the IMF as the high price it had to pay to secure access to the World Bank's development loans, the most precious treasure the new multilateralism offered. In this respect, there was no difference between Argentina and other Latin American countries that regarded the IMF as the stick in international finance and the World Bank as the carrot.[142]

The first World Bank mission arrived in Buenos Aires on February 1, 1960. Its main goal was to conduct an in-depth examination of transportation and energy issues.[143] Notwithstanding local expectations, this mission refrained from formulating definite recommendations.[144] Needless to say, Argentina had no choice but to continue to deepen its relationship with the IMF.

Alongside this new phase in Argentine–World Bank relations, four IMF missions visited Buenos Aires in 1960. The first and most prolonged mission, headed by G. Dorrance, lasted from November 1959 to January 1960. The other three were headed by Costanzo. The second mission arrived in February, and the third, which was part of the annual consultation, arrived in May. Members of the May mission met not only with Alsogaray but also with prominent figures in the infrastructure sector, including the directors of Agua y Energía (the Argentine water and energy utility company), the minister of infrastructure, the managing director of the national railway company, and other state bodies. The fourth mission arrived in November 1960 to conduct the preliminary negotiations for the third SBA.

The IMF's massive presence in Buenos Aires did not excuse Argentine representatives from having to meet IMF executives in Washington. In March 1960, Campos and Klein met Per Jacobsson at the IMF headquarters and updated him on the progress of the stabilization program.[145] Per Jacobsson, who was well versed in the details, put his guests in a tight spot when he asked what had been done with respect to the promises to drastically cut import taxes. Per Jacobsson was disappointed with the answers he received and immediately dispatched a letter to Alsogaray, emphasizing that he expected continued liberalization of imports to Argentina.[146] The letter irritated Alsogaray, who responded that Argentina was moving toward a policy of "progressive liberalization of imports, while avoiding the creation of distortions or social problems." He added: "Please believe me that in this respect, our position is firm, although the lack of comprehension within and outside Argentina undoubtedly makes our goal much more difficult to achieve. In referring to lack of comprehension from outside, I do not exclude the IMF, which we expected to stand firmly by our side, in complete understanding of this effort, which is personal to a large extent, and whose success depends on many diverse factors which cannot be measured purely by general standards."[147]

Alsogaray's personal and emotional reply was far from impetuous, as it was sent twenty days after Per Jacobsson's communication had been received. There is no doubt that Alsogaray, who agreed with the IMF about the need to liberalize the economy, felt hurt by the impatience shown toward his country in general, and toward him in particular. However, Per Jacobsson's conduct suggests that, as the ideological affinity between Argentina's economic leadership and the IMF grew, so did the IMF's demands.

Still, it seems that both the deepening and the widening of professional and personal ties between Argentine economists and IMF officials, and the ongoing consolidation of a common working routine, were not enough to mitigate or eliminate the IMF's doubts whenever Argentina failed to meet agreed timetables

or strict procedures. As Costanzo warned, "The delays and omissions in sending information to Washington while I was away . . . make me suspicious about
intentions."[148]

In short, Frondizi's efforts to attract foreign capital certainly bore fruit—at
least, in the short term. The remarkably intensive second cycle demonstrated a
fast growth rate in heavy industry (power, steel and iron).[149] The tightened links
with the international financial community, which were propelled by the IMF's
seal of approval, led to a sharp increase in the volume of direct investment in
Argentina, which totaled $427 million in 1959.[150] In the domestic sphere,
despite the very slow improvements in wage levels, the declining rate of inflation
did rein in the social unrest brought about by the stabilization program. In light
of these positive developments, which helped to dispel the initial doubts, the
IMF recommended the signing of yet another SBA with Frondizi's administration as early as November 1960.[151]

The Third Cycle, 1960:
The IMF and Its Local Agents

In September 1960, in what had already become a ritual, Argentina announced
its desire to sign a new SBA with the IMF worth $100 million. Contrary to previ-
ous years, Argentina declared that the purpose of the arrangement would be "to
maintain confidence, and there is no intention to draw funds unless an unfore-
seen heavy loss of reserves occurs."[152] This declaration, which reflected a common IMF practice, indicates that toward the end of 1960, Argentina needed the
IMF's seal of approval more than its actual dollars. In effect, Argentina ended
up drawing only $60 million of the $100 million granted and in this way got
another chance to continue implementing the stabilization program.[153]

But not everything that glittered was gold in Argentina in those days. Along
with the economic recovery of 1960, the loan agreements signed by Frondizi led
to a growing sense that a rope was being tightened around Argentina's neck. The
SBA of December 1960 included a new clause titled "Rescheduling," a novelty
designed to mitigate what could no longer be denied: the eventual need to repay
the debts. Argentina was not the only Latin American debtor that faced serious
difficulties with repayment and rescheduling, however, and its situation at times
was better than that of other nations in the region.

Because SBAs were designed to solve temporary problems, they were supposed to expire after twelve to eighteen months. In reality, however, between
1952 and 1962, several Latin American borrowers, Argentina among them, were
plagued by "recidivism"—that is, the signing of SBAs for three or even more
than five consecutive years.[154] This cyclical succession of SBAs (and complementary loans) created situations in which borrowers needed new SBAs to meet
their commitments and repay previous loans.

In September 1960, Argentina asked to be allowed to start repaying the IMF after five years instead of the originally stipulated three years. The request was easy to justify: In 1961, Argentina had to repay $29 million to the IMF ($15 million in April, $4 million in July, and $10 million in October), plus the equivalent of $60 million to European creditors.[155] Without debt rescheduling, Argentina's repayments in 1961 and, particularly, in 1962 would have amounted to $265 million—that is, about a third of Argentina's total exports at the time.[156] In all, Argentina's external debt was estimated at $1.448 billion in September 1960 (compared with $575 million at the time of the coup in 1955). Of this amount, $768 million were Central Bank commitments to the IMF, U.S. administration agencies, and the Paris Club; $644 million were debts of Argentine government bodies; and the remaining $35 million were private debts with government or Central Bank guarantees.[157] Partially because of these figures, the IMF leaned toward granting Argentina's request and even assisting the country to reach similar arrangements with U.S. and European banks and the Paris Club.[158]

It was under these circumstances that a new mission, headed by Costanzo, left for Buenos Aires in November 1960.[159] Costanzo's final report was positive. On December 9, 1960, the IMF approved a $100 million SBA to Argentina.[160] The steps the Argentine government was required to take were no different from the ones stipulated in the agreements signed in 1958 and 1959 and later on in 1961.[161] The letter of intent dispatched by Alsogaray echoed the promises listed in previous letters, especially in regard to efforts to stabilize and liberalize the economy and to put an end to bilateralism.[162]

Unlike in previous years, Argentina did not apply for supplementary stabilization loans.[163] Nevertheless, during 1961, several development loans were granted to the country and were allocated toward the expansion of local infrastructure and industry.[164] For instance, on April 11, the Export-Import Bank, jointly with the Chase Manhattan Bank, approved a $610,000 loan to Yacimientos Petrolíferos Fiscales (YPF), the Argentine national oil company.[165] In May, the Export-Import Bank approved another loan, worth $40 million, to improve road infrastructure.[166] Most important, on June 30, the World Bank announced its first loan to Argentina: $48.5 million for highway development and to import road maintenance equipment. That loan was planned to be repaid over sixteen years, at an annual interest rate of 5.75 percent.[167] In late July, the World Bank announced that, jointly with the U.S. administration, it would grant Argentina a $205.5 million loan for industrial development.[168] In addition, a newly established institution, the Inter-American Development Bank (IDB), announced a $15 million loan to be invested in the agriculture, mining, and industry sectors.[169] On October 9, 1961, the IDB approved a further $700,000 loan, which was transferred to Tool Research Argentina of Santa Fe, an automotive concern jointly owned by Argentine and U.S. investors.[170] Perhaps contrary to what could be expected from a nationalist leader, numerous U.S. banks, companies, and private investors had been increasing their activities in Argentina considerably during Frondizi's tenure.

In broad terms, it seems that U.S. President John F. Kennedy's intentions to encourage economic development in Latin America through the Alliance for Progress, combined with the IMF's desire to maintain good relations with its strongest member (the United States) and Argentina's difficulty in meeting its repayment commitments, led to several changes in the economic aspects of the routine of dependency. At the core of these changes were the IMF's willingness to make repayment schedules flexible and an increasing inflow of development loans. As we shall see, these changes did not significantly alter what began to emerge as an established and firm routine of dependency.

The monitoring process that followed the loan approved in December 1960 was not as close and intensive as usual. During 1961, only two IMF missions visited Argentina. The first, in August, was headed by Jorge del Canto, the experienced and influential head of the Western Hemisphere Department.[171] The second, which arrived in October, was coordinated by Costanzo, David Finch, and Harris Jafri.[172] This was actually the first mission ever to combine the "annual consultation" with discussions on renewing the SBA.[173] The two missions were highly satisfied with their findings and referred to Argentina's economy as "a boom causing an increase in production and investment."[174]

Although the mission's reports secured the renewal of the SBA, they highlighted several unresolved issues. They stressed that, although Argentina was in the midst of negotiations to join the General Agreement on Tariffs and Trade (GATT), the road to full economic and trade liberalization was still long.[175] In addition, the reports severely criticized what the IMF regarded as Argentina's obstinacy in continuing to impose high taxes and tariffs on imports, and condemned the salary raises approved in 1960.[176] To complicate matters, the mission warned against a renewed worsening in Argentina's balance of payments and a sharp rise in its external debt, which climbed to $1.7 billion in September 1961.[177] In other words, despite the economic progress and personnel changes in the Argentine administration, and regardless of the political price Frondizi had to pay for the stabilization measures, the IMF expected more.

At the same time, the decrease in the number of IMF missions visiting Argentina did not translate into reduced involvement of the institution in the national arena. On the contrary, not only did the Fund gradually augment its direct and indirect presence in Argentina, but the willingness of certain Argentine officials to cooperate with the IMF was also expanding. For instance, Costanzo and his entourage were invited to meetings not only at the Central Bank and the Ministry of Economy, but also with senior representatives of a very wide range of government agencies and bodies, such as the Secretariats of

Industry, Fuel and Energy, Trade, and Agriculture; the Ministries of Infrastructure and Public Projects and Labor; and the Banco de la Nación.[178]

The reasons for the decreased number of IMF missions were varied. Because the wheels of the joint working machine were firmly on track, the IMF might have assumed they could remain in motion without continually being pushed. The departure in late 1960 of the IMF's resident delegation from its offices at the Central Bank may confirm this hypothesis. In addition, Argentina did not use the entire sum granted to it by the new SBA, depriving the IMF of a reason to conduct assessments before every draw. Moreover, it should be remembered that in 1961, political and social agitation in Argentina reached new peaks. Hence, it is not implausible that IMF representatives did not wish to be identified by Argentine and U.S. observers with the dramatic events that took place in the country at the time—particularly with the personnel changes at the Ministry of Economy, the Ministry of Foreign Relations, the Central Bank, YPF, and the Railway Board. Following a personal request by Frondizi, for instance, Alsogaray was replaced by Roberto Alemann in April.[179] The appointment of Alemann, who had been playing a crucial role in Argentina's relationship with the Paris Club, the Bretton Woods institutions, and the U.S. administration, could not have been more lauded by all of these bodies. At that point, then, the IMF opted to monitor events from afar, mainly through Argentine radio and press reports.[180] Already familiar with the frequent personnel changes in Argentina's government, the IMF (rightly) did not regard the events as a threat to the stabilization program.[181]

In the third cycle, thus, the IMF's satisfaction with the developments in Argentina, along with its own wish to stay out of the limelight in the volatile local arena, appears to have led to a notable decrease in the number of missions to Buenos Aires. This relative physical disappearance, however, did not herald a total disappearance of the IMF. To be sure, until 1961, two main reasons were given for the Fund's massive presence in Buenos Aires: the need and desire of both parties to disseminate and assimilate "proper" working procedures and the need to consolidate and implement austerity measures. During 1961, however, the impression was that these two goals were close to being achieved, so continued surveillance could no longer be justified. In addition, the IMF's growing concern about its image among the member countries in general, and in the United States and Latin American countries in particular,[182] led it to try to avoid being perceived as overly involved in internal Argentine affairs. It is safe to assume that the IMF felt secure in lowering its profile in Argentina because it was confident that its work would be done by others. Indeed, the recurrent personnel changes at the highest echelons, driven by the relentless progress toward liberalization, created a situation in which the reins remained in the hands of economists such as Alemann and Klein, who not only overtly identified with the Fund's monetarist doctrine but also to a certain, though informal, extent acted as its prime agents.

Conclusion

The origins of Argentina's dependence on the IMF can be traced back to the inception and establishment of the Bretton Woods institutions. Before its incorporation into those institutions in September 1956, Argentina's dependence was shaped by the efforts that Washington expected it to make to gain entry into the IMF and World Bank. Once it became a member, the dependency went far beyond the numbers and statistics registered on the Central Bank's balance sheets. In effect, the strictly economic aspects of this asymmetric partnership were no more than small pieces in a big and complex puzzle. Thus, the analysis of the close ties between Argentina and the IMF uncovers a larger picture that had been so far overlooked, a picture composed of the *intimate* facets of dependency, the fabric of which was being incessantly woven behind the scenes through formal and informal contacts.

It is true that before 1958, Argentina had been accumulating a long record of loans and debts.[183] It is also true that Argentina had never enjoyed absolute autonomy and that on too many occasions its leaders had no choice but to consider external factors while shaping domestic economic plans. However, nothing in the past resembled the relationship that evolved with the IMF. The fact that countries such as Argentina were members of a multilateral institution from which they received loans did not liberate them from dependency. On the contrary: Membership in the IMF deepened Latin America's vulnerability to external pressures and influence.

A close examination of the creation and entrenchment of the demanding routine of dependency during the 1957–1961 period raises the question of why this process took place mostly under Frondizi's rule. This question is even more fascinating if one keeps in mind that Frondizi's "multilateral experiment" had bittersweet consequences for Argentina. Indeed, it cannot be denied that the stabilization program had several positive outcomes in the short term, even though it negatively affected vast sectors of Argentine society. For example, by 1959 the fiscal deficit had been significantly reduced. After a short recession in that year, Argentina's gross domestic product rose by 7.9 percent, and inflation was reduced to an annual rate of 27.1 percent.[184] Despite these encouraging figures, Frondizi's administration accumulated a dramatic level of foreign debt, which almost quintupled from $575 million in late 1955 to $2.649 billion when Frondizi was ousted in early 1962.

Like many of his counterparts in Latin America, Frondizi perceived cooperation with the IMF as a precondition for gaining access to development loans from the World Bank. In addition, there is no doubt that Frondizi believed that a stable relationship with the IMF could help Argentina improve its image, and its ties, with Washington. In this respect, the Cold War and the need of the United States to keep Latin America in its area of influence facilitated the establishment of friendly relations between Frondizi and Presidents Dwight Eisenhower and John F. Kennedy.[185]

Yet the relationship with the IMF also soon became an efficient instrument to reach both international and national political goals. Indeed, the relationship seemed to be crucial to securing Frondizi's political survival by conveying a message of change to diverse opposition groups, including the military and the local establishment, who supported stabilization.[186]

Unlike Perón, who was personally and directly involved in the negotiations with the Bretton Woods institutions, Frondizi was almost completely absent from contacts with the IMF. This stands in stark contrast to Frondizi's involvement in the not always successful negotiations with the World Bank.[187] The documents that are available to researchers do not reveal the reasons for his absence. However, three main hypotheses can be posed. First, due to Frondizi's personal interest and participation in the implementation of the development agenda, he chose to relegate the management of the financial issues—among them, relations with the IMF—to the Ministry of Economy and the Central Bank. Second, to secure his political survival, Frondizi renounced his involvement in the contacts with the IMF, thereby letting an orthodox team of economists liberalize the economy almost without interference. Third, Frondizi used the rotating officials at the top economic institutions as scapegoats to be blamed for the implementation of austerity measures that sometimes contradicted the principles of developmentalism. I tend to believe that the strengthening of the relationship between the IMF and Frondizi was the result of a combination of these three hypothesized courses of action. In addition, it is not unreasonable to presume that, at the time, neither Frondizi nor other members of his government could be fully aware of the deep and long-term impact of a very active membership in the IMF, and especially of the routine of dependency.

As this chapter had demonstrated, the economic aspects of Argentina's relations with the IMF—namely, the loan agreements and stabilization programs—were a central but not unique aspect of the routine of dependency. It was actually the creation of an epistemic community of experts—or, even more, the gestation of an unwritten ideological alliance between groups from two unequal parties who happened to see eye to eye on Argentina's reality—that had the most significant impact on Argentina's political and economic life.

The working routine with the IMF did not remain immune to the political instability in Argentina, however. From 1962 on, the relationship had many ups and downs—not because the IMF had qualms about signing agreements with dictatorships but, rather, because of the weakness of Argentina's political institutions.

4

Fluctuations in the Routine of Dependency

Argentine–IMF Relations in a Decade of Political Instability, 1962–1972

tand-by arrangements, as shown in Chapter 3, serve as the platform for establishing a solid joint working routine for the IMF and its borrowers. The fact that the majority of borrowers sign a series of consecutive SBAs (e.g., Chile has signed ten consecutive agreements; Uruguay, thirteen; and Haiti, twenty-one) may create the impression that this routine can only deepen and become increasingly institutionalized.[1] That impression, however, is only partially accurate. As explained below, the routine of dependency is by no means an unalterable or deterministic mechanism.

Argentina provides a privileged prism through which to examine how national political instability is fueled by and, at the same time, shapes the relationship with the IMF. Until now, we have seen how events in Argentina—the overthrow of Perón, the election of Frondizi—led to the formation of the routine of dependency. This chapter, by contrast, focuses on instances in which the political, economic, and social situation in Argentina triggered a slowdown or temporary halt in the routine of dependency. We shall see how President Arturo Illia (October 1963–June 1966)—whom opponents sarcastically nicknamed "the Turtle" for his alleged sluggishness and indecision—became the first president to distance Argentina from the IMF. Since then, only Néstor Kirchner (May 2003–December 2007) and, to a certain extent, the incumbent president of Argentina, Cristina Fernández de Kirchner, have followed in Illia's footsteps and considerably narrowed the routine of dependency. It should be mentioned that in the 1980s, President Raúl Alfonsín, perhaps encouraged by key figures on his economic team who had worked with Illia in the 1960s, also tried to replicate Illia's autonomist position, though only for a short time and less successfully.

This chapter, then, describes the pendulum swings that characterized the relationship between Argentina and the IMF in 1962–1972, one of the stormiest times in Argentina's contemporary history. While doing so, it highlights the junctures where the routine of dependency was disrupted, only to rise again, stronger than ever, like the phoenix from the ashes. In effect, I argue that crises, as well as political changes at the national level, create fluctuations in relations not so much with the entire financial community as with the IMF. Since Argentina was far from being the only country to be plagued by instability, the patterns described here are highly relevant for other Latin American borrowers. During the decade from 1962 to 1972, six presidents and nine economic ministers were replaced in quick succession in Argentina, three presidents and eleven finance ministers were replaced in Chile, six presidents and twenty finance ministers were replaced in Brazil, and four presidents and nine finance ministers were replaced in Peru.

The analysis of the fluctuating relations between the IMF and an unstable Argentina reveals that the IMF was usually eager (sometimes more so than Argentina) to resume its intervention as soon as local conditions permitted. To reactivate the routine mechanisms that had been temporarily reduced to a minimum or even neglected, the IMF more than once adopted astoundingly flexible positions toward Argentina. By "flexible" I mean that in certain cases, the IMF was ready to forgive Argentina for its poor economic performance or for deviating from program targets to rationalize the approval of a new SBA.

The IMF's flexibility could be explained in two ways. First, there is no doubt that the economic failure of a borrower is—at least, to some degree—also the failure of the IMF. In other words, when a loan is not repaid, the IMF's financial stability is endangered, and the institution becomes vulnerable to criticism for its inability to prevent an economic crisis or, even worse, for having instigated a breakdown. Second, the professional and personal ties that develop between IMF officials and local technocrats can lead the IMF to overlook short-term economic failures or incompliance. To be sure, the IMF's flexibility cannot be understood without taking into account the far-reaching consequences of the routine of dependency—consequences that propel the IMF's staff to keep the working routine at as intense a level as possible. The final goal of the routine of dependency is not merely to solve balance-of-payments shortfalls but, rather, to lead IMF member states to abandon "old economic models" such as populism, interventionism, statism, developmentalism, socialism, and communism in favor of the "right" model (liberalism). But economic paradigms that are deeply rooted in a given society (as statism was in Argentina and Brazil, as socialism was in Chile, and as communism was in the former Soviet states) cannot be instantly erased. Changes in economic policies and, especially, in economic thought require time. Indeed, only persistent hard work in the form of countless interactions between IMF technocrats and local economists can guarantee that a strong epistemic community of convinced experts capable of managing a stable market economy will be created. As Sarah Babb has shown, the IMF's "educational" role in Mexico was considerably reinforced by a more direct strategy of ideological socialization, implemented through the professional training of new generations of economists at U.S. schools of economics, particularly the University of Chicago. This systematic socialization facilitated the shift from the socialism of the Mexican Revolution (both in its early expression of the 1910s and after its revival under Lázaro Cárdenas in the 1930s and early 1940s) to neoliberalism.[2] A similar process took place in Chile, where a young generation of so-called Chicago Boys helped the dictator Augusto Pinochet to abandon the socialist policies implemented by Salvador Allende and embark on a deep liberalization of the economy.[3] The Chilean case is particularly interesting. It is not unreasonable to believe that the presence of ECLAC's headquarters in Santiago de Chile strengthened the monetarists' will to create a cadre of liberally oriented economists to counterbalance the strong presence of developmentalist economists in the local scene.

Careful scrutiny of the relationship between Argentina and the IMF during this decade and the one immediately following (discussed in Chapter 5) also enables us to assess empirically how the type of regime (e.g., democracy versus dictatorship) may or may not affect a country's interactions with the Fund. This question is also tragically relevant to most Latin American countries, where democratic regimes have been deposed by national armed forces that have established authoritarian regimes—Brazil in 1964–1985, Chile in 1973–1990, Colombia in 1953–1958, and Uruguay in 1973–1985, to name just a few. The academic literature that has addressed this question offers sometimes contradictory findings. On the one hand, scholars such as Kenneth Schultz and Barry Weingast point to a "democratic advantage," according to which democratic regimes' chances of getting loans from international organizations such as the IMF are higher because those regimes are more inclined to repay their debts.[4] On the other hand, some scholars maintain that democracies have more difficulty consolidating favorable agreements with international lenders. For instance, Sebastian Saiegh argues that among developing countries, democratic governments are at higher risk to reschedule their debts or to proclaim default, consequently reducing their chances of getting loans at low interest rates.[5]

Against this background of theoretical models, the Latin American case in general and the Argentine case in particular reveal that the type of regime is not a key criterion for assessing the loan agreements signed with the IMF; nor does it provide the most appropriate prism through which to examine borrowers' relationships with the Fund. In fact, an analysis of the cyclical nature of the relations with the IMF—specifically of the sequence of periods of intense activity and temporary detachment—yields two distinct and complementary criteria for understanding the IMF–borrower relations: the ideological criterion and the personal and bureaucratic criterion.

Cracks in the Routine of Dependency and the
Last Nail in Frondizi's Political Coffin

The harmony that marked the formative years of Argentina's relationship with the IMF did not last for long. During the months leading up to Frondizi's ousting in March 1962, the joint working routine began to erode, creating what I call a "temporary episode of detachment." In general, such episodes were initiated by Argentina and by the IMF. When Argentina was the initiator, the motives were largely ideological, as during Illia's presidency, or tactical, as in the case of President General Alejandro Lanusse (analyzed below). When the IMF initiated the detachment, these episodes reflected, above all else, the Fund's aspiration to avoid being identified or associated with the political and social crises that erupted in Argentina. Broadly, all of the temporary episodes of detachment were infused with varying degrees of pragmatism of all of the parties involved.

The first episode of detachment was initiated by the IMF and took place at a particularly delicate time, from Argentina's point of view—namely, during the coup d'état that ended Frondizi's rule. In October 1961, as part of the ongoing monitoring of the loan arrangement of December 1960, an IMF mission landed in Buenos Aires. The mission's report was positive, which enabled Argentina to request its fourth consecutive SBA. On November 2, Roberto Alemann (who had replaced Álvaro Alsogaray as the minister of economy), sent a letter of intent to the IMF. The letter was accompanied by a personal and cordial missive to Jorge del Canto, still head of the Western Hemisphere Department, with whom Alemann had maintained working ties in previous years. Through that letter, Alemann asked to participate in the meeting in which the SBA was to be approved.[6] Alemann was confident that the arrangement was in the bag. He was right. On December 8, 1961, the IMF Executive Board approved a new $100 million loan to Argentina.

At first glance, the new loan was yet another seal of approval for the economic policy that had been implemented by Frondizi, with the IMF's support, since late 1958. Unlike on previous occasions, Alemann's letter of intent stated: "The Argentine government desires a stand-by arrangement with the [IMF] to provide a secondary line of reserves to be used only if the decline in gold and exchange reserves is unduly rapid."[7] It also stated that this time, Argentina was interested not in supplementary stabilization loans but, rather, in development loans, which Frondizi wished to secure from European and U.S. sources.[8] With this goal in mind, Alemann met with Robert F. Woodward, assistant secretary of state for inter-American affairs in the Kennedy administration, and negotiated with the World Bank and the Export-Import Bank.[9] Frondizi also met with President John F. Kennedy to secure access to funds from the Alliance for Progress.[10]

Nevertheless, as Argentina's international economic relations were gradually stabilizing, Frondizi's leadership was deteriorating. Between March and December 1961, driven by a hope to guarantee the continuation of democratic rule, Frondizi asked former President Pedro Eugenio Aramburu to run as the Radical Civic Union's candidate in the elections scheduled to take place in 1964.[11] His failure to convince Aramburu contributed to the government's increasing instability. The follow-up for the SBA of December 1961 was thus conducted under the shadow of an imminent military coup.

In the meantime, the military's suspicion of Frondizi continued to escalate, especially during 1961, when the president seemed to tolerate the return of the Peronists to the helm of the trade unions and he expressed intentions to reassume diplomatic relations with Cuba, despite demands from Washington, DC, to sever all ties with Fidel Castro's regime. Argentina's economic deterioration, which began in late 1961, along resentment in staunch conservative circles due to Alsogaray's discharge from the Ministry of Economy in April 1961, had also eroded Frondizi's position. Finally, the elections of March 18, 1962, which led to the Peronists' victory in ten out of fourteen Argentine provinces and to a subsequent desperate attempt to annul the results, were the last straw.[12]

The IMF was not indifferent to the political events in Argentina. In fact, in its own way the Fund added fuel to the flames. On March 19, just one day after the elections that triggered the crisis, the IMF decided to deny Argentina the right to keep drawing money within the framework of the SBA that had been signed only three months earlier.[13] Contrary to all of its previous declarations, the IMF now claimed that Argentina had breached its obligations when, to finance its expenditures, it drew credit from the Central Bank in sums that exceeded the agreed on ceilings, causing a significant depletion in its foreign currency reserves.[14]

The IMF is surely entitled to withhold funds from its borrowers if it deems that the country is failing to fulfill its obligations. Moreover, the conditions attached to the loan were specifically designed to guarantee the Fund's right to do so. However, in examining this specific decision, we should remember that since its establishment, the IMF had been considerably flexible when dealing with its borrowers. Even if Argentina did exceed its credit limits in early 1962, there was no substantial reason to expect the IMF to impose sanctions on the country—and certainly not in the midst of a coup. But the IMF opted not to stay on the sidelines. Thus, the suspension of the arrangement cannot be seen as a purely economic decision. It was, rather, a tactical political move by the IMF to gain the trust of Argentina's future rulers. It is worth noting that, during the same period, the IMF was warning Colombia that it had violated its SBA, but the Fund did not freeze its agreement with that country. Unlike Buenos Aires, Bogotá by that time had severed its diplomatic ties with Cuba and lined up behind the Kennedy administration's desire to consolidate a hemispheric foreign policy toward Castro.[15]

The IMF's decision to suspend the SBA made waves not only in Argentina but also within the U.S. administration, which was already viewing Frondizi not as a moderate statesman who deserved help but, instead, as a suspect ultra-nationalist.[16] This perception of Frondizi constituted a serious problem because, as Vanni Pettinà indicates, in the context of the Cold War the U.S. administration, highly influenced by the CIA, interpreted the rise of nationalism in Latin America (as well as in Asia and the Middle East) as strongly linked to the advance of socialism and therefore as an unmatched opportunity for Moscow to extend its influence in the region.[17] In any event, the day after the IMF announced the SBA's suspension, U.S. Ambassador Robert McClintock declared that the events in Argentina were causing a reconsideration of financial assistance to the country. Voices in the background in Argentina were calling for a devaluation of the peso. The government's deficit grew, and by the end of March 1962, its debts had nearly doubled.[18] According to data form the Argentine Central Bank, state's and the private sector's debts totaled $2.8 billion in December 1963.[19]

On March 29, 1962, less than two weeks after the elections in which leaders of the Peronist party (except Perón) were allowed to submit their candidacy for the first time since 1955, Frondizi was overthrown by a military coup. The new rulers were faced with a hard task: regaining the international financial community's trust in Argentina's economy. As shown below, the IMF quickly reversed its attitude toward Argentina, and the routine of dependency was restored.

Temporary Solutions for a Temporary Government: The Stand-by Arrangements during Guido's Presidency

Following the coup in March 1962, a debate broke out in military circles between the Colorados (Reds), who aspired to follow the principles of the Liberating Revolution and increase influence of the military in state affairs, and the Azules (Blues), who wanted a limited democracy. Finally, it was decided to establish a semiconstitutional regime and appoint as president not a military figure but a civilian: the lawyer and politician José María Guido of the Radical Civic Union, who had served as president of the Senate under Frondizi. Guido, however, failed to restore order in Argentina.[20] In a desperate attempt to remain in office, he made a series of concessions that left power in the army's hands. Among other measures, Guido committed to annulling the elections of March 1962, dissolving Congress, and retaining the ban on the Peronist party. As if this were not enough, he agreed to establish an anti-Peronist, anti-Frondizist, and reactionary cabinet.[21]

The economic leadership of Guido's government was highly unstable. During its 562 days in power, from March 1962 to October 1963, there were five different ministers of economy, with the first two lasting less than a month in office. These ministers, who were all liberally oriented, were (in chronological order) Jorge Wehbe, Federico Pinedo, Álvaro Alsogaray, Eustaquio Méndez Delfino, and José Alfredo Martínez de Hoz. Strikingly, instead of jeopardizing the relationship with the IMF, the frequent changes in the Ministry of Economy contributed to its consolidation. For instance, in early April 1962, rumors reached the IMF that Pinedo would be appointed (for the third time) as economic minister, while Guillermo Walter Klein would serve as his secretary.[22] These rumors raised great expectations in Washington. In a matter of days, Klein (who until very recently had served as the representative of the Southern Cone on the IMF's Executive Board), summoned Jorge del Canto to an urgent meeting to get his blessing for a new stabilization program. Not coincidentally, the program was publicized in Argentina on April 11, two days after Klein's meeting with del Canto.[23] According to del Canto, "Dr. Klein suggested that I accompany the mission during the weekend to discuss a plan of immediate action that the Government was contemplating to deal with the exchange crisis that Argentina was confronting. . . . Dr. Pinedo and Dr. Klein wanted the [IMF] mission to make comments on their own ideas as to how to deal with the present situation. . . . Overall, the outlook seems very promising in terms of developing a new program that would justify Argentina's support of the [IMF]."[24]

Klein's attempts to strengthen the ties with the IMF, and especially with top executives with whom he had established professional and personal ties while representing his country, soon bore fruit. Without delay, Managing Director Per Jacobsson gave Argentina the green light to apply for a new SBA,[25] brushing aside the pretexts the IMF had used for suspending the arrangement a month earlier. On April 23, 1962, del Canto landed once again in Buenos Aires. On April 25, in the midst of the negotiations, Pinedo resigned and was replaced by Álvaro Alsogaray.[26] Del Canto was confident that Alsogaray would come to terms with the IMF.[27] As expected, the letter of intent was quickly finalized. On June 6, the IMF approved a $100 million SBA that was almost identical to the one signed with Frondizi in 1961. The main difference was that it established a stricter framework regarding the Central Bank's level of reserves.

As in previous instances, Argentina was granted complementary loans, mainly from the U.S. government. It should be noted that while IMF loans to Latin American states tended to be followed by U.S. loans, there were some exceptions. For example, in December 1954, the IMF approved a $25 million credit to the Colombian dictator Gustavo Rojas Pinilla (June 1953–May 1957), but the State Department did not authorize a $25 million loan from the Federal Reserve.[28] This initial refusal was somewhat surprising, because during the Cold War, Washington used foreign loans to foster economic integration and anticommunist policies all over the continent. Once Colombia began fully implementing the austerity measures promoted by the IMF and World Bank, however, the United States renewed its financial assistance to the country.

In any event, Argentina was fortunate. On June 7, the U.S. Treasury approved a $50 million loan to Guido's administration.[29] At the same time, Alsogaray strove to raise $130 million from the Alliance for Progress, as Frondizi and Kennedy had discussed.[30] However, shortly after the SBA was approved, Alsogaray sent a frank letter to Per Jacobsson expressing dissatisfaction with the agreement because, he said, he had not been familiar with the details when he signed it.[31] Alsogaray's frustration is easily understood: The arrangement had been consolidated by his predecessor, Pinedo (who had served for barely nineteen days), and signed by Alsogaray on his second day in office. Adding insult to injury, Alsogaray opined that the IMF mission in April had failed to grasp the gravity of the economic crisis plaguing Argentina.[32] Claims that IMF reports contained substantial inaccuracies—especially when such inaccuracies were meant to conceal serious economic problems—were heard not only in Argentina but also in other countries, such as Peru, where the Fund was accused of praising the local economy until the very moment that it collapsed in 1967–1968.[33] The disturbing novelty here is that such a worrying claim had been voiced not by opposition leaders, but by the signatory to the agreement.

Although Alsogaray was not entirely satisfied with the economic developments, Guido's government had no difficulty in cultivating the routine of dependency. And even while Argentina kept adhering to practices that were clearly incompatible with the IMF's policies (especially regarding credit and trade), the IMF had no qualms about renewing its assistance. Curiously, the IMF's good will and tolerance toward Argentina's new military rulers was remarkably unlike the strictness that it manifested toward Frondizi's dying government in March 1962. This selective flexibility, so it seems, stemmed from the Fund's desire to ensure the ratification of the SBA, as this financial instrument has become an indispensable platform for establishing an efficient and influential joint working routine. The same flexibility appears to have characterized IMF–Peruvian relations, as well, especially in the late 1960s, when Lima made considerable efforts to implement stabilization policies.[34]

Nevertheless, the renewed, idyllic ties with the IMF did not lead to a substantial improvement in Argentina's economy. Each of the changing ministers of economy attempted to improve the relationship with the IMF and to apply the same orthodox formulas, which centered on deregulation of the exchange market, significant cuts in government expenditure, and tightened credit restrictions.[35] However, none of them was able to solve acute financial problems and rein in inflation. All that the ministers managed to achieve, with the IMF's advice, was a decrease of about 9 percent in industrial production and about 11 percent in per capita consumption, along with a 30 percent drop in investment in equipment and machinery.[36] The routine of dependency may have been recovered, but the Argentine economy most certainly had not.

To avoid a crisis, Guido's cabinet set several economic goals: to reach monetary stability, to control inflation, to reduce the fiscal deficit, to stop the devaluation of the peso, to improve the balance of payments, and to reschedule the foreign debt. It should be noted that at the time, debt rescheduling had become a common goal of countries, such as Bolivia, Chile, Ecuador, and Peru, that since the late 1950s had been borrowing from the IMF to pay short-term debts while sinking more deeply into foreign debt. In the Argentine case, as well as in other countries that were granted loans from the same lenders, the government declared that the goals had to be attained without government intervention in the economy and through cooperation with the United States, the Bretton Woods institutions, private banks, and the Paris Club.[37] Cooperation with the IMF was promptly secured.

Predictably, the SBA of June 1962 opened the floodgates for the arrival of a succession of IMF missions. During that year, seven missions visited Argentina, attracting the interest of prominent figures in the national economic leadership, as well as of interest groups, who often approached the IMF representatives to try to influence the content of the loan agreements. For instance, the Association of Manufacturers of Agricultural Machinery and Spare Parts contacted the mission of July 1962, and the president of the Argentine Industrial Union met with the mission of November 1962.[38]

Not only was the number of missions much greater than ever before, but they also remained in Argentina for longer periods of time: only two days in July, but about twenty days in August, and then from mid-October until mid-November, from late November until late December, and for nearly two months in January–February 1963. Furthermore, most missions were headed by senior IMF officials such as David Finch, Eugenio Bertens, and Jorge del Canto, who, as was already explained, were intimately familiar with the national and regional reality and key government officials.

Overall, the missions' reports seem to indicate that the IMF continued to approve financial assistance even when it was clear that the national economy was far from recovering and that the government was unable or unwilling to meet its standing commitments. In actuality, and more than anything else, the new loans provided a strong pretext to tighten the surveillance process. In this manner, on August 5, a high-ranking IMF mission arrived in Buenos Aires to hear Alsogaray's detailed explanation of his new economic plan.[39] The plan covered the central challenges of the hour, such as debt rescheduling, a drastic improvement in the balance of payments, and substantial reductions in state expenditures.[40] Although no one in the mission believed that the economic minister would be able to implement his plan, the IMF went ahead and approved a further $50 million loan, increasing the overall amount of the SBA to $100 million.[41]

In October, another mission arrived in Argentina.[42] In mid-November, the IMF defined Argentina's situation as critical and on the brink of a major economic crisis.[43] In January 1963, yet another mission visited the country. Although this mission was unable to embellish the dismal picture it saw, it began to elaborate a new SBA. IMF officials also warned about a number of fundamental problems, especially the national budget. Their impression was that the situation had "deteriorated further" compared with the "highly adverse state of affairs" they had found on their previous visit.[44] To make matters worse, the mission concluded that the various ministers in Guido's cabinet were in disagreement and that no concerted effort was made to implement the stabilization plan.[45] Even while the mission was elaborating a relatively "soft" stabilization plan, it reported that "it is uncertain that even this program can be implemented, as the Minister of Economy is not strong and may fail to achieve even this degree of action. It is also possible that after adoption, his weakness would lead to departures even from a seemingly realistic program."[46] Still, the Fund's intense skepticism regarding Argentina's ability to meet its goals was not an obstacle to signing a new arrangement.

The IMF was well aware of the volatile state of Argentina's politics. Therefore, and despite its flexible approach, it insisted that some of the steps stipulated in the draft letter of intent be implemented before the loan was approved. In fact, this was the first time the IMF had ever applied *ex ante* conditionality (or prequalification criteria) and not just *ex post* conditionality (monitoring of program implementation) in Argentina. Likewise, and in a deviation from the norm, it was agreed that the letter of intent should be approved not only by the economic minister or the president of the Central Bank, as was customary, but "by the full Cabinet, including particularly the Secretaries for the Armed Forces, the Minister of the Interior, and the Minister of Public Works."[47] The IMF may have treated Guido's regime with exaggerated tolerance, but its technocrats were certainly neither blind to Argentina's problems nor naïve. As I show especially in Chapter 6, this was not the last time that the IMF's Executive Board of Directors and the IMF technocrats disagreed over the stance to be adopted toward a country in crisis that had limited political will and ability to implement economic policies backed by the Fund.

In urgent need of the IMF's indispensable seal of approval to reopen negotiations with the Paris Club, Argentina had no choice but to accept its novel and somewhat offensive demands. But it soon turned out that an IMF's loan was not necessarily a guarantee for securing loans from other creditors, as those creditors were less flexible and more cautious than was the Fund. In effect, Alsogaray's efforts to reschedule the debt to the Paris Club were fruitless. His failure, alongside his deteriorating reputation with the IMF—along with growing tension between him and certain sectors of the military and of the Argentine business community—drove Alsogaray to resign barely six months after taking office.[48] Eustaquio Méndez Delfino, the liberal economist who had served as president of the Central Bank until May 1962, stepped into Alsogaray's shoes on December 10, 1962, and soon informed the European lenders of the negotiations with the IMF.[49] Méndez Delfino knew that there was no ground for cultivating great expectations, since the formal and informal reports sent by the IMF to the creditor states were adverse.[50]

Meanwhile, the stand-by negotiations dragged on, and Argentina's hopes gradually evaporated. In a desperate move, Argentina asked the IMF for a modest gesture: to extend until October 6, 1963, the arrangement that was scheduled to be in force until June 6—a scheme that originally was proposed by Finch.[51] In a meeting on March 27, 1963, attended by Luis Otero Monsegur, the president of the Central Bank of Argentina and close colleague of Méndez Delfino, and former Economic Minister Roberto Alemann, who had been appointed Argentine ambassador to the United States, the IMF approved a $100 million SBA to Argentina.[52] As requested, the arrangement was scheduled to expire in October 1963, when a new government, to be established after general elections, would "be free to continue its relationship with the IMF."[53] Through this short-term SBA, the IMF laid the foundations that would allow Guido's successor to approach the Fund with a request for a new $100 million arrangement.[54] Despite Argentina's skepticism, information about complementary aid worth $65 million from the U.S. Treasury, the Export-Import Bank, and the Alliance for Progress began to circulate.[55]

The arrangement approved in early 1963 did not meet with unanimous support from the IMF's Executive Board. The European creditors were among its strongest opponents, and the United States was its most enthusiastic supporter.[56] This situation, in which the U.S. view finally prevailed, coincides with the realistic approach that perceives international organizations as bodies that reflect the interest of their most powerful member states.[57] In this particular case, where the United States and Europe disagreed, the model elaborated by Strom Thacker, in which states with geopolitical proximity to Western shareholders in general and to the United States in particular enjoy preferential treatment from the IMF, seems to be particularly relevant.[58] As Jon Kofas consistently argues, especially during the Cold War and under the shadow of the Cuban Revolution, Washington used IMF and World Bank loans as leverage to implement economic reforms and prevent communism from gaining strength in the region.

In sum, the IMF was keen to tighten its relationship with any government, democratic or authoritarian, that was willing to adopt its recommendations and foster a close joint working routine with it. Whether a given government really could or would meet its obligations to the IMF was often a secondary matter. In this respect, it seems that while dealing with IMF-friendly governments or local experts in particular, the Fund tended to perceive incomplete compliance with program targets as mere glitches that would be ironed out in due course. As we shall see, some of those glitches turned into unexpected temporary episodes of detachment.

The Struggle for Independence: Arturo Illia and the First Attempt to Stop the Routine of Dependency

Presidential elections took place in Argentina on July 7, 1963. The winner was the physician Arturo Humberto Illia, candidate of the UCRP (Unión Cívica Radical del Pueblo), and one of the most forceful critics of former President Frondizi.[59] His vice-president was Carlos Humberto Perette, whom the U.S. State Department regarded as an opportunist and an ultranationalist.[60] Illia carried 2.44 million votes—that is, only 25.15 percent support. Second in the race were 1.7 million empty envelopes representing Peronists who in 1958 had voted for Frondizi. The rest of the votes were divided among nine opposition parties that filled some two-thirds of the seats of a highly split Parliament.

The comparisons between Illia and Frondizi are unavoidable. They both grew up in the Radical Civic Union and rose to power in semidemocratic elections in which the Peronist party was outlawed. Yet there were essential differences between them. First, thanks to his pact with Perón, Frondizi won 52 percent of the votes, whereas Illia was a minority president. There were also wide gaps in their economic views. While Frondizi invested considerable efforts in stabilizing and developing Argentina's heavy industry, relying on foreign capital to do so, Illia adhered to independentist economic nationalism.[61] Illia aspired to reach gradual and balanced growth, abandoning the exclusive focus on heavy industry. Based on this approach, two complementary programs were consolidated: (1) a short-term plan designed to restore monetary stability and promote consumption and growth; and (2) a National Development Plan to be implemented in a second phase, intended to secure steady and sustained growth through the effective use of existing resources.[62]

In terms of international economic relationships in general, and the ties with the IMF in particular, there was practically an abyss dividing Illia and Frondizi. Argentina's trade relations during Illia's tenure were based on the premise that markets lack ideological boundaries, so concrete steps were taken toward commercial multilateralism. Trade with the traditional commercial partners (the United States and Western Europe) declined, while trade with Latin American countries, the Communist bloc, and China increased. In addition, Frondizi and Illia differed greatly in how they conducted Argentina's economic relations with the United States, especially with regard to the polemical oil contracts. Loyal to developmentalist models, Frondizi signed contracts with North American corporations out of the conviction that this was a necessary step toward development and economic independence. Illia, by contrast, annulled these contracts, condemning them as a symbol of dependence on foreign capital.[63] As we shall see, Illia's struggle for economic independence was not limited to the termination of the oil contracts. It also implied the adoption of an uncompromising stance vis-à-vis the IMF.

God Is in the Details: The Characteristics of Illia's Detachment from the IMF

Illia's move into the Casa Rosada on October 12, 1963, made the IMF anxious, because key officers in his government held nationalist and statist stands and opposed the previously implemented stabilization plans backed by the IMF. Among them were Eugenio Blanco, the new minister of economy; Félix Gilberto Elizalde, the president of the Central Bank; and Bernardo Grinspun, Illia's trade secretary.[64]

At first, the IMF carefully analyzed Illia's inaugural speech, although he did not allude to the Fund even once. Although Illia referred explicitly to an emergency plan to come out of the recession and announced the annulment of the "plainly illegal" oil contracts signed by Frondizi (thereby causing profound apprehension in the United States and Britain because similar declarations were also made by Brazil and Peru at the time), the IMF concluded that "the tone of the address was moderate, and while most of the campaign promises were repeated, there was little to suggest any intention of following extreme policies or making radical departures from the present line."[65]

This rosy interpretation of Illia's intentions was quite unrealistic. The IMF misunderstood Illia's stiff position even when he refused to hold an introductory meeting with the Fund's representatives before entering the presidential palace.[66] This kind of introductory meeting, in which IMF technocrats presented their analysis of Argentina's economy to the new government officials, had already became customary in Argentina (see Chapter 3). Illia's refusal therefore was not accidental, and it deprived the IMF of one of its instruments of influence. Moreover, once Illia was in power, Argentina unilaterally altered its treatment of the Fund. The changes were manifest in every single facet of the routine of dependency, including the permanent presence of IMF representatives at the Central Bank, the hosting of IMF missions, the furnishing of information, and compliance with the obligations outlined in the SBAs.

Overall, Illia pushed the IMF into a reactive rather than a proactive position toward Argentina. The correspondence between Jack Guenther, the IMF's permanent representative at the Central Bank, and the Fund's headquarters is a powerful illustration of this new balance of power. Guenther arrived at the Central Bank in December 1962 to provide technical assistance. The agreement between Argentina and the IMF concerning Guenther's duties stipulated that his mission would be completed in September 1963. In addition, as is common in contracts of this kind, the accord specified that the cost of his stay in Buenos Aires would be paid in equal parts by the IMF and the Argentine government.[67]

When Guenther's contract expired in September 1963, the IMF faced a dilemma: Should it call him back to Washington or instruct him to remain in Argentina in the hope that his contract would be renewed? Eventually, the IMF decided to wait until after Illia had selected the new appointees to the Central Bank. Notwithstanding the IMF's patience, several Central Bank officials considered Guenther's continued presence too fundamental for him to wait for a government response and put the issue directly on Illia's desk.[68] But Illia was in no particular hurry to make a decision on the issue, which elevated the IMF's concern. On the one hand, the Fund feared that Guenther's presence would be construed by anti-IMF Argentines as an external imposition; on the other, it strove to avoid a situation in which the departure of its technician would be interpreted as unwillingness to cooperate with Illia.[69] Guenther, of course, was aware of the tension his stay provoked in both official and opposition circles. Most disturbing in his opinion was the fact that several political groups, including the reactionary Christian Democratic Party and several factions within the ruling party, were urging a termination of the relationship with the IMF.[70] Unsurprisingly, the contract was not renewed, and Guenther moved back to Washington.

The "Guenther episode" is illuminating. Several scholars have implied that Guenther's contract was not renewed because of indecision or negligence on Illia's part, but this appears to be misleading.[71] Historical evidence suggests that Guenther's contract was not extended as part of a consistent or conscious strategy aimed to minimize the Fund's presence in Argentina. That Illia simply forgot or was unable to make a decision on such a central issue that was brought to his personal attention several times seems improbable. Moreover, in a sharp departure from the past, the two missions that visited Argentina during 1964 were not allocated rooms at the Central Bank; this reflects nothing other than an intentional shift in Argentina's approach to IMF representatives. By 1963, the working practices of IMF officials in Argentina were so firmly established and unquestioned that only explicit instructions could have changed them radically—as happened during Illia's presidency. Moreover, in yet another salient sign of the new times, IMF missions complained about now having to rent for their office space instead of getting it for free at the Central Bank.[72] More important, the number of IMF missions to Argentina was sharply reduced. In the twelve months that preceded the elections in 1963, seven IMF missions had arrived in Argentina; during the almost three years of Illia's presidency, by contrast, only six missions visited the country (two in 1964, three in 1965, and one in 1966). Evidently, a different wind was blowing in Argentina.

Setting new norms and boundaries for the relationship with the IMF was not limited to the missions. It also spread to other facets of the routine of dependency. As mentioned, the short-term SBA was going to expire in October, and the discussions about its renewal provided fertile ground for a clash between the IMF and Argentina. As attested by Enrique García Vázquez, the vice-president of the Central Bank at the time, "The IMF's narrow monetarism was inconsistent with Illia's policy; he implemented a short-term economic plan centered on increased credit and public spending," with a statist flavor far more pronounced than the IMF was ready to swallow.[73] Meanwhile, the president and vice-president of the Central Bank were assigned the task of negotiating with the renowned French economist Pierre-Paul Schweitzer, who became the managing director of the IMF on September 1, 1963. Following brief discussions, Schweitzer refused to grant Illia an SBA or to renew the short-term arrangement that was in effect, but he promised to recommend to European governments the rescheduling of Argentina's debt—a promise that he kept.[74] Although it was the IMF that decided not to open formal loan negotiations, the fact cannot be ignored that Illia left the Fund no other choice.

Despite the profound change in IMF–Argentine relations, Illia's administration was not interested in a total rupture with the Fund. Therefore, Economic Minister Eugenio Blanco declared publicly, "The fact that under certain circumstances—and in special cases—the government does not see the situation eye to eye with the IMF does not mean [it is] departing from the Fund."[75] Without loan agreements in force, however, several long-standing components of the routine of dependency began to deteriorate. For instance, soon after he was reappointed as a director on the IMF's Executive Board, Walter Klein wrote a letter to the president of the Argentine Central Bank listing del Canto's complaints about faults in the regular updates that Argentina had been dispatching to the IMF. Del Canto arrogantly demanded an advance draft of any bill or ordinance pertaining to the national budget or fiscal reform that was to be discussed by the Argentine Congress.[76] There is no doubt that del Canto, who was used to serving as an unofficial but de facto adviser to several Argentine economic teams, was reluctant to relinquish that privileged role. Unfortunately for him, though, this last demand was rejected.

The steps Argentina took to distance itself from the IMF were accompanied by mounting tension with the World Bank. The disputes with the Bank focused on an agreement signed in January 1962 that granted to Argentina $95 million for the state-owned electric company Servicios Eléctricos del Gran Buenos Aires (SEGBA). The problem arose when, in late 1963, SEGBA still had not updated its tariffs and failed to introduce a comprehensive organizational reform, as the World Bank had requested.[77] It is important to note that assistance from the World Bank was conditioned on deep reforms in the energy and infrastructure sectors not only in Argentina but also in other Latin American countries. It is striking, for example, to examine how the Bank promoted the same organizational reforms in the roads, airports, and electric power facilities and finance corporations in Colombia during the 1950s and 1960s.[78]

In December 1963, George Woods, president of the World Bank, urged Blanco to meet the provisions of the agreement. Blanco, a socialist and nationalist, defiantly replied that the issue would be reconsidered, but Argentina would have the last word.[79] Blanco's attitude enraged Woods, who sent a heated letter to Illia warning that solving the SEGBA problem was a prerequisite for discussing any further projects.[80] To resolve the crisis, Burke Knapp, vice-president of the World Bank, arrived in Argentina in February, accompanied by a financial adviser and an energy expert.[81] However, even the personal involvement of Woods and Knapp fell short in moderating Argentina's uncompromising stance.

While Illia's administration did not borrow from the IMF, it opted to secure (more expensive) loans from other foreign lenders who did not impose conditions and whom Illia and the Argentine public considered less controversial than the Fund. For instance, in October 1963, the Inter-American Development Bank (IDB) granted a $92.6 million credit to Argentina for development and educational projects.[82] In early 1965, the IDB approved another $15 million for local industry and $15 million to the Argentine Industrial Bank.[83]

After Illia's first year in office, the IMF could not ignore that Argentina was determined to detach itself from its technocrats, conditional lending, and intervention. This was not merely another "temporary episode of detachment" caused by a sudden crisis on the national level. It was a major decision by Illia. In the IMF's view, however, Blanco was the sole person responsible for the unfavorable situation. Not only was the minister against foreign capital—the IMF included—but he also implemented policies that contradicted the Fund's dictates. At the center of these policies was a substantial increase in state intervention in the economy, which led to, among others things, serious restrictions on the use of imported spare parts in the auto industry; the approval of special credits to companies that reduced their reliance on imported raw materials; and the passing in June 1964 of the Minimum Wage Law (*Ley de salario mínimo, vital y móvil*) and the Supply Law (*Ley de abastecimiento*), which was designed to freeze the price of a family's basic household expenses, retirement allowances, and pensions. In addition, unlike Elizalde, Blanco objected to the arrival of yet another IMF mission in May.[84] As del Canto reported during his visit to Argentina in June 1964:

> I believe that we developed a better understanding about the Fund and our desire to help Argentina on the part of some members of the so-called "economic team," such as the President of the Central Bank [Elizalde] but the Minister of Economy [Blanco]. . . could not be characterized as a champion of the Fund. The position of the Minister vis-à-vis the Fund is difficult, because the party in power ran an anti-Fund platform and he, like many others, associates the Fund with what they call the deflationary policies of the earlier Government and the recession

of 1962–63. The present Government is well-intentioned, but rather in-experienced and somewhat nationalistic.[85]

Finally, in 1963, the question was (and still is): To what extent and for how long can a Latin American nation disengage from the IMF? As Illia probably understood, and as recently suggested by the IMF's slow return to Argentina under President Cristina Fernández de Kirchner in her second term, a total disengagement is neither a realistic nor a prudent option.

The Turtle's Race to Independence

In August 1964, the sudden death of Blanco and the appointment of the prag-matic and moderate attorney Juan Carlos Pugliese in his place facilitated certain improvements in Argentina's relations with the World Bank and especially with the IMF. In the background, a marked upturn in the Argentine economy began to take place. An internal IMF report from January 1964 applauded the relative progress in the country's balance of payments and economic activity, the stabil-ity of the peso, and the increase in Central Bank's reserves from $126 million in late 1962 to $280 million a year later. At the same time, the IMF insisted that the primary problem of Argentina had always been the budget deficit, which had reached a monthly rate of 2–2.5 percent.[86]

Illia's administration, however, was still reluctant to fully restore the work-ing routine with the IMF. For its part, the Fund was prepared to compromise and even continue to turn a blind eye to economic measures that were inconsis-tent with the liberal model it strove to promote. Prominent among these mea-sures were Illia's refusal to adopt a stabilization program and his adherence to a gradual plan in which, according to Keynesian precepts, the budget deficit was considered a marginal problem compared with unemployment and recession.

Unlike the IMF, the World Bank initially refused to relax its conditions as long as Argentina failed to meet its obligations in the SEGBA affair. As if this were not enough, Gerald Alter, the director of the World Bank's Western Hemi-sphere Department, explained to del Canto, his counterpart at the IMF, how disappointed he was in light of the fund's "exaggerated" rapprochement with Argentina.[87] Alter made it clear that he found no justification for signing an SBA with Illia's government.[88] The tension between the Bretton Woods institu-tions regarding Argentina was evident. In the end, the World Bank announced its readiness to reconsider its support for new projects in the country.[89] The apparent turn in the World Bank's position seems to have derived, at least par-tially, from competition between the institutions over prestige and areas of influence and from the Bank's fear of losing as important a client as Argentina. In this respect, one should note that Illia managed to locate alternative sources for development loans (especially the IDB), which threatened the World Bank's prominence in the region.

Nevertheless, neither the appointment of Pugliese nor the IMF's willingness to restore its working routine with Argentina was sufficient to persuade Illia's government to come closer to the Fund. It was only in 1965, and especially after the ruling party's defeat in the congressional elections in March, that Argentina began to contemplate knocking on the IMF's door. As del Canto reported, "The Argentine authorities probed, on an informal basis, Mr. Sacchetti [the head of the IMF's mission to Argentina] on what the reaction of the management would be to an approach by Argentina regarding a stand-by."[90] Del Canto estimated that Argentina would soon request a new arrangement.[91] However, his forecast was mistaken. During a visit to Washington, Pugliese declared that Argentina had decided not to succumb to the IMF's pressures, because adopting the Fund's rigid recommendations would lead not just to recession but to "the suicide of Argentina's democracy."[92] The IMF's reaction to Pugliese's statement was immediate and furious.[93] Thus, quite systematically, Illia became the first Argentine president to prove that it was possible to create a "routine of detachment" instead of a routine cycle of negotiations, loan arrangements, stabilization programs and surveillance.

Illia's independentist aspirations affected not only Argentina's relations with the IMF but also the character of the economic plans that were implemented during his presidency, which differed profoundly from the stabilization plans of Frondizi and Guido. In June 1965, Pugliese launched a five-year National Development Plan designed "to achieve, within a framework of growing monetary stability, a high and sustained growth in national production, as well as to solve the structural problems that have impeded the economic development of the country for years."[94] The plan applied to the years 1965–1969, and its cost was estimated at $1,738.6 million, of which $1,030 million would come from the private sector, and only about 10 percent of the total would be provided by foreign creditors and investors.[95] As Pugliese stated at the time, "A stand-by arrangement with the IMF could be beneficial, [but it is] not vital."[96] Importantly, before the plan was officially launched, Pugliese announced that he would publicize it in full—first in Argentina, and later in foreign forums.[97] Far from being a curiosity or a mere caprice of the minister, the announcement signified a sharp departure from the past. As shown in Chapter 3, from 1956 until 1963, all of the Argentine government's economic plans had been formulated jointly with the IMF and publicized in Argentina only after the Fund approved them.

By late June 1965, even without signing an SBA with the IMF and despite Britain's and France's reservations, Argentina had rescheduled its debt to the Paris Club and reach similar arrangements with Japan and the United States.[98] It would be inaccurate, however, to conclude that this was achieved without external assistance. Indeed, the negotiations with the Paris Club succeeded (although with moderate results) only when the United States approved the postponement of Argentina's loan repayments to the Export-Import Bank, thus setting a precedent that Europe was quick to imitate. In addition, although no SBA was in force, one cannot ignore that the IMF's attendance at the meetings held between Argentina and the Paris Club members represented a critical seal of approval.[99] The IMF's presence at these meetings was far from passive. It was actually responsible for creating the economic and financial reports on Argentina that served as the basis for negotiations with the Europeans.[100] It should be emphasized, however, that Argentina did not choose to invite the IMF to take part in its discussions with the Paris Club. On the contrary, Argentina consented only after an explicit demand by the Europeans.[101] But Argentina was not alone in having to involve the IMF in its negotiations. In the early 1970s, the Paris Club made the approval of an SBA with the IMF a condition for holding debt negotiations with Chile. This was a harsh condition, as the President Salvador Allende (November 1970–September 1973) was reluctant to pay the high political price of entering an SBA.[102] Obviously, the international financial community was not inclined to forgo the services and expertise of the IMF. Thus, refusing to sign SBAs was not enough to liberate borrowing states from the IMFS's intervention in its economic affairs.

The years 1964–1965 brought economic recovery to Argentina, with the gross national product rising at an annual rate of 10 percent and unemployment declining from 8.8 percent in July 1963 to 4.6 percent by the end of 1965. The increase in exports, the result of both Illia's monetary policy, and bumper crops in 1964–1965, prevented a crisis in the balance of payments. In addition, unlike Frondizi, Illia resisted the temptation to accumulate short-term liabilities.[103] The economic results for 1966 were less encouraging, but there were no signs of recession or problems in the balance of payments. Nevertheless, the feeling among the Argentine public was that the country was on the brink of an economic crisis and headed for another coup.[104]

In early 1966, in an attempt to evade an economic crisis and appease proliberal opponents, including those in military circles, Argentina requested financial assistance from the IMF. Simultaneously, Pugliese committed to liberalizing the exchange market. The IMF promptly allowed Argentina to purchase $30 million to avoid overly diluting its foreign currency and gold reserves through debt repayment.[105] Although this was the lowest amount ever transferred by the IMF to Argentina, and while this was not an SBA but an almost automatic purchase within the framework of the gold tranche, the move signaled a minor rapprochement with the Fund. Research at the IMF Archives reveals that the same kind of temporary detachment, followed by a similarly limited joint working routine that included very few mutual visits and the use of IMF funds but not within the framework of conditional lending, also characterized the relations between the IMF and Chile during Allende's presidency.[106] In other words, Illia's and Allende's model of (more independent) IMF membership was not an "accident." It was a very real and plausible option that they strove to pursue.

As IMF's reports indicate, del Canto interpreted Illia's refusal to request a new SBA not as a matter of principle but, rather, as pragmatism. He opined that it would be risky for Illia to send a letter of intent to the IMF in an election year, when political agitation was on the rise.[107] There is no doubt that he was correct in assuming that an agreement with the IMF carried a high political price at the time, not only on the volatile Argentine scene, but in the region as a whole. Latin Americans' discontent with the IMF appeared to be so profound, in fact, that even officials who represented their governments at the Fund did not hide their criticism. For instance, Jorge González del Valle, the alternate executive director representing Guatemala, declared at an IMF meeting that the Fund constituted "a new form of imperialism in its desire to dictate policies to the Latin American countries."[108]

But Illia's unequivocal stance vis-à-vis the Fund was not enough to save him from his expected ouster, and he was humiliatingly overthrown on June 28, 1966. The 1966 coup, like previous ones, was not the result of an economic crisis. As a matter of fact, Illia was successful not only in overcoming the recession inherited from Guido, but also in managing the external debt. While Argentina's debt to the IMF amounted to $238 million in December 1963, it had been reduced to $190 million by December 1964, to $146 million by December 1965, and to $117.5 million by December 1966.[109] The motivation behind the coup was largely political.[110] The aggressive opposition against Illia was broad and diverse, encompassing trade unions; political parties (including factions within the Radical Civic Union); the military; the media; the agricultural-exporting sector, which opposed the government's involvement in regulating beef prices; and the Industrialist Association, which rejected the Minimum Wage Bill.[111] The common argument conveyed by the opposition was that Illia's government was ineffective, making it relatively easy for the military to present itself as a modern, professional, and capable alternative.[112]

Contrary to these efforts to de-legitimize Illia's government, his attitude toward the IMF, along with many actions that he took—including annulling the contracts signed with foreign oil companies by Frondizi, passing the minimum wage bill, launching a comprehensive development plan, and refusing to dispatch armed forces to join the Peace Corps in Santo Domingo (contrary to U.S. expectations)—clearly attest to his determination and his readiness to take political risks. It is therefore improbable that the routine of detachment from the IMF was due to negligence or incapacity. The working routine that had evolved with the IMF since 1957 was so intensive that it is practically inconceivable that it could simply have been ignored. The multifaceted interactions and practices that had been routinized for years could not have stopped all by themselves, without a guiding hand.

Again, as in the case of Allende in Chile in the early 1970s and as in many Latin American countries today (e.g., Argentina, Bolivia, Ecuador, Uruguay, and Venezuela), Illia's detachment from the IMF was not total and never threatened Argentina's membership or formal status in the Fund. In effect, in 1965, in the midst of an episode of profound detachment, the IMF approved an increase in Argentina's quota, from $280 million to $350 million.[113]

As we shall see, temporary episodes of detachment do not necessarily lead to permanent detachment from the IMF. Indeed, the clear signs of independence during Illia's term were promptly obliterated by his successors.

The Dependency Pendulum under the "Argentine Revolution"

After President Illia was ousted, a new era began in Argentina. What the conspirators called the "Argentine Revolution" differed considerably from the earlier Liberating Revolution. The heads of the new regime rejected the label "provisional" and declared their intention to remain in power indefinitely.

As a result of the professionalization process the Argentine army had undergone in the early 1960s (with U.S. aid), the senior echelon now perceived itself as the only power capable of managing the republic. The Argentine Revolution, which initially encountered no resistance (or even significant protest), soon revealed its true authoritarian nature. In an attempt to intimidate potential opponents, the regime outlawed political parties, imposed severe censorship, intervened in the state universities, dismantled the labor unions, and transferred all power and authority to one person—President General Juan Carlos Onganía. Unparalleled in its brutality, the Argentine Revolution did not hesitate to point its guns at real and imagined adversaries. The event known as the Night of the Long Police Sticks in July 1966, when faculty and students demanding academic freedom and autonomy for the universities were beaten up and arrested, was clear evidence of the regime's violence. In May 1969, another bloody popular confrontation between citizens and military forces in the city of Córdoba (an event known as the Cordobazo) marked the beginning of the end of the dictatorship that remained in power until May 1973.[114]

Onganía's policy was largely based on the model of the military regime that was established in Brazil in 1964 and on the National Security Doctrine, which Washington actively disseminated in the region. According to the doctrine, in addition to its traditional duty (fighting external wars), the army had to carry out internal wars against subversive elements, which, in line with Cold War tensions, were perceived as striving to detach the underdeveloped countries from the Western world and draw them closer to communism. Since the military believed that the enemy was steadily encroaching in every possible arena, the internal war had to be fought on the ideological, economic, and political fronts.[115] In line with this reasoning, subversion was fueled by the conditions associated with underdevelopment, so the economic front soon became a central focus.[116]

Onganía actually established what the political scientist Guillermo O'Donnell defined as a bureaucratic-authoritarian (BA) state. In such states, the top positions are occupied by figures with extensive records in large organizations, especially the military. The BA state creates a unique blend of liberal principles and exclusionary economic practices, thereby isolating state power and excluding political and interest groups, especially the weaker social classes. The government's neglect of the lower socioeconomic sectors and its determination to depoliticize social demands eventually bring about the entrenchment of so-called peripheral capitalism, in which an underdeveloped state enjoys a high level of industrialization but at the same time remains directly dependent on core countries.[117] Argentina under Onganía certainly met O'Donnell's definition. However, it depended not only on core states (the United States and Western European nations), but also on the IMF and World Bank, two institutions highly influenced by those same rich states and wielding unprecedented power.

The Argentine Revolution perceived the IMF both as a source of financial resources and international legitimacy and as an organization whose professionalism and rationality Argentina had to internalize to be modernized. Therefore, and probably more than in any previous regime, its members were eager to collaborate with the Fund and become respected as members of its epistemic community of rational, efficient, and liberal economists. This kind of a priori affinity also appeared in Argentina in the 1970s, under President Jorge Rafael Videla and his neoliberal economic minister, José Alfredo Martínez de Hoz, as well as during President Carlos Saúl Menem's tenure in the 1990s. The close relationship forged after 1974 between the IMF and the Chilean dictator General Augusto Pinochet, whose young Chicago Boys implemented a neoliberal economic plan, is another prominent example of this symbiotic partnership.[118]

The new Argentine leadership, as shown below, found sympathetic partners at the IMF. Thus, with Onganía in power, the IMF abandoned the reactive stance it had adopted during Illia's tenure and directed its best efforts at building an alliance with the new dictatorial administration. Nonetheless, even this alliance could not remain immune to the changing Argentine reality.

Del Canto's Renewed Ties with Argentine Economists

Shortly after the coup, the flow of IMF missions into Argentina resumed. The first mission was scheduled for October but postponed until November, at Argentina's request. This mission was supposed to complete the Article IV

Consultation that had begun in March 1966, during Illia's presidency.[119] Although the mission was not charged with any extraordinary task, del Canto opted to head it personally. Clearly, he regarded the revitalization and tightening of the relationship with Argentina as paramount.

In the course of his frequent encounters with Economic Minister Jorge N. Salimei, a young industrialist, and his ideologically heterogeneous staff, del Canto offered a plan that had been devised by his department—a plan that no one in Argentina had requested, even when the government found it hard to consolidate a coherent economic strategy of its own. The Fund's plan was comprehensive and dealt with exchange and fiscal policy, credit, wages, tariffs, and external debt. But that was not all. In an additional effort to restore old routine mechanisms that had been altered or suspended by Illia, del Canto made any future discussion of a new SBA conditional on the appointment of a new IMF resident representative at the Central Bank, as had become customary in the region.[120]

Del Canto did not really have to impose conditions, though, because in January 1967, Salimei, who had been subjected to constant criticism by several economists and businessmen, most vehemently Álvaro Alsogaray, resigned from the Ministry of Economy after only six months in office. Onganía replaced him with Adalbert Krieger Vasena and charged the new economic minister with elaborating and implementing a stabilization plan. From Onganía's perspective, Krieger Vasena was a smart choice. He was not only a liberal pragmatist and an old friend of the IMF; he was also known in Washington because of his business connections with U.S. companies that had invested in Argentina.[121] In addition, the new minister surrounded himself with a team of professional economists, including Pedro Real and Egidio Ianella, president and vice-president, respectively, of the Central Bank.

Krieger Vasena promptly took significant steps to restore and consolidate Argentina's ties with the international financial community. On January 25, he presented his economic plan at the Inter-American Committee on the Alliance for Progress, a key forum to discuss Latin American economic affairs.[122] He then informed the IMF that the Argentines "would like to have the assistance of the [IMF's] staff in preparing this program, and they wish to have the program supported by a stand-by arrangement."[123] As early as January 30, 1967, then, two IMF technicians headed for Argentina, to be joined later by del Canto, to gather data for a report that would serve as the basis for negotiations.[124]

Del Canto and his entourage remained in Buenos Aires until March 10.[125] When the mission finally left Argentina, Krieger Vasena declared war on inflation and announced a 40 percent devaluation of the peso that was aimed at attracting foreign investors.[126] Concurrently, he announced strict guidelines on wages in the private and public sectors and a 50 percent reduction in import taxes.[127] Just as the economic plan was made public, rumors began to spread of a new SBA with the IMF.[128] Toward the end of March, Krieger Vasena initiated a complementary loan-raising campaign in the United States and Europe.[129] Discussions were held with all the European creditors, but unlike during Illia's days in office, they were attended not by anonymous IMF technocrats but by del Canto himself.[130] Del Canto's massive involvement was a clear sign of the IMF's return to Argentina, as well as of the Fund's consolidation as a central pillar and ultimate arbiter in the economic global sphere.

Argentina was granted $100 million from European commercial banks (in descending order by loan volume, from Germany, Britain, Italy, Switzerland, Belgium, France, the Netherlands, Spain, and Sweden) and $5 million from Canadian banks. All of the loans were to be repaid in four years, with a one-year grace period, at an annual interest rate of 2 percent.[131] In addition, the U.S. Treasury approved a $75 million loan.[132] The private and government loans accorded with the United States were negotiated mainly by Álvaro Alsogaray, who was serving as Argentina's ambassador to Washington.[133] In addition, Krieger Vasena embarked on a series of negotiations with the World Bank to solve the SEGBA conflict and obtain new loans for the energy sector.

Following del Canto's request, in early March the IMF and Argentina agreed on the appointment of Marcelo Caiola as the IMF's permanent representative at the Central Bank. Caiola, who was treated much better than his predecessor, Guenther, was given a spacious office and secretarial services.[134] Although he was stationed at the Central Bank, he was soon "cooperating with the Ministry of Finance's technical staff on all matters related to the implementation of the stabilization plan."[135] On May 1, 1967, a new $125 million SBA was signed. The agreement was designed to support the ongoing implementation of the stabilization plan that was intended to reduce inflation, improve the balance of payments, and create favorable conditions for sustained growth.[136] Together with the complementary loans, Argentina managed to raise $400 million.

Interestingly, Argentina did not intend to, and never did, withdraw a single dollar within the framework of the arrangements signed with the IMF in 1967 and 1968. This situation, as mentioned in Chapter 3, was not uncommon—in Argentina or elsewhere. For instance, Peru signed consecutive SBAs between 1954 and 1969 but drew nothing between 1959 and 1967.[137] Thus, one can safely conclude that the IMF's limited financial assistance was not an economic imperative at the time. Rather, the signing of SBAs was a vital means to reach other immediate and important goals. In effect, the agreement helped rehabilitate Argentina's economic and political image in the international arena, serving as a bridge to access a wide range of credits and investments. On the other hand, it facilitated a further entrenchment of the partnership with the IMF—a goal that was important in its own right. Furthermore, and from a national perspective, it seems conceivable that the Argentine Revolution could use the IMF's involvement in the launching of the stabilization program as a scapegoat—that is, to justify the application of austerity measures that otherwise would be impossible to apply because of their high social price tag. It is hard to believe that the regime ignored the labor unrest, street protests, and strikes that had been provoked by the application of belt-tightening plans supported by the IMF since the late 1950s in Bolivia, Chile, and Colombia.[138]

Nevertheless, the signing of the SBA in May marked the complete reactivation of the joint working routine. In July, Caiola and the first monitoring mission landed in Buenos Aires.[139] The mission was satisfied with the recent economic developments and with the fact that Argentina had followed its recommendations to the letter.[140] Unsurprisingly, in January 1968, another mission, headed once again by del Canto, was on its way to Argentina to negotiate the renewal of the SBA. Del Canto's intervention proved useful, and in March 1968, Argentina submitted a new letter of intent. The Argentines justified their request based on what they presented as the success of the economic plan of 1967, their readiness to fight inflation, and the fact that Argentina had not drawn any funds.[141]

In general, the IMF was impressed with Argentina's economy, especially with its financial stability, improvement in the balance of payments, wage policy, and creation of growth conditions. The IMF considered the ongoing implementation of the stabilization plan vital, and in April 1968, it approved a new $125 million arrangement.[142] In May, as an additional indication of the apparent success of the IMF-supported economic plan, Argentina repaid its pending debts to the IMF in advance.[143] When it signed the agreement for 1968, Argentina asked the IMF to continue to post a resident representative at the Central Bank.[144] Caiola, whose one-year contract had just expired, was immediately replaced by Hernán Mejía.[145]

In short, with the renewal of the SBA, Argentina and the IMF fully and enthusiastically reactivated their joint working routine. However, as we shall see, as political instability snowballed in Argentina, it affected the routine of dependency.

Good Will Is Not Always Enough . . .

The economic program implemented from 1967 to mid-1969 succeeded in stabilizing prices and sustaining an average annual growth rate of 5 percent. By early 1968, inflation had reached single-digit figures. A re-equipping program of national industry, with distinct traces of developmentalism, was launched. Public investment and industrial output increased, and unemployment rates modestly diminished. Despite these figures, Argentina's political and social situation deteriorated, eventually damaging the working routine with the IMF.

Argentina's economic performance and the repression exerted by the regime did not silence the opposition. Nationalist groups within and outside the military, as well as broad sectors of civil society (such as students and industrial workers), protested against the rapid emergence of foreign capital as a major factor in Argentina's economy. The most prominent symbol of the denational-ization of the economy was the acquisition of local companies by foreign corpo-rations, with banking, automobile and tobacco manufacturing the biggest lures. For instance, the tobacco company Massalin y Celasco was purchased by Philip Morris, and Imparciales was purchased by Reval. In banking, the Banco Argen-tino de Comercio became the Chase Manhattan Bank, and Citibank bought up Banco Argentino del Atlántico and Banco de Bahía Blanca. The automobile plant Acinfer was taken over by Ford.[146] In the ranking of most profitable com-panies during Onganía's presidency, the top thirteen were founded or owned by foreigners. The construction of several monumental projects, such as the under-water tunnel connecting the cities of Santa Fé and Paraná and the Zárate-Brazo Largo Bridge (both inaugurated in the early 1970s), as well as the nuclear power station in Atocha, did not placate the critics.[147]

In February 1969, while tensions in Argentina were increasing, two missions arrived in Buenos Aires: one from the IMF, and one from the World Bank.[148] Oddly, as the World Bank's relations with Argentina were improving, Argen-tina and the IMF began to shape a less intensive and, more important, less visible joint working routine. Criticism of the growing role of foreign capital in the country appear to have made Argentina's ties with the IMF even more con-troversial than they had been in the past. At the same time, it is likely that the IMF wanted to avoid a situation in which its name would (again) be associated with upheavals in the (again) explosive Argentine arena.

The World Bank's activity in Argentina at the time was intense. In December 1968, the Bank approved a twenty-five year loan for $82 million to build a power station and was considering granting another $25 million for upgrading the road infrastructure.[149] While the task of the World Bank's mission's was to assess further projects, the IMF delegation headed by the indefatigable del Canto (which consequently had the mandate to make decisions) limited itself to the elaboration of a mere report. The mission concluded that the Argentine econ-omy was thriving and that the plan for 1969 had great potential.[150] But as soon as del Canto left, and probably in an attempt to show the critics that the Argen-tine government was indeed distancing itself from the IMF and foreign capital, the Ministry of Economy announced that the SBA would not be renewed.[151]

The World Bank loans and positive IMF report paved the road to signing agreements with a wide range of supplementary financiers. In July 1969, an agreement for a $50 million loan was reached with five private U.S. banks, and an additional $25 million was under consideration.[152] In addition, Argentina signed an agreement for $27.3 million with a group of German banks.[153] To-ward the end of 1972, when the economic deterioration began, Argentina was granted another loan from a group of New York banks.[154] In development funds, and in addition to the World Bank loans, the Argentine Revolution was granted a $25.5 million loan from the IDB to improving its marine transportation system. In 1969, the IDB approved a series of extra loans to finance the purchase of modern agricultural equipment, to upgrade energy and transportation infrastructures, technological education projects, and to combat cattle diseases that jeopardized beef exports.[155] In 1972, it approved another $50 million loan for the construction of a power station in the Andes.[156] In short, the Argentine Revolution began to be more selective in choosing its financial sources. In fact, in 1969, only one element was missing in this complex network of lenders: the controversial IMF.

Aside from the economic front, in 1969 the first deep fractures in the Argentine Revolution appeared. Krieger Vasena became one of the most prominent political victims of the riots that erupted not only in Córdoba but also in the cities of Corrientes and Rosario in May 1969. Interestingly, and as additional proof of his close ties with and outstanding reputation in international circles, after he was forced out of office in Argentina, he was appointed to the position of chief executive of Deltec International, based in the Bahamas, and later held key positions at the World Bank.[157] Krieger Vasena was replaced by José María Dagnino Pastore, a graduate of Harvard University and a professional economist with no declared political affiliation (as numerous IMF officials, who hold doctoral degrees in economics from prestigious universities in English-speaking countries, mainly the United States).[158] At the same time, the dissidents' actions—most significantly, the kidnapping and assassination of former President General Pedro Aramburu in May 1970—further eroded Onganía's shaky position. He was finally ousted in July by General Roberto Levingston, a relatively anonymous officer who had served as a military attaché in Washington.

At the same time, the economic situation continued to worsen, and inflation took off. In an effort to imitate Krieger Vasena's strategy, Levingston's first economic minister, Carlos Moyano Llerena, devalued the exchange rate, subjected exports to a withholding tax, lowered import duties, and proposed a voluntary agreement on prices. Nevertheless, without labor's support, it was impossible to freeze wages. Moreover, since the devaluation was not seen as a one-off step, financial speculation increased.[159]

Levingston aspired to restore calm in Argentina. In an address to the nation, he condemned "terrorist acts" by citizens and announced his intention to introduce a gradual increase in wages and pensions, which would benefit the weakest groups in society.[160] This was a blatant shift from the original tenets of the Argentine Revolution. In October 1970, in a rather surprising move, Levingston appointed Aldo Ferrer as his economic minister. Ferrer, a former disciple of Raúl Prebisch and a fervent defender of industrial protectionism, sought to recover and revitalize nationalized industry by, among other things, passing laws that would oblige all government authorities and agencies to purchase only Argentine products and by renewing credits to local industry.[161] Despite these attempts, the economy continued to weaken.[162]

Unable to bring about the yearned for calm, in March 1971, Levingston was overthrown by General Alejandro Lanusse, who presided over the country for almost two years, during which three different economic ministers held office. The instability in the economy certainly contributed to the regime's decline. The growth rates registered in previous years were completely erased, while the budget deficit and inflation rate tripled. Export prices were the only component of the Argentine economy that showed any sign of improvement, which temporarily prevented an acute crisis in the balance of payments. Under these conditions, the IMF had no option but to take a step back and considerably reduce its public, and even its behind-the-scenes, presence in Argentina. The Argentine Revolution, for its part, had to change its economic orientation to survive. In actuality, a new and inevitable episode of temporary detachment between the IMF and Argentina was taking shape.

The IMF's Ambivalent Stance at the Fall of the Argentine Revolution

In July 1969, another IMF mission arrived in Argentina.[163] For the first time in a very long while, del Canto chose not to join it. This is understandable, especially since echoes of the Cordobazo and its brutal repression were still resonating in Argentina and abroad. Interestingly, the mission did not believe that the recent changes at the Ministry of Economy would lead to a profound shift in Argentina's policy. Moreover, it anticipated that central components of the joint working routine would remain intact, even in the absence of a loan arrangement. The mission's forecast was certainly realistic. In effect, the mission introduced to the Argentines the next resident representative at the Central Bank, Ángel Serrano, who arrived in Buenos Aires in August 1969, and whose contract, as suggested by the IMF, was later extended for six more months. In February 1970, another mission arrived to hold what the Fund called "informal consultations." In June, the IMF began to prepare another "informal mission" to examine the factors that had led to yet another devaluation of the peso.[164]

The initial attempts to safeguard the joint working routine regardless of the political crisis in Argentina were not restricted to the missions. For instance, when the IMF evaluated the quotas of all member states in late 1970, it decided to raise Argentina's from $350 million to $440 million,[165] indicating that, just as in Illia's days, fluctuations in the relationship with the IMF were not necessarily obstacles to the preservation of—or even to slight improvements in—Argentina's formal status in the Fund. In addition, toward the end of 1971, when the IMF was trying to lower its visibility in Argentina, local newspapers reported that Buenos Aires appeared to be on the verge of requesting financial assistance from the Fund.[166] The rumors became news when Carlos Brignone, the president of the Central Bank, flew to Washington hoping to raise an unprecedented $440 million from the IMF, $600 million from commercial European and U.S. banks, and $150 million from foreign companies operating in Argentina.[167] Brignone's reasons for the trip were crucial: He had to ensure that Argentina would have the $600 million needed to repay the debts that were due on July 1973. With Central Bank reserves dwindling to $150 million, returning to the arms of the IMF was indeed a reasonable option.

And yet before he left for Washington, Brignone sent the IMF an official request for an urgent mission to examine the economic plan for 1972.[168] The IMF agreed, and the parties promptly began intensive negotiations and drafted a letter of intent.[169] The Fund, however, had difficulty trusting Argentina's ability to meet its obligations. Particularly disturbing was the prospect of rampant inflation that would subvert the country's ability to preserve mobility in exchange rates.[170] Likewise, the political reality of the Argentine Revolution was too fragile and volatile for the IMF to risk its reputation by becoming involved in it. Eventually, the IMF refused to grant Argentina another SBA, pressing it to improve its reserve level by using special drawing rights (SDRs), an international reserve asset created by the IMF in 1969 to supplement its member countries' official reserves.[171] In other words, in light of the political tsunami that was sweeping away all traces of economic and institutional stability in Argentina, the IMF and Argentina had no alternative but to adopt a careful course of action that allowed them to continue their joint activity while avoiding binding and politically costly SBAs.

Finally, despite Lanusse's efforts to bring about democratization, and regardless of the far-reaching steps he took—which included returning the body of Eva Perón to Argentina for burial, inviting Juan Perón to return to Argentina from exile in 1972, and establishing the Gran Acuerdo Nacional (Grand National Accord),[172] he was left with no choice but to put an end to this sad chapter in Argentine history. Lanusse called for democratic presidential elections in which, for the first time since 1946, the Peronist party was allowed to take part. In May 1973, the Peronist candidate, Héctor Cámpora, became president of Argentina, and more turbulent years awaited the country.

Conclusion

The routine of dependency that began to develop between Argentina and the IMF in 1957 soon became a constant and central component of the country's economic and political life. However, in a changing political reality in which presidents, ministers, economic models, and ideologies continuously rose and fell, it was impossible for the joint working routine to remain unharmed. True, the numerous and varied mechanisms that constitute the routine of dependency underwent different types and degrees of variation and alteration. Such alterations, which under certain circumstances became temporary episodes of detachment between the parties, were initiated by the IMF, as in the case of the suspension of the SBA in March 1962, or by Argentina, as during Onganía's presidency, especially in late 1968. The detachment applied mainly, but not exclusively, to the signing and completion of loan agreements. In most cases, the reciprocal visits and several technical interactions, such as the dispatch of weekly updates to IMF headquarters, continued to take place at changing levels of regularity. It is important to note that the temporary episodes of detachment generally ended without having to negotiate the renewal of formal joint activities. Moreover, these episodes never threatened Argentina's membership in the IMF or its chance to obtain financial assistance within the framework of the first and even second tranche.

Nevertheless, the deliberate and profound disengagement initiated and maintained by President Illia during his term in office shows unequivocally that borrowing states can regulate the intensity of their interactions with the IMF. A diminished and restricted routine of dependency, however, does not necessarily mean complete autonomy from the IMF. In effect, even while Illia refrained from signing SBAs, and even as he fundamentally altered Argentina's attitude toward the IMF's representatives, the IMF never ceased to play a significant role in Argentina's economic life. Not only did the international financial community request the IMF's involvement in bilateral and multilateral negotiations with Argentina, but some Argentine government officials and businessmen managed to keep the Fund's delegates directly or indirectly involved in the local realm.

Initiating a minor or major episode of detachment has always been difficult for both parties. From Argentina's point of view, the biggest challenge has always been to maintain the fragile dividing line between detachment and crisis so it does not lose the indispensable seal of approval that the IMF, and sometimes the World Bank, can confer. In addition, and from a strictly economic perspective, the Argentine case indicates that refraining from requesting IMF loans has led to signing more expensive loan agreements with other creditors and lenders. Thus, while the political and electoral cost of the IMF's SBAs sometimes seems extremely high, less controversial alternatives also are costly.

The routine of dependency has been so intensive that the need to assess and determine, again and again, whether to cultivate it or hold it back has become a permanent issue on borrowers' economic and political agendas. Nurturing the working routine with the IMF demands enormous efforts on a borrower's part. Tracking the endless trips made by Argentina's economic ministers, who are often accompanied by senior ministry and Central Bank officials and ambassadors, and the time devoted to the IMF missions visiting Buenos Aires begs a question: What could these chronic borrowers have achieved if they had been freed from the need to constantly foster this routine?

From the IMF's point of view, the puzzling question is: What made such a highly professional organization grant loans to unstable states that could not or did not truly intend to keep their commitments, especially when it was not at all clear that the debts would ever be repaid? In the case of Argentina, there seem to be two main explanations. One is that the IMF regarded SBAs and, more important, their associated monitoring mechanisms as a privileged admission ticket to local economic power structures—a convenient means of exerting its influence on domestic economic policy and thought. The other is that the IMF must grant loans to justify its very existence. During the period discussed in this chapter, the so-called Bretton Woods regime was coming to an end—the collapse of the fixed exchange rate system in the early 1970s would bring it down—and the IMF desperately needed to redefine its mission. The interaction between the parties, while distinctly asymmetric in nature, appears to have been based not only on Argentina's dependence on the IMF, but also on the IMF's dependence on its Latin American clients, especially those with large and strategically important economies, such as Argentina, Brazil, Chile, and Mexico. It is therefore not surprising that the IMF (like some U.S. administrations) made no distinction between democratic and dictatorial regimes when it decided to tighten or relax its links with Argentina and Chile. The main issue for the IMF has always been whether a regime is ready and willing to commit—at least, on paper—to economic liberalization. The identity of the signatory to a loan agreement, whether an elected president or a tyrant, has been a marginal issue.[173]

Argentina's incorporation into the IMF in 1956—in particular, the establishment of a joint working routine during Frondizi's presidency—forged the basis for a dependency that differed substantially from Argentina's relation with the parties from which it had been borrowing since the early nineteenth century. Borrowing from the IMF created an ongoing, deep, and daily dependency that soon became one of the very few constants in the politically and economically tumultuous country. From 1958 forward, only two options were left: to renounce membership in the Bretton Woods institutions or to try to regulate the intensity of the routine of dependency. So far, no Latin American nations—except for Cuba, which left the Bretton Woods institutions in 1964—has ever taken option one.

5

All Regimes Are Legitimate

*The IMF's Relations with Democracies
and Dictatorships, 1973–1982*

The joint working routine between Argentina and the IMF has had many ups and downs. The fluctuations in the relationship in general, and the occasional episodes of detachment in particular, were most often initiated by Argentina. Contrary to the IMF's enduring image as an inflexible body, an examination of the intimate aspects of the relations between the parties suggests that the IMF has been ready and willing to compromise to retain its influence in Argentina's economy. This has held true not only for governments that have been sympathetic to the Fund, but also for administrations that have opposed the routine of dependency, as in the case of President Arturo Illia.

This chapter delves deeply into the fluctuations in the dependency relations between the IMF and Argentina, during a singular period in the region's and the country's contemporary history. From the late 1960s to the 1980s, several Latin American countries underwent parallel political and economic processes, in which democratically elected leftist administrations that aspired to reverse the course of IMF-backed liberalization were overthrown by violent military dictators who resumed and intensified the implementation of neoliberal policies. This pattern, which was observable, among others, in Argentina, Brazil, Chile, and Uruguay, significantly affected the ties with the IMF. In addition, this period was marked by the eruption of the debt crisis in 1982, which hit most Latin American nations and, ironically, paved the road to the most massive regional intervention ever by the IMF.

In Argentina, this period began with the arrival of Juan D. Perón in Buenos Aires on November 17, 1972, after eighteen years of exile. During his brief stay in Argentina, Perón founded the Frente Justicialista de Liberación (FREJULI), a multipartisan front led by the Peronist party that encompassed proponents of Frondizi's developmentalism, Christian Democrats, populist conservatives, former Socialist Party and Radical Civic Union members, and several provincial parties. Perón and Alejandro Lanusse then negotiated Argentina's return to democratic rule.[1] Because Perón was banned from running in the general elections of March 11, 1973, he chose Héctor Cámpora, a left-wing Peronist, and Vicente Solano Lima, a member of the Popular Conservative Party, as FREJULI's candidates for president and vice-president.[2]

In the first round, FREJULI won 49.5 percent of the votes, while Ricardo Balbín, the Radical Civic Union's candidate, trailed far behind, with 21.2 percent.[3] In light of the huge gap, the radicals bailed out of the second round, and FREJULI was proclaimed the winner.[4] A day after the elections, Perón declared, "We all have one goal in common, and it is called the homeland (*patria*)."[5] However, the "Montoneros," the most radical wing of the Peronist movement, did not heed Perón's call to stop the armed struggle. Between the elections and May 25, when Cámpora entered the Casa Rosada, the number of terrorist attacks increased daily. Perón vainly tried to stop the violence from Madrid; on June 20, 1973, he returned to Argentina for good.

The period known as the late Perón era was marked by government instability and incompetence. President Cámpora held the reins for only seven weeks; new elections were held in July 1973. FREJULI won an overwhelming majority of 61.9 percent of the votes. Between July 13 and October 12, Raúl Lastiri, the chairman of the Chamber of Deputies and a FREJULI member affiliated with the conservative Peronist factions, officiated as interim president. In October 1973, Lastiri delivered the government to Perón and to his vice-president, María Estela Martínez de Perón (Isabel or Isabelita), Perón's third wife.

When Perón died from an illness in July 1974 at seventy-eight, he was succeeded as president by Isabel. A leadership vacuum formed, however, that eventually was filled by José López Rega, then the minister of welfare and a cabinet secretary. Notorious for his fascist ideology, López Rega established the paramilitary secret organization the Argentine Anticommunist Alliance (Triple A) in November 1973, which kidnapped and murdered hundreds of leftist militants. Under these tragic circumstances, Isabel rescheduled the general elections for October 1976. By late 1975, though, her days were clearly numbered. On March 24, 1976, a military coup installed a dictatorial regime that remained in power until 1983.

This chapter thus focuses on temporary episodes of detachment and rapprochement between the IMF and Argentina at a period in which countries throughout the region experienced sharp turns in their political and economic structures. The Argentine case is especially illuminating, as during the unstable late Perón era, Argentina's attitude toward foreign capital, the United States, and the IMF fluctuated. This period is also unique because the military rulers, especially in Argentina and Chile, encouraged increasing intervention by the IMF in the national economies.

Finally, the chapter addresses two interrelated issues that are often raised by political scientists and that I discussed briefly in the previous chapter: the IMF's so-called political neutrality. The military regimes that followed the coup of 1964 in Brazil, of 1973 in Chile, and of 1976 in Argentina, with their systematic violation of human rights, provide fertile ground for analyzing this issue, confirming the IMF's (problematic) claim that it was consistently impartial and never distinguished between democracies and dictatorships.

No Second Chance for a First Impression: The Routine of Detachment during the Late Perón Era

In response to a staff question about future relations between Argentina and the Fund, Mr. [Alfredo] Gómez Morales [the president of Argentina's Central Bank] said that visits of Fund missions had frequently caused upheaval in Argentina, and that some way should be found to make the contacts more discreet. Particularly, he said the staff should avoid contacts outside the official sector. While these comments were rather general, . . . at one point Gómez Morales seemed to be suggesting that staff visits to Argentina should be replaced by periodic consultations in Washington. . . . (All of this was stated in a quite moderate and amicable way.)[6]

This account, part of a report of a meeting that took place after Cámpora resigned in August 1973, points to two central components of the dependency ties at the time. First, the IMF was represented by Jorge del Canto, the experienced economist who was in charge of relations with all Latin American member states from the 1940s until his retirement in 1977. Argentina was represented by Gómez Morales, a veteran economist who had worked closely with Perón. His return to a key government position was certainly symptomatic, reflecting the revolving-door environment in which a small group of economists would serve in high-ranking positions, return to the private sector or take prestigious positions abroad (sometimes at the Bretton Woods institutions), and then return to the Ministry of Economy or the Central Bank. Gómez Morales, for example, was president of the Central Bank in 1949–1951 and 1973–1974, as well as economic minister under Perón in the 1940s and under Isabel in October 1974–July 1975. Álvaro Alsogaray and Roberto Alemann also served as economic ministers and ambassadors to Washington and, between these appointments, developed private businesses.

Second, as the head of a delegation to Washington, Gómez Morales strove to make the working routine with the IMF less intensive, conspicuous, and controversial than usual. Therefore, he asked the Fund to hold all future bilateral meetings only in Washington. One can assume that Gómez Morales wanted not only to reduce the IMF's visibility on the local scene to avoid criticism but also to decrease the Fund's direct involvement in decision making in Argentina. Further, Gómez Morales was probably anxious to prevent the (not always official) meetings that members of IMF missions held with government officials and representatives of interest groups and businessmen in Argentina.

Due in part to a history of mutual suspicion (see Chapter 2) and the Peronists' traditionally anti-imperialist stand, the IMF decided to wait on the sidelines. Although Gómez Morales belonged to the liberal faction of Peronism, he failed to gain the Fund's trust. The IMF's reservations were understandable: During his stay in Washington, Gómez Morales declared, "My country was not part of the IMF during the first two terms of General Perón because that institution did not reflect the aspirations of the developing world."[7] Rhetoric aside, what may have aroused the Fund's suspicion was that behind Gómez Morales loomed Economic Minister José Ber Gelbard.

Gelbard's economic thinking noticeably contradicted that of the IMF. A staunch supporter of interventionism and an enemy of foreign capital, Gelbard became the first president of the General Economic Confederation (CGE), established by Perón in 1952 to unite owners of small and medium-size businesses and industrialists. He served as an official and unofficial adviser to democratic presidents and dictators alike; he was also a minister without portfolio in the early Perón era and later became the owner of a major industrial concern.[8] Gelbard managed to keep his post as economic minister under four consecutive presidents: Cámpora, Lastiri, Juan D. Perón, and Isabel Perón.

When Gómez Morales arrived in Washington demanding changes in the joint working routine, the IMF was already concerned about the transformations in Argentina's economy. In effect, Cámpora's nationalist economic team was determined to annul any law that it considered detrimental to the national interest. In June 1973, Gelbard promoted a Law of Foreign Investment that stipulated that all new foreign investments would be conditioned on the participation of at least 51 percent domestic capital and that existing investments would gradually be nationalized.[9] This law, which enraged the IMF and the U.S. government, was by no means an isolated challenge to the liberalization process that the IMF had been sponsoring for decades. Gelbard, indeed, worked toward strengthening state-owned companies, reversing privatization and "de-Argentinization" processes that had been the norm in previous years. In addition, he established maximum prices for agricultural produce; raised the property tax; and exempted shoes, textile manufacturing, and other products from duties.[10] In 1973, he convinced the workers and industrialists to sign "The Social Pact," which, among other things, led to a 15 percent raise in wage and a moratorium on prices. The same year, he launched a three-year economic plan that stressed income redistribution and the need to develop national industry and that favored the interests of the national bourgeoisie over those of the agricultural-export sector and multinational companies.[11]

The IMF was not alone in its concern over the reforms initiated by Gelbard. The U.S. administration did not rule out the possibility of a real about-face in Argentina's economy and foreign affairs. For instance, despite U.S. opposition, Cámpora announced his wish to establish diplomatic relationships with the Democratic Republic of Vietnam, North Korea, and Cuba, and his support of Panama's demands in the conflict with the United States.[12] Despite these provocative declarations, however, Washington—like the IMF—made conscious efforts to avoid conflict with Buenos Aires.[13] The appeasing reactions by the United States and the IMF were fruitful, as Argentina soon tried to moderate its foreign policy. In November 1973, Perón was scheduled to meet with President Richard Nixon, but an illness forced him to postpone the visit. Then it was agreed that the two presidents would meet in December, but Perón died before the meeting could take place. Argentina also launched alternative channels to approach the U.S. administration. Foreign Minister Alfredo Vignes maintained contact with Secretary of State Henry Kissinger, for instance, that yielded a bilateral agreement between the two countries in which, in line with the expectations of the United States and the IMF, Argentina committed to promoting gradual relaxation of the draconian Law of Foreign Investment.[14]

Alongside its efforts to reintegrate into the international arena, the Peronist administration was reluctant to accommodate the IMF. Argentina irritated the Fund when, in a meeting convened by the IMF in Rome in January 1974, Gómez Morales, now serving as the minister of economy, made a pact with oil-producing Arab countries. The pact was signed during the oil crisis, when members of the Organization of Petroleum Exporting Countries (OPEC) proclaimed an oil embargo in response to the U.S. decision to resupply the Israeli military during the Yom Kippur War of October 1973. Because the IMF was demanding that OPEC's members lower oil prices, Argentina's move was especially infuriating.[15]

It is important to note that at least part of Argentina's challenging stand toward the IMF reflected an approach common throughout the region at the time. During the 1970s, Argentina was not the only Latin American nation that attempted to avoid IMF-supported stabilization programs and ended up borrowing from commercial and multilateral lenders. From 1979 to 1981, only a third of the region's countries were under IMF SBAs.[16] This trend, as argued below, was later reversed by the military regimes partly for ideological reasons but also because of the debt crisis of 1982.

While the mistrust provoked by the Peronist administration was far from groundless, the IMF, as usual, refrained from total detachment from Argentina. The IMF's initial moderation, though, was by no means passive or endless. Soon after the elections of March 11, 1973, the IMF was once again looking for ways to exert its influence on the elaboration of the economic plans of the new administration. To that end, in late March the IMF held a meeting in Washington with senior Argentine officials, including the incumbent Economic Minister Jorge Wehbe and Jorge Bermúdez Emparanza, the president of the Central Bank. The IMF proposed to prepare a document analyzing Argentina's economic evils and suggesting solutions, to be officially submitted to the new government. Obviously, there was nothing new in that proposal. Back in 1966, the IMF had elaborated a detailed plan that nobody in Argentina had ever requested (at least, officially). In any case, Wehbe, formerly a member of Frondizi's and Lanusse's cabinets and therefore familiar with the IMF's programs, opined that the Frondizist factions of FREJULI could be interested in such a guideline. By contrast, Bermúdez Emparanza, who originally was affiliated with Frondizi's faction of the Intransigent Radical Civic Union, firmly believed that any attempt by the IMF to exercise influence on the Peronists would prove useless.[17] As it soon turned out, the Peronist administration was ready to consider external proposals, but not from the IMF. Indeed, Cámpora promptly adopted the CGE's plan, which was titled, "Suggestions by National Industry Captains for a Governmental Program."[18]

It seems, thus, that while Argentina attempted to create a temporary episode of detachment, the IMF endeavored to avert it. In late 1973, in an attempt to please Gómez Morales and respond to his demands to alter the nature of the monitoring process, the IMF offered to postpone the beginning of the Article IV Consultation until March or April 1974. Such extraordinary postponement, IMF officials argued, could save the administration from serious political embarrassment.[19] The Fund's offer was surely generous and created an unprecedented situation in which no consultations with Argentina were conducted for twenty-two months, from June 1972 to April 1974. Recognizing that this rescheduling would not sway the Argentines, the Fund also proposed an original solution for the location issue, as Gómez Morales had requested that all meetings be held in Washington. Recurring to its flexibility, the IMF offered to begin with preliminary talks in Washington and move to Buenos Aires later. According to this formula, the meetings in Argentina would last no more than a week and be attended by what can be labeled a "mini-mission" of two or three IMF representatives. Although Gómez Morales promised to discuss this proposal with his superiors, he never responded to del Canto, leaving him astonished and resentful.[20] As the IMF sensed that Argentina was procrastinating, it comforted itself with the hope that the new ambassador to Washington, Alejandro Orfila—a representative of the agricultural export sector and industrial elite who had developed excellent working ties with the IMF while serving as economic attaché in Washington during Frondizi's presidency—would help restore the relationship.[21] Despite the deep fissures in the routine of dependency, a total detachment between the parties was never on the IMF's or Argentina's agenda.

And so it happened that Gelbard, the "archenemy" of foreign capital, soon found himself at the discussion table with the IMF.

One Step Forward, Two Steps Back: The First Consultation with the Peronist Administration

Argentina's determination to lessen its interactions with the IMF did not exempt it from certain procedures that were part and parcel not only of membership but also of the institution's working routine. In effect, during 1974–1975, the Peronist regime had to cope with the consultation process and with the updating of quotas.

Argentina's Article IV Consultation began in Washington in April 1974, as suggested by the IMF.[22] It was then decided that the next meetings would be held in Argentina, on July 9–12. Although del Canto feared that Perón's death on July 1 would be used as a pretext for halting the process, there were no delays or unexpected changes. The mini-mission that landed in Argentina at a very singular time—a week after Perón's death and a day before Argentina's Independence Day—comprised del Canto, Jack Guenther, and a secretary. Still, del Canto's willingness to show flexibility toward Argentina was not infinite. He adamantly refused the Ministry of Economy's request to hold only one concluding meeting in Argentina, arguing that even the two meetings that had already been scheduled would not suffice for gathering the information needed to produce an in-depth report on Argentina's economy.[23]

Perón's passing marked a watershed in Argentine history, as well as in the IMF's attitude toward Argentina. From mid-1974 on, del Canto grew increasingly rigid toward Buenos Aires. He was convinced that with Perón's death, Argentina desperately needed the IMF to convey a message of institutional, political, and economic stability to the entire international financial community.[24] Naturally, the ties with the IMF had a profound impact at the national level, as well. Powerful interest groups (such as the agricultural export sector, businesses directly related to foreign capital, and parts of the military) regarded the tightening of relations with the IMF as of paramount importance. It is therefore reasonable to assume that Argentina's decision to proceed with the consultation process soon after Perón's widow, Isabel, officially assumed the presidency was a sign of the government's need to appease its liberal opponents. It should be noted, however, that the contacts with the IMF remained secret (as they had been in the first Perón era), because they could fuel the fury of the leftist and most radical factions inside and outside the Peronist party.

Eventually, del Canto's position prevailed, and two intensive and amicable, but almost clandestine, meetings with IMF representatives were held in Argentina. They were attended by Gelbard and Gómez Morales. As the consultation process evolved, Gómez Morales changed his initially chilly attitude toward the

IMF, opting instead to take a conciliatory approach that was at odds with Gelbard's belligerence. The second phase of the consultation focused on problems in the balance of payments, with special emphasis on wheat and meat prices; the levels of foreign currency reserves ($2 billion as of June 1974); the annual deficit (estimated at $2.3billion); the import and export policy, which was characterized by considerable state intervention, especially in import quotas, customs, and tariffs; the increasing inflation; and the energy crisis, and so on.[25] It should be stressed that at no point did any of the participants raise the issue of IMF aid to Argentina. This suggests that there was an attempt by both parties to maintain a real or pretended correct relationship—or, in other words, to establish a routine of dependency on a much smaller scale—while refraining from discussing sensitive issues such as a new SBA.

But the Peronist administration's attempts to convey a sense of stability were to no avail. In July 1974, a new round of personnel changes began in government institutions, including, of course, the Ministry of Economy. One of the first ministers to pay the price of the regime's facelift was Gelbard, whose policy had exasperated not only the agricultural, industrial, and multinational sectors, but also the middle classes and small industrialists and businessmen, who saw their chances to prosper and survive slimming rapidly. In addition, the CGE, Gelbard's source of power, quickly weakened, and the General Federation of Labor (CGT) demanded Gelbard's dismissal.[26] On October 21, 1974, Isabel appointed the moderate Gómez Morales to head the Ministry of Economy. His short term, which ended in June 1975, represented a transition between two conflicting approaches: the nationalist and interventionist approach promoted by Gelbard and the approach known as "shock policy" (analyzed in the following section), which was applied by economic minister Celestino Rodrigo. The IMF followed these transitions closely. It was particularly interested in the attempts to control inflation and prices, even while it anticipated that Isabel's government would lead to a relaxation of price control.[27] The IMF also believed that Argentina had failed to consolidate a comprehensive strategy to eradicate inflation and that its wage policy was fundamentally flawed.[28]

Gómez Morales believed that attracting foreign capital was the only way to tackle the deterioration of Argentina's terms of trade and the Central Bank's plummeting reserve levels. He therefore amended the Law of Foreign Investment that had been passed by Gelbard. While Gelbard blocked credits to foreign companies operating in Argentina, Gómez Morales equated their status to that of domestic companies, thereby giving them access to financial assistance.[29] As in the 1950s, Gómez Morales regarded the international financial organizations as legitimate sources of loans and credit. Accordingly, he held negotiations with the World Bank, the IDB, and the IMF. In March 1975, Ricardo Cairoli, president of the Central Bank, announced that if foreign currency reserve levels kept falling, negotiations with the IMF about financial assistance would be inevitable.[30]

In early 1975, largely due to the oil crisis, the IMF increased its financial resources through a 33.6 percent general increase in its quotas.[31] As in previous periodic updates, the IMF was entitled to decide that certain countries would be assigned the average rate of increase—the majority of member countries fell into that category—while the quotas of others would be upgraded or downgraded at varying rates. As one might expect, most of the members that enjoyed higher-than-average upgrades at the time were oil-producing countries. In May 1975, Argentina was notified that its name was not included in the list of countries awarded special upgrades. Following this, Ambassador Alejandro Orfila convened several IMF officials, including del Canto, for an unofficial dinner. He used the gathering to inform del Canto of Argentina's concern that, unlike Brazil, Mexico, and Venezuela, its quotas would not be raised above the general average. Orfila warned that he intended to contact the managing director of the IMF, the Dutch economist Johannes Witteveen, directly to demand a revised decision, but del Canto tried to talk him out of that idea.[32] The next day, Gómez Morales sent a telegram to Witteveen highlighting the problematic aspects of disrupting the existing balance among Latin American countries.[33] It took about two weeks for Witteveen to reply that the update list was a true reflection of the actual economic situation and that he saw no justification for revising Argentina's quota.[34] Argentina was not granted any special upgrade, and its quota was raised by the general 33.6 percent. The increase from 440 million to 535 million SDRs was ratified only after the coup on December 5, 1977.[35]

To sum up, the mini-consultation satisfied neither the IMF nor Argentina. When del Canto's patience ran thin, the Fund went back to pulling the strings. Once again, political turmoil in the national arena shaped the routine of dependency and triggered a new temporary episode of partial detachment. In the meantime, plagued by instability and terrorism, Peronist Argentina strove to obtain the IMF's seal of approval, which could either help it to survive or, alternatively, contribute to its downfall.

Early Attempts to Normalize the Relationship with the IMF

The recurrent changes in Argentina's leadership have often led to renewed rapprochement between the parties. Gómez Morales's dismissal from the Ministry of Economy on June 2, 1975, and Celestino Rodrigo's appointment in his place is a prominent example of this phenomenon.[36] During his brief time in office (June 2–July 21, 1975), Rodrigo promoted the so-called shock policy, which was remarkably receptive to foreign capital and devoid of social sensitivity.

When Rodrigo took office, Argentina was expected to repay $2 billion in debts in 1976 and higher sums in 1977 to U.S. and European banks, the World Bank, and the IDB.[37] Argentina was determined to repay its debts as scheduled, but in July 1974, outbreaks of hoof-and-mouth disease in Europe prompted bans on imported Argentine beef, causing an immediate decrease in exports and risking Argentina's balance of payments. Rodrigo concluded that the most viable option would be to obtain new loans.[38] That is, even while Argentina was struggling with the heavy burden resulting from its continued reliance on foreign loans, it was not deterred from signing new stabilization and development loan agreements. Thus, in late 1974, the World Bank examined the possibility of extending financial aid to increase Argentina's electricity production capacity.[39] In May 1975, a tripartite agreement was signed with the IDB and Uruguay for the construction of a dam to generate hydroelectric energy (Salto Grande).[40] Concurrently, the World Bank granted a $134 million loan for agricultural development.[41]

But Argentina's keenness to revitalize its activity vis-à-vis the international financial community was not just the result of pragmatism; it was also part of a comprehensive plan. During his brief term, Rodrigo revoked the "Social Pact" and implemented a shocking austerity plan known as the "Rodrigazo." The plan represented an attack on wage earners by drastically curtailing their purchasing power. In the first phase, Rodrigo announced a 160 percent devaluation of the peso; a doubling of the rates charged by public utility corporations, which pushed general prices higher still; and a limit of 50 percent on wage increases. Contrary to traditional Peronist policy, Rodrigo deregulated the prices of most of the basic products in the average family's shopping basket, leaving only about thirty products under state regulation.[42] While the devaluation benefited exporters, it wreaked havoc on the imports of vital industrial inputs. The unions responded to the Rodrigazo with the first general strike ever under a Peronist government. In mid-June 1975, collective labor agreements were negotiated that promised an initial wage increase of 45–100 percent. The furious reactions to Rodrigo's plan and the promises of a real wage increase led to his resignation.[43]

Although Rodrigo's plan was never completed, it is worth noting that it included collaboration with the IMF as a means to rebuild ties with foreign capital.[44] In fact, as soon as Rodrigo took office, he dispatched two senior representatives to hold negotiations at IMF headquarters. Del Canto welcomed the Argentines, who expressed their intention to hold further meetings with the IMF, provided that the meetings would be kept secret.[45] This request suggests that Rodrigo feared his contacts with the IMF would be the last straw. The request to keep the negotiations confidential is even more intriguing when compared with the transparency of the interactions between the IMF and Chile during the regime of Salvador Allende (November 1970–September 1973) and of IMF–Brazilian relations during João Goulart's presidency (September 1961–April 1964). A loyal Marxist, Allende fully understood the antagonism that intervention by the IMF raised in socialist and communist circles, but he did not hesitate to invite IMF missions to Santiago and to let the local press report freely on every encounter or transaction with the Fund.[46] The same was true for Goulart, a left-wing member of the Brazilian Labor Party, who implemented a nationalist economic policy and sought closer relations with communist countries. Nevertheless, he wanted to restore the working routine with the IMF. In December 1961, he invited a mission to conduct the annual consultation—in fact, the first consultation to be held in Brazil since March 1959[47]—thus ending a temporary episode of detachment but without trying to avoid the scrutiny of Brazilian public opinion. As could be anticipated, the IMF soon began to work with Brazilian economists on elaborating a stabilization plan and agreed to reschedule Brazil's repurchases.[48] As Witteveen stated, "The Fund is most eager to be of help to Brazil in reaching a solution to [its] problems."[49]

In any event, Rodrigo's days in office were short, and he was replaced by Pedro José Bonani, who served as economic minister for less than a month (July 22–August 11, 1975). On August 14, Bonani was replaced by Antonio Cafiero, an old-school Peronist who in the 1940s was plainly averse to Argentina's joining the Bretton Woods institutions. Cafiero stayed in office until February 3, 1976. His ties with the IMF, as will be shown, were ambivalent.

Endless Zigzagging: Cafiero and the IMF

Rodrigo failed (or simply did not have enough time) to put Argentina's relationship with the IMF back on track. The country's instability at the time precluded a total rapprochement between the parties, although some joint activity continued to take place sporadically and secretly. Yet despite the difficulties, and even when Isabel, suffering from a nervous breakdown, absented herself from the presidency (September 13–October 17, 1975),[50] the IMF supported the granting of financial aid to Argentina. The IMF's willingness to assist Argentina seems to have increased with the publication of Cafiero's stabilization program. The program stipulated a succession of measured and gradual devaluations (in contrast to Rodrigo's plan) and contained an implied promise that state employees would not lose their jobs. The IMF applauded the plan. In fact, when Argentina was granted 76.1 million SDRs (about $117 million) in October 1975 within the framework of the "oil facility" (a lending instrument created by the Fund in 1974 to help oil importers in the face of increasing oil prices), the IMF opined:

> Mr. [A.W.] Yaméogo [executive director of the IMF's Executive Board] expressed his sympathy with the Argentine authorities in the extremely difficult circumstances in which they found themselves. . . . The long delay in adopting effective corrective measures seemed to have been due to difficult internal political problems, and many internal and external circumstances beyond the control of Argentine authorities. He was

therefore pleased to note the new determination of the authorities to restore the economy with Fund assistance. . . . [H]e hoped that the Fund would recognize the efforts embodied in the stabilization program.[51]

Thus, contrary to its habit of blaming borrowers for their economic problems, the IMF excused Argentina from some responsibility for its poor economic performance. It is not surprising, then, that the Executive Board hoped that Argentina would eventually apply for an SBA or for a purchase from the conditional upper tranches.[52] At this point, Managing Director Witteveen instructed his staff to make Argentina's consent to launch another consultation a condition for granting financial aid. After all, the IMF was much more interested in the monitoring process than in the loan itself.

In light of Argentina's efforts to erase all traces of the last temporary episode of detachment, del Canto was ready once again to adopt a more tolerant and patient position toward Argentina. As he explained in December 1975:

During the past week, the Argentine authorities have contacted us through various channels to bring us up to date on recent developments. . . . I think with all honesty that we can tell the Board on Friday that Argentina has been cooperating with the Fund in the sense of keeping us informed. As far as we can judge, performance on the program to date is mixed, but I think all Board members agree that 'cooperation' does not require proof of complete success in carrying out policies.[53]

Following del Canto's recommendations, the IMF concluded that Argentina was eligible to be granted soft financial assistance in the form of the compensatory financing facility (CFF).[54] The CFF was created in 1963 to assist countries that were experiencing either a sudden shortfall in export earnings or an increase in the price of cereal imports caused by fluctuating global commodity prices. CFFs (unlike SBAs) do not carry surcharges or binding conditions. Thus, in December 1975, during Cafiero's term, the IMF approved a drawing of 110 million SDRs (about $126 million) under the CFF.[55] It estimated that the assistance would facilitate Argentina's negotiations with other lenders, especially commercial banks.[56]

From a regional perspective, approving soft and almost automatic loans was a strategy the IMF adopted broadly to accommodate leftist and populist regimes that were nationalist and anti-imperialist in essence. These new instruments allowed the IMF to remain active in Latin America at a time that numerous governments were refraining from signing controversial SBAs. Peronist Argentina was certainly not alone in using the oil facility, the CFF, or first tranche purchase transactions. During Allende's term, Chile did exactly the same. For instance, in July 1972, Chile requested a gold tranche purchase in Deutsche

Marks equivalent to 1,500,671 SDRs,[57] and in December 1972, it asked to purchase the equivalent of 39.5 million SDRs under the CFF.[58]

Overall, during 1975 Argentina was able to repay its debts to the IMF as scheduled, as it had in 1973 and 1974.[59] Despite the relative economic improvements, Cafiero resigned in February 1976, having found himself in a no-win situation in which he had to make decisions under contradictory pressures from opposing circles inside and outside the administration, inside and outside the Peronist ruling party.[60]

Replacing Cafiero with Emilio Mondelli was a last effort by Isabel and her advisers to rebuild the "Social Pact" and strengthen ties with the international financial community. An economic liberal and devout Christian, Mondelli had never been a member of the Peronist party. He began his public career in 1973 as an adviser to Gómez Morales. In October 1974, he was appointed president of the Central Bank. As the minister of economy, as we shall see, Mondelli pursued the course outlined by his predecessor vis-à-vis the IMF. However, he also had failed to sign an SBA with the Fund.

A Last-Ditch Attempt: Mondelli and the
Failed Negotiations with the IMF

When Mondelli joined the Ministry of Economy, Isabel's government was already doomed. It thus is not surprising that Mondelli failed to appease either the local and international financial community or the Argentine workers. A number of organizations in the areas of commerce, construction, and agribusiness, including the Sociedad Rural Argentina—the cattle ranchers' association that had long controlled Argentina's export economy—disparaged him before he even managed to publicize his economic plan. On February 16, a massive general strike took place.[61] Mondelli's announcement regarding his intention to hold meetings at the IMF headquarters infuriated the trade unions.[62] Unlike Cafiero, and unlike the traditional Peronist strategy, Mondelli refused to conduct the negotiations with the IMF in secret.

Although Mondelli was determined to reinstate the relationship with the IMF, he initially refrained from requesting an SBA. On February 22, in response to an explicit demand by the IMF's managing director, an IMF mission, headed once again by Jack Guenther, arrived in Buenos Aires to discuss exchange rates and the international trade restrictions imposed by Argentina. It should be stressed that at the time, Argentina was using a multiple exchange rate system that the IMF disapproved. At the end of the day, the mission got the impression that the "big picture" was positive, even if there was still a long way to go.[63]

While the mission was in Argentina, Mondelli finalized his economic program. On February 25, he submitted the plan not only to the government, but also to the commanders of the Navy, Air Force, and ground forces, a perturbing

indication of the immense pressure exerted by the military and of the last desperate attempts to stop—or, at least, postpone—the inexorable coup.[64] Mondelli's plan, which like Rodrigo's scheme was described by the Argentine press
as pure "shock politics," stipulated harsh belt-tightening measures, which would
rattle the entire economic system. The key problems were inflation (estimated
at an annual rate of 635 percent) and the budget deficit. In addition, during
February and March 1976, Argentina had to make several debt repayments.
While the Central Bank reserves as of late December 1975 totaled $618 million,
the anticipated repayments reached $1.8 billion.[65]

Central points in Mondelli's program included the setting of new tariffs for
services provided by the state and maximum prices for basic products; wage
increases according to the raise in public service tariffs; and a ninety-day "cease-
fire" among various sectors of the economy. As the local media noted, the publication of the economic program during the IMF mission's visit was no coincidence; rather, it was part of Mondelli's attempt to rehabilitate Argentina's image
in the eyes of the Fund and other lenders.[66] Moreover, although there is no solid
evidence for it, Mondelli may well have shared his final deliberations on the plan
with IMF representatives.

Clearly, the IMF regarded a sound economic program and political stability
as critical preconditions for negotiating substantial financial assistance. The IMF
was not entirely against granting loans to Peronist Argentina, but it certainly was
in no hurry to approve them, either. Indeed, during the mission's stay in Argentina, it was agreed that discussions on an SBA would not commence before
April.[67] This holdup could not have been accidental, because in Argentina's
volatile politics, two months were an eternity. I believe that the IMF assumed
that, sooner or later, the Peronist regime would be history, allowing it to hold
negotiations with a more stable and amenable administration. By mid-1975,
and indubitably in early 1976, the fact that the military was planning a coup
was far from secret. Furthermore, from a very early stage of the preparation,
rumors abounded about potential pro-liberal candidates to staff the position
of economic minister. According to the rumors, Roberto Alemann and Álvaro
Alsogaray were even summoned for interviews by the conspiracy's leaders, with
the favorite candidate being the orthodox José Alfredo Martínez de Hoz.[68] It is
also obvious that the U.S. administration was fully aware of the imminent coup.
It is known that Washington actively supported the removal of a series of democratically elected presidents in Latin America, including Isabel, Allende, and
Goulart. Moreover, by early 1976, the assessment that Isabel would soon be
overthrown became a hot topic in leading U.S. newspapers.[69] For all of these
reasons, it seems implausible that the IMF would fail to consider the impending
coup in its decisions regarding its course of action vis-à-vis Argentina.

Although this was a failure foretold, on March 6, 1976, Eduardo Zalduendo,
the president of the Central Bank, visited the IMF accompanied by several tech-

nocrats. At that stage, the IMF stressed that, to gain access to the upper credit tranches, Argentina would have to introduce "substantial" changes, mainly in its fiscal policy and tax collection and state revenue mechanisms.[70] Zalduendo's chances to persuade the IMF that Argentina was indeed worthy of an SBA were close to nonexistent. Already during Cafiero's term, the IMF had stipulated three conditions for "leaving the door open for the first tranche" (a loan worth 25 percent of the quota): a reduction in the budget deficit; a decrease in oil imports through reform of the energy sector; and the adoption of norms that would bring about a streamlining of the fiscal system. Argentina's failure to meet the commitments given by Cafiero, along with a further wage increase, made the Fund's approval absolutely unfeasible.[71] But the failure of Zalduendo's mission was much greater. Not only did the IMF refrain from even initiating a negotiation of an SBA, it even refused to renew purchases equivalent to $40 million under the oil facility. The sole consolation was the granting of a $127 million credit due to decrease in exports (CFF), which had already been arranged before Zalduendo's visit.[72] The IMF was not alone in refusing to help Argentina. By March 1976, all of Argentina's requests for loans from European banks had been refused.[73]

To sum up, late Peronism constituted one of the most chaotic periods in contemporary Argentine history. The political, economic, and personal upheavals since the first military coup took place in 1930 were aggravated by ferocious terrorist activity—first by radical groups that sprouted within the ranks of Peronism,[74] and later by state terrorism. As in the first Perón era, the Peronism of the 1970s gradually grew apart from its uncompromisingly nationalist and anti-imperialist economic position to conciliate and attract foreign capital, albeit ambivalently and without much success. But the situation in the 1970s was completely different from that in the 1950s, when, had he not been overthrown, Perón might have become the first Argentine president to sign a loan agreement with the IMF. Indeed, it is conceivable that if the coup had not taken place in March 1976, the Peronist administration would have found itself involved in a profound episode of detachment not only from the IMF but also from the entire international financial community.

Since May 1973, when Cámpora rose to power, the IMF had been willing to compromise to keep its relationship with Argentina as intact as possible. The IMF also showed flexibility during the relatively long term of Minister Gelbard, whose economic policy was staunchly nationalist. His successor, Gómez Morales, was in fact the first economic minister to have made some effort to curtail the deterioration of the relationship between the parties. He was also the first Peronist to ask for and be granted the Fund's financial assistance. While Cafiero tried even harder to rebuild the ties with the IMF, he could not overcome strong domestic opposition. When, in a desperate move, Mondelli attempted to negotiate an SBA, his request was rejected out of hand.

A close examination of archival evidence reveals that it was as Isabel's time was running out that the IMF actually turned its back on Argentina. The detachment created between the Peronist administration and the IMF was largely initiated by and the result of the confrontation between irreconcilable worldviews within the Peronist movement, the military, the administration, and Argentine society as a whole. To be sure, democratically elected regimes have been challenged by the urgent need to conciliate sometimes contradictory pressures from different sectors of society, a challenge that often convinced the authorities to renounce the IMF's assistance to increase their chances of political survival. This does not necessarily mean that dictators totally ignore popular pressure; rather, it means that the political risks of collaborating with the IMF are much higher for democratic than for military regimes.

For its part, the IMF has always been eager to enter the Argentine arena through any possible door, regardless of who has held the keys. It has been the military regimes, however, which as a rule have been more economically liberal, that have welcomed foreign capital (except for Carlos Saúl Menem, who adopted the same approach, although he was democratically elected). It is for this reason that I find the claim that the IMF has preferred totalitarian regimes inaccurate, if not altogether erroneous.[75] In fact, as far as the Argentine and Chilean cases are concerned, it has actually been the military authorities who have initiated and encouraged the IMF's intervention in the national economy. To put it simply, the IMF and authoritarian regimes were equally active partners, with full agency, in the creation of the ideological and economic alliances that had catastrophic consequences for broad sectors of Argentine society.

The Renewal of the Relationship between the IMF and Argentina during the "Process of National Reorganization"

As early as January 1976, the heads of the three military forces began to discuss the nature of the regime they were soon to establish.[76] The two major issues were the division of power between the forces and the scope and nature of repression measures, which they believed would put an end to what they perceived as chaos. Chief of Staff Jorge Rafael Videla and Naval Commander-in-Chief Emilio Eduardo Massera disagreed about the organizational structure of the future regime. Massera's position, in which each of the three forces would be in charge of 33 percent of the government ministries, provinces, state-owned companies, and every other state-owned asset, finally prevailed.[77]

The coup of March 24, 1976, launched what the conspirators called the Proceso de Reorganización Nacional (Process of National Reorganization). Power was handed over to a junta comprising Videla (as president), Massera, and Orlando Ramón Agosti. The coup was by no means a caprice of a handful of military officers; nor did it take place in a vacuum. On the contrary: It enjoyed strong support from both inside and outside Argentina. There is broad consensus among scholars that Secretary of State Henry Kissinger, as well as other U.S. officials, sanctioned the ousting of Isabel.[78] Further, President Gerald Ford (1974–1977) promptly recognized the junta. Like his predecessor, President Richard Nixon (1969–1974), Ford had no qualms about establishing close relations with ruling generals in Central and South America. In fact, the only deviation from this policy came under President Jimmy Carter (1977–1981), who launched a human rights campaign that led to the denial of economic and military assistance to the brutal dictatorships in Argentina, Chile, and Guatemala.[79] But perhaps most notably, the military marched to the presidential palace with the encouragement and endorsement of anti-Peronist groups, while some of these groups supported neoliberal economic precepts. José Alfredo Martínez de Hoz, the junta's economic minister, was a prominent representative of such groups. A well-known figure in Argentina, he came from a landed family associated with the Sociedad Rural Argentina and served as minister of economy under President Guido in 1963. Until the coup, he was president of the Consejo Empresario Argentino (Argentine Business Council).

When he took power in March 1976, Videla declared that the new regime marked the end of one historical cycle (Peronism) and the beginning of a new one. In this spirit, the junta waged a vicious internal war on subversion (known as the Dirty War); demolished many of the institutions created by the Peronists (especially the CGT and the unions); outlawed all political opposition and relinquished all due process of law. The brutal repression was facilitated by a state apparatus that was responsible for illegal arrests, torture, kidnapping, assassinations, and the 'disappearance' of at least 10,000 people.[80]

With Martínez de Hoz, the junta's objective of restoring order was translated into the economic arena. Once in office, he promised to put an end to rampant and counterproductive speculation. The main goal was to bring about a fundamental change in the Argentine economy. At the core of this change was dismantling state interventionism; deregulation; implementing monetary controls to curb inflation; promoting open competition; correcting price distortions; creating new financial markets; broadening the industrial infrastructure, and revitalizing and diversifying the export sector. Martínez de Hoz played a major role in this process, which went far beyond its strictly economic aspects. Equipped with academic degrees in economics and law, he helped to create the image of skill, ethics, and self-discipline the regime sought to attribute to itself.[81]

According to the liberal paradigm that prevailed at the time not only in Argentina but elsewhere in Latin America and in other regions of the world, all of the goals defined by the new regime could be achieved through the aggressive pursuit of foreign investment. Under these circumstances, the implementation of a strict stabilization program and close collaboration with the IMF appeared to be the most natural choice for the junta. Martínez de Hoz's friendship with David Rockefeller, as well as with other U.S. bankers, certainly facilitated the $1 billion IMF loan and supplementary loan agreements he soon secured.[82] As we shall see, the coup marked the beginning of a new and tragic era in Argentina's history, as well as a renewed and even stronger alliance with the IMF.

The IMF's Prompt Return to Argentina

On the very day the military took over the Casa Rosada, the incumbent economic minister, General Joaquín de las Heras (who remained in office for barely four days), informed the IMF of Argentina's intention to go ahead with the procedure to secure an SBA based on the request submitted a few days earlier by Mondelli.[83] On March 30, Martínez de Hoz was appointed economic minister, and the junta gave him complete freedom to recruit his own professional team. He filled the highest positions in his ministry and at the Central Bank with figures who had won the trust and sympathy of the international business, financial, and banking community, including Juan Alemann (businessman and brother of Roberto Alemann), Guillermo Walter Klein (Martínez de Hoz's close friend and right hand, as well as the legal representative of several foreign banks in Argentina, who had been involved for years in Argentina's official economy),[84] and Mario Cárdenas de Madariaga (a lawyer who championed agribusiness during the presidencies of Guido and Lanusse). Martínez de Hoz also appointed Adolfo Diz, who held a doctorate in economics from the University of Chicago and had studied under Milton Friedman, as president of the Central Bank. In 1967–1968, Diz had been an executive director at the IMF. When he returned to Argentina, he cultivated ties with other Chicago Boys in Latin America. For his part, Martínez de Hoz had been a member of the international board of the Chase Manhattan Bank in the early 1970s and was thus well known in financial circles in Washington, New York, and Europe.[85]

Immediately upon his appointment, Martínez de Hoz announced several major changes, including equating the status of foreign capital to that of domestic capital. He also announced that Argentina would approach the IMF only after the stabilization program had been consolidated and made into law.[86] The plan, implemented after April 1976, aimed to bring about "liberalization, openness, and modernization of the economy."[87] According to Martínez de Hoz, liberalization meant opening the domestic market to outside competition (and not necessarily the development of local industry to compete in international markets).[88] As a result of the total eradication of interventionism that was so ingrained in Argentina's economy and society, and its replacement with a one-way liberalization that allowed foreign goods to inundate the country, the dictatorship that ended in 1983 brought about massive destruction of national industry on an unprecedented scale.[89] Liberalization—Martínez de Hoz's style—was evident in many provisions of the economic plan, including the revocation of the payment of advances for agricultural exports; the abolition of subsidies for nontraditional (industrial) exports and credit lines to encourage industrialization; increased tariffs for state utilities; liberalization of the foreign exchange market; reductions in state expenses; and amendments to the Law of Foreign Investment.[90] All of these measures earned him powerful supporters in Washington—particularly Henry Kissinger (who as the former secretary of state visited Argentina in June 1976) and William Rogers, assistant secretary of state for Latin America.[91]

It should be mentioned that Argentina's economic plan was somewhat more gradual (except in its fiscal aspects) and less shocking than Chile's plan. For instance, Videla did not privatize oil reserves or social security, as Pinochet did. There were several reasons for the difference between the economic policies of these two regimes, which cooperated in the political arena as well as in the Dirty War. Among other things, Pinochet enjoyed almost absolute power and autonomy while Videla (Martínez de Hoz's major supporter) faced criticism from members of the junta. In addition, it should be stressed that several sections of Argentina's military supported statism and therefore opposed some of the reforms proposed by Martínez de Hoz. And last but not least, the Chicago Boys were much more radical (and numerous) in Chile than in Argentina, perhaps because Martínez de Hoz himself was not a classic Chicago Boy, and perhaps because after Allende's term, the liberal economists in Chile saw themselves as brave "counter-revolutionary" and anticommunists agents.[92] In March 1975, when inflation in Chile was at 375 percent and the economy was deteriorating, Pinochet called Milton Friedman and Arnold Harberger (who, like Friedman, had trained a generation of young Chilean economists) for help. The two experts strongly urged Pinochet to apply "shock treatment," stressing that gradualism was not viable.[93] While Martínez de Hoz perceived the Chilean shock as a model to be imitated to some extent, he was a pragmatist and opted for a somewhat more gradual plan that he hoped would generate less social unrest.[94]

Argentina's new economic policy, the nature of its relationship with the IMF, and the imminent approval of the first SBA in years attracted the attention of Argentina's creditors and lenders. The British Embassy in Buenos Aires, for instance, approached Klein in an attempt to learn about the new program. Klein responded that the decision whether to apply for an SBA would be made only after the IMF mission had left town and emphasized that the Ministry of Economy was elaborating a foreign investment law designed to attract as many investors as possible.[95] The impression at the British Embassy was that Argentina was willing to follow the IMF's prescription in full, regardless of its harshness.[96] Indeed, the president of the Industrialist Board, Eduardo García, claimed that "the Minister of Finance would do whatever the IMF wishe[d] in order to get its money."[97] In actuality, as seen below, the IMF did not have to impose anything. After twenty years of activity in Argentina, its work was being done by its Argentine allies.

The Full Return of the Routine of Dependency:
The First Mission

The first mission after the coup, headed again by Jack Guenther, landed in Argentina in May 1976. This was in fact the first ordinary consultation since 1972. According to a later account by Vito Tanzi, a senior economist in the IMF's Fiscal Department who participated in all of the missions to Argentina during the dictatorship years, this first visit had been "among the most dramatic missions [he] participated in."[98] The most disturbing and depressing fact, according to Tanzi, was that from the moment of landing at Ezeiza Airport, the mission was escorted "by a large group of individuals carrying weapons, including machine guns [that] belonged to the national police and would be our body-guards for the three weeks we would stay in Buenos Aires. There were twenty-four such guards assigned to protect us from assassination attempts."[99] It is interesting to note that Tanzi explained these safety measures as an attempt to protect the mission, never hinting at other motivations, such as the military's wish to prevent IMF staff from seeing for themselves the situation in Buenos Aires during the cruel repression and harsh economic blows.

In my opinion, the protection and effective isolation of the IMF mission served two major goals. One was to prove to the visitors that the new regime was holding the reins in a professional and efficient manner, as opposed to the chaos of previous years; the other was to remove any political hesitation the IMF may have had in its consideration of providing assistance to dictatorial Argentina. I must emphasize that I found dozens of newspaper articles on human rights violations in the region in the files at the IMF Archives but no trace of intra-organizational discussion of that issue. If my assessment is accurate, and Martínez de Hoz was indeed apprehensive about the potential conflating of political and economic considerations, then this is an intriguing point, because nothing in the IMF's relationship with dictatorships in the region indicates that it ever discriminated against those regimes. Moreover, the IMF itself, and certainly its representatives, were specifically instructed to avoid political considerations. As Tanzi states:

> The Fund was supposed to follow closely the economic developments of countries but not the political ones, and to deal with whether the government was in control at the time. The nature of these governments, whether democratic or authoritarian, was considered irrelevant. The economists working at the Fund were not encouraged to get involved in, or even to become knowledgeable about, political issues. . . . As long as a government was firmly in power, the Fund was expected to be indifferent to its political nature. It was expected to be politically neutral.[100]

Despite the difficult political environment in Argentina, the mission performed its task as anticipated. Not only did it take part in the consolidation of the new economic plan, it also fully reinstated the working routine that had been nearly cut off in previous years. After three years of mostly clandestine, hurried, and irregular contacts, the end of the last temporary episode of detachment reflected the interest of both Argentina and the IMF to return to "business as usual." The IMF was determined to resume its role as an influential player in Argentina's economy. The military regime, in turn, could not forgo the IMF's seal of approval, which (as argued in previous chapters) had not only economic but also political value.

Whether the IMF truly sought to be politically neutral or had a preference for democratic or military regimes are not the most relevant questions for understanding the Fund's particularly close interactions with the oppressive military regimes in Argentina, Brazil, Chile, or Uruguay. The intensive working routine that evolved between the IMF and the authoritarian regimes in Latin America in the 1960s and 1970s seems to derive, more than anything else, from the IMF's willingness to work with any administration interested in implementing a liberal economic agenda that was consistent with its prescribed policy. The political nature of economically pro-liberal regimes was relegated to a marginal place or ignored altogether.

Thus, as part of the continuous intensification of the joint working routine, the May mission paved the road for a host of reciprocal visits. A few days after the consultation in Argentina was completed, the minister of economy and the president of the Central Bank were on their way to Washington.[101] The frequent meetings were highly productive and led to the elaboration of a preliminary and partial draft of a letter of intent for a loan worth 159.5 million SDRs ($184 million), the equivalent of the first extended tranche. The letter was not finalized, but not because of disagreement between the parties. Argentina needed more time to determine how to allocate the funds and which sectors would suffer cutbacks. To complete the letter, it was agreed that two weeks after the first mission returned to Washington, another mission would visit Argentina.[102] It should be noted that the first mission was only authorized to conduct negotiations regarding the first tranche, but during the discussions, Argentina raised the possibility of applying for two tranches at once ($368 million). The rationale was that only a significant IMF loan would guarantee the approval of larger loans by private lenders.[103]

As agreed, on June 29, 1976, the second mission, led by Guenther and Caiola, who had previously served as permanent IMF representatives in Argentina, ventured out to Buenos Aires. Del Canto authorized the mission to negotiate relatively large sums—up to about 260 million SDRs ($300 million), the equivalent of the first tranche (159 million SDRs) plus 100 million SDRs from the second tranche.[104]

When approval of the IMF loan seemed secure, Martínez de Hoz traveled to Europe and the United States to assemble a complementary loan package. When he returned on June 25, however, he was unable to show any real successes (especially in Europe), except for the rescheduling of debts originally due for repayment in early 1976. Supplementary loans were still on hold, awaiting the IMF's approval.[105] Among the key potential lenders were a number of private U.S. and Canadian banks. According to estimates, the American banks were expected to grant loans worth about half a billion dollars, whereas the Canadian banks were supposed to furnish $50 million–$100 million.[106]

Adhering to protocol, on July 8, Martínez de Hoz and Diz submitted an official request for an SBA worth 250 million SDRs ($300 million)—the maximum the mission could negotiate.[107] Attached to the letter of intent was a document describing the economic plan for 1976.[108] It outlined the measures the new administration had already taken to address several acute problems: the sharp increase in the cost of living (800 percent from April 1975 to late April 1976); the balance-of-payments deficit (close to $700 million), the budget deficit (13 percent of the gross national product), and the recession. The Argentine government claimed that the economic plan of April 1976 had led to a significant and rapid change in many areas—it slowed the inflationary process, therefore removing the risk that Argentina would be forced to declare default. In addition, the government declared its intention to eradicate the multiple exchange rates system.[109] The importance of the memorandum was immense because it implied the continuous application of *ex ante* conditionality.

On August 6, 1976, the IMF's Executive Board approved an SBA that was valid for a year for the sum of 260 million SDRs or ($300 million).[110] The loan, as the Ministry of Economy boasted, was "the largest . . . ever granted by the IMF to a Latin American country, and in effect, twice the sum of any loan ever given to any country in the region."[111] Following the signing, Argentina reached further agreements with foreign private banks. It received $500 million from U.S. banks, $66 million from Canadian banks, about $61 million from Swiss banks, and $60 million from British banks. Smaller amounts, amounting to $110 million, were granted by Dutch, Scandinavian, French, Belgian, Spanish, and German banks.[112] Overall, Martínez de Hoz raised a much larger sum than expected—about $800 million—in addition to the IMF's $300 million.

Approval of the arrangement was largely based on a promise given by Martínez de Hoz that Argentina would move toward economic liberalization and put an end to interventionism.[113] This promise was soon backed by action. On August 13, 1976, the Argentine government ratified a new Law of Foreign Investment.[114] The IMF certainly did not need to impose economic liberalization on Videla's government. As Martínez de Hoz concluded in retrospect: "Our economic program was even more severe than the IMF demanded. There were no disagreements or debates with the IMF. It was easy."[115] Obviously, this was not the first time Argentina attempted to establish a free-market economy, but as Martínez de Hoz argued, until that time the free-market doctrine had been implemented only partially and inconsistently—neither Aramburu nor Frondizi or Onganía had ever committed to it in full.[116] Martínez de Hoz therefore regarded the ascent of the military regime as a golden opportunity to bring in the necessary changes. Interestingly, years later he remained convinced that de facto governments encounter greater difficulties than democratic regimes in attempting to implement structural reforms, because they lack the support of political parties. He believed that while Videla's and Menem's administrations adopted the same economic policy, Menem's task was easier because he enjoyed his party's support.[117]

The Entrenchment of the Routine of Dependency: The Surveillance of the 1976 Stand-by Arrangement

The close surveillance of the loan in 1976 reflected the desire of both parties to further tighten their collaboration. To that end, and in addition to the missions, Argentina asked the IMF to dispatch a technician who would be based at the Central Bank for about three months to assist in tariff calculations and address the external debt.[118] Del Canto approved the request not only because it implied the return of IMF resident representatives to the Central Bank, but also because he believed that there were not enough professional economists in Argentina to perform all of the tasks that he demanded. This time, del Canto appointed the IMF economist Claudio Loser to the job.[119] An Argentine national, Loser received his doctorate from the University of Chicago in 1971 and joined the IMF in 1972. He would direct the Western Hemisphere Department in 1994–2002.

At the heart of the monitoring procedures, as usual, were multiple consultations and reciprocal visits. Shortly after the SBA was approved in October 1976, Diz flew to the United States to sign loan agreements for $500 million with New York banks and to meet IMF officials to discuss implementation of the stabilization plan.[120] That month, Martínez de Hoz, accompanied by a group of Argentine bankers and industrialists, traveled to Manila to attend the annual meeting of the IMF and World Bank—meetings that were already considered a golden opportunity to tighten the contacts with other world leaders, with the executives of the Bretton Woods institutions and with bankers and influential people in the world of business and international finance. In Manila, Martínez de Hoz held personal conversations with IMF Managing Director Johannes Witteveen, World Bank President Robert McNamara, and U.S. Treasury Secretary William Simon.[121]

The IMF was very pleased with the figures presented by the Argentines. The only difficulties the Fund pointed out were inflation and the budget deficit. It is important to note that Diz used the meeting to invite Witteveen to pay an official visit to Argentina. The IMF responded that, if and when the managing director decided to visit Latin America, he would accept an invitation from the Argentine government. Diz also asked whether Buenos Aires could be elected to host the IMF's annual meeting in 1979.[122] These inquiries, as the IMF should and could easily understand, stemmed from the Videla government's need for international legitimacy. As one can assume, "political neutrality" is by no means a synonym for naiveté.

In December 1976, a mission headed by Caiola arrived in Argentina to monitor the implementation of the stabilization plan and assess the next drawings within the SBA. In addition, the mission had the mandate to examine the economic plan for the coming year.[123] Although the mission was not expecting any special difficulties, it recognized that not all of the national leadership was in a cooperative mood.[124] For instance, the mission reported that while Diz was abroad, they felt tension that was defused only when he returned from a series of meetings in Mexico.[125] The IMF officials reported fundamental differences among the Argentine economic team, especially concerning fiscal policy. These inner tensions were resolved only toward 1978, when the military decided that Videla would stay in office until 1980—a decision that strengthened the already solid position of Martínez de Hoz and his team.[126]

The internal conflicts did not discourage the IMF. In January 1977, a new mission arrived in Argentina, and it was immediately followed by another one that lasted from late February to mid-March 1977. During these visits, it was concluded that having drawn the equivalent of 160 million SDRs ($184 million) by December 1976, Argentina would be entitled to draw the rest of the amount in two installments of 50 million SDRs each. The mission regarded Argentina's performance as mixed and felt that it should have met all of its commitments in every key issue on the agenda: fiscal deficit, inflation, liberalization of the foreign currency market and international trade, tax collection, and so on.[127]

On April 14, as scheduled, Martínez de Hoz and Diz dispatched to the IMF Managing Director Witteveen a detailed report on the country's economic situation. The document outlined all of the measures taken by the end of 1976 and included a list of obligations to be implemented during 1977.[128] As contacts with the IMF intensified, Argentina was granted two World Bank loans. The first, in May 1977, was earmarked for the development of transportation infrastructure; the second, in July, went to SEGBA. Also in July, the third IMF mission for 1977 arrived in Argentina, and it was once again headed by Caiola, whose goal was to draft a letter of intent that could easily receive the IMF's blessing.[129]

In September 1977, Argentina formally requested a new SBA worth 159 million SDRs ($215 million).[130] As part of the arrangement, which was similar to the previous one, Argentina committed to examine, jointly with the IMF, whether by the end of 1977 the implementation of the arrangement would still be required. The SBA was approved on September 16, 1977. Although it was endorsed by the United States, the representatives of Western European countries had difficulty approving it.[131] Contrary to what one might expect, given the recurrent reports about human rights violations in Argentina at the time, no political or humanitarian issues were raised in the heated debate over the arrangement's approval.[132] In any event, based on the partial improvement in Argentina's economic situation, the arrangement was terminated, by mutual agreement, in December 1977. Also, it should be stressed that due to the initial economic recovery, Argentina refrained from drawing IMF funds. Martínez de Hoz's most significant achievement that year was an improvement in the balance of payments, with the level of reserves reaching $1.2 billion by the end of the year, especially due to an increase of up to 51 percent in exports. In terms of the macroeconomic figures, the only problem left unsolved was the rampant inflation.[133]

Nevertheless, and regardless of the positive data presented by Argentina, one must not ignore the fact that concurrently—and beyond the harsh social consequences of the economic plan—the external debt kept swelling. The debt amounted to $7.8 billion in 1975; by 1976, it had risen to $8.2 billion, and in 1977, it soared to $9.6 billion.[134] In 1980, the external debt was estimated at $27 billion, and in 1983 it was close to $45 billion.[135] Overall, during the years of dictatorship, Argentina's external debt increased by 364 percent. The external debt problem and the breakout of the first economic crisis in March 1980 created widespread panic; at the same time, it gave rise to speculative activity.[136] But as we shall see, these problems did not destabilize the routine of dependency.

The Routine of Dependency in the Absence of Stand-by Arrangements

By 1978, the Argentine economy was again in recession, and inflation had risen to 175 percent. In February, a consultation under the 1977 SBA took place.[137] Even when Dante Simone, the Argentine representative at the IMF, declared at an Executive Board meeting in early April that "due to the improvement in its balance of payments and reserve situation, Argentina is considering the possibility of not requesting a new SBA when the current one expires," the working routine continued.[138] In June, the Central Bank requested technical assistance from the IMF in using computers for economic analysis.[139] In September, the Fund elaborated a new report on Argentina's economy.

During 1978, Martínez de Hoz implemented a series of drastic reforms that significantly affected the state-owned companies, triggering discontent among workers. In early 1978, fourteen state-owned companies were receiving government subsidies; by the end of the year, however, only two of them were still being supported by the government (the telecommunications company Entel and the railroads).[140] Fearing social unrest, Martínez de Hoz issued relatively generous wage guidelines. Public sector wages and salaries were incremented by 40–50 percent in January 1978, by 35 percent in May, by 36 percent in September, and by 36 percent again in December. In real terms, however, salaries remained unchanged.[141] One should keep in mind that the eyes of the world were turned on Argentina, host of the Mundial (FIFA World Cup) in 1978. Eager to use the competition to show the world that Argentina was an efficient, modern, and unified nation, the junta was ready to make concessions to avert riots.[142] Interestingly, these measures were criticized by conservative factions of the military, who feared that the new wage policy might lead to even higher inflation.

Martínez de Hoz then introduced two controversial measures that served as fertile ground for what later emerged as the debt crisis: the liberalization of financial markets and the so-called *tablita* (simple list). Part of the economic plan announced on December 20, 1978 (inspired by a similar monetarist program elaborated in Chile), the *tablita* was a preannounced devaluation of the exchange rate based on a monthly declining rate of devaluation.[143] The plan was initially successful in that the rate of inflation fell from 444 percent in 1976 to 175 percent in 1978 and to about 100 percent in 1980. The fiscal deficit fell to 5–6 percent of the gross domestic product (GDP).[144] Nevertheless, the *tablita*, which the IMF perceived as a wrong strategy for reducing inflation, fell short of generating the needed credibility to make it work. The IMF mission headed by Caiola that visited in March 14–19, 1979, stated, "It is disappointing that fiscal, credit and wage policies are not well articulated," and warned that "the entire program would collapse."[145] Despite the critics, Caiola's report was the first ever to open with the comment that "the mission received very good collaboration at the technical level."[146] This remark is especially illuminating because it demonstrates that after long years of constant complaining by the IMF about the poor quality of the data furnished by the Argentines, the Central Bank had finally generated information according to the international standards imposed by the Fund. The long-standing routine of dependency, combined with the incorporation of a number of Chicago Boys into the Central Bank and Ministry of Economy, certainly facilitated Argentina's compliance with the new norms of international finance.

In late 1979, the IMF stated that "during the first half of 1979 the Argentine economy expanded strongly, the rate of unemployment was the lowest in recent years, and the strong balance of payments performance led to a substantial buildup of net international reserves. On the other hand, the inflation rate showed no signs of abatement."[147] Thus, apart from the inflation, the IMF found no major difficulties. The inflow of capital from a flood of foreign investments was so large that Argentina was able to repay all of its obligations to the IMF during 1978.[148] Nevertheless, hard times were still ahead for Argentina.

Argentine–IMF Relations under the Shadow
of the Debt Crisis

The debt crisis that Argentina faced in the early 1980s was common to other less-developed countries (LDCs). The crisis began on August 12, 1982, when Mexico's finance minister notified the U.S. Federal Reserve and Treasury and the IMF that Mexico would be unable to meet its obligation to repay $80 billion in debts in August. By October 1983, twenty-seven countries that owed $237 billion had rescheduled or were in the process of rescheduling their debts. Sixteen were Latin American countries, and the "big four"—Mexico, Brazil, Venezuela, and Argentina—owed commercial banks 74 percent of the LDCs' total outstanding debt. The first signs of the crisis appeared in the late 1970s, with Latin America's rapid debt accumulation and increasing capital flight due to overvaluation. Nevertheless, most Latin American nations, including Argentina, continued to borrow heavily.

In 1980–1982, there was a serious outflow of capital from Argentina to US banks, where deposits earned tax-free income. In addition, by 1980 the Argentine peso had become one of the most overvalued currencies in the world. Its high purchasing power abroad (which created an illusion of prosperity for the middle and upper classes) soon had many referring to it as "sweet money" (*plata dulce*). In addition, due to the overvaluation of the currency and the gradual reduction of import tariffs, domestic products lost their competitive edge to massive cheap imports, accelerating the country's deindustrialization. Moreover, overvaluation encouraged a risky speculative lending and borrowing boom. Banks and public and private corporations could reap annual profit margins of up to 80 percent by borrowing in dollars in international markets and lending the funds domestically in pesos.[149] From the time the financial system was liberalized in June 1977 until late 1980, the number of commercial banks and financial companies (*financieras*) in Argentina almost doubled. By early 1980, Argentina had become dangerously dependent on continuous borrowing from foreign banks.

In March–April 1980, external shocks, such as the spike in oil prices that followed Ayatollah Ruhollah Khomeini's rise to power in Iran and the tightening of U.S. monetary policy, along with internal problems generated a banking crisis in Argentina that spurred panic among depositors. Amid the crisis, however, the IMF notified Argentina that its quota had been increased by 267.5 million SDRs.[150] In April 1980, the Central Bank promulgated new regulations governing adjustable loans to stop capital flight and strengthen the financial system—regulations that the IMF considered appropriate.[151] In June, a new mission led by Caiola was concerned about the banking crisis but remained optimistic about Argentina's economic prospects.[152] In the same month, the

Central Bank requested IMF technical assistance, and in July, two IMF technicians arrived at the Central Bank for a short visit.[153]

In February 1981, Martínez de Hoz announced a sharp devaluation of the national currency and revoked the *tablita*. The economic program suffered a last blow when the military decided to limit Videla's presidential term to five years. In March 1981, Videla was succeeded by General Roberto Eduardo Viola. He appointed Lorenzo Sigaut to head the Ministry of Economy; Sigaut and his close friend Domingo Cavallo then attempted to reverse Martínez de Hoz's policies. These changes did not alter the working routine with the IMF, however. Argentina kept the Fund updated on the new economic measures, and between August 27 and September 16, an Article IV Consultation took place. The mission warned the Argentines about the danger if measures were not taken to reduce the fiscal deficit and control monetary growth.[154]

Viola's term was brief. His position was at once imperiled by a deep financial crisis and by infighting within the armed forces. On December 10, 1981, Viola was ousted by a coup led by the Argentine Army's intransigent commander-in-chief, Lieutenant-General Leopoldo Galtieri, who became president. As minister of economy Galtieri appointed none other than Roberto Alemann, who faced an external debt that had tripled in three years. Alemann wanted to implement an even more orthodox policy than his predecessors, focusing on inflation, the denationalization of domestic industry, the privatization of state owned-companies, deregulation, and wage freezes, regardless of the inflation.

Galtieri, whom President Ronald Reagan viewed as a wall against communism in Latin America, visited Washington in November 1981 and offered the United States military bases in Patagonia in return for investments in a new gas pipeline and Argentina's oil industry.[155] While Galtieri enjoyed a favored position with the Reagan administration, his standing at home was fragile. He was unable to get support from opposing factions within the military, and social unrest mounted. In March 1982, the unions organized a mass demonstration to protest the state of the economy. The Argentine invasion of the Malvinas (Falkland Islands) on April 2, 1982, and the beginning of an extremely expensive war against Britain (which prompted further capital outflows and the freezing of Argentine assets in the U.K.) made it impossible to implement any economic plan.[156] In 1981 and 1982, the Argentine economy had contracted sharply, at an annual rate of −6.2 percent and −5.2 percent, respectively.

Argentina's surrender on June 14 ended a war that lasted twenty-seven days, claimed almost two thousand casualties, and whose chief purpose was short-term political gain for both Galtieri and British Prime Minister Margaret Thatcher. Increasing protests in Argentina (especially against amnesty for members of the armed forces involved in repression) marked the end of Galtieri's brief term. General Reynaldo Bignone emerged as the new *de facto* president and soon realized that he had no choice but to call for democratic elections.[157]

Throughout the war and its tumultuous aftermath, the IMF and Argentina continued their routine interactions. On May 11, Alemann met with the Managing Director Jacques de Larosière (June 1978–January 1987) and other top IMF officials. Following Galtieri's resignation, the IMF reported, Alemann was replaced by José María Dagnino Pastore, who had been "well known to the [IMF] staff from the time he was minister . . . in the late 1960s, and who remained in touch with the staff since." Pastore, the report continued, "has now indicated he would like the mission to arrive in Buenos Aires in mid-July."[158] The third mission for 1982 remained in Argentina for two weeks (July 14–28). It should be mentioned that Pastore officiated for barely a month, having been eclipsed by the influential Domingo Cavallo from the very beginning. He was replaced by another known figure in Argentina and in international banking circles: the neoliberal Jorge Wehbe.

Although President Bignone initially did not express any interest in requesting assistance from the IMF, the Fund predicted that Argentina would soon realize the political and economic wisdom of such a move.[159] This prediction was based not only on assessment of Argentina's explosive situation, but also on the fact that the debt crisis that had erupted in Mexico had been spreading across Latin America. In September 1983, Julio González del Solar, the president of the Central Bank, unofficially informed a top IMF official that, in close consultations with a multiparty group, it had been agreed "to seek the [IMF]'s financial assistance in the upper credit tranches" and that he "urged the Fund to give a sympathetic hearing to his request."[160] In November, E. Walter Robichek, director of the Western Hemisphere Department in 1977–1981, approved the economic plan that Argentina was to begin implementing before the IMF gave the go-ahead for a new SBA.[161] Robichek favored a fifteen-month arrangement rather than an extended SBA, as Argentina preferred. Obviously, Robichek feared that there was not enough political support in Argentina to implement an effective program, especially in view of the upcoming democratic elections. By the end of September, the military was simultaneously negotiating with Robichek, the politicians who were likely to form a new government after the elections, foreign creditors, and the Bank for International Settlements (BIS).[162] In November, González del Solar and his staff held several meetings at IMF headquarters, and an IMF mission visited Argentina in December. At the core of these meetings were the new economic program and the new letter of intent.[163]

It should be stressed that the main creditor banks' high level of exposure propelled governments in the developed countries to take a special interest in the Latin American debt crisis. Under the leadership of the Reagan administration, and with the aim of avoiding a major international banking crisis, the private and official lenders organized into "advisory committees" to deal with debtor countries. In the cases of Mexico and Argentina, these committees were headed by Citibank and held several meetings with the IMF. By December 31, an agreement was reached with the committee, and on January 7, 1983, Argentina officially requested an SBA.[164] On January 24, the IMF approved an SBA of 1,500 million SDRs (equivalent to approximately $2 billion)) for the period from January 24, 1983, to April 23, 1984.[165]

The monitoring of this SBA was particularly tight because the managing director had instructed his staff during the crisis to keep him up to date on developments in Argentina, Brazil, and Mexico.[166] On April 17, an IMF mission arrived in Argentina to evaluate its performance under the SBA.[167] A second mission arrived on May 10.[168] The third mission, which arrived in June, concluded that "performance under the program has been fairly satisfactory," and while there had been some improvements in the balance of payments and GDP, inflation averaged 12.8 percent a month.[169] Also in June, González del Solar visited the IMF to discuss the recent rise in inflation rates and the social pressures for significant wage increases.[170] In July, another mission arrived in Argentina.

Throughout these months, the IMF stayed in close contact with Citibank, the coordinator of the advisory committee, regarding bridge and medium-term loans that the banks had granted to Argentina.[171] These contacts implied a transformation in IMF relations with private bankers. As shown in previous chapters, during the 1960s and 1970s, private banks withheld new credits until the IMF approved an SBA with the borrowing country. During the crisis in the 1980s, the bankers attempted to reduce their exposure by adopting a collective-action strategy that considerably increased their influence over the IMF. This process corroborates Erica Gould's argument concerning the growing role played by private financiers in the elaboration of conditional loan arrangements.[172] Without doubt, the Latin American debt crisis took the routine of dependency to a new peak.

Remarkably, once the crisis began, the IMF acquired a higher profile than it had ever enjoyed in Latin America. True, during the 1970s Latin American countries tried to avoid conditional IMF loans and signed agreements with other lenders. In 1979–1981, just one-third of Latin American countries were under an SBA. By 1983, however, when countries were seeking short-term relief and IMF aid in negotiating long-term loans, three-quarters of them entered into some sort of arrangement with the Fund.[173] The close cooperation between the IMF, the World Bank, and creditor governments soon began to crystallize into a coherent vision of what creditors considered appropriate for the region—that is, the "Washington Consensus," which I discuss in the next chapter.[174]

The military's return to the Casa Rosada thus marked a shift not only in Argentina's political and economic life, but also in the fabric of its relationship with the IMF. Although the routine of dependency has been especially welcomed and powerful on many occasions since 1957, the military regime in general, and Videla's term in particular, significantly strengthened it. On the one hand, this derived from the regime's urgent need to gain international legitimacy. On the other, it was surely a direct result of the same long-standing routine of dependency that the IMF had cultivated so patiently and consistently with every regime that was ready, for whatever reasons, to liberalize its economy. The intensive IMF working routine in dictatorial Argentina was the culmination of a long-term process. In effect, it was no coincidence that Martínez de Hoz could appoint a relatively homogeneous group of liberal economists to key positions at the Ministry of Economy and Central Bank. Rather, it was a consequence of IMF's ongoing involvement and ideological influence. Similar processes, as already mentioned, were also under way in Chile and Mexico, pointing to the expansion and entrenchment of the routine of dependency at both the national and the regional level. Not only was there strong ideological affinity between broad sectors of the military and the IMF in Argentina, but the regime was also powerful and stable enough to implement its policies and the IMF's recommendations almost without a hitch.

Conclusion

The relationship between the IMF and its member states has always been the result of dynamic interplay between changing political and economic circumstances on the national, regional, and international levels, on the one hand, and the IMF's changing priorities and needs, on the other. The routine of dependency—including episodes of detachment and rapprochement, as well as periods of intense collaboration—both shapes and is shaped by the participating actors. However, one thing seems to have remained almost unalterable: the IMF's readiness to compromise and keep the routine of dependency active at all costs. Whether the regime involved is a democracy or a dictatorship and whether the administration dealing with the IMF is stable or not appear to have been secondary, or even irrelevant, questions.

The case of Argentina is especially illuminating, because its political and economic instability, especially in the 1960s and 1970s, seriously challenged the IMF's flexibility, as its relations with the country in the late Perón era amply demonstrate. As several economic ministers attempted to fundamentally alter key components of the joint working routine—by asking to conduct consultations only in Washington, for instance, or to keep consultations confidential, if not secret—the IMF consistently adapted to local needs and limitations. But this flexibility was by no means a sign of weakness. On the contrary: The temporary and tactical concessions the IMF made resulted from its mounting power and centrality in the global arena, its pragmatism, and its willingness to sacrifice immediate gains to achieve long-term goals. In other words, the professional and highly stable IMF staff could afford to be patient, justly confident that Argentina was firmly on the course of economic liberalization, and that sooner or later a "local agent"—an ideological ally of the IMF—would take the helm at the Ministry of Economy and cooperate fully with the Fund. Furthermore, as the years went by, the routine of dependency continued to evolve, and the assimilation of liberal economic ideas consolidated, the chances that a neo-liberal, pro-IMF economist would become the minister of economy steadily increased. Indeed, the epistemic community of local economists and IMF technocrats broadened and deepened, especially when Martínez de Hoz was in charge of the economic portfolio. It is quite possible, then, that the establishment of Videla's government was good news for the IMF, just as it was for the United States. As argued in previous chapters, the IMF had a long history of fruitful relationships with military regimes in Latin America, which were often inclined to embark on economic liberalization.

Even if the IMF was indeed politically neutral and did not distinguish between democracies and dictatorships, the question that should be asked is: How could an international organization that in 1947 became a specialized agency of the United Nations have had such close relationships with governments that systematically violated human rights? I believe that while the IMF was politically neutral, it was far from ideologically neutral. Simply put, the IMF's self-imposed political neutrality exempted the institution from having to ask itself thorny questions about the nature and the legitimacy of its ties with brutal dictatorships. As mentioned above, documents in the IMF Archives demonstrate that both IMF officials and representatives of its member states were aware of the Argentine military's atrocities. However, I found no evidence of any discussion of the political and moral implications of collaborating with that dictatorship. And even if such a discussion ever did take place, it is clear that the IMF ultimately prioritized economic over moral and political considerations.

6

Routine of Dependency
or Routine of Detachment?

Looking for a New Model of
Relations with the IMF

T he 1980s are usually considered Latin America's "lost decade." This char-
acterization refers, more than anything else, to the state of the economy.
In effect, at the same time that the region experienced the worst economic
crisis since the Great Depression, it underwent a profound process of political
transformation that resulted in the largest series of free elections in its history
until then. Moreover, those nations that returned to democracy in the 1980s and
1990s have remained democratic to the present day.

This chapter thus begins with this lost decade, paying special attention to
several heterodox experiments undertaken in the mid-1980s in Argentina under
President Raúl Alfonsín (1983–1989), as well as in other countries, such as Brazil under President José Sarney (1985–1990) and Peru under President Alan
García (1985–1990). It then turns to the shift toward market economics, especially through an examination of the case of Carlos Saúl Menem in Argentina
(1989–1999). Finally, it briefly refers to the attempts by several nations in the
region at the beginning of the twenty-first century to create not just a new temporary episode of detachment from the IMF but actually a new model of interaction with it.

While the previous chapters focused on the making, evolution, and entrenchment of the routine of dependency during 1944–1982, this chapter makes no
claim to provide a detailed account of the routine of dependency in the post-
1983 period. As historians are aware, archival material relating to recent years
has not yet been declassified. Hence, it is impossible at this point to examine
fully the inner workings of the latest stages of the IMF's relations with its borrowers. Nonetheless, recent events in the region point to an important research
agenda for scholarship once the archival materials become available. Among

them are the massive implementation of IMF-backed market reforms in the 1990s and the repayment of debts to the Fund by countries such as Argentina and Brazil in 2005. Observed through the prism of the "routine of dependency," these critical processes cannot easily be perceived as mere accidents of history. Rather, they are the consequences of an ongoing, though not linearly evolving, process of Latin America's integration into the global economy.

Following Mexico's default in August 1982, countries in Latin America confronted acute problems in repaying billion-dollar debts with only limited access to external financing. Living standards fell across the region, while unemployment and poverty levels soared. By the late 1980s, the average per capita product of Latin America was 8 percent lower than it had been at the beginning of the decade, and hyperinflation plagued Argentina, Bolivia, Brazil, Nicaragua, and Peru. Even Mexico and Venezuela, both rich in petroleum resources, suffered economic crises due only partly to declining oil prices in international markets. The outflow of capital continued at an annual rate of $25 billion.[1]

Given these adverse conditions, debtor countries and the international financial community devised a strategy to deal with the debt crisis and with what Cheryl Payer has termed the "debt trap,"[2] with the U.S. government taking several initiatives to address the growing problem. Indeed, at the IMF and World Bank meeting in Seoul in October 1985, James Baker III, secretary of the treasury in Ronald Reagan's administration (1981–1989), announced a new strategy to combat the debt crisis. The Baker Plan aimed to induce heavily indebted developing countries (ten of them in Latin America) to apply market reforms that would incorporate them into the global economy. In exchange, multilateral development agencies (especially the World Bank and the IDB) and commercial banks would increase loans by $26 billion in a three-year period.[3] This plan yielded scant results, however, mainly because commercial banks were reluctant to take more risks. The failure of the Baker Plan coincided with the appointment of the French economist Michel Camdessus as managing director of the IMF in January 1987. Camdessus supported debt reduction for the most heavily indebted countries, a stance that the U.S. administration and the Federal Reserve initially opposed. In January 1989, Nicholas Brady, treasury secretary under President George H. W. Bush (1989–1993), launched a new strategy based on significant debt reductions for developing countries and offered U.S. support to debtor nations that committed to adopting market-based economic measures. The Brady Plan led to policy-based (conditional) lending agreements with Mexico, Costa Rica, Venezuela, Uruguay, Argentina, and Brazil. Overall, the plan did not yield significant debt reduction.[4]

As for Argentina, for decades it had been the country with the highest standard of living and per capita income in Latin America. However, after experiencing periods of neoliberal economic policies—accompanied by several irregularities and mistakes in the implementation of economic programs—its economy collapsed, pushing 54 percent of the population under the poverty line by the late 1990s. This process, which drastically changed Argentina's socioeconomic structure, took place while the IMF was particularly active in Latin America and Argentina was considered an example of neoliberalism. Some scholars refer to this period as a break or even as a revolution in Argentina's and Latin America's history.[5] However, it appears that the events that characterized the post-debt crisis period were not so much a rupture as the corollary of processes (economic, social, political, ideological, and bureaucratic) that had been under way nationally, regionally, and globally since the Bretton Woods institutions were established. In effect, the deep neoliberalization that Argentina—and other Latin American nations—experienced in the mid-1980s and especially in the 1990s was largely facilitated by decades of routine of dependency.

True, during Reagan's administration in the United States and Margaret Thatcher's in Britain, and with Ann Krueger serving as chief economist of the World Bank between 1982 and 1986, neoliberal policies were promoted more aggressively worldwide than they had ever been. Nevertheless, in some cases, neoliberalism had clearly been the political and economic choice of certain Latin American presidents, and Menem is a good case in point. In other words, the neoliberalization of economic thought and policies was not necessarily and not invariably imposed on Argentina (and on other Latin American nations) from abroad. To a large extent, it was the result of disillusionment with previous economic policies and of years of intensive and almost constant, welcomed, and desired interactions between members of the epistemic community of U.S.-trained or U.S.-inspired local economists, on the one hand, and Washington-based officials, on the other. Ironically, as we shall see, it was precisely the zealous implementation of neoliberal structural reforms in the 1990s that paved the way to the abandonment of neoliberalism in the early 2000s.

The Failed Rebellion: Raúl Alfonsín and the IMF

Alfonsín was the first democratically elected president in Argentina following seven years of military rule that were plagued with violence, corruption, and deep changes in the economy. Alfonsín won the general elections that had been called in October 1983 by the last de facto president, Reynaldo Brignone, with nearly 52 percent of the votes that came from and beyond traditional Radical Civic Union supporters. A lawyer from the city of Chascomús, in eastern Buenos Aires Province, Alfonsín owed his political career to Ricardo Balbín, one of the most prominent figures of the Radical Civic Union, who later became one of his most bitter rivals. In 1963, Alfonsín was elected to the Chamber of Deputies, becoming a strong supporter of President Illia. In 1972, he established the moderate, left-of-center Movimiento de Renovación y Cambio (Movement for Renewal and Change).

When Alfonsín assumed the presidency in December 10, 1983, Argentina's economy was in the midst of an unprecedented crisis. In 1983, the inflation rate rose to 433.7 percent (double the rate in 1982). The GDP was barely equivalent to that in 1970. Fixed investment had fallen more than 30 percent compared with the average in the previous decade. The purchasing power of wage earners was below that in the 1960s. The public sector deficit in 1983 was estimated at 11.1 percent of the GDP.[6] In addition, an adverse external situation characterized by the collapse of prices of agricultural products, the paralysis of external credits, and the increment of international interest rates only worsened Argentina's economic position.[7] The most pressing problem, however, was an astronomical foreign debt of about $46 billion.

Alfonsín's presidency fueled hopes that the return to democracy would be accompanied by a return to economic stability. After running a nationalist and anti-imperialist campaign, he was expected to cure the ills created by the previous regime, not only in the political, economic, and social fields, but also in the area of human rights. Once in office, Alfonsín took several measures aimed at shedding light on the dark events that had taken place during the Dirty War and punishing members of the armed forces who had violated human rights. In December 1983, he established the national truth-finding commission CONADEP and charged it with collecting evidence on the fate of the *desaparecidos* (missing people). In addition, Alfonsín allowed criminal indictments to be brought against central figures of the military regime, including Videla, Viola, Massera, and Galtieri. At the same time, the government cut military spending drastically.[8] Nevertheless, the political consequences of Alfonsín's human rights policy were mixed. On the one hand, it provided him with popular support, but on the other, it left him exposed to the permanent threat of the army and of the most reactionary groups in society.

Despite the immense expectations raised by the return to democracy, the new administration elaborated its economic policies with little consultation with civil society. While it was clear from the outset that the economic elites would not be the beneficiaries of his programs, Alfonsín failed to garner wide popular support. Moreover, the government soon found itself in a permanent conflict with the unions, which traditionally have been associated with Peronism. In fact, Alfonsín was able to establish needed alliances with neither the working class and the unions nor the elites.[9] This situation significantly limited his ability to implement a coherent economic plan.

Alfonsín appointed Bernardo Grinspun as minister of the economy and Enrique García Vásquez as president of the Central Bank, two economists who had also served under Illia. Partly based on a misunderstanding of the real scope of the structural changes that Argentina underwent during the dictatorship, Grinspun tried to follow the same Keynesian premises that he had adopted in the 1960s. Indeed, he tried to implement statist measures—such as controls over prices, exchange rates, and interest rates—that were at odds with the IMF's prescriptions. Grinspun maintained the dollar at a very high value to support national industry, which had been neglected by the previous regime. More than anything, he was determined to establish an equitable distribution of income.

Interestingly, as soon as Alfonsín was elected, he invited Raúl Prebisch to return to Argentina as senior economic adviser to the new administration—an invitation that Prebisch delightedly accepted. Even though Prebisch and Alfonsín had met on only a few occasions by then, a number of factors made ties between them somewhat foreseeable. Prebisch knew former President Illia and almost all of Alfonsín's team, many of whom had been Prebisch's students before 1948 or had worked with him at ECLAC, UNCTAD, and other international agencies. As Edgar Dosman notes, there is no doubt that Prebisch's involvement established—or was aimed at establishing—a direct link between Alfonsín's and Illia's presidencies.[10]

Prebisch returned to Argentina and was given an office at the same Central Bank that he had helped to found in the 1940s. He reported directly to Alfonsín and worked closely with the Ministry of Economy, the Central Bank, the Ministry of Finance (headed by Juan Sourrouille), and the Ministry of Foreign Affairs (under Dante Caputo).[11] In addition to his professionalism and experience, as well as his reputation not only as an economist but also as a thinker and theorist in economics and development,[12] Prebisch actually played a key role as intermediary in the first contacts between the government and the international financial institutions.[13] Prebisch's intervention was crucial: Soon after taking office, Alfonsín announced his intention to withhold loan repayments (as did Brazil in 1987) and to reconsider the legitimacy of the debts accumulated by the dictatorship. Oddly, the U.S. Treasury was the only body that was ready to make concessions to Alfonsín, granting Argentina a bridge loan to help it pay part of the repayments that were due in 1984.[14] The bridge loan (*crédito puente*) was a short-term loan aimed at allowing Argentina to meet urgent obligations until funds coming from sources such as multilateral agencies and private banks could be disbursed.

Assuming, then, that Alfonsín wanted to create continuity between his government and Illia's, it should not be surprising that he initially adopted a confrontational strategy toward the IMF—a strategy similar to the one Alan García adopted when he assumed the presidency of Peru in 1985. In reality, democratic regimes, such as Alfonsín's and García's, could not afford to overlook the strong public opposition to the IMF, because such opposition could easily be translated into social unrest and electoral defeat. As Kendall Stiles points out, additional considerations may have driven Alfonsín to confront the IMF. In the national arena, the Senate Budget Committee was dominated by Peronists who would not approve any agreement with the Fund. In the international sphere, Argentina had more to gain than to lose from an anti-IMF strategy. As a prospective leader of the Non-Aligned Movement, Argentina could certainly enhance its reputation among Third World nations through open confrontation with the IMF.[15] Thus, partly as a continuation of Illia's stance and partly because of national and international circumstances, Alfonsín initiated a temporary episode of partial detachment from the IMF.

The detachment was indeed partial. Even before Alfonsín became president, Enrique García Vásquez asked for an appointment with the IMF's managing director "to discuss the situation and prospects of Argentina's financial arrangement with the Fund."[16] The IMF responded that it would "thus seem advisable that a fact-finding mission travel to Buenos Aires to bring back to headquarters up-to-date information on the economic situation for the discussion with Mr. García Vásquez. This work would also assist in the preparation of our position for any future negotiation with Argentina, which may start early next year."[17]

The fact-finding mission stayed in Argentina from December 12 to December 16. As soon as it arrived, a "Ministerial Resolution was issued establishing a five-person committee in the Ministry of Economy for liaison with the Fund staff and prohibiting any contact of Ministry employees with the Fund staff except through this committee."[18] This unusual step, one can safely suppose, was expected to avoid the almost natural unofficial interactions with IMF staff, especially if we take into account that more than a few of the Chicago Boys still held key government posts and were eager to work with the IMF's representatives. Nevertheless, as the IMF mission reported, "The initial defensive attitude of some members of the committee soon disappeared. . . . The transition did, however, result in difficulties in obtaining fiscal data and analysis."[19] The mission also emphasized that "one area that remains unclear is the role of the Ministry vis-à-vis that of the Central Bank in dealing with the Fund. It appears that the intention may be to shift the locus of contact and discussions with the Fund to the Ministry."[20] This comment reveals that Alfonsín rightly perceived the relationship with the IMF as not only economic in nature, but also as essentially political. This is why the new administration preferred to put the management of the routine of dependency into the hands of a small, controllable group in the highly politicized Ministry of Economy and to curb the freedom of action of the more professional and technical Central Bank officials.

At this time, the SBA that was signed on January 1983 was still in force, which forced Grinspun to cooperate in a close monitoring process. The December mission concluded that Argentina had complied with fiscal and balance-of-payments targets until the end of September but diverged from the program substantially in the last quarter of 1983, especially in the areas of price and wage controls.[21] The mission also considered some of the data furnished by the Argentines partial and dubious. Argentina nonetheless was interested in finding the way to gain access to IMF funds but without paying the potentially explosive political price of such a strategy. After all, while the arrangement in 1983 was for a total of 1.5 billion SDRs (equivalent to approximately $2 billion), by December 1983 Argentina had only purchased the equivalent of 600.51 million SDRs.[22] However, on the eve of the meeting with the Central Bank's president, the IMF had already resolved that, regardless of any explanation García Vásquez would offer to justify Argentina's non-compliance with the IMF's SBA, "It is not possible to maintain the fiction that the original architecture of the stand-by can be re-established."[23] Simply put, the IMF was determined to suspend the 1983 SBA. For reasons that still remain obscure, on January 21, 1984, national authorities officially informed the IMF that Argentina was revoking the arrangement.[24] Rather than creating a crisis, however, the revocation actually facilitated the opening of a new and relatively blank page between the parties.

In late January 1984, preparations began for a new mission that would stay in Argentina for almost a month. The main goal was "to negotiate *ad referendum* a program of one year to 18 months that could qualify Argentina for access to Fund resources for up to a maximum of 2,086.88 SDRs or 187.5 percent of quota. . . . The mission will also hold the 1984 Article IV Consultation."[25] The mission was expected to focus on, among other things, strategies to curb inflation to one-digit rates by late 1984, wage control in the private sector, and improvement in the balance of payments. The mission was also instructed to "discuss with the authorities the possibility of stationing a resident representative in Buenos Aires."[26]

After a month in Argentina, the mission left almost empty-handed. In a meeting with the highest-ranking IMF authorities and representatives of the Federal Reserve Board, including its influential chairman, Paul Volcker, the mission complained about the poor quality of the data compiled by Argentina and about what it regarded as the lack of a coherent economic plan. As the IMF's managing director opined, "The situation appeared to be very dim, and all of the elements of a disaster seemed to be falling into place."[27] Joaquín Ferrán, a Spanish economist who headed numerous IMF missions to Latin America, reported, "Just before the mission left, the Minister was still optimistic that an agreement could be reached in the near future. He hoped to have a complete set of projections ready by March 16 and expected that on that basis the mission could return to Buenos Aires to agree on a letter of intent in the week of March 19."[28] Understanding the significant technical work that Argentina would still have to do to supply the requested data, Ferrán considered the minister's schedule too optimistic. Alfonsín was aware of the obstacles to reaching an agreement with the IMF. Thus, on March 21, he asked Prebisch to be his personal representative at negotiations in Washington.[29] While Prebisch's visit to Washington created a solid platform for an agreement with the IMF, it reactivated old anti-Prebisch sentiments in Argentina. Not only did local newspapers criticize Prebisch's involvement in negotiations with the Fund, but Vicente Saadi, the Peronist senator from Catamarca, stated that his party did not share the government's positive opinion of Prebisch because Prebisch had only served to deepen colonialism and slavery of Latin American nations.[30]

In the meantime, to maintain an uncompromised position vis-à-vis the international financial community, Alfonsín felt he had to form a "debtors' cartel" capable of negotiating with the Western creditors and the IMF on behalf of developing countries. After several months of lobbying for the idea, however, Mexico, Brazil, Venezuela, and Colombia—who were negotiating the rescheduling of their own debts—joined the creditors in calling on Argentina to adopt the formula of case-by-case negotiation. In March 1984, fearing that an Argentine moratorium would be detrimental to their own talks, those four Latin American countries lent Argentina $300 million for three months. That sum was followed by $100 million from Washington.[31] It should be underlined that, despite his failure to create a debtors' cartel, Alfonsín did not relinquish the attempt to bring about stronger regional integration. Indeed, in 1985, he signed the Argentina–Brazil Integration and Economic Cooperation Program (PICE) with Brazilian President José Sarney, which served as the basis for establishing the Southern Common Market (Mercosur) among Argentina, Brazil, Paraguay, and Uruguay in 1991.

During this time, interactions with the IMF continued. In April 1984, Grinspun and García Vásquez held several meetings at the Fund's headquarters.[32] In May, at Argentina's request, three technicians arrived in Buenos Aires "to continue technical work with officials."[33] In early May, Grinspun insisted on having "a full negotiation mission as soon as possible and . . . indicated the hopes he [would] not have to send unilaterally a letter of intent to the Fund."[34] The IMF answered that this request was impossible to fulfill, because Argentina was unwilling to change its fiscal policy. Grinspun responded that he had "no more political room to maneuver, and that within two days he would have to report to the [Argentine] Congress on negotiations with the Fund."[35] Grinspun threatened that without a mission, he would be forced to break negotiations. The IMF considered several alternatives, and finally, partially out of fear that Grinspun would accuse the IMF of having forced him to interrupt the talks, a three-week mission arrived on May 12.[36] Predictably, the parties were unable to reach an agreement.

In June 1984, Grinspun submitted a "made in Argentina" letter of intent to the IMF that, for the first time ever, was not the result of the firmly established negotiation process in which the IMF staff would draft a letter that was later signed by local authorities. The new letter prioritized domestic growth over debt repayment—an unthinkable strategy from the IMF's perspective. Among other things, it referred to a 6–8 percent wage raise, an increase in the money supplied beyond IMF guidelines, and limits on interest payments to avoid drastic cuts in imports. Defiantly, the letter stated that its submission did "not signify the adoption of commitments that would restrict [Argentina's] sovereignty in the management of its domestic problems."[37] Grinspun added, "The policy described here entails the adoption of measures and targets that are indispensable for the rehabilitation of the national economy and that will be implemented and attained over and above any agreement to be reached with the IMF."[38]

In other words, Alfonsín's administration persisted in going after financial assistance from the IMF but without accepting economic prescriptions that were incompatible with Argentina's political and social reality. In doing so, he was following in Illia's footsteps, but only partially. Illia presided over a country that was in a better economic situation than Alfonsín's Argentina and could afford to take the economic risks that significant detachment from the IMF would entail. Alfonsín, by contrast, had to confront the immense challenge of obtaining IMF funds without committing political suicide.

It should be noted that Alfonsín was not the only regional leader at the time who refused to fully accept the existing rules of the game. Peruvian President Alan García also defied the IMF. The Fund, however, was more intolerant toward Peru than toward Argentina. As Grigore Pop-Elleches argues, García (contrary to Alfonsín) apparently overestimated Peru's importance to Western economic interests. The IMF (and Western creditors) was ready to compromise to avoid a debt moratorium in Argentina; Peru's debt, however, was too small to convince the Fund to treat it with the same flexibility with which it treated Argentina.[39]

As should be expected, the IMF and the U.S. administration were astonished when they received Argentina's unilateral letter of intent and asked Enrique José Candioti, the Argentine ambassador to Washington, to contact the Fund for clarification. Candioti explained that he had "been talking to the U.S. Treasury that morning and Mr. Volcker that afternoon. Minister Grinspun wanted . . . to make clear to the Managing Director that the Argentine Letter of Intent did not have a confrontational aspect at all."[40] He added that "the Managing Director had to understand the extremely charged political atmosphere in Argentina to see the letter in its proper context. . . . It was thus impossible to rule the country without the agreement of the Peronists."[41]

On the surface, then, Argentina wished to demonstrate to the IMF and to a generally anti-IMF public at home that Alfonsín's administration could have its cake and eat it. Behind the scenes, though, Argentina was very far from imposing its will on the IMF. From May 6 until June 13, an IMF mission stayed in Argentina, but no agreement was reached. On June 22–23, two Argentine representatives met with IMF officials in Washington. On that occasion, the IMF asked the visitors to inform Grinspun that it was impossible for the Fund to support Argentina's economic plan as described in the letter of intent.[42]

In mid-July, as requested by Argentine authorities, a two-week IMF mission visited Buenos Aires. Sourrouille, then Argentina's secretary of planning, informed the mission: "There has been a complete review of the estimates of the fiscal outcome for the first half of 1984 . . . , including substantial reductions in spending and revenues and some decline in the estimates of the overall deficit."[43] As usual, there were still deep discrepancies over wages. In general, average real wages among the national government employees declined from December 1983 to July 1984; real wages of provincial government employees remained unchanged; and real wages in the public sector as a whole rose 4 percent. Issues such as balance-of-payments targets, exchange rates, and interest rates also remained unresolved.[44]

Finally, because of weighty international pressure, an agreement with the IMF was reached on September 18, 1984. Grinspun and García Vásquez signed an amended letter of intent that was more in line with the IMF's requirements.[45] The austerity program delineated in the letter included standard measures, such as a sharp reduction in inflation (from 1,200 percent a year to 150 percent), the elimination of price controls, a significant reduction of the public sector deficit, and liberalization of foreign trade restrictions. In November 1984, Grinspun visited the IMF's headquarters to discuss delicate issues, especially wage policy, price controls, and exchange rates.[46] In early December, a new mission visited Argentina to elaborate the final details of the agreement.[47] While the mission was organizing its visit, Argentina submitted a request for a CFF equivalent of 275 million SDRs, or 24.7 percent of its quota) to meet the shortfall from the 20 percent export reduction in 1982–1983. On December 4, the request was approved.[48] On December 28, the IMF approved a fifteen-month SBA to Argentina based on the letter of intent from September 25.[49] All of these agreements, the result of significant compromise and efforts by both parties, demonstrate that at the time neither Argentina nor the IMF could afford to relinquish the joint activities: Argentina urgently needed the IMF's funds, and the IMF needed to revitalize its activity in the region.

But the SBA was insufficient to solve all of the acute economic problems that affected Argentina. On January 15–16, a group of officials headed by Grinspun met in Paris with sixteen creditor countries from the Paris Club to discuss Argentina's request to reschedule its external debt service obligations. Unsurprisingly, representatives of the IMF, the World Bank, the IDB, UNCTAD, the European Community, and the OECD attended the meetings as observers. The Paris Club members, as was customary, asked the IMF to explain Argentina's situation and the economic program backed by the 1984 SBA.[50] Clearly, all of the participants in the multilateral talks considered the IMF the "responsible adult" whose opinion ultimately would determine Argentina's fate. The very fact that Argentina was under a valid SBA at the time was enough to convince the creditor nations to provide the much needed debt relief. This was extremely important, as the payments due between January 1 and December 31, 1985, were estimated at about $2 billion.[51]

The new economic program was soon endangered by wage raises, a 24 percent price increase, and accelerating inflation during the first quarter of 1985. Grinspun and García Vásquez were first in line to pay the price for the economic deterioration: Both men resigned on February 18, 1985. Grinspun was replaced by Juan Sourrouille, a self-described heterodox and Harvard-trained economist who had been serving as planning secretary under Alfonsín. In light of Argentina's non-compliance with the plan's conditions, the IMF and the commercial banks suspended new loans in March 1985. Nevertheless, even while Argentina appeared unable and unwilling to implement the Fund's orthodox prescriptions, the IMF staff continued to adhere to its traditional, flexible approach.

The IMF's Ongoing Compromise: New Economic Plans and Increasing Political Instability

Although Alfonsín's economic policy ran counter to the IMF's advice, the Fund, as it had been on so many other occasions in the past, was willing to compromise to keep the joint working routine vigorous. This was not an easy task.

By mid-April, Sourrouille, Mario Brodersohn, and José Luis Machinea (all of whom were supporters of developmentalism), presented the draft of their economic program to the IMF, the U.S. Treasury, and the Federal Reserve Bank in a meeting held at the IMF's headquarters.[52] Guided by the need to curb inflation without triggering a serious recession (as used to be the case with IMF-backed stabilization programs), Sourrouille launched the heterodox Austral Plan in June 14, 1985. In general, a heterodox program implies a reasonable balance between price and income policy, on the one hand, and a focused attack on the underlying causes of inflation, on the other. Heterodox plans are based on a temporary price freeze designed to thwart widespread expectations of ever increasing inflation and on state intervention to break inflationary inertia.[53] Similar programs, it is worth noting, were adopted by Peru in 1985, Brazil in 1986, and Mexico in 1987. Evidence suggests that Mexico was the only country to register a successful stabilization by 1988. Others, like Argentina, experienced initial positive results, followed by renewed deterioration. In the case of Brazil, for example, inflation dropped from 228 percent in 1985 to 58 percent in 1986 but then soared to 1,000 percent in 1988.[54]

At the core of the Austral Plan was the creation of a new currency—the austral—which replaced the peso at a rate of 1 austral per 1,000 pesos, with the exchange rate devalued 18 percent in relation to the dollar. The creation of new currencies, such as the austral in Argentina, the cruzado in Brazil (1986–1989), and the inti in Peru (1985–1991), is important for both economic and psychological reasons, because it has the power to suppress memories of inflation. In addition to launching the austral, the plan imposed a freeze on wages and prices, reduced the budget deficit, increased state utility prices, and committed not to print inflationary quantities of money.[55] It implied a departure from Grinspun's economic policy and a shifting of the focus from income redistribution to stabilization and adjustment. Even though it was far from being a classic IMF-supported plan, the search for stabilization won approval from the Fund, creditor governments, international financial institutions, and powerful economic groups in Argentina.[56] This broad support was manifested in a $400 million bridge loan that Argentina obtained from the United States, Spain, Colombia, and Venezuela, which was used to pay overdue obligations on Argentina's foreign debt.[57]

It should be noted that the IMF used the Austral Plan as a pretext for resuming the disbursement of credits on the SBA that had been suspended in March. As Pop-Eleches indicates, there are several explanations for the IMF's support of a heterodox plan. One obviously derives from what the Fund perceived as a welcome shift in Alfonsín's economic policy. Another is related to the economic and political importance of Argentina to Western nations and to the fact that the West in general, and the United States in particular, has had a strong influence on the IMF's policies. In this specific case, the IMF could not ignore that Volcker had praised the plan and promised direct U.S. support for Argentina's negotiations with private banks and the international financial institutions. Other explanations are based on the sheer size of Argentina's economy—one of the largest in Latin America. In countries with much smaller economies and relatively small foreign debts, such as Bolivia or Peru, as previously mentioned, the international financial community could afford to make certain financial concessions or be inflexible, depending on the circumstances, because the potential losses were minimal. In the case of Argentina, the losses could have been huge. In fact, the IMF's best possible course of action was to be flexible to ensure that Alfonsín's administration would continue to repay Argentina's debts.[58]

While these explanations are sound and practical, to fully understand the IMF's consistent flexibility toward Argentina and other debtor nations we must take into consideration its need and desire to preserve and entrench the routine of dependency. Indeed, the IMF's determination to steadily cultivate the ties among the members of the epistemic community of IMF and local technocrats as a way to influence the local scene has made the Fund more prone to forgo short-term goals to achieve long-term objectives. To be sure, the IMF's relations with its borrowers are not just the result of the interplay between its member states. Such relations are also fundamentally shaped by the fact that the Fund is a bureaucratic organization whose highly skilled staff has developed its own agenda. The IMF's staff is ready to compromise because compromises ensure the continued existence of the routine of dependency, and the routine of dependency in turn guarantees the IMF's survival. As Argentine President Néstor Kirchner declared in 2004, borrowing countries can live without the Fund, but without its borrowers, the Fund would lose its raison d'être.

During the first six months of implementation, the Austral Plan brought inflation down. However, it could not stabilize the economy more permanently. Despite its achievements, the program received harsh criticism. Diverse sectors of society, including the Sociedad Rural Argentina, the Argentine Industrial Union, the banking sector, and the combatant CGT labor federation, all pressed the government to revise the plan. From mid-1985 until January 1987, the CGT staged eight general strikes to protest the economic policy. In April 1986, Sourrouille announced a second phase of the Austral Plan, which was more moderate, gradual, and flexible than the first phase. Accordingly, the government authorized modest wage raises and a reduction of price controls. These measures, however, led to a new wave of inflation, an increase in the budget deficit, and deterioration in the balance of payments.[59] Still, the IMF was quite satisfied with the results.[60]

By early 1987, Alfonsín's political situation worsened when the CGT created an alliance with senior clergy of the Argentine Roman Catholic Church, which had opposed Alfonsín's initiative to legalize divorce. At the same time, the government's relations with the military deteriorated. Due to strong pressures exerted by the military and reactionary groups, the National Congress passed the *Ley de Punto Final* (Full Stop Law) on December 24, 1986, which stipulated the end of investigations and prosecution of members of the armed forces accused of crimes during the Dirty War. Alfonsín initially refused to approve the law, but the threat of a new coup left him no choice. After a series of military rebellions, Alfonsín made further concessions to the armed forces, increasing social discontent.[61] Nonetheless, as explained bellow, the social and political turmoil in Argentina did not alter the routine of dependency.

Keeping the Routine of Dependency Alive: New Economic Plans and More SBAs

Although post-1985 files at the IMF Archives are not yet open to researchers, several hints in public sources shed light on the working routine in the second half of Alfonsín's term. For instance, Article IV Consultations were held in Buenos Aires on August 28–September 20, 1985, and October 29–December 4, 1985. Also, Argentine officials made several visits to the IMF's headquarters between December 1985 and February 1986.[62] In March 1986, Argentina requested "IMF technical assistance in evaluating the effects of [the] recent tax reform package and determining the direction of future tax reform."[63] Most important, in May 1986, the IMF approved Argentina's request to extend the

SBA that was scheduled to expire on May 31, 1986, until June 30, 1986.[64] This short-term extension was very significant, as it allowed Argentina to withdraw funds that were still available under the framework of the previous stand-by.

During 1987, the economic situation began to fade again. On January 12, 1987, Sourrouille and José Luis Machinea, now president of the Central Bank, submitted a request to the IMF for an SBA totaling 1,113 million SDRs for a period of fifteen months. The request was based on "the magnitude of the economic effort that is being undertaken toward the consolidation of low inflation and economic growth, and on the financing needs that Argentina is facing."[65] The letter mentioned that the Argentine government intended to "enter into discussions with the international financial community to secure a restructuring of its debts and to obtain new external financing, and attaches great importance to assistance from the Fund in its efforts."[66] This was important, as Argentina's total external debt was expected to reach an exorbitant $51.5 billion by the end of the year, including obligations to the Fund.[67] But the only novelty in the situation—which also applies to the agreement signed in 1984—was that the commitments and conditions were so numerous that they were no longer an integral component of the letter of intent; instead, they were incorporated into a twelve-page "memorandum of understanding on economic policy." On January 29, 1987, Argentina was granted a CFF, and on February 23, 1987, the IMF approved the SBA.[68]

Toward late 1987, the Austral Plan became increasingly unsustainable as inflation resurged, reaching a monthly rate of 3 percent. In addition, the political situation worsened. On September 6, 1987, legislative elections were held. The Peronists won 41 percent of the votes and sixty seats in Congress, while the Radical Civic Union got only 37 percent of the votes and fifty-two seats. This defeat destroyed the last vestiges of self-confidence of a highly criticized government, set political opposition out of control, and led to regrettable economic measures under the umbrella of the Plan Primavera (Spring Plan) of August 1988–February 1989. Conditioned by the ongoing negotiations on Argentina's foreign debt, free collective wage bargaining, and tax revenues, the plan was designed to achieve electoral, rather than economic, objectives. Indeed, the most urgent need of the Alfonsinism at the time was to secure reasonable price stability until the elections in May 1989.[69] The plan consisted of a temporary understanding between the government and the Industrial Union regarding prices, a 30 percent increase in public utility tariffs, and a 12 percent devaluation of the austral. The plan ignored the agricultural sector and wage earners, and their outrage made the social and political situation even more volatile.

The plan did not help. In its first two months, the inflation rate remained at 42.5 percent, and Alfonsín was unable to obtain foreign financing for the plan's continuation. To make matters worse, in June 1988, the IMF declared that Argentina was not in compliance with the agreement and suspended all further disbursements. Deprived of the Fund's assistance and of private lending, Argentina looked to the World Bank as its only remaining source of international financing. Although James Baker had pushed the Bank to support Argentina while he served as treasury secretary, his resignation from the position in August to manage George W. Bush's presidential campaign led the World Bank to suspend its activity in Argentina in early 1989.[70] In addition, tax collection soon reached its lowest point in months, and the value of the dollar jumped 45 percent on the free market. Sourrouille resigned, and on March 31, 1989, was replaced by Juan Carlos Pugliese, a former minister of economy under President Illia.[71]

The presidential elections of May 14, 1989, took place in the midst of an economic and institutional crisis. The winner was the Peronist candidate, Carlos Saúl Menem, a lawyer and the governor of La Rioja Province. On May 29, Alfonsín declared a state of siege that lasted thirty days due to violent food riots that erupted in the cities of Rosario, Quilmes, Bernal, and San Miguel. These incidents, which caused fourteen deaths and hundreds of arrests, alongside an acute economic crisis and the disintegration of his political power, led President Alfonsín to resign on July 12, five months before his term expired.[72]

Alfonsín's entry into the Casa Rosada raised expectations that the return to democracy would be accompanied by an improvement in the economy and in the standard of living of those sectors of society that the previous dictatorship had left behind. However, the three economic programs that were launched under Alfonsín (Sourrouille's plan, the Austral Plan, and the Spring Plan) and supported by two SBAs (in December 1984 and February 1987) and two CFFs (in December 1984 and February 1988) failed to stabilize the economy.

While Alfonsín's electoral campaign had strong nationalist and anti-imperialist content, archival documents suggest that from the outset his regime was ambivalent and not as hostile toward the IMF as was Illia's government in the 1960s. In effect, even before taking office (or before discovering the real magnitude of the economic disaster), Alfonsín's economic team had contacted the IMF to assess its chances of being granted financial assistance. If we take into consideration these early contacts initiated by Argentina, followed by Alfonsín's failure to create a regional front to negotiate the foreign debt and the imminent debt repayments, the relatively quick accord with the IMF should not be surprising. Argentina surely needed financial support.

The lack of viable strategies to solve pressing economic problems while confronting upcoming debt repayments forced Alfonsín to sign controversial SBAs that carried serious political and social risks—and Alfonsín certainly paid the price. The IMF resorted to its traditional flexibility to provide Argentina with financial assistance and thereby maintain the routine of dependency. To be sure, after several years of little activity in the region, the IMF was ready to support even heterodox economic programs that deviated from its standard orthodox principles. As we shall see, Alfonsín's successor brought the alliance with the IMF to a new, and perhaps unexpected, high.

Menem and the Transformation of Argentina

When asked about the IMF's support of the massive privatizations that took place under Menem in a sometimes disorderly and even corrupt way, Claudio Loser, the Argentine who headed the IMF's Western Hemisphere Department from 1994 to November 2002, explained: "There was too much dogma and too little attention to how things were done. Because the ideological precepts were followed, nobody looked at the practical implementation. . . . Those were the predominant ideas [the Washington Consensus]. And Menem was totally sympathetic with them. He was, as had always been said, a model student."[73]

Menem's investiture on July 8, 1989, represented the first constitutional transfer of presidential power in Argentina since 1928. At the time, the anticipated monthly inflation rate was 200 percent; foreign exchange reserves were virtually exhausted; public sector spending was financed by printing currency; real wages were low; prices were high; and there was a deep recession in all non-export activities. This critical constellation, and especially the inflation, provided Menem with ample justification for implementing harsh economic measures.[74] As Kurt Weyland convincingly points out, Menem—as well as Fernando Collor de Mello in Brazil (1990–1992) and Alberto Fujimori in Peru (1990–2000)— learned from their predecessors' failure and used political populism to gain broad support and impose economic liberalism, which in turn strengthened their populist leadership. Thus, they pragmatically and effectively created a complex and counterintuitive connection between neopopulism and neoliberalism.[75]

After an electoral campaign plagued by vague promises of a "productive revolution" and a "*salariazo* (huge wage increase)," Menem's first term in office surprised many in Argentina, not only because of his extravagant personal style, but also because the economic policies he promoted were clearly at odds with traditional Peronist principles. Nonetheless, partially encouraged by the collapse of communism and the emergence of a unipolar world order under U.S. hegemony, Menem seemed to have abandoned old Peronist stands in the area of foreign relations, as well. With Menem in power, Argentina automatically aligned itself with Washington. Among other things, and breaking with its highly controversial neutrality, Argentina sent troops to the Gulf War, redesigned its policy on nuclear weapons, and, in 1991, left the Non-Aligned Movement.[76] As Vicente Palermo and Marcos Novaro argue, with Menemism, old dichotomies that had characterized Argentine politics and economics for decades—such as Peronism and anti-Peronism, statism and privatization, and nationalism and liberalism—seemed suddenly to become irrelevant.[77] But was this blurring of old concepts as sudden and unexpected as Palermo and Novaro maintain? Did the economic policies adopted by Menem carry important affinities with the "shock doctrine" advanced by Pinochet in Chile and with the so-called Fujishock that had been pursued by Alberto Fujimori in Peru since August 1990?[78] Is it possible to trace a line between Videla's and Menem's economic policies? Would it be inaccurate to describe Menem's neoliberal project as the corollary of a long-term process that some of his predecessors tried but could not fully implement? Based on what is generally known and on publications by key Argentine and IMF insiders, the following are some grounded speculations that emphasize the ongoing impact of the routine of dependency.

Menem and the Washington Consensus

By 1989, when Menem took office, Argentina was in a state of shock. It had experienced a traumatic Dirty War; it had lost the Malvinas (Falklands) War; and it had saw several episodes of hyperinflation—sometimes, such as during Alfonsín's term, triggering bloody social riots. These elements created an ideal situation for the application of what Menem described as a "major surgery without anesthetic,"[79] which inevitably brings to mind the shock treatment to which Naomi Klein refers to in *The Shock Doctrine*.[80] Moreover, the unprecedented political power Menem managed to concentrate significantly increased his capacity to implement fundamental reform in Argentina.[81] Despite the blank check he received from his voters, however, Menem's first months in office were characterized by confusion and inconsistency, especially in the economic realm. But through a series of key appointments and controversial measures, he (unlike most of his predecessors) soon secured the broad support and power needed to implement a wide-ranging reform of the state.[82]

The Menem decade can be divided roughly into two stages of a single process through which the last traces of statism and government intervention were eradicated and replaced with free-market policies and an increasingly influential private (national and foreign) sector. The Convertibility Law of Economic Minister Domingo Cavallo in 1991 was the watershed between two major phases of Argentina's transformation.[83]

During Menem's first year in office, three different economists took the reins at the Ministry of Economy. The first two, Miguel Ángel Roig (who died after a week in office) and Néstor Mario Rapanelli (later replaced by Antonio Erman González), were former vice-presidents of Bunge and Born, Argentina's largest multinational company, one of the biggest agribusinesses in the world, and a symbol of aristocratic power in the eyes of Peronists. These appointments, which brought key figures from the private sector into the centers of government power, were indicative of Menem's pro-market orientation and his desire to create an alliance with the business community. Another significant appointment that was even more appealing to right-wing sectors was that of Jorge Triaca as minister of labor. As the head of the Plastic Workers Union, Triaca had closely collaborated with the last dictatorship.[84] In December 1990, to consolidate his political leadership and on the pretext of national reconciliation, President Menem pardoned the leaders of the dictatorship of the 1970s who had been imprisoned during Alfonsín's presidency. This highly controversial step helped Menem obtain the support of the military and the most reactionary groups in society.[85]

Once Menem formed a multifaceted support base, he embarked on an ambitious project of state transformation that went far beyond the economic sphere. His project, as Loser has argued, was based on the emerging "Washington Consensus," a term coined in 1989 by the economist John Williamson to describe a set of economic policy prescriptions that the IMF, the World Bank, and the U.S. Treasury considered the standard reform package needed for crisis-wracked developing countries. These prescriptions included macroeconomic stabilization, economic opening in trade and investment, and the expansion of market forces within the domestic economy. Today, the term is commonly used to refer to a strongly market-based approach or neoliberalism.

In practical terms, the prescriptions of the Washington Consensus can be divided into three complementary categories. First, they call for reduction and revision of the economic role of the state. In that regard, Latin American governments are expected to exercise fiscal discipline; concentrate their resources not on social subsidies but on health, education, and infrastructure; and deregulate the economy, allowing market forces to operate without political or bureaucratic obstacles. Second, they support the private sector, which means that countries should sell state-owned enterprises and remove restrictions on foreign capital. Third, they call for Latin American governments to drastically revise trade policies, look outward for markets, reduce tariffs on trade, and eliminate protectionism.[86] As we shall see, Menem's administration followed these prescriptions religiously, not necessarily as a result of U.S. pressure, but because of its own convictions.

Argentina for Sale: Privatizations and the First Stand-by Arrangement of Menemism

When he took office, Menem, along with Minister of Public Works Norberto Dromi, outlined a plan "to reform the state and to transform the nation" based on the implementation of a "Popular Market Economy." The plan's main goals were national unity, realism, planning, participation, popular market economy, private initiative, conjectural state enterprise (in other words, the state would act as the main player in the business area or would complement private enterprise, according to changing circumstances), just and efficient public services, decentralization, and integrality.[87] As the plan stated, "*Popular economy,* because it rewards work, . . . guarantees social and distributive justice and safeguards the intervention, orientation, planning and promotion of the state as the guard of the common well-being. *Market economy,* because it guarantees economic freedom, recognizes private initiative, promotes competition, and demands efficiency."[88] In effect, Menem's administration assigned the state a key role in advancing a market economy.

The plan became a reality in August 1989, when the National Congress passed the State Reform Law. It authorized the executive to liquidate or privatize, partially or wholly, almost all public companies including (but not limited to) telecommunications, airlines, television and radio stations, gas, electricity, subways and railways, petrochemicals, and steel, as well as the federal highway system.[89] In September, the Administrative Emergency Law (known as the Dromi Law) was approved by Congress. It suspended all government subsidies for 180 days and, more important, allowed the executive to impose economic measures related to wages, taxes, and tariffs by decree.[90] That law paved the way for approximately 350 decrees related to privatization, deregulation, appointment of judges, and the right to strike. More than anything else, though, it led to an unprecedented concentration of power in the executive.[91]

These reforms, along with improvements in short-term macroeconomic imbalances, secured Menem the support of the IMF, the World Bank, and the Bush administration.[92] While details surrounding the interaction between the IMF and Menem's administration remain unclear because pertinent IMF documents have not been released, it seems that the first IMF mission arrived in Argentina in July 1989. The second arrived in September. In between, and later, Argentine representatives met with IMF officials in Washington. These frequent meetings were aimed at conducting the Article IV Consultation "in conjunction with discussions on an economic program that could be supported with a stand-by arrangement."[93] As became routine, and inevitably between ideological partners, the parties worked together on the details of an economic plan that Menem had envisioned on his own. The IMF applauded Menem's plans, especially the privatizations that would create "an environment in which markets function freely, which [would] involve the reduction of the scope of government regulations, including in particular those that limit competition from abroad. Thus, the import regime is to be liberalized and foreign direct investment is to be given the same treatment as domestic investment."[94] The IMF stated, "The government of Argentina has embarked on an ambitious macroeconomic program and far-reaching structural reforms. The staff welcomes the measures already taken by the authorities and believes that prompt Fund support for Argentina's program is essential for the resolution on Argentina's severe external payment difficulties."[95] After years of collaboration, therefore, a true alliance had finally emerged.

Encouraged by the IMF's stance, Rapanelli and Javier González Fraga, president of the Central Bank, submitted a request for an SBA on October 12.[96] The arrangement allowed Argentina to draw $1.57 billion (99.2 percent of its quota) until March 31, 1991. The memorandum on economic policy stipulated: "To deal with the deep-rooted imbalances of the economy, the Government has put in place a rigorous plan of structural and macroeconomic policy reforms, for which there is a great deal of social support in Argentina."[97] The strategy that had been adopted, it added, "involves the withdrawal of the state from activities that can be undertaken by the private sector."[98] The goal was to rapidly reduce the public sector deficit from 16 percent of the GDP in 1989 to 1.25 percent in 1990 and to reduce inflation to a monthly rate of less than 2 percent by the end of 1989 and further toward international levels by the end of 1990.[99]

In May 1990, a new IMF mission visited Argentina. Interestingly, the IMF's initial enthusiasm evaporated as the mission realized that Argentina was not following the plan as expected. In December 1989, the major problems were the growth of money supply and the fiscal deficit. The IMF's report indicated that "real wages remain low by historical standards and public and private sector unions have been staging work stoppages, slowdowns, and protests."[100] However, on the pretext that the results during the first months of the plan's implementation were good, the IMF finally agreed to approve several revisions to the SBA, especially in the fiscal area.[101]

Increasing social turmoil caused by the return of hyperinflation and disagreements among the official economic team led in December 1989 to the replacement of Rapanelli with Antonio Erman González, a Peronist who had served as vice-president of the Central Bank and worked with Menem when he was governor of La Rioja. On December 18, González announced the elimination of price controls and the free floating of the austral, a measure that aimed at completely freeing the foreign exchange market. Then, with the IMF's and U.S. support, and on the advice of Domingo Cavallo, González launched the so-called Plan Bonex that made obligatory the conversion of time deposits of more than 1 million australs (approximately $500 million), bank reserves in the Central Bank, and short-term government debt to ten-year dollar-denominated bonds (*bonos externos,* or BONEX), at an exchange rate of 1,830 australs per dollar. The BONEX would pay 9 percent interest per year.[102] This plan replaced most of the short-term, public-sector domestic debt with medium-term external debt.

Despite these efforts, the GDP declined by 2.7 percent during the first quarter of 1990, and the IMF temporarily suspended the release of funds to Argentina. It is important to understand that the BONEX had a serious social impact, as it denied depositors access to their savings. As if this were not enough, the plan failed to stop capital flight and to curb the inflation rate, which by February 1990 had reached 100 percent.[103] Overall, 1990 was challenging for Menem's administration, as it ended with a 2,000 percent annual inflation rate and a constantly soaring dollar exchange rate. At the same time, Argentina faced a coup attempt by Colonel Mohamed Ali Seineldín, the controversial pardons granted to the perpetrators of the previous dictatorship, and a series of corruption scandals. As we shall see, these internal problems, on the one hand, and the support of the international community (including President Bush's visit to Buenos Aires on December 5, 1990[104]), on the other, were the scenario for the second stage of transformation of Argentina's state and economy.

The Convertibility Plan: Economic Stability at All Costs

In February 1991, Menem called Cavallo, his minister of foreign affairs since 1989, to replace Erman González as minister of economy. When Cavallo took office, privatizations had been proceeding so quickly that by October 1990, almost all of the companies mentioned in Dromi's plan were already out of state hands. Until 1991, many privatizations were done with a profound sense of urgency, and some state-owned companies were sold at rock-bottom prices and with little or no regulation (paving the way for private monopolies). However, Cavallo conducted the final phases of privatization more carefully.[105]

On April 1, 1991, after eighteen months of rampant inflation, Cavallo launched the Convertibility Plan, which stipulated free convertibility of the austral into U.S. dollars at an exchange rate of 10,000 australs to the dollar, fully backed by foreign exchange reserves. The plan had three basic features: it established the convertibility system in law; it abolished price indexation; and it allowed contracts to be denominated in foreign currencies and foreign currencies to be used as alternative means of payment.[106] In other words, it paved the way for the *dollarization* of the economy.

Initially, few people believed the plan could succeed. However, the initial results were encouraging: inflation dropped to single-digit rates in 1993; prices stabilized almost overnight; and the index of real GDP rose by 28 percent cumulatively between 1990 and 1993. The plan created confidence at home and abroad and attracted large inflows of capital. In addition, as Cavallo indicated, "The IMF, under pressure from the U.S. government (since the Fund did not support the Convertibility Plan), started to cooperate with the implementation and financing of the program."[107] In effect, in June 1991 the IMF approved an SBA for 780 million SDRs, which was replaced in March 1992 by an Extended Fund Facility (EFF) of 2.438 million SDRs (or 161 percent of quota). This assistance paved the way to debt-relief agreements under the Brady Plan—agreements that would be in place on a permanent basis for years, even after the end of Menem's second mandate. In this respect, it should be emphasized that the EFF was extended in December 1992 and in December 1993, and again in April 1995, as part of the IMF's response to the Mexican Crisis of 1994. In early 1996, when it was no longer possible to renew the EFF, the IMF suggested that Argentina apply for a new SBA. On March 14, 1996, Cavallo sent a formal request to Managing Director Michel Camdessus, and the arrangement was approved on April 12, 1996. This SBA ended on January 11, 1998, and on February 4, 1998, it was replaced by an EFF that was in effect until March 10, 2000.[108]

Overall, the Convertibility Plan reduced inflation. With the help of capital inflows, it stabilized the economy and led to a brief economic boom. However, this rosy picture did not last long. When the Mexican Crisis of December 1994 erupted, it spread to Argentina. The banking system lost 18 percent of its deposits in three months; credit contracted, leading to an increase in unemployment. In the second quarter of 1995, Argentina once again entered a recession.[109]

It was in this atmosphere of crisis that the presidential elections of May 14, 1995, took place. Menem (who had reformed the constitution to allow incumbent presidents to be run) was reelected by almost 50 percent of the votes. There are at least two complementary explanations for these results. The first is that the reelection was an expression of support for Menem's reforms. The second is that it was the fear of economic instability that helped Menem to get reelected, the notion being that the president and his team were the most capable officials to lead the economy at times of uncertainty.[110] And, of course, one cannot ignore the roughly 50 percent of the voters who did not want Menem to be reelected. It is reasonable to assume that among these opponents were not only anti-Peronists, but also citizens who had suffered—directly or indirectly—the social cost of neoliberalism. In effect, Menem's reforms included restricting workers' rights, dismantling the public health system and public education, and increasing inequality, as well as the number of people living below the poverty line. As early as December 1993, serious riots had erupted in Santiago del Estero and La Rioja during protests by public employees against Menem's economic policy and government corruption.[111] In mid-1995, none other than Minister of Economy Cavallo publicly denounced the influence of mafias in the government sphere and the lack of transparency of Menem's administration.[112] Obviously, these serious charges reflected growing tension between Cavallo and Menem, which led to the president's decision to appoint the ultraliberal Roque Fernández as minister of economy during his second term instead of reappointing Cavallo.[113]

Menem's second term witnessed growing discontent with neoliberalism in Argentina. Even as the national economy recovered relatively from the recession provoked by the Mexican Crisis, the growth did not return to the levels of Menem's first term. In addition, Argentines began to protest more massively the impact of neoliberalism, especially the stagnation of real wages, increasing unemployment (which reached about 19 percent in 1995 and 14 percent in 1999), and high poverty levels. As Argentina's foreign debt increased, especially during Menem's second term, the national production underwent a deep process of de-Argentinization. Alongside the privatization of the gas and electric utilities, as well as the state-owned oil company YPF, foreign investors bought more than four hundred well-known Argentine firms in a wide variety of industries, including Terrabusi, Ginebra Bols, Baglei, Fargo, Musimundo, El Ateneo, Alfajores Havanna, Hotel Libertador, Jardín de la Paz, Noblex, and Villavicencio. A similar process took place in banking, where foreign investors acquired a host of small and provincial banks.[114]

Interestingly, even as Argentines grew skeptical about Menem's ability to keep the economy growing, the international financial community and the IMF continued to praise him. Many people recall Menem's invitation to give a speech at the annual meeting of governors of the IMF and World Bank in Washington in October 1998. The Argentine press emphasized how exceptional the invitation was, calling it a sign of the international financial community's support for Menem's policies.[115] Menem's speech surprised Latin American representatives by completely overlooking the regional agenda and instead responding to U.S. President Bill Clinton's call to increase the IMF's funds in light of the crisis then under way in Asia.[116] Menem focused on "the keys to achieving this absolute economic miracle [of Argentina's economy]" and went on to say, "We worked side by side with the IMF, the World Bank, and the IDB to achieve macroeconomic stability, deepen structural reforms, and adopt policies aimed at improving the economic fortunes of the poorest members of society."[117]

The de-Argentinization of the economy, the impoverishment of millions of Argentines, and the recurrent scandals and cases of corruption all combined to increase the already mounting resentment toward Menem's administration and neoliberalism. The losses Peronism suffered in the parliamentary election of 1997, and its defeat in the presidential elections of 1999, verified this resentment. After a decade of deep structural reforms, a large number of Argentines were once again looking for a new economic strategy.

To sum up, Menem took office six years after the return to democracy, when Argentina was still trying to recover from traumatic events. Unlike Alfonsín, whose political power had gradually eroded, Menem benefited from the Peronist majority in the National Congress, the weakness of the discredited radical opposition following the poor economic results of Alfonsín's administration, and his own ability to consolidate a comprehensive base of support. Ironically, Menem used this extraordinary support not to apply traditional Peronist policies, as most of his voters and political rivals had probably expected, but to relinquish the nationalism and statism that were so deeply rooted in Argentina. There is no doubt that Menem's political and economic break with the Peronism of the 1940s–1950s and of the 1970s was also propelled by an international context marked by the collapse of communism and the emergence of the Washington Consensus. In this respect, it is important to note that Menem's adherence to the Washington Consensus was self-reinforcing: It provided him with the full support of the United States and the IMF, which in turn facilitated the deepening of neoliberal reforms.

Menem's administration may not have needed the IMF to impose its liberalization measures: The president was determined to adopt a market economy anyway. Menem appears to have been interested in the IMF's (and Washington's) seal of approval to gain recognition from not only the international community but also the business community at home. The IMF did not disappoint Menem. Although the extent to which the IMF was blind to the messy and sometimes harmful way in which Menem's reforms (especially the privatizations) were conducted, one cannot but assume that some of the technocrats were at least partly aware of the situation in Argentina and feared the potential economic and social consequences of such deep and fast transformation. If, as Claudio Loser testified, he and others in his department tried to convince the Executive Board to reconsider its support of Menem's regime, it would not be unreasonable to imagine two main scenarios. In the first scenario, the IMF was indeed consciously and deliberately oblivious (as Loser's quote at the opening of this section indicates) because it prioritized dogma over economic performance. In the second, and not necessarily contradictory, scenario, some at the IMF did realize that the situation in Argentina was too risky, but they could not turn off the engines of the routine of dependency because a new economic crisis in Argentina would certainly be perceived as an IMF failure coming on the heels of the crises in Mexico and Asia. In other words, the IMF could not let its model student fail. This notion of the IMF being trapped in a situation that it helped create seems to be confirmed by the Fund's (perhaps irrational) support of Menem's successor, Fernando de la Rúa, and of the nation's sinking economy.

From Routine of Dependency to Routine of Detachment: De la Rúa and Kirchner

De la Rúa, a politician who had taught criminal law at the University of Buenos Aires and served as an adviser to the Ministry of Internal Affairs under President Illia, won the elections in October 24, 1999, with 48.4 percent of the votes. He took office as president on December 10. From the outset, de la Rúa lacked the political power needed to successfully confront the economic and social crisis that hit Argentina. Like Alfonsín, de la Rúa was a minority president, as the Senate was dominated by Peronists. In addition, although de la Rúa belonged to the Radical Civic Union, he had never been the party's leader. He was elected as the candidate of the Alianza, a left-center electoral coalition created in 1994 from the old Radical Civic Union and the Front for a Country in Solidarity (FREPASO), which he did not organize or coordinate.[118]

De la Rúa inherited from Menem skyrocketing foreign debt, reduced access to financing, a $7.2 billion fiscal deficit, and, as he stated publicly, a serious social and moral deficit.[119] Paradoxically, de la Rúa intended to solve these problems by applying the very same policies that Menem had pursued. He maintained the Convertibility Law and tried to embark on new structural reforms. In this sense, he chose a path that was incompatible with his promise to "break out from a time in which the government turned a cold shoulder to the people."[120] In fact, one of the first steps that he and Economic Minister José Luis Machinea (who had served as president of the Central Bank under Alfonsín) took was to raise taxes to solve the deficit problem.[121]

The *impuestazo* (huge tax increases) was not enough. The deficit continued to increase. Steeped in debt, Argentina once again turned to the IMF, hat in hand, hoping that new loans (and more debt) would cure its chronic ills of inflation, deficit, and debt repayment. The IMF, it seems, shared those hopes and made significant efforts to save its star pupil. On March 10, 2000, it approved a three-year SBA of $7.2 billion (255 percent of Argentina's quota). The arrangement emphasized tax reform, spending cuts, renewal of structural reform, and maintenance of the Convertibility Law.[122] Nevertheless, on May 2000, de la Rúa admitted that the deficit had failed to reach the levels agreed on with the Fund.[123] The same month, to reduce public spending, Machinea launched a plan that in practice deepened Menem's reforms and involved reorganizing the state bodies responsible for, among other things, pensions, health, education, taxes, and social insurance.[124]

It was also in May that the recently elected managing director of the IMF, the German economist Horst Köhler, accompanied by several high-ranking IMF officials (including the Argentine Claudio Loser), visited Argentina and other Latin American countries. On May 16, Köhler met with de la Rúa, Machinea and his advisers, and the President Pedro Pou of the Central Bank. During a press conference, Köhler stated: "The policy applied in Argentina is the correct one, and the economic program is evolving well."[125] When de la Rúa begged Köhler to take into consideration Argentina's social problems, Köhler responded that the measures adopted by the government (especially the *impuestazo*) were crucial to increasing investors' confidence.[126]

Soon after the IMF officials' visit, and in light of the ongoing economic and social crisis, de la Rúa launched an austerity plan that, as had been promised to the IMF, would reduce the budget deficit from $6.5 billion to $4.5 billion. The strategy consisted of a drastic cut in public spending, a 12 percent reduction in salaries for public employees, the elimination of labor benefits, tax increases (affecting especially the middle classes), and other measures. There is no doubt that these steps exacted a high social price and therefore disappointed de la Rúa's voters. According to a detailed account by Michael Mussa, who served as economic counselor and director of the IMF's Research Department in 1999–2001, the IMF was extremely concerned as the recession deepened, the fiscal deficit continued to grow, and default on Argentina's sovereign debt became possible.[127] Despite the growing worries, however, the heads of the IMF, as well as of the World Bank and the IDB, publicly backed the measures Machinea announced.[128]

By November, it had become clear that Argentina once again would not be able to meet its deficit target. The IMF could have used this as an excuse to suspend its financial assistance, but instead, during November–December 2000, intensive negotiations were held by Argentina, the Fund, and private banks to assemble a package aimed at helping the country reduce its growing debt burden and avoid a dangerous crisis of confidence. On January 12, 2001, the IMF approved an increase to the SBA first approved on March 2000 to about $14 billion, or an astonishing 500 percent of Argentina's quota. In addition, Argentina was granted supplementary financing from the World Bank, IDB, Spain, and commercial banks.[129] The package, which totaled $39.7 billion, was the largest rescue effort by the IMF since it had shored up Brazil in 1998 at the end of the Asian Crisis.[130]

The unavoidable question is: Why did the IMF continue to support Argentina? First, as shown in previous chapters, only in very few cases did the Fund suspend its financial assistance to Argentina. In addition, as Mussa argues, "For a country of the importance of Argentina that was making some constructive efforts to address its policy deficiencies, it would have been unusual—but not unprecedented—for the Fund to announce publicly a suspension of its support."[131] In other words, at this stage, both Argentina and the IMF seemed to be trapped in a vicious circle of mounting loans, debts, and unresolved economic problems. There is no doubt that the economic and political risks of economic collapse were too high, not only for Argentina, but also for the IMF. Although it cannot be supported by documentation, it is sound to presume that the commercial banks, which tried to avert a situation in which Argentina stopped repaying its debts, also played a role in the IMF's decision to continue to support a drowning debtor.

In return for the agreement signed in January 2001, Argentina once again committed to balancing its budget and reducing the fiscal deficit. Perhaps the message that Argentina and the IMF wanted to convey more than anything else was that Argentina would continue to honor its debts. Nonetheless, investors soon showed their reluctance to return to Argentina.[132] In light of his failure to solve the economic and political crisis, Machinea was replaced on March 5 by the economist Ricardo López Murphy, a University of Chicago graduate. The new minister intended to proceed with the reforms accorded with the Fund. In addition, he insisted on the privatization of the Banco Nación and on other contentious measures to reduce the deficit, including the implementation of tuition fees at public universities.[133] As could be expected, López Murphy's adjustment plan brought social protest, reinforced political opposition, and aggravated tension within the Alianza. On March 19, after merely two weeks in office, he was replaced by Cavallo, whose appointment was perceived by Argentines as a last-ditch attempt to resume the reforms initiated by Menem.[134]

Once in office, Cavallo secured parliamentary approval for wide-ranging special emergency powers of the president to enact economic measures by decree (as in Menem's term). He soon introduced a financial transactions tax, which was gradually increased and intended to raise tax revenues. From the beginning, it was clear that this and other measures aimed at promoting growth and attracting investment were not enough to meet the goals stipulated in the SBA. Aware of the situation, the IMF sent a new mission to Argentina in mid-April and finally modified the fiscal deficit target for the second quarter of 2001.[135]

As the economic situation continued to deteriorate, Cavallo took several unilateral steps, apparently without consulting with the IMF. In mid-April, he made a sudden change in the Convertibility Plan: Rather than being pegged at parity to the U.S. dollar, the peso would instead be pegged 50 percent to the dollar and 50 percent to the euro. Then he found a pretext to replace his opponent Pedro Pou as president of the Central Bank. Most important, Cavallo initiated a mega-swap (*mega-canje*) of the foreign debt. The effect of the swap was to exchange about $30 billion of the face value of existing Argentine sovereign debt for new sovereign obligations. Interests and payments due between 2001 and 2005 were reduced by the swap, at the expense of substantially higher interest and payments due over the next twenty-five years.[136] The IMF considered the mega-swap a serious risk to Argentina's economy because in effect it only postponed (as opposed to solved) the repayment of debts. However, the Fund publicly supported Cavallo's move,[137] and the mega-swap was completed in June.

In July 2001, Cavallo tried a new strategy known as the Zero-Deficit Plan, under which the federal deficit would be eliminated completely by August 2001.[138] In August, Cavallo announced that the results of the plan were mixed, but he remained optimistic. Despite—or perhaps because of—the ongoing crisis and the increasing worries among IMF economists, the IMF increased the existing SBA with Argentina by $8 billion on August 21.[139] The revenues continued to fall.[140] When on September 7 it became quite certain that Argentina was on the brink of an economic meltdown, the IMF, as had become routine, approved an increase of $7 billion (to about $22 billion) of the SBA initially approved in March 2001.[141]

The parliamentary and provincial elections of October 14, 2001, in which the Peronist party was the big winner, ended de la Rúa's chances to implement a new economic plan. Cavallo had no choice but to request debt rescheduling. In November, as de la Rúa continued to lose support, Cavallo announced his intention to visit the IMF's headquarters to discuss further disbursements, but the Fund responded that he would not be received by the staff. One can just imagine that at the time, the IMF began to seriously reconsider its policy not only toward Cavallo but toward Argentina's economy in general.

In late November, Argentine banks were losing about $1 billion per day. Investors and ordinary citizens were trying to get away from the risks related to an imminent devaluation of the peso. Then, in an unprecedented and traumatic move known as the *corralito* (small corral), the government closed the banks and announced that when they reopened, withdrawals would be limited to $250 a week.[142] This desperate attempt to avoid a run on the banks, along with profound popular discontent after three years of recession and more than 20 percent unemployment, led to widespread riots.[143] The chaos also led to Cavallo's resignation. On December 20, 2001, after violent demonstrations that were brutally repressed by the police, leaving twenty-five people dead and hundreds wounded around the country, de la Rúa, devastated by the social and economic crisis and devoid of political support, resigned.[144]

The Routine of Detachment: The Beginning of the End?

De la Rúa was replaced by Senator Ramón Puerta, who served as the interim president until Adolfo Rodríguez Saá, the Peronist governor of San Luis Province, took office. In his inaugural speech, Rodríguez Saá announced that Argentina would not repay the $18 million that was due the following day; Argentina thus went into default on December 24.[145] After barely a week in office, Rodríguez Saá resigned. In January 2002, the Peronist Senator Eduardo Duhalde was appointed by the Legislative Assembly to serve as president until December 2003. At his inauguration, he declared: "The [neoliberal] project failed. . . . Argentina is in bankruptcy."[146]

Duhalde soon ratified the default on most of the public debt and revoked the Convertibility Law. He appointed the heterodox and pragmatic economist Jorge Remes Lenicov, a member of the Peronist party since the 1970s, as minister of economy; Remes Lenicov devalued the peso, retained the *corralito,* and forged the *pesification* of the economy, thereby reversing the previous dollarization.[147] Most notably, Remes Lenicov attempted to negotiate a new rescue package from the IMF. During a visit to Washington, he said, "The story with the Fund is like in ancient times when people said that all roads lead to Rome. Today, all roads lead to the IMF. . . . [A]ll of our allies tell . . . us to go to the Fund."[148] But the road to the IMF was longer than expected. It was only on January 17, 2003, after a year of negotiations, that the Fund approved an SBA of about $2.9 billion for eight months to cover Argentina's payment obligations through August 2003. It also agreed to extend for a year the repayment of an additional $3.7 billion that would be owed to the IMF by August.[149] Simply put, Argentina was granted new loans to repay its previous loans. In addition, it is not unreasonable to suggest that this loan helped to create the relative stability that was needed to facilitate the transition to a new elected government.

The Entrenchment of the Routine of Detachment:
The Kirchner Era

Presidential elections took place on April 27, 2003, ending an electoral campaign marked by economic crisis and social turmoil (and with $178 billion in debts). Of the seven presidential contenders, three belonged to different factions of the Peronist movement: former presidents Carlos Saúl Menem and Adolfo Rodríguez Saá and Governor Néstor Kirchner of Santa Cruz Province. Kirchner generally adhered to a social democratic discourse that differentiated him from Menem and de la Rúa. Menem won the elections but with only 24.4 percent of the votes (much less than the majority stipulated by Argentine law). Consequently, a second round of elections was needed. Menem withdrew from the second round, however, and Kirchner, who had won only 22.2 percent of the votes in the first round, was nominated as president. Kirchner worked with three ministers of economy. The first, Roberto Lavagna, had held the same position under President Héctor Cámpora in the 1970s, as well as under Alfonsín and Duhalde. In November 2005, without a clear explanation, Lavagna was replaced by Felisa Miceli, a former student of his and, at the time, president of the Central Bank. In July 2007, facing suspicion of scandal and corruption, Miceli resigned and was replaced by Miguel Peirano. In any event, the press and the public felt that economic ministers (except perhaps, Lavagna) played a secondary role in the new government, because Kirchner administered the economy himself.[150]

It is important to understand that when Kirchner entered the Casa Rosada, disillusionment with pro-market reforms was widespread throughout Latin America. Neoliberal governments that had taken power in the 1990s were being replaced with different types of leftist (or, in some cases, neopopulist) governments—for example, those of Hugo Chávez in Venezuela (1998), Lula da Silva in Brazil (2002), Lucio Gutiérrez (2002) and Rafael Correa (2006) in Ecuador, Tabaré Vázquez in Uruguay (2004), Evo Morales in Bolivia (2005), and Alan García in Peru (2006).

In sharp contrast to the sense of confusion that characterized Menem's first months in office and the constant vacillation of de la Rúa, Kirchner took several immediate and visible steps. He cashiered the top commanders of the armed forces, began the process of impeaching the Supreme Court, reorganized the Federal Police, and reopened intelligence files on the bombing of the Argentine Israelite Mutual Association's building in 1992, which had been suspiciously sealed by Menem. He showed the same determination in the economic arena, and his measures drastically reduced poverty and unemployment. In June 2003, the managing director of the IMF visited Argentina to meet personally with Kirchner and publicly admitted that Argentina's economy was recovering without the IMF's intervention.[151] Paradoxically, the fact that Argentina was in default placed Kirchner in a relatively privileged bargaining position vis-à-vis the IMF, as the international financial community was eager to put its books in order.

At the annual meeting of Board of Governors of the IMF and World Bank on September 22, 2003, the IMF announced that it had agreed to make a $12.5 billion emergency loan available to Argentina. This accord, which deferred repayments of debt to multilateral institutions until after 2006, was innovative because it had no attached conditions, and the IMF did not consult commercial banks while negotiating it.[152] The actual details of the negotiations are uncertain, but they appear to reflect a shift in how discussions with the Fund are conducted and, perhaps, in the balance of power between the parties. Instead of punishing Argentina for the longest default in history, the IMF provided unconditional financial assistance. Kirchner, in fact, appears to have found an ingenious formula that allowed Argentina to use IMF funds without the complete routine of dependency that was part and parcel of conditional lending.

Kirchner was indeed determined to change Argentina's power relations with the IMF without letting the economic asymmetry between the parties turn into political asymmetry. In March 2004, in a move that inevitably brings to mind Alfonsín's efforts to create a debtors' cartel, Kirchner recruited the support of President Lula of Brazil, President Ricardo Lagos of Chile, and José Luis Rodríguez Zapatero, the recently elected socialist prime minister of Spain, in demanding that the IMF stipulate fiscal targets that would not be detrimental to economic growth and that would not lead to cuts in public spending on infrastructure.[153] Moreover, Kirchner often attacked the IMF in public. In July 2004, when referring to the alleged self-criticism of the Fund in relation to Argentina's collapse in 2001, he stated that the IMF's mistakes had driven 15 million Argentines below the poverty line.[154] In September 2005, after the agreement signed between the parties in early 2004 was revoked, Kirchner harshly criticized the IMF in a speech at the United Nations, at which Rodrigo de Rato of Spain, the new managing director of the IMF, also was present.[155] In that speech, Kirchner demanded that the Fund revise its policies in Latin America.

Tensions between Kirchner's administration and the IMF increased as the Fund expected Argentina to restructure its debt and embark on structural reforms. During a visit to Germany in April 2005, Kirchner warned: "I received an Argentina devastated by an economic program supported by the IMF, [but] there is life after the IMF, and it's a very good life. . . . Being in the embrace of the IMF isn't exactly like being in heaven."[156] It did not take long for Kirchner to translate his words into action. On December 13, 2005, Brazil announced that it would repay its entire debt of $15.5 billion due to the IMF over the next two years. The timing of this announcement derived largely from President Lula's need to gain the support of leftist groups in the coming presidential elections in Brazil as rumors of corruption in his administration were circulating. Two days later, Kirchner declared that Argentina would repay $9.8 billion to the Fund. This would save Brazil $900 million and Argentina $842 million in interest payments.[157]

To sum up, a combination of factors facilitated Kirchner's drastic and defiant detachment from the IMF—a detachment that only Arturo Illia had been willing and able to implement before him and that his widow, Cristina Fernández de Kirchner, who succeeded him as president, maintains. These factors included broad political support at home; favorable internal and external economic conditions; the capability of creating an anti-IMF alliance with other Latin American debtors; and increasing criticism of the IMF, globalization, and neoliberalism, even in Washington, with Joseph Stiglitz as one of the key intellectual mentors of this process. The detachment initiated in the early 2000s by a large number of Latin American nations is indeed still in place today.

Conclusion

The years after 1983 witnessed deep transformations in Latin America in general, and in Argentina in particular. In effect, the so-called lost decade was characterized by economic crises, on the one hand, and transition to stable democracies, on the other. Despite what in retrospect seems to have been unrealistic expectations, the transition to democracy did not necessarily move forward hand in hand with a transition to economic stability and growth. Thus, administrations that were responsible for reinstalling democracy in the region paved the way for new democratic regimes looking for new economic horizons. Indeed, in the 1990s, echoing worldwide trends, most Latin American nations embarked on economic liberalization. To a certain extent, that process resumed the liberalization that had been promoted by military rulers in the 1970s, but it took it several steps further. The 1990s marked the final abandonment of the import-substitution industrialization models that had been implemented in the region over decades, along with the full implementation of market reforms that changed the economic and social fabric of several countries. At the dawn of the twenty-first century, Latin American nations, disenchanted with neoliberalism, began to look for new, homemade economic strategies. These strategies, so far, include flat refusals to restore the demanding and overwhelming joint working routine with the IMF.

The Argentine case definitely reflects—and, at times, even shapes—the processes that have been under way at the regional level. In the 1980s, Raúl Alfonsín became Argentina's first democratically elected president after a particularly brutal and devastating military regime. However, his heterodox economic plans, which aimed to reverse some of the policies implemented by the previous regime, fell short of solving the country's acute economic and social problems. Inflation and the burden of a contentious and astronomical foreign debt not only led to Alfonsín's gradual shift to orthodoxy, but it also endangered the very existence of his regime. When Carlos Saúl Menem became president in 1989, Argentina was still trying to heal the wounds inflicted by the dictatorship and by the economic crisis that had erupted at the end of Alfonsín's term. Instead of adhering to nationalist, statist, and anti-imperialist Peronist precepts, as could be expected, Menem embarked on a liberalization process that transformed not only the economy but also the state as a whole. Unlike his Peronist predecessors, Menem aligned himself with the U.S. administration and became a poster boy for neoliberalism. By implementing the prescriptions of the Washington Consensus, Menem carried out the deepest de-Argentinization of the Argentine economy in history, thereby creating a new model of integration in a global neoliberal order. At the same time that Argentina was privatizing its state-owned companies and natural resources, transferring them in most cases into foreign hands, millions of suffered the consequences of extreme neoliberalism. Certainly, an unthinkable 54 percent of Argentines found themselves living below the poverty line and half of them below the indigence line.

The massive, hurried, disordered, corrupt, and often violent ways in which the market reforms were implemented may have be a main factor behind Menem's defeat in the presidential elections of 1999, in which he hoped to be reelected for a third consecutive term. Fernando de la Rúa, the winner, replaced Menem as president and raised hopes for change not only in the economy but also in the management of national institutions. Like Illia and Alfonsín before him, de la Rúa was considered an exceptionally honest and decent politician. Unfortunately, though, he was unable to gain broad political support and soon found himself in the midst of a dangerous social and economic crisis that led him to resign. After months of political instability and default, Kirchner was elected president. He seems to have been determined to differentiate himself from Menemism, Alfonsinism, and the inefficacy of de la Rúa. His reproaching of the IMF reached an unprecedented level when he, along with other presidents in the region, unilaterally decided to repay all of the country's debts to that institution and put an end to—or, at least, diminish—the routine of dependency.

Strikingly, throughout the years clouded by economic and mounting social problems, the IMF had been deeply involved in Argentina. While the real scale of the Fund's involvement since the mid-1980s remains a mystery waiting to be revealed, from the return to democracy in 1983 until 2003, Argentina signed nine agreements with the IMF for a total of about $40 billion. To be sure, throughout these tumultuous years—as was the case after 1956—Argentina's economy has been under close surveillance by the IMF. This has been true not only in periods in which Argentina has followed the IMF's advice to the letter, but also when it has applied economic programs that have had little in common with IMF policies and that the Fund could have used as a pretext for withdrawing from the collapsing country. But the IMF—in some cases under strong pressure by the United States—decided to keep providing financial and technical assistance to Argentina. It is true that Argentina's economy has always been too large to be allowed to fail; but it is also true that the IMF was never interested in completely stopping the routine of dependency. To put it simply, when it comes to Argentina, not only the IMF's prestige, but also its very existence, was as stake.

Conclusions

For millions of Latin American citizens, as well as for a legion of scholars and politicians in the region and around the world, IMF–Latin American relations are synonymous with intrusive conditional loan agreements, skyrocketing debt, and imposed economic liberalization. This is perhaps why academic research has focused almost exclusively on the economic aspects of these relations. In contrast with this traditional approach, this book focuses on the unexplored, "intimate" aspects of the relationship between the IMF and its borrowers. In doing so, it reveals what I term the "routine of dependency"—a dependency that goes beyond the size of the loans and debts accumulated by borrowing states to account for more comprehensive and nuanced processes. The "routine of dependency" is composed of a wide spectrum of activities and interactions—including the dispatch of detailed weekly reports from national central banks to IMF headquarters, visits by borrowing countries' presidents and ministers to Washington, the periodic arrival of IMF missions and high-ranking officials in the capital cities of borrowing countries, and, at certain times, the permanent presence of IMF representatives in governments' most influential economic institutions—all these activities and interactions continue even when no loan agreements are in effect.

By uncovering the array of nearly permanent, behind-the-scenes interactions and mechanisms that have emerged as a core component of both borrowers' and the IMF's daily existence, this book challenges several old truisms and conventional dichotomies that have shaped our perception of IMF–Latin American relations. Indeed, contrary to the common wisdom that portrays Latin American borrowers as passive, inefficient, easily manipulated, and even childish or corrupt clients of an omnipotent and imperialist IMF, this book highlights the mutual, though asymmetrical, nature of relationships between equally active and sovereign parties.

As I have argued, all of the parties to the routine of dependency are guided not only by economic considerations, but also by ideological, political, bureaucratic, and propagandist motives. One of the main implications of this perspective is that the routine of dependency is not God-given. As several Latin American nations clearly demonstrated by repaying their debts to the IMF in full in late 2005 and early 2006, and as several leaders in the region have proved by initiating temporary episodes of detachment from the Fund, countries do have the mandate and capability to regulate the intensity of their joint working routine with the IMF.

To fully understand the making and institutionalization of the routine of dependency, including the pendulum swings between periods of harmonious and intense activity and temporary episodes of partial detachment, this book had analyzed IMF–Latin American relations from their starting point at the Bretton Woods Conference of July 1944 to the widespread debt repayments in 2005. As I have argued, Latin American nations, which had been seeking alternatives to the United States as a source of funding since the 1930s, joined the IMF and the World Bank with great expectations. However, their hopes soon vanished. Latin American nations were not only relegated to secondary roles during the founding of the IMF and World Bank; they were also given inferior voting power in the first international institutions to reject the "one country–one vote" principle. The U.S. government's decision to exclude the neutral Argentina from the fortunate group of original members of the Bretton Woods institutions deprived the region as a whole of the chance to gain influence in the management of these multilateral organizations.

Latin America's asymmetrical relations with the IMF began to gestate at Bretton Woods in 1944. The generation of the routine of dependency, however, coincided with the launching of the IMF's financial activities in the region— namely, with the granting of the first stand-by arrangement to a Latin American nation, Peru, in 1954. The scope and significance of this routine, as both an analytical tool and a real behind-the-scenes mechanism, can be wholly understood only when it is followed year by year, day by day, loan by loan, and interaction by interaction. I put the intriguing case of Argentina under the magnifying glass to show how critical the mechanisms that constitute the routine of dependency are to the IMF's own functioning and survival and to reveal patterns that are common to the Fund's interactions not only with Argentina, but also with other borrowers.

My detailed examination of IMF–Argentine relations has revealed findings that are often surprising and even counterintuitive. First, managing the country's relations with the IMF has been a top priority on the agenda of every single Argentine president since 1944. This is true both for presidents who signed loan agreements with the Fund and for those who, for whatever reasons, did not request or use the IMF's financial assistance. Even President Juan Domingo

Perón, invariably described in the literature as the archenemy of the IMF, made considerable and systematic efforts to gain entry for Argentina into the Bretton Woods institutions. President Cristina Fernández de Kirchner provides a striking example of the high intensity that an exceptionally partial, malfunctioning, and tense joint working routine with the IMF can reach in the absence of valid loan agreements and debts. In fact, during the past few years, Argentina has had no choice but to reactivate part of its collaboration with the Fund as a precondition for negotiating debt rescheduling with the Paris Club.

Second, close examination of the Argentine case seems to corroborate the IMF's claim (which is problematic in itself) that it is determined to adhere to economic neutrality by not discriminating by types of regimes. A look at the long list of presidents who have signed loan agreements with the IMF shows that the routine of dependency has never been the exclusive patrimony of a certain political party or regime. As soon as an administration expresses its intention (not necessarily its willingness or capability) to adopt IMF-backed stabilization and adjustment plans—or, in other words, as soon as an administration makes an ideological turn toward liberalism—the IMF is ready to open loan negotiations. As I have shown, Arturo Frondizi, who came to power through free elections and subscribed to developmentalism, signed the first conditional IMF loan to Argentina in 1958. The transitional and authoritarian government of President General Juan Onganía approved another SBA in 1967. A new loan agreement, in 1977, was negotiated during the administration of General Jorge R. Videla, who became de facto president and led one of the cruelest dictatorships Argentina ever experienced. Videla's liberal and orthodox economic minister, José Alfredo Martínez de Hoz, signed SBAs that not only considerably increased the burden of the foreign debt but also significantly strengthened the ideological and strategic alliance with the IMF and the international financial community.

With Argentina's return to democracy in 1983, leaders from a variety of political and ideological backgrounds signed SBAs. Raúl Alfonsín, the head of the Radical Civic Union, was granted IMF loans within the binding framework of SBAs in 1984 and 1987. Carlos Saúl Menem, an atypical Peronist leader, entered into conditional loan agreements with the Fund in 1989, 1991, 1992, 1993, 1995, 1996, and 1998. The IMF granted Fernando de la Rúa, who emerged from the ranks of the Radical Civic Union and was elected as the representative of a multipartisan political alliance, an SBA in 2000. Peronist President Eduardo Duhalde signed the last SBA in 2003.

The reasons for this sequence of loans, in which each agreement served as a stepping stone to the next, are varied. In the case of Argentina, the loans point to a high level of pragmatism and to the growing influence of liberally oriented, pro-IMF government officials and technocrats, alongside a lack of more convenient alternatives. In the past few years, however, this situation seems to have been partially reversed. Indeed, Argentina, along with other Latin American nations, is not only reluctant to adopt another neoliberal economic program, but it is being awarded credits and loans from alternative sources, mainly Venezuela and China.

For the IMF's part, it is worth noting that the approval of consecutive loans is so routine a practice that Graham Bird refers to it as "recidivism."[1] Nevertheless, the sheer size of Argentina's economy undoubtedly has reinforced the Fund's readiness to approve financial assistance as long as the government undertakes stabilization efforts. The rationale behind the ongoing financial support to large but turbulent economies has always been that the risk of a domino effect if they were to collapse are too huge to ignore, as the Mexican Crisis of 1982 clearly demonstrated. The support provided by the IMF to the sinking Argentine economy in 2000, during de la Rúa's brief presidency, provides an excellent example of this phenomenon. Another equally significant reason for the granting of so many loans to Latin American borrowers, Argentina among them, is the tendency of the IMF's largest shareholders to support the granting of aid to borrowing member states that maintain close relations with them, and especially with the United States.

It should also be stressed that the IMF, as well as its borrowers and creditor member states, is by no means a monolithic organism. As an in-depth analysis of Argentine–IMF relations suggests, the Fund is not only a multilateral organization that represents the interest of its (strongest) member states but also a bureaucracy composed of a highly professional and quite homogeneous staff of economists that has developed its own goals, norms, and beliefs. As the Argentine case demonstrates, the granting of loans to certain borrowers had provoked internal conflicts at the IMF. In most cases, the Executive Board, composed of twenty-four representatives of individual member states or groups of member states, has served as a stamp of approval for the recommendations brought to it by the technocrats of the Western Hemisphere Department. However, sometimes (e.g., during the discussions of IMF support for Cavallo's Convertibility Plan of the late 1990s) the opposite seems to occur—that is, the economists urge the board to stop granting loans, but the board, often under pressure from Washington and private lenders, ignores the specialists' recommendations.

In any event, the intense and almost constant activity of the IMF in Latin America cannot but raise questions about whether nations in the region became addicted to the cyclical signing of loan agreements whose economic results were mixed, if not harmful to their national interests. Furthermore, one must ask the same question about the IMF itself. After all, the readiness and, at times, almost inexplicable flexibility of the IMF toward unstable economies prompts one to wonder whether the Fund developed a voracious appetite for the very mechanisms that constitute the routine of dependency—mechanisms that reach their peak precisely when loan agreements are in place.

Surely, as claimed in this book, the flow of financial and technical assistance to unstable countries such as Argentina—and, moreover, the broader complex of IMF–borrower relations—cannot be fully understood without taking into consideration the self-reinforcing dynamics of the routine of dependency and the influential epistemic community that is simultaneously a result and a main promoter of that routine. In effect, it was the creation of knowledge-based networks of technocrats in the IMF and its borrower member states who shared a liberal economic ideology that paved the way for the IMF's growing, long-term, and not necessarily unwanted influence in the region.

The origin and consolidation of this epistemic community to a large extent was a natural result of multiple official, and sometimes semiofficial or unofficial, encounters between economists from the IMF and its borrowers. As this book shows, the same IMF officers meet time and again with the same national representatives, who remain involved in the ongoing management of the national economy even under very different administrations. Undoubtedly, epistemic communities grow more quickly in the fertile ground of shared economic beliefs—in this case, economic orthodoxy. This was certainly the case in Chile and Mexico, where generations of Chicago Boys who filled key positions at Ministries of Economy and Central Banks were keen to collaborate with and learn from their peers at the IMF. The Argentine case appears to have been a bit different—and, perhaps, more challenging from the perspective of the IMF— because the University of Chicago's economic training programs were far less popular in Argentina than in other Latin American nations. In addition, during the 1950s and 1960s, students and followers of the renowned Argentine economist Raúl Prebisch, whose influence resonated into the 1980s in the heterodox programs of President Raúl Alfonsín, still occupied key positions in central government institutions.

When Claudio Loser, the Argentine who directed the IMF's Western Hemisphere Department, was asked about the Fund's relations with Argentina's changing ministers of economy, he acknowledged that his staff had maintained much more intense dialogue with liberal Argentine economists like Ricardo López Murphy than with others, such as Juan Sourrouille.[2] Non-orthodox economists in Argentina, according to Loser, "in general propose plans that are technically weak."[3] Although the lack of local alternatives to the neoliberal programs imported from the United States (directly or via the Bretton Woods institutions) has been a reality, there is no doubt that the desire of local economists to intensify their collaboration with IMF technocrats led to the Fund's growing influence and impact in Argentina. Indeed, as Peter Hass explains, the members of an epistemic community share not only beliefs but also a common policy enterprise.[4] In other words, through a variety of interactions, IMF technocrats and their local allies and partners jointly elaborate reports that are rich in economic data (and in line with the international standards stipulated by the

Fund), which Argentina—except during the terms of General Jorge Rafael Videla in the 1970s and Carlos Saúl Menem in the 1990s—has found almost impossible to produce and furnish on its own. These reports (which have led to systematic shrinking of the state apparatus and intervention in the economy) are then presented to decision makers at the IMF and the borrowing country, serving as the basis for designing economic programs and for approving loan agreements. As the Argentine case reveals, this technical process was led for decades mainly by IMF staff, who were more stable and sometimes more knowledgeable about Argentina's economy than the constantly changing local staffs.

The routine of dependency and the evolution of the epistemic community of IMF and local technocrats definitely played a major role in triggering and preserving the IMF's intervention in debtor countries such as Argentina. But the routine of dependency should not be painted in deterministic colors. National leaders could, and often did, consciously regulate its intensity; further, the routine has never been totally immune to internal and external influences. As this book has shown, every turn or crisis in the national, regional, or global sphere has had the potential to affect or to be used as a pretext to alter the joint working routine with the IMF. As I have shown, the IMF rarely chooses to interrupt SBAs, because they guarantee the continuation and deepening of the routine of dependency. Nevertheless, the Fund did so when the political situation in Argentina became intolerable, as occurred in March 1962 during the coup that overthrew President Arturo Frondizi. A similar situation occurred in 2001, just before President Fernando de la Rúa announced his resignation. In most cases, however, it was the Argentine leaders who decided to reduce the IMF's presence in the country. While President Arturo Illia and President Néstor Kirchner present the most drastic cases, the case of Alejandro Lanusse, who served as de facto president in the early 1970s, indicates that even dictatorial regimes cannot completely ignore the political and social opposition that the ties with the IMF provoke.

Regional influences are clearly of paramount importance. The political pendulum in Latin America has always been accompanied by another pendulum that swings between different, and often contradictory stances, vis-à-vis the IMF. Simply put, in the same way that Latin American nations concurrently experience cycles of populism, dictatorship, and neoliberalism, they also desire tightening and loosening of their joint working routine with the IMF. As shown, the dictatorships of the 1970s tended to be friendly to the Fund, while the leftist administrations of a large number of Latin American countries today have maintained the confrontational stance adopted in late 2005.

Whether Argentina and other Latin American countries will continue to pursue their current independent approach vis-à-vis the IMF remains unclear. The experience of Brazil demonstrates that a different model of interaction with the Fund is indeed possible: Rather than confronting or opposing the Bretton

Woods institutions, President Lula da Silva managed to translate the country's flourishing economy into increased voting power within the IMF and the World Bank. Under the most recent reform of the quotas, which was approved by the IMF and World Bank in 2010, Brazil is expected to become the first Latin American nation to enter the institutions' exclusive top ten. However, the chances that this model of interaction will be successfully adopted by countries whose economies are not experiencing growth similar to Brazil's remain dim.

At this point, all we can do is speculate. The episode of detachment provoked by the debt repayments to the IMF in 2005–2006 is ongoing. The current and prolonged detachment has created an ideological vacuum that could be filled by new and homemade economic programs. And discontent with neoliberalism is growing globally, as reflected in the emergence of social protest in the form of "*indignados*" in Spain, Occupy Wall Street movements in the United States, and other protest movements in Portugal, Greece, Israel, and Britain. All of this raises questions about whether there is room for establishment of a new Latin American school of economic thought—or, alternatively, whether there is room for renewal of ECLAC or for the emergence of a new generation of economists who can elaborate a new set of policies that are more in line with the political and social realities of what appears to be the dawn of a post-neoliberal era. As this book has tried to demonstrate, money is just one part of the story. The time has come to develop new ideas and more symmetrical patterns of interaction among members of the global economic community to improve the lives of millions of people, not only in Latin America but also in the world as a whole.

Notes

INTRODUCTION

1. Joseph Stiglitz, "Argentina, Shortchanged: Why the Nation That Followed the Rules Fell to Pieces," *Washington Post,* May 12, 2002.

2. See, e.g., José Antonio Ocampo, "Poverty Increased in Lost Half-Decade," *ECLAC Notes,* no. 25, November 2002.

3. Sarah Babb, *Managing Mexico: Economists from Nationalism to Neoliberalism* (Princeton, NJ: Princeton University Press, 2001); Jeffrey Chwieroth, *Capital Ideas: The IMF and the Rise of Financial Liberalization* (Princeton, NJ: Princeton University Press, 2009).

4. On the Argentine case, see Eduardo Amadeo, *La salida del abismo* (Buenos Aires: Editorial Planeta, 2003); Paul Blustein, *And the Money Kept Rolling In (and Out): Wall Street, the IMF, and the Bankrupting of Argentina* (Washington, DC: Public Affairs, 2005); Marcelo Bonelli, *Un país en deuda: La Argentina y su imposible relación con el FMI* (Buenos Aires: Editorial Planeta, 2004); Luigi Manzetti, *The International Monetary Fund and Economic Stabilization: The Argentine Case* (New York: Praeger, 1991); Naum Minsburg, *Los guardianes del dinero* (Buenos Aires: Norma, 2003); Michael Mussa, *Argentina and the Fund: From Triumph to Tragedy* (Washington, DC: Institute for International Economics, 2002); Ernesto Tenembaum, *Enemigos* (Buenos Aires: Norma, 2004). On the Chilean case, see Naomi Klein, *The Shock Doctrine: The Rise of Disaster Capitalism* (New York: Picador, 2007), esp. pts. 1–2. On the Mexican case, see Devesh Kapur, "The IMF: A Cure or a Curse?" *Foreign Policy,* no. 111 (1998): 114–130; Miguel Ramirez, "The Latest IMF-Sponsored Stabilization Program: Does It Represent a Long-Term Solution for Mexico's Economy?" *Journal of Interamerican Studies and World Affairs* 38:4 (1996): 129–156; Ngaire Woods, *The Globalizers: The IMF, the World Bank, and Their Borrowers* (Ithaca, NY: Cornell University Press, 2006), chap. 4. On other cases, see Ariel Buira, ed., *Challenges to the World Bank and IMF: Developing Country Perspectives* (London: Anthem Press, 2003); Anthony Payne, "After Bananas: The IMF and the Politics of Stabilisation and Diversification in Dominicana," *Bulletin of Latin American Research* 27:3 (2008): 317–332; Grigore Pop-Eleches, *From Economic Crisis to Reform: IMF Programs in Latin America*

and Eastern Europe (Princeton, NJ: Princeton University Press, 2009); Ednei Roza, "The IMF and the Effects of Structural Conditionalities in Brazil: What Is About to Happen?" *Law and Business Review of the Americas* 14:2 (2008): 347–365.

5. Jon V. Kofas, *The Sword of Damocles: U.S. Financial Hegemony in Colombia and Chile, 1950–1970* (London: Praeger, 2002); Thomas Scheetz, *Peru and the International Monetary Fund* (Pittsburgh: University of Pittsburgh Press, 1986).

6. Luigi Manzetti, *The International Monetary Fund and Economic Stabilization: The Argentine Case* (New York: Praeger, 1991); Raúl García Heras, *El Fondo Monetario y el Banco Mundial en la Argentina. Liberalismo, populismo y finanzas internacionales* (Buenos Aires: Lumiere, 2008); Noemí Brenta, *Argentina atrapada. Historia de las relaciones con el FMI, 1956–2006* (Buenos Aires: Ediciones Cooperativas, 2009).

7. Joseph Stiglitz, *El malestar en la globalización,* trans. Carlos Rodríguez Braun (Buenos Aires: Taurus, 2002), 82.

8. Quoted in Tenembaum, *Enemigos,* 44.

CHAPTER 1

1. For one of the few exceptions, see Jon V. Kofas, "The Politics of Foreign Debt: The IMF, the World Bank, and US Foreign Policy in Chile, 1946–1952," *Journal of Developing Areas* 31, no. 2 (1997): 157–182.

2. Eric Helleiner, "The Development Mandate of International Institutions: Where Did It Come From?" *Studies in Comparative International Development* 44 (2009): 189–211.

3. Rosemary Thorp, "The Latin American Economies in the 1940s," in *Latin America in the 1940s: War and Postwar Transitions,* ed. David Rock (Berkeley: University of California Press, 1994), 41–58.

4. Victor Bulmer-Thomas, *The Economic History of Latin America since Independence* (New York: Cambridge University Press, 1994), 267.

5. Eric Helleiner, "Reinterpreting Bretton Woods: International Development and the Neglected Origins of Embedded Liberalism," *Development and Change* 37, no. 5 (2006): 943–967.

6. Helleiner, "The Development Mandate," 207–208.

7. Richard Gardner, *Sterling–Dollar Diplomacy: Anglo-American Collaboration in the Reconstruction of Multilateral Trade* (Oxford: Clarendon, 1956), 52–53, 68.

8. David Green, *The Containment of Latin America: A History of the Myths and Realities of the Good Neighbor Policy* (Chicago: Quadrangle, 1971), 87–90.

9. Gardner, *Sterling–Dollar Diplomacy,* 4.

10. Jane Asherman, "The International Monetary Fund: A History of Compromise," *Journal of International Law and Politics* 16 (1984), 235–304; Harold James, *International Monetary Cooperation since Bretton Woods* (New York: Oxford University Press, 1996), 33–35.

11. Leslie Bethell, "Britain and Latin America in Historical Perspective," in *Britain and Latin America: A Changing Relationship,* ed. Victor Bulmer-Thomas (New York: Cambridge University Press, 1989), 1–26.

12. See, e.g., Mario Rapoport, "La política británica en la Argentina a comienzos de la década de 1940," *Desarrollo Económico* 16, no. 62 (1976): 203–228.

13. Anthony Eden to Her Majesty's Representatives in Latin America, attachment to "Bones of Contention in Latin America," memorandum, April 22, 1943, Foreign Office (FO) 371/33929, U.K. National Archives, Public Records Office, Kew (hereafter, NAKEW).

14. Perowne to Walley, December 21, 1942, attached to FO 371/33929, NAKEW.

15. Bethell, "Britain and Latin America," 1–24.

16. Warren F. Kimball, "'The Juggler': Franklin D. Roosevelt and Anglo-American Competition in Latin America," in *Argentina between the Great Powers, 1939–46*, ed. Guido di Tella and D. Cameron Watt (London: Macmillan, 1989), 18–33.

17. For an analysis of both plans from the standpoint of monetary theory, see Filippo Cesarano, *Monetary Theory and Bretton Woods: The Construction of an International Monetary Order* (New York: Cambridge University Press, 2006), esp. chap. 6.

18. "The Keynes Plan," February 11, 1942, reprinted in J. Keith Horsefield, *The International Monetary Fund, 1945–1965: Twenty Years of International Monetary Cooperation*, 3 vols. (Washington, DC: International Monetary Fund, 1969), 3:3–18.

19. Gerald M. Meier, *Problems of a World Monetary Order*, 2d ed. (New York: Oxford University Press, 1982), 32–33.

20. "The Keynes Plan," April 1943, reprinted in Horsefield, *The International Monetary Fund*, 3:19–36.

21. The united nations were Australia, Belgium (and Congo), Brazil, Canada, China (and Manchuria), Costa Rica, Cuba, Czechoslovakia, Dominican Republic, El Salvador, Ethiopia, Greece, Guatemala, Haiti, Honduras, India, Iran, Iraq, Luxembourg, Mexico, Netherlands, Netherlands East Indies, New Zealand, Nicaragua, Norway, Panama, Philippines, Poland, Union of South Africa, Union of Soviet Socialist Republics, United Kingdom, United States, and Yugoslavia. The associated nations were Bolivia, Colombia, Chile, Ecuador, Egypt, Iceland, Liberia, Paraguay, Peru, Uruguay, Venezuela, and, by early 1943 (in a special status), France and Italy: see IMF and World Bank quota calculations (quota equals one-half foreign trade in 1938), April 16, 1943, box 31, file 291-303, Bretton Woods Conference Files (1940–1947) (hereafter, BWC), IMF Archives. (The United Nations as an organization was established in 1945). "The Keynes Plan" (April 1943), 3:21.

22. "The White Plan," April 1942, reprinted in Horsefield, *The International Monetary Fund*, 3:37–82.

23. Ibid., 3:62–72.

24. Ibid., 3:62.

25. *New York Times*, April 23, 1944.

26. On the divergences between Britain and the United States, and especially on the economic and political perspectives shared by experts from both sides, see G. John Ikenberry, "A World Economy Restored: Expert Consensus and the Anglo-American Postwar Settlement," *International Organization* 46, no. 1 (1992): 289–321.

27. Henry Morgenthau Jr. to Cordell Hull, March 1, 1943, box 39, Records of the Bretton Woods Agreements (1938–1946), entry 360 O, RG 56: U.S. Department of the Treasury Department NARS A-1, U.S. National Archives and Records Administration (hereafter, NARA-BWA).

28. Despite France's exclusion at this stage, it was finally decided that French representatives, as well as those of other European governments in exile, had to be invited to the Bretton Woods Conference: ibid.

29. Adolf A. Berle, Jr. to Morgenthau, Jr., March 2, 1943, box 39, NARA-BWA.

30. For the complete list of countries, see Treasury Department press release 36-3, April 7, 1943, in box 26, NARA-BWA. The same document is in box 14, file 143-140, Luxford Ansel series, BWC, IMF Archives.

31. Secretary of State [Hull] to the Ambassador in the United Kingdom (Winant), April 5, 1944, 800.515/1029a, in *Foreign Relations of the United States* (hereafter, *FRUS*) (1944), 2:107–108.

32. Cordell Hull to U.S. Embassy in London, urgent telegram (3077), April 17, 1944, in NARA-BWA, box 23; Secretary of State to the Ambassador in the United Kingdom (Winant), April 17, 1944, 800.515/1010c, *FRUS* (1944), 2:118–119.

33. Secretary of State to the Ambassador in the United Kingdom (Winant), April 17, 1944.

34. On Brazil's strong cooperation with the United States, see, e.g., Joseph Smith, "Brazil: Benefits of Cooperation," in *Latin America during World War II*, ed. Thomas Leonard and John Bratzel (Lanham, MD: Rowman and Littlefield, 2007), 144–162.

35. Frank D. McCann, "Brazil and World War II: The Forgotten Ally. What Did You Do in the War, Zé Carioca?" *Estudios Interdisciplinarios de América Latina y el Caribe* 6, no. 2 (1995), available online at http://www.tau.ac.il/eial/VI_2/mccann.htm (accessed July 1, 2012).

36. Thorp, "The Latin American Economies," 44–45.

37. Ngaire Woods, *The Globalizers: The IMF, the World Bank, and Their Borrowers* (Ithaca, NY: Cornell University Press, 2006), 15–28.

38. See, e.g., *New York Times,* April 23–24, June 9, June 21, 1944; *Newsweek,* July 3, 1944; B. H. Beckhart, "The Bretton Woods Proposal for an International Monetary Fund," *Political Science Quarterly* 59 (1944): 489–528; Jack N. Behrman, "Political Factors in U.S. International Financial Cooperation, 1945–1950," *American Political Science Review* 47 (1953): 431–460; Edward E. Brown, "The International Monetary Fund: A Consideration of Certain Objection," *Journal of Business of the University of Chicago* 17 (1944): 199–208; John H. Williams, "The Postwar Monetary Plans," *American Economic Review* 34 (1944): 372–384.

39. "Joint Statement by Experts on the Establishment of an International Monetary Fund," April 1944, reprinted in Horsefield, *The International Monetary Fund,* 3:128–135.

40. G. John Ikenberry, *After Victory. Institutions, Strategic Restraint, and the Rebuilding of Order after Major Words* (Princeton, NJ: Princeton University Press, 2001), 199–203.

41. Horsefield, *The International Monetary Fund,* 1:79–80.

42. Acting Secretary of State [Stettinius] to the Ambassador in the United Kingdom (Winant), March 1, 1944, 840.50/3559a, in *FRUS* (1966), 2:17–18.

43. Viscount Halifax to Foreign Office (no. 397 Remac), May 29, 1944, Treasury (T) 231-359, NAKEW.

44. Ibid.

45. Horsefield, *The International Monetary Fund,* 1:79.

46. Viscount Halifax to Foreign Office (no. 410 Remac), June 1, 1944.

47. Helleiner, "The Development Mandate," 207–208.

48. President Roosevelt to the Secretary of the Treasury, draft letter, June 9, 1944, 800.515/1201c, in *FRUS* (1944), 2:134–135.

49. Donald Moggridge, ed., *The Collected Writings of John Maynard Keynes* (London: Macmillan, 1980), 26:42.

50. Andrés Cisneros and Carlos Escudé, eds., *Historia general de las relaciones exteriores de la República Argentinas,* 15 vols. (Buenos Aires: Neuvohacer, 1992), 8:61–71.

51. Harold Molineu, *U.S. Policy toward Latin America: From Regionalism to Globalism* (Boulder, CO: Westview, 1986); Bryce Wood, *The Making of the Good Neighbor Policy* (New York: Columbia University Press, 1961).

52. It must be noted that at the same time, President Roberto M. Ortiz proposed that Argentina should join the Allies: see Carlos Escudé, "Un enigma. La 'irracionalidad' Argentina frente a la Segunda Guerra Mundial," *Estudios Interdisciplinarios de América*

Latina y el Caribe 6 (1995): 5–35; Joseph Tulchin, "The Argentine Proposal for Non-Belligerency, April 1940," *Journal of Inter-American Studies* 11 (1969): 571–604.

53. On the State Department's analysis of the Argentine situation after President Castillo took office, see Under Secretary of State (Welles) to the Ambassador in Argentina (Armour), Washington, DC, June 28, 1943, in *FRUS* (1943), 5:419–424.

54. Michael Francis, *The Limits of Hegemony. United States Relations with Argentina and Chile during World War II* (Notre Dame, IN: University of Notre Dame Press, 1977), esp. chap. 3; Bryce Wood, *The Dismantling of the Good Neighbor Policy* (Austin: Texas University Press, 1985), 1–2.

55. For the text of the statement published at the end of the Rio de Janeiro Conference, see Rio de Janeiro Meeting of Foreign Affairs of the American Republics, January 15–28, 1942, in *A Decade of American Foreign Policy: Basic Documents, 1941–49* (Washington: United States Government Printing Office, 1950), 412–414. For an analysis of Chile's neutrality, see, e.g., Graeme S. Mount, "Chile: An Effort at Neutrality" in Leonard and Bratzel, *Latin America during World War II,* 163–182.

56. Cordell Hull, *The Memoirs of Cordell Hull,* vol. 2 (London, 1948), 1378; John Blum, *From the Morgenthau Diaries: Years of War, 1941–1945* (Boston: Houghton Mifflin, 1967), 194–206.

57. For an analysis of Argentinean neutrality, see, e.g., Guido di Tella and D. Cameron Watt, *Argentina between the Great Powers, 1939–46* (London: Macmillan, 1989); Mario Rapoport, "Argentina y la Segunda Guerra Mundial. Mitos y realidades," *Estudios Interdisciplinarios de América Latina y el Caribe* 6 (1995), available online at www.tau.ac.il/eial/VI_1/rapoport.htm (accessed July 1, 2012).

58. Memoria del Ministerio de Hacienda, vol. 3 (Buenos Aires: Ministerio de Hacienda, 1945), 289–290.

59. Callum MacDonald, "The Politics of Intervention: The United States and Argentina, 1941–1946," *Journal of Latin American Studies* 12 (1980): 365–396.

60. Randall Woods, "Hull and Argentina: Wilsonian Diplomacy in the Age of Roosevelt," *Journal of Interamerican Studies and World Affairs* 16, no. 3 (1974): 350–371.

61. The Ambassador in Argentina (Armour) to the Secretary of State, Buenos Aires, April 8, 1943, in *FRUS* (1943), 1:829–830.

62. *Economic Survey,* April 20, 1943. *Economic Survey* was a respected weekly journal with a liberal outlook specializing in economic matters. It was published in Buenos Aires and run by Rodolfo Katz, an expert in agricultural economy. Well-known economic liberal figures who later became Argentine economic ministers and official advisers, such as Roberto Alemann and Adelberto Krieger Vasena, also contributed to the journal.

63. Escudé, "Un enigma."

64. David Sheinin, *Argentina and the United States: An Alliance Contained* (Athens and London: University of Georgia Press, 2006), 82.

65. Ambassador Armour to Secretary of State Cordell Hull, telegram (2:28 PM), April 16, 1943, in box 29, file 276-283, BWC, IMF Archives.

66. Ibid., telegram (5:25 PM), April 16, 1943, box 29, file 276-283, BWC, IMF Archives.

67. Cordell Hull to the U.S. Embassy in Buenos Aires, letter, April 26, 1943, box 29, file 276-283, BWC, IMF Archives.

68. Ibid.

69. See, e.g., K. G. Grubb to J. Victor Perowne, March 17, 1943, FO 371/33558, NAKEW.

70. Ibid., March 19, 1943.

71. British Ministry of Information to J. Victor Perowne, March 17, 1943, FO 371/33558, NAKEW.

72. For the pressure exerted on the British government by Hull, see, e.g.,: Foreign Office to Viscount Halifax, May 3, 1944, in Cabinet (CAB) 122/952, NAKEW. For a discussion of the different positions of the United States, Britain, the Soviet Union, and Germany toward the neutral countries of World War II, see Roberto Russell and J. G. Tokatlian, "Los neutrales en la Segunda Guerra Mundial," *Ciclos* (2000), 19, 7–50.

73. On the British efforts to moderate U.S. pressure on Argentina, see, e.g., A. Gallop to Hadov, July 20, 1944, FO 371/37705, NAKEW. British documents refer extensively to Britain's "admitted dependence on supplies" from Argentina and the "great interests that our (British) investors and exporters have" in the country: see, e.g., Sir David Kelly to Foreign Office, January 28, 1944, CAB 122/951; Anthony Eden to Viscount Halifax, January 21, 1944, CAB 122/951; Halifax to Foreign Office, May 1, 1944, CAB 122/952, all in NAKEW.

74. Blum, *From the Morgenthau Diaries,* 1202–1204.

75. *Economic Survey,* May 16, 1944.

76. For the full text of the invitation to the Bretton Woods conference, see United Nations Monetary and Financial Conference (released to the press by the White House on May 26, 1944), *Department of State Bulletin,* vol. 10, no. 257, May 27, 1944, 498; *Proceedings and Documents of the United Nations Monetary and Financial Conference,* Department of State, Publication no. 2866 (Washington, DC: U.S. Government Printing Office, 1948), 1:4–5.

77. *Proceedings and Documents of the United Nations Monetary and Financial Conference,* 1:3.

78. International Monetary Fund, "Table of U.S. and U.K. Proposed Quotas," May 4, 1944, T 160/1287, NAKEW.

79. Foreign Office to Washington on quotas, May 15, 1944, T 160/1287, NAKEW.

80. Hull to certain American diplomatic representatives, May 25, 1944, 800.515/1087a., *FRUS* (1944), 2:132–133.

81. These neutral countries also waited a relatively long time before they were allowed to join the Bretton Woods institutions. Turkey joined in 1947; Sweden joined in 1951, the same year the Swedish economist Ivar Rooth was chosen as the second director of the IMF; Ireland joined in 1957; Spain joined in 1958; and Portugal joined in 1961.

82. Edward Mason and Robert Asher, *The World Bank since Bretton Woods* (Washington, DC: Brookings Institution Press, 1973), 33.

83. Decree 3.185/46, January 31, 1946, in *Boletín Oficial de la República Argentina,* vol. 54, no. 15.512, June 26, 1946. (Archive of the Ministry of the Interior, Buenos Aires).

84. Ibid.

85. Decree 3.185/46, January 31, 1946, in box 5, file 420-710, Central Files Collection, Country File series, Argentina subseries (hereafter, CFC–Argentina), IMF Archives.

86. A–C/F—Mr. Collado, CFD—Mr. Young, April 4, 1946, in CFC–Argentina, IMF Archives.

87. *New York Times,* May 7, 1946; *Washington Post,* May 7, 1946.

88. For the IMF's official definition of quotas, see http://www.imf.org/external/about/quotas.htm.

89. "Articles of Agreement of the International Monetary Fund," July 22, 1944, reprinted in Horsefield, *The International Monetary Fund,* 3:199–200.

90. J. Keith Horsefield, "Derivation and Significance of the Fund's Resources," in Horsefield, *The International Monetary Fund,* 2: 349–380.

91. Horsefield, *The International Monetary Fund,* 1:129.

92. *Clarín,* September 26, 1956.

93. Memorandum of a meeting on the International Stabilization Fund in White's Office, June 2, 1943, in box 31, file 291-303, BWC, IMF Archives.

94. Bulmer-Thomas, *Economic History of Latin America,* 263.

95. Memorandum of a meeting on the International Stabilization Fund.

96. Russell Porters, "Morgenthau Sees Monetary Accord," *New York Times,* July 9, 1944.

97. Ibid.

CHAPTER 2

1. Juan D. Perón, *La hora de los pueblos* (Buenos Aires: CS Ediciones, 2005), 59. The book was originally published in 1968.

2. The surprisingly few historical studies that examine the relationship of Argentina with the Bretton Woods institutions begin their story, without exception, in the post-Perón era: see, e.g., Noemí Brenta, *Argentina atrapada. Historia de las relaciones con el FMI, 1956-2006* (Buenos Aires: Ediciones Cooperativas, 2009); Roberto Frenkel and José M. Fanelli, "La Argentina y el Fondo en la década pasada," *El Trimestre Económico* 54 (1987): 75-131; Raúl García Heras, *Presiones externas y política económica: El Fondo Monetario Internacional y el Banco Mundial en Argentina, 1955-1966* (Bogotá: Universidad De los Andes, Cátedra Corona, 2000); Luigi Manzetti, *The International Monetary Fund and Economic Stabilization: The Argentine Case* (New York: Praeger, 1991).

3. See Leslie Bethell and Ian Roxborough, "Latin America between the Second World War and the Cold War: Some Reflections of the 1945-8 Conjuncture," *Journal of Latin American Studies* 20 (1988): 167-189.

4. Perón to Alberto E. Asseff, October 28, 1967, in Juan D. Perón, *Correspondencia* (Buenos Aires: Corregidor, 1983), 1:156.

5. The IMF began to develop the principle of conditionality in 1952. Stand-by arrangements (characterized by conditional clauses) were created in 1956 and implemented beginning in 1957.

6. By the time Argentina joined in 1956, the number of member states had reached sixty. Today, there are 188 members of the IMF and World Bank (compared with 192 members of the United Nations).

7. The IMF initially established a system of fixed exchange rates for the currency of all member countries as a part of the Bretton Woods agreement. This par value was based on the value of gold and the U.S. dollar, and the dollar was valued at $35 per ounce of gold.

8. Assistant Secretary of State (Braden) to Ambassador in Mexico (Messersmith), March 8, 1946, 835.00/2-2846, *FRUS* (1946), 11:232-233.

9. For an analysis of bilateral agreements as opposed to the Bretton Woods system, see García Heras, *Presiones externas y política económica,* 18-23. On the Third Position, see, e.g., Andrés Cisneros and Carlos Escudé, eds., *Historia general de las relaciones exteriores de la República Argentina,* 15 vols. (Buenos Aires: Nuevohacer, 1998-2003), 13:81-191.

10. For an analysis of Perón's industrialization policies and connections to the industrial sector, see James Brennan, "Industrialistas y Bolicheros: Business and the Peronist Populist Alliance, 1943-1976," in *Peronism and Argentina,* ed. James Brennan (Wilmington, DE: Rowman and Littlefield, 1998), 79-125; Pablo Gerchunoff and Lucas Llach, "Capitalismo industrial, desarrollo asociado y distribución del ingreso entre los dos gobiernos peronistas: 1950-1972," *Desarrollo Económico* 15, no. 57 (1975): 3-54; Graciela

198 Notes to Chapter 2

Mateo, "El gobierno de Domingo Mercante. Expresión singular del peronismo clásico," *Estudios Interdisciplinarios de América Latina y el Caribe* 15, no. 2 (2004): esp. 178–187; Mónica Peralta-Ramos, *The Political Economy of Argentina: Power and Class since 1930* (Boulder, CO: Westview Press, 1992), 26–34. On the social policies that benefited broad sectors of Argentine society, see, e.g., Jeffrey Sachs, "Social Conflict and Populist Policies in Latin America," National Bureau of Economic Research working paper no. 2897, March 1989, available online at http://www.nber.org/papers/w2897 (accessed April 13, 2009).

11. On the myths and realities of debt repayment, see Noemí Girbal-Blacha, *Mitos, paradojas y realidades en la Argentina peronista (1946–1955): Una interpretación histórica de sus decisiones político-económicas* (Buenos Aires: Universidad Nacional de Quilmes, 2003), 31–33; "Transmisión radial con motivo del rescate de la deuda externa. 20 Julio 1946," *Habla Perón* (Buenos Aires: Alea, 1949), 150–151.

12. *Time,* July 21, 1947.

13. On the role and influence of Friedman in the IMF and World Bank, see Robert W. Oliver, *George Woods and the World Bank* (Boulder, CO: Lynne Rienner, 1995), 96–116.

14. "Meeting in Mr. Friedman's Office, August 27, 1947. Subject: Meeting with Economic Counselor and Secretary of the Argentine Embassy," in box 5, files 1–20, file title 420-710, CFC–Argentina, IMF Archives.

15. Ibid.

16. Margaret Garritsen de Vries, *The IMF in a Changing World, 1945–85* (Washington, DC: International Monetary Fund, 1986), 21.

17. Margaret Garritsen de Vries, "The Retreat of Bilateralism," in *The International Monetary Fund, 1945–1965: Twenty Years of International Monetary Cooperation,* ed. J. Keith Horsefield (Washington, DC: International Monetary Fund, 1969), 2:297–316. On the position of the IMF regarding bilateralism in Latin America through the middle of the 1950s, see Johan H. C. de Looper, "Recent Latin American Experience with Bilateral Trade and Payments Agreements," *IMF Staff Papers* 4 (1954–1955): 85–112.

18. "Article 14, Articles of Agreement of the International Monetary Fund (22 July 1944)," in Horsefield, *The International Monetary Fund,* 3:185–214.

19. "Meeting in Mr. Friedman's Office, August 27, 1947."

20. McCloy, a lawyer by profession who had served as assistant secretary of war in the U.S. government, was president of the World Bank for just two years. During his brief time in office, he increased both the formal and the de facto power of the institution's president.

21. "Meeting in Mr. Friedman's Office, August 27, 1947.

22. Jon V. Kofas, *The Sword of Damocles: U.S. Financial Hegemony in Colombia and Chile, 1950–1970* (London: Praeger, 2002), 6.

23. Latin America's interest in the World Bank and misgivings regarding the IMF have not disappeared. Despite the present crisis in the world economy, none of the Latin American countries currently has an agreement with the IMF, as some have with the World Bank.

24. *Washington Post,* May 13, 1948.

25. See, e.g., Carlos Escudé, "The U.S. Destabilization and Economic Boycott of Argentina of the 1940s, Revisited," Universidad del Centro de Estudios Macroeconómicos de Argentina, Serie de Documentos de Trabajo no. 323, Área de Ciencia Política, July 2006.

26. R. L. Horne to Camille Gutt, "Argentina," letter, June 24, 1948, box 5, files 1–20, file title 420-710, CFC–Argentina, IMF Archives.

27. R. L. Horne to Mr. Mendels, "Argentina—Approximate Terms of Membership," letter, June 24, 1948, box 5, files 1–20, file title 420-710, CFC–Argentina, IMF Archives.

28. Ibid.

29. Horsefield, *The International Monetary Fund,* 1:217.

30. *Wall Street Journal,* November 5, 1948.

31. "Mr. Gutt's Meeting with Mr. Miranda," EBD/378 (November 29, 1948), box 5, files 1–20, file title 420-710, CFC–Argentina, IMF Archives.

32. "Report on Latin America," EBM/390 (January 5, 1949), box 5, files 1–20, file title 420-710, CFC–Argentina, IMF Archives.

33. Ibid.

34. M. M. Mendels to Eugene Black, confidential letter, September 8, 1949, box 5, files 1–20, file title 420-710, CFC–Argentina, IMF Archives.

35. Bethell and Roxborough, "Latin America between the Second World War and the Cold War," 171–172.

36. See, e.g., Mario Rapoport and Claudio Spiguel, *Estados Unidos y el Peronismo. La política norteamericana en la Argentina, 1949–1955* (Buenos Aires: GEL, 1994), 75–77.

37. Edward Miller to Ellsworth Bunker, Confidential Official-Informal Letter, November 13, 1951, box 1 of 14, Assistant Secretary of State for Latin American Affairs (Edward J. Miller), 1949–1953, A–B, entry lot 53D 26, RG 59: General Records of the State Department, NARA (hereafter, NARA–Miller).

38. Henry Dearborn, Division of the River Plate Affairs, memorandum, May 23, 1949, *FRUS* (1949), 2:500–504.

39. Raúl García Heras, *El Fondo Monetario y el Banco Mundial en la Argentina. Liberalismo, populismo y finanzas internacionales* (Buenos Aires: Lumiere, 2008), 18.

40. Internal disagreements abounded in the Perón government. In the economic area, see, among others, Claudio Belini, "D.I.N.I.E. y los límites de la política industrial peronista, 1947–1955," *Desarrollo Económico,* 41, no. 161, (2001), 97–119. On other aspects of the internal debates, see Raanan Rein, *In the Shadow of Perón: Juan Atilio Bramuglia and the Second Line of Argentina's Populist Movement* (Stanford, CA: Stanford University Press, 2008).

41. "Visita del Señor Edward G. Miller, Secretario de Asuntos Latinoamericanos del Departamento de Estado de EE.UU.A.," Consejo Económico Nacional, Análisis de la Situación Económica 1950–1952, February 1950, 30–32, in Biblioteca Prebisch, Banco Central de la República Argentina.

42. "Factors in Economic Relations with Argentina," press release, May 17, 1950, in *Department of State Bulletin* 22, no. 569 (May 29, 1950): 860–861.

43. "Proposed Export-Import Bank Loan of $61 Million in Argentina," National Advisory Council doc. 88, Action 162, March 1, 1955, box 2, NAC Actions (August 21, 1945–December 31, 1968), 671–1073 (1954–1957), Records of the Office of the Assistant Secretary for International Affairs, entry no. 360 D, RG 56: General Records of the Department of the Treasury, NARA (hereafter, NARA-NAC); Clarence E. Birgfeld, Division of East Coast Affairs, memorandum of conversation, June 5, 1950, 835.10/6-550, *FRUS* (1950), 2:725–727; *Washington Post,* April 5, 1950.

44. Ivan B. White, Economic and Finance Adviser, Bureau of Inter-American Affairs, memorandum of conversation, February 9, 1950, 835.10/2-950, *FRUS* (1950), 2:691–692.

45. "Department's Recommendation that the Export-Import Bank Give Sympathetic Consideration to an Argentine Request for Financial Assistance," confidential letter from Edward Miller to Thorp, November 25, 1949, in box 1, NARA–Miller.

46. Jon V. Kofas, "The Politics of Foreign Debt: The IMF, the World Bank, and U.S. Foreign Policy in Chile, 1946–1952," *Journal of Developing Areas* 31, no. 2 (1997): 157–182.

47. Jon V. Kofas, "The Politics of Austerity: The IMF and U.S. Foreign Policy in Bolivia, 1956–1964," *Journal of Developing Areas* 29, no. 2 (1995): 213–236; Jon V. Kofas,

"Stabilization and Class Conflict: The State Department, the IMF, and the IBRD in Chile, 1952–1958," *International History Review* 21, no. 2 (1999): 352–385.

48. "Minutes of the 156th Meeting of the National Advisory Council on International and Financial Problems," May 16, 1950, NAC Files, lot 60D 137, *FRUS* (1950), 2:717–724.

49. The GATT was created in 1947 to replace the International Trade Organization, which was proposed but not approved at the Bretton Woods Conference. Argentine membership in the GATT was finalized in July 1968.

50. Edward Miller to Ellsworth Bunker, confidential letter, November 13, 1951, in box 1, NARA–Miller.

51. Robert Potash, *The Army and Politics in Argentina, 1945–1962* (Stanford, CA: Stanford University Press, 1980), 143–144; Eprime Eshag and Rosemary Thorp, "Las políticas económicas ortodoxas de Perón a Guido (1953–1963). Consecuencias económicas y sociales," in *Los Planes de Estabilización en la Argentina*, ed. Aldo Ferrer, Mario Brodersohn, Eprime Eshag, and Rosemary Thorp (Buenos Aires: Paidós, 1974), 64–132. For an innovative examination of this plan from the point of view of consumption policies, see Eduardo Elena, "Peronist Consumer Politics and the Problem of Domesticating Markets in Argentina, 1943–1955," *Hispanic American Historical Review* 87, no. 1 (2007): 111–149. For the full text, see "Plan Económico de 1952," Consejo Económico Nacional, 1952, Banco Central República Argentina, Biblioteca Tornquist, Buenos Aires.

52. "Radiation de capitals extranjeros. Ley no. 14.222, sancionada el 21 de Agosto de 1953," *Memoria Anual del Banco Central 1953—Decimonoveno Ejercicio*, Banco Central, Buenos Aires, 1954, 133–144.

53. *La Nación*, March 15–17, 1954.

54. Ibid., March 17, 1954.

55. *El Economista*, March 27, 1954.

56. Ibid.

57. Ibid.

58. "U.S.–Argentina Economic Relations," memorandum of conversation, March 15, 1955, in box 1, RG 59: General Records of the State Department, Assistant Secretary of State for Inter-American Affairs (Henry F. Holland), 1953–1956, Country File Argentina-Bolivia, entry lot 57 D 295, NARA (hereafter, NARA–Holland).

59. "Argentina—Mr. Black's Visit, March 15–17, 1954," April 22, 1954, IMF Archives.

60. "Call of Ambassador Paz on Mr. Holland," memorandum of conversation, May 19, 1954, box 1, NARA–Holland.

61. "Recognition of New Government of Argentina," press release, September 25, 1955, *Department of State Bulletin* 33, no. 850 (October 10, 1955): 560.

62. Pablo Gerchunoff and Lucas Llach, *El ciclo de la ilusión y el desencanto. Un siglo de políticas económicas argentinas* (Buenos Aires: Ariel, 1998), 233; Potash, *The Army and Politics in Argentina*, 214–226.

63. Celia Szusterman, "The 'Revolución Libertadora', 1955–8," in *The Political Economy of Argentina, 1946–1983*, ed. Guido di Tella and Rudiger Dornbusch (Pittsburgh: University of Pittsburgh Press, 1989), 89–103.

64. David Sheinin, *Argentina and the United States: An Alliance Contained* (Athens: University of Georgia Press, 2006), 110–113.

65. Mario Rapoport, Eduardo Madrid, Andrés Musacchio, and Ricardo Vicente, *Historia económica, política y social de la Argentina (1880–2000)* (Buenos Aires: Ediciones Macchi, 2000), 539. For a comprehensive account of Prebisch's life, see Edgar Dosman, *The Life and Times of Raúl Prebisch, 1901–1986* (Montreal: McGill–Queen's University Press, 2008).

66. Roberto Cortés Conde, "Raúl Prebisch: his years in government," *CEPAL Review,* 75 (2001), 81–86; Katherine Sikkink, "The Influence of Raúl Prebisch on Economic Policy-Making in Argentina, 1950–1962," *Latin American Research Review* 23, no. 2 (1988): 91–114.

67. Sikkink, "The Influence of Raúl Prebisch," 94. Article XIV Consultations with Argentina, Merle Cochran to Coromina-Segura, March 5, 1957, box 6, files 1–18, file title 720-810, CFC–Argentina, IMF Archives. "Argentina Economic Mission: United Nations Mission to Argentina," memorandum of conversation, February 2, 1956, box 1, NARA–Holland.

68. Raúl Prebisch, *Informe preliminar acerca de la situación económica* (Buenos Aires: Secretaría de Prensa y Actividades Culturales de la Presidencia de la Nación, 1955), 11, 14–15, 35–36.

69. Roberto Cortés Conde, *Progreso y declinación de la economía argentina. Un análisis histórico institucional* (Mexico City: Fondo Cultura Económica, 1998), 65; Gerchunoff and Llach, *El ciclo de la ilusión y el desencanto,* 237; J. C. Portantiero, "Political and Economic Crisis in Argentina," in di Tella and Dornbusch, *The Political Economy of Argentina,* 16–24.

70. Prebisch, *Informe preliminar,* 71–72.

71. *El Economista,* December 15, 1956.

72. "Consultation on Various Economic and Political Problems," confidential memorandum of conversation from Department of State, March 7, 1956, in NARA, Holland Files, box 1.

73. Jorge del Canto to Ivar Rooth, letter, November 28, 1955, in box 5, files 1–20, file title 420-710, CFC–Argentina, IMF Archives.

74. Memorandum from the Assistant Secretary of State for Inter-American Affairs (Holland) to the Undersecretary of State (Hoover), November 15, 1955, U.S. Department of State, Central Files, 835.10/11-2055, *FRUS* (1955–1957), 7:384–385.

75. Ibid., 385–386.

76. Memorandum by the Assistant Secretary of State for Inter-American Affairs (Holland), January 26, 1956, *FRUS* (1955–1957), 7:401–403.

77. Dispatch from the Ambassador in Argentina (Nufer) to the Department of State, December 9, 1955, U.S. Department of State, Central Files, 033.1120/12-955, *FRUS* (1955–1957), 7:388–393.

78. British Embassy in Buenos Aires to Foreign Office, letter 218-1039/4/55, December 6, 1955, FO 371/114026.

79. "Argentina—Summary of Dr. Prebisch's Economic Report," November 10, 1955, box 4, files 1–11, file title 320-420, IMF Archives.

80. "Argentina—The Prebisch Report," November 16, 1955, in ibid.

81. David Pollock, Daniel Kerner, and Joseph Love, "Entrevista inédita a Prebisch. Logros y deficiencies de la CEPAL," *Revista de la CEPAL* 75 (2001): 9–24.

82. Dispatch from Ambassador in Argentina (Nufer) to the Department of State (December 9, 1955), 7:393–394.

83. G. A. Costanzo to J. González del Solar, letter, November 22, 1955, box 5, files 1–20, file title 420-710, CFC–Argentina, IMF Archives.

84. Articles of Agreement of the International Monetary Fund, July 22, 1944, reprinted in Horsefield, *The International Monetary Fund,* 3:196–197.

85. Research Department, in consultation with Western Hemisphere and Legal Departments, to the Managing Director, "Fund Relations with Argentina: Statistical Questions," December 14, 1955, box 5, files 1–20, file title 420-710, CFC–Argentina, IMF Archives.

86. Argentina's Membership in the IMF and Problem of Latin American Representation on the Executive Board, November 22, 1955, box 5, files 1–20, file title 420-710, CFC–Argentina, IMF Archives.

87. *Clarín,* September 26, 1956.

88. "Consultation on Various Economic and Political Problems," confidential memorandum of conversation from Department of State, March 7, 1956, box 1, NARA–Holland.

89. Ibid.

90. Síntesis de la conferencia de prensa del Sr. Ministro de Finanzas en la que se informó que el gobierno provisional ha resuelto adherer a los convenios constitutivos del Fondo Monetario Internacional y del Banco Internacional de Reconstrucción y Fomento, April 19, 1956, Colección Dr. Zalduendo, Carpeta 13: 1957—Informe Verrier, Instituto Di Tella, Buenos Aires, Argentina.

91. D. 7103, April 19, 1956—Gestiones para el ingreso de la Argentina al Fondo Monetario Internacional y al Banco Internacional de Reconstrucción y Fomento (B.O. 30/IV/56), *Anales de Legislación Argentina,* Tomo XVI-A, 1956, Decretos, República Argentina.

92. See decree no. 3.185/46, January 31, 1946, *Boletín Oficial de la República Argentina,* vol. 54, no. 15.512 (June 26, 1946), Archive of the Ministry of Interior, Buenos Aires; D. 7103, April 19, 1956.

93. Memorandum of a Conversation, Department of State, Washington, DC, April 25, 1956, U.S. Department of State, Central Files, 735.00/4-2556, *FRUS* (1955–1957), 7:408–411.

94. *La Nación,* April 20, 1956.

95. *Noticias Gráficas,* April 20, 1956.

96. *El Economista,* December 15, 1956.

97. For Prebisch's response, see, e.g., Prebisch, Desarrollo económico y política social. *Mesa Redonda en la Universidad de Córdoba,* 1956; *El Economista,* April 28, 1956.

98. *El Mundo,* October 28, 1956.

99. *La Prensa,* April 20, 1956.

100. Ambassador Adolfo A. Vicchi to IMF Managing Director Ivar Rooth, official letter, May 15, 1956, box 5, files 1–20, file title 420-710, CFC–Argentina, IMF Archives.

101. J. Del Canto, acting director, WHD, to Ivar Rooth, managing director, office memorandum, May 23, 1956, in box 5, files 1–20, file title 420-710, CFC–Argentina, IMF Archives.

102. García Heras, *Presiones externas y políticas económica,* 9.

103. *El Economista,* May 19, 1956.

104. Del Canto to Rooth (May 23, 1956).

105. "Arrangements for Meeting Argentine Mission," letter from R. L. Horne (World Bank) to Mr. Van Campenhout, June 27, 1956, box 5, files 1–20, file title 420-710, CFC–Argentina, IMF Archives; Carlos A. Coll Benegas to Mr. Van Campenhout, letter, June 28, 1956, box 5, files 1–20, file title 420-710, CFC–Argentina, IMF Archives.

106. "Argentina: Membership in the IBRD and the IMF," national advisory document no. 88, action no. 898, June 29, 1956, box 2, NARA-NAC.

107. "Report on the Admission of the Argentine Republic to Membership in the Fund," from the Secretary to members of the Committee on Membership—Argentine Republic, August 9, 1956, box 5, files 1–20, file title 420-710, CFC–Argentina, IMF Archives.

108. D. Ley 15.970, August 31, 1956—Aprobación de los convenios sobre Fondo Monetario Internacional y Banco de Reconstrucción y Fomento, *Anales de legislación Argentina* 16-A (1956): 943–979; *La Nación,* September 1, 1956.

109. Gesualdo Costanzo to J. González del Solar, letter, November 22, 1955, box 5, files 1–20, file title 420-710, CFC–Argentina, IMF Archives.

110. Pragmatism, above all else, guided the World Bank, which apparently took the initiative in the case of Argentina. On the Bank's pragmatism under McCloy and Black see, among others, Devesh Kapur, John P. Lewis, Richard Webb, eds., *The World Bank: Its First Half Century* (Washington, DC: Brookings Institution Press, 1997), esp. chap. 3.

CHAPTER 3

1. For technical reasons, Haiti entered the IMF and World Bank only in late 1953.

2. John Ikenberry and Charles A. Kupchan, "Socialization and Hegemonic Power," *International Organization* 44, no. 3 (1990): 283–315.

3. See, e.g., Rogelio Frigerio, *Las condiciones de la Victoria* (Montevideo: Editorial A. Monteverde y Cia, 1963; Rogelio Frigerio, *Desarrollo y subdesarrollo económicos,* (Buenos Aires: Paidós, 1984); Rogelio Frigerio, *Estatuto del Subdesarrollo* (Buenos Aires: Librería del Jurista, 1983). On Frigerio's background, see Hugo Gambini, *Frondizi. El estadista acorralado* (Buenos Aires: Editorial Vergara, 2006), 173–178.

4. For an in-depth discussion of developmentalism, with a special focus on Argentina, see, e.g., Marcelo Cavarozzi, "El 'Desarrollismo' y las Relaciones entre Democracia y Capitalismo Dependiente en Dependencia y Desarrollo en América Latina," *Latin American Research Review,* 17:1 (1982), 152–165; José Ocampo, "New Economic Thinking in Latin America," *Journal of Latin American Studies* 22, no. 1 (1990): 169–181; Raúl Prebisch, "Five Stages in My Thinking on Development," in *Pioneers in Development,* ed. Gerald Meier and Dudley Seers (New York: Oxford University Press, 1984), 175–191; Julio Nosiglia, *El desarrollismo* (Buenos Aires: Centro Editor de América Latina, 1983), esp. chaps. 2–3; Celia Szusterman, *Frondizi and the Politics of Developmentalism in Argentina, 1955–62* (London: Macmillan, 1993), esp. chaps. 4–6.

5. Jon V. Kofas, *The Sword of Damocles: U.S. Financial Hegemony in Colombia and Chile, 1950–1970* (London: Praeger, 2002), 7.

6. Mario Rapoport, "La Argentina y la Guerra Fría. Opciones económicas y estratégicas de la apertura hacia el Este, 1955–1973," *Ciclos* 5, no. 8 (1995): 91–122.

7. For a discussion of this alliance, see, e.g., Roberto Porsecanski, "The Alliance for Progress or Alianza para el Progreso? A Reassessment of the Latin American contribution to the Alliance for Progress," unpublished master's thesis, Tufts University, Medford, MA, 2005, available online at http://fletcher.tufts.edu/research/2005/Porzecanski.pdf (accessed April 2, 2011); Raúl Saez, "The Nine Wise Men and the Alliance for Progress," *International Organization* 22, no. 1 (1968): 244–269; Joseph Tulchin, "The United States and Latin America in the 1960s," *Journal of Interamerican Studies and World Affairs* 30, no. 1 (1988): 1–36.

8. For this point, see British Embassy in Buenos Aires to Her Majesty's Treasury, London, letter, April 5, 1957, FO 371/126166/AA1102/8, NAKEW.

9. Margaret Garritsen de Vries, "The Consultation Process," in *The International Monetary Fund, 1945–1965: Twenty Years of International Cooperation* (Washington, DC: International Monetary Fund, 1969), 2:229–248.

10. See "Articles of Agreement of the International Monetary Fund (July 22, 1944)," reprinted in Horsefield, *The International Monetary Fund,* 3:203.

11. "Article XIV, Consultation with Argentina, H. Merle Cochran to R. Corominas-Segura, March 5, 1957, box 6, files 1–18, file title 720-810, CFC–Argentina, IMF Archives.

12. See "Articles of Agreement of the International Monetary Fund (July 22, 1944),"
reprinted in Horsefield, *The International Monetary Fund,* 3:197.

13. "The Attitude on the Argentine Partners' Side toward Their Bilateral Agreements
as quoted from Fund Consultation Papers," memorandum, April 15, 1957, box 6, files
1–18, file title 720-810, CFC–Argentina, IMF Archives. Today, the Paris Club is an informal group of nineteen official creditors from some of the world's biggest economies, whose
role is to find coordinated and sustainable solutions to the payment difficulties experienced
by debtor countries. Its traces its origin to 1956 when Argentina agreed to meet its public
European creditors in Paris.

14. Horsefield, *The International Monetary Fund,* 1:429; *New York Times,* April 16,
1957. A *purchase* is a transaction in which a member country buys the currency of another
member from the Fund in exchange for its own currency. For a detailed definition, see
"Articles of Agreement of the International Monetary Fund (July 22, 1944)," in Horsefield,
The International Monetary Fund, 3:191–192.

15. "The Argentina Multilateral Trade and Payments System," report sent by the
Ministry of Finance, Republic of Argentina, ERD-14, 606, translation, January 17, 1958,
IMF Archives.

16. "Meeting No. 24: Final Meeting on Policy Discussions at the Office of the Minister
of Economy at 11:00 AM on July 15, 1958," in box 2, Argentina (1956–1958) file, folder 4,
Western Argentina Country Files Hemisphere Department Immediate Office Records
(hereafter, WHD–Argentina), IMF Archives.

17. Banco Central de la República Argentina, *Actas de Directorio,* no. 34-155 (December 11, 1957–July 3, 1958), 21–22.

18. "Meeting No. 24."

19. *Economic Survey,* September 30, 1958.

20. Director of International and Financial Development Affairs (Adair) to the Assistant Secretary of State for Economic Affairs (Mann), memorandum, September 24, 1958,
FRUS (1958–1960), 5:510–512.

21. *New York Times,* October 26, 1958.

22. Emil G. Spitzer, "Stand-by Arrangements: Purposes and Forms," in Horsefield,
The International Monetary Fund, 2:468–491.

23. Kofas, *The Sword of Damocles,* 32.

24. Emil G. Spitzer, "Factors in Stabilization Programs," in Horsefield, *The International Monetary Fund,* 2:492–510.

25. Luigi Manzetti, *The International Monetary Fund and Economic Stabilization: The
Argentine Case* (New York: Praeger, 1991), 200.

26. Roberto Frenkel and Guillermo O'Donnell, "The 'Stabilization Programs' of the
International Monetary Fund and Their Internal Impacts," in *Capitalism and the State in
U.S.-Latin American Relations,* ed. Richard R. Fagen (Stanford, CA: Stanford University
Press, 1979), 171–216.

27. Ikenberry and Kupchan, "Socialization and Hegemonic Power," 283–285.

28. *El Nacional,* November 23, 1958; *La Nación,* November 22, 1958.

29. *La Nación,* November 23, 1958.

30. *La Prensa,* December 21, 1958; "The 'Mood' of Argentina for Stabilization: Report
by Jorge del Canto to the Managing Director and the Deputy Managing Director," memorandum, November 6, 1958, in box 4, files 1–11, file title 320-420, CFC–Argentina (Stabilization Program), IMF Archives.

31. Raúl García Heras, "El plan de estabilización económica de 1958 en la Argentina,"
Estudios Interdisciplinarios de América Latina y el Caribe 11, no. 2 (2000): 137–149.

32. *La Nación,* October 28, 1958.

33. Frank Southard Jr. to Secretary Robert B. Anderson, "Argentina: Tentative Views of IMF Mission," memorandum, November 26, 1958, in box 25, Records of Secretary Robert B. Anderson, International Development Association—International Matters (Argentina–USSR), entry 198, RG 56: General Records of the Department of the Treasury, NARA (hereafter, NARA–Anderson).

34. *La Prensa,* December 1, 1958.

35. Director of Office of East Coast (Bernbaum) to the Assistant Secretary of State for Inter-American Affairs (Rubottom), memorandum, December 9, 1958, *FRUS* (1958–1960), 5:521–522.

36. Emilio Donato del Carril to Per Jacobsson, letter of intent, EBS/58/76 (December 18, 1958), supp. 1, IMF Archives; Joseph Gold, *Stand-by Arrangements* (Washington, DC: International Monetary Fund, 1970), 41.

37. EBS/58/76, supp. 2, attachment 1, IMF Archives.

38. Ibid., 41.

39. *La Prensa,* December 11, 1958.

40. Ibid., December 17, 1958.

41. Ibid., December 14, 1958.

42. "Argentina—Stand-by Arrangement," EBS/58/76 (December 18, 1958), supp. 2, IMF Archives.

43. Ibid.

44. Thomas Scheetz, *Peru and the International Monetary Fund* (Pittsburgh: University of Pittsburgh Press, 1986), 97–101.

45. "Argentina—Stand-by Arrangement."

46. Joint announcement by the Export-Import Bank of Washington, eleven U.S. commercial banks, the U.S. Treasury Department, and the Development Loan Fund, December 29, 1958, in box 4, files 1–11, file title 320-410, file 5, CFC–Argentina, IMF Archives; Ambassador Hurtado to Secretary Robert B. Anderson, letter, December 29, 1958, in box 25, Records of the Office of the Assistant Secretary for International Affairs (1958–1963), entry 70 A 3232, RG 56: General Records of the Department of the Treasury, NARA.

47. Raúl García Heras, *El Fondo Monetario y el Banco Mundial en la Argentina. Liberalismo, populismo y finanzas internacionales* (Buenos Aires: Lumiere, 2008), 65–68.

48. Erica Gould, *Money Talks: The International Monetary Fund, Conditionality, and Supplementary Financiers* (Stanford, CA: Stanford University Press, 2006), esp. chap. 2.

49. Andrés Cisneros and Carlos Escudé, dirs., *Historia general de las relaciones exteriores de la República Argentina,* 15 vols. (Buenos Aires: Nuevohacer, 1998), 11:89–93.

50. Ibid., 13:249.

51. "Mensaje radiofónico del señor presidente de la Nación doctor Arturo Frondizi, transmitido el 19 de Febrero de 1959, por la red nacional de radiodifusión y T.V.," in Presidencia de la Nación, *Trabajadores y empresarios frente al programa de estabilización* (Buenos Aires: Biblioteca Tornquist, 1959).

52. For a discussion of the loans and stabilization programs adopted by these countries from the 1950s on, see, e.g., Jon V. Kofas, "The IMF, the World Bank, and U.S. Foreign Policy in Ecuador, 1956–1966," *Latin American Perspectives* 28, no. 5 (2001): 50–83; Jon V. Kofas, "The Politics of Austerity: The IMF and U.S. Foreign Policy in Bolivia, 1956–64," *Journal of Developing Areas* 29, no. 2 (1995): 213–238; Karen Remmer, "The Politics of Economic Stabilization: IMF Standby Programs in Latin America, 1954–1984," *Comparative Politics* 19, no. 1 (1986): 1–24.

53. Gold, *Stand-by Agreements,* 36–40.

54. Benjamin Cohen, "Balance-of-Payments Financing: Evolution of a Regime," *International Organization* 36, no. 2 (1982): 457–478.

55. Horsefield, *The International Monetary Fund*, 1:432.

56. Gold, *Stand-by Arrangements*, 67–84.

57. "Argentina—Stand-by Arrangement."

58. Gesualdo Costanzo to Eugenio Bertens, letter, February 4, 1959, in box 6, files 1–18, file title 720-810, CFC–Argentina, IMF Archives.

59. Ibid.

60. Eugenio Bertens to H. Merle Cochran, confidential letter no. 4, January 3, 1959, in box 6, files 1–18, file title 720-810, CFC–Argentina, IMF Archives.

61. Ibid.

62. Ibid.

63. Eugenio Bertens to the Sub-Secretario de Finanzas, Mario O. Mendevil, letter, January 5, 1959, box 6, files 1–18, file title 720-810, CFC–Argentina, IMF Archives.

64. Eugenio Bertens to H. Merle Cochran, confidential letter no. 4, January, 3 1959, box 6, files 1–18, file title 720-810, CFC–Argentina, IMF Archives.

65. Ibid.

66. Acting Secretary to the Members of the Executive Board, "Argentina—Stabilization Program—Progress Report," EBS/59/10 (February 18, 1959), IMF Archives.

67. This mechanism is now officially established. The representatives, responsible for "technical assistance," are called "resident representatives" and "resident specialists." They remain stationed at the destination country for short or longer terms, according to the circumstances of each particular case.

68. "Technical Assistance," IMF Factsheet, updated March 10, 2010, available online at http://www.imf.org/external/np/exr/facts/tech.htm (accessed April 4, 2011).

69. Jeffrey Chwieroth, "'The Silent Revolution': Professional Training, Sympathetic Interlocutors, and IMF Lending," Paper presented at the University Seminar on Global Governance and Democracy," Duke University, Durham, NC, April 2008.

70. Peter Hass, "Introduction: Epistemic Communities and International Policy Coordination," *International Organization* 46, no. 1 (1992): 1–35; Emanuel Adler and Peter Hass, "Conclusion: Epistemic Communities, World Order, and the Creation of a Reflective Research Program," *International Organization* 46, no. 1 (1992): 367–390.

71. Eugenio Bertens to H. Merle Cochran, confidential letter 3, December 28, 1958, box 6, files 1–18, file title 720-810, CFC–Argentina, IMF Archives.

72. "Argentina—Article XIV, Consultation," SM 61/85 (November 24, 1961), IMF Archives.

73. Kofas, *The Sword of Damocles*, 32.

74. Frank Southard Jr. to Otero Monsegur, letter, December 20, 1962, box 4, Argentina (1960–1962) file, folder 3, WHD–Argentina, IMF Archives.

75. Gesualdo Costanzo to IMF Headquarters, confidential letter, February 8, 1960, box 6, files 1–18, file title 720-810, CFC–Argentina, IMF Archives.

76. Eugenio Bertens to H. Merle Cochran, confidential letter 4, January, 3 1959, box 6, files 1–18, file title 720-810, CFC–Argentina, IMF Archives.

77. Ibid.

78. IMF, "Conditionality in Fund-Supported Programs: Policy Issues," prepared by the Policy Development and Review Department, approved by Jack Boorman, February 2001, available online at http://www.imf.org/external/np/pdr/cond/2001/eng/policy/021601.pdf (accessed April 5, 2011).

79. Ibid.

80. Edgar Jones to H. Merle Cochran, confidential letter 5, January, 20 1959, box 6, files 1–18, file title 720-810, CFC–Argentina, IMF Archives.

81. Edgar Jones to H. Merle Cochran, "Argentina—Briefing for Stand-by Follow-up," memorandum, April 17, 1959, box 6, files 1–18, file title 720-810, CFC–Argentina, IMF Archives.

82. Ibid.

83. Pablo Gerchunoff and Lucas Llach, *El ciclo de la ilusión y el desencanto. Un siglo de políticas económicas argentinas* (Buenos Aires: Ariel, 1998), 261–266.

84. Edgar Jones to H. Merle Cochran, "Argentine Bilateral Payments Policy," confidential letter, May 5, 1959, box 6, files 1–18, file title 720-810, CFC–Argentina, IMF Archives.

85. Eugenio Bertens to H. Merle Cochran, confidential letter 18, May 22, 1959, box 6, files 1–18, file title 720-810, CFC–Argentina, IMF Archives.

86. Mario Rapoport, *El laberinto argentino. Política internacional en un mundo conflictivo* (Buenos Aires: Eudeba, 1997), 356–357; Assistant Secretary of State for Inter-American Affairs (Rubottom) to the Ambassador in Argentina (Beaulac), letter, May 30, 1959, *FRUS* (1958–1960) 5:568–570.

87. On Chile, see Naomi Klein, *The Shock Doctrine: The Rise of Disaster Capitalism* (New York: Picador, 2007), esp. pts. 1–2. On Mexico, see Sarah Babb, *Managing Mexico: Economists from Nationalism to Neoliberalism* (Princeton, NJ: Princeton University Press, 2001), esp. chap. 8.

88. Edgar Jones to the Managing Director, "Argentina—Report on Mission, May 1959," memorandum, May 29, 1959, box 6, files 1–18, file title 720-810, CFC–Argentina, IMF Archives; *Economic Survey,* May 27 1959.

89. Department of State, Washington, memorandum of conversation, October 6, 1959, *FRUS* (1958–1960), 5:601–604.

90. Ibid.

91. Mario Rapoport, Eduardo Madrid, Andrés Musacchio, and Ricardo Vicente, *Historia económica, política y social de la Argentina, 1880–2000* (Buenos Aires: Macchi, 2003), 553–554.

92. Eugenio Bertens to H. Merle Cochran, secret letter 22, July 3, 1959, box 6, files 1–18, file title 720-810, CFC–Argentina, IMF Archives.

93. Gary Wynia, *Argentina in the Postwar Era* (Albuquerque: University of New Mexico Press, 1978), 90–94.

94. Ibid., 96; Ambassador in Argentina (Beaulac), memorandum, August 26, 1959, *FRUS* (1958–1960) 5:591–599.

95. Gerchunoff and Llach, *El ciclo de la ilusión y el desencanto,* 266.

96. Bertens to Merle Cochran (July 3, 1959).

97. *Department of State Bulletin,* no. 1048, July 19, 1959, 117; *Economic Survey,* July 14, 1959.

98. Eugenio Bertens to H. Merle Cochran, confidential letter, July 25, 1959, in box 6, files 1–18, file title 720-810, CFC–Argentina, IMF Archives.

99. Guillermo Walter Klein's laws offices were the official representatives of several foreign banks in Argentina. Beginning in 1976, Klein was the right-hand man of Finance Minister Alfredo Martínez de Hoz. During Martínez de Hoz's term in office, the number of foreign banks represented by Klein's law offices, where Martínez de Hoz's son was an employee, increased considerably: see "Entrevista a Norberto Galazo," *Página 12,* June 21, 2004.

100. Bertens to Merle Cochran (July 25, 1959).

101. Ibid.

102. *Economic Survey*, August 19, 1959.

103. Jeffrey Chwieroth, *Capital Ideas: The IMF and the Rise of Financial Liberalization* (Princeton, NJ: Princeton University Press, 2009), 115.

104. Bertens to Merle Cochran (July 25, 1959).

105. *Economic Survey*, July 14, 1959.

106. Minutes of meeting with Mr. Alsogaray, August 5, 1959, in box 6, files 1–18, file title 720-810, CFC–Argentina, IMF Archives.

107. Large passages from the report were cited by the Argentine press: see, e.g., *La Nación*, September 28, 1959.

108. Gesualdo Costanzo to the Managing Editor, "Argentina—Notes for Meeting with Mr. Alsogaray," memorandum, October 5, 1959, box 18, files 1–10, file title 1750-1760, file 6, CFC–Argentina, IMF Archives.

109. *Economic Survey*, October 13, 1959.

110. Ibid.

111. *La Nación*, November 11, 1959.

112. Ibid., November 12, 1959.

113. Ibid.

114. Ibid., November 16, 1959.

115. Ibid.

116. Ibid., November 17, 1959.

117. Álvaro Alsogaray to Per Jacobsson, "Argentina—Request for Stand-by Arrangement, Annex to Stand-by-Arrangement" [letter of intent], EBS/59/105 (November 18, 1959), IMF Archives.

118. *La Nación*, November 20, 1959.

119. Ibid., November 22, 1959.

120. Ibid., November 23, 1959.

121. Ibid., November 27, 1959.

122. R. L. Horne, Secretary, to Eustaquio Méndez Delfino, Alternate Governor, IMF, letter, November 25, 1959, box 15, files 1–24, file title 1110-1430, file 11, CFC–Argentina, IMF Archives.

123. The revision of the quotas leads to an increase in the IMF's funds, from $9.2 million to $14 billion: see Margaret Garritsen de Vries, *The IMF in a Changing World, 1945–1985* (Washington, DC: International Monetary Fund, 1986), 69; "Enlargement of Fund Resources through Increases in Quotas: Report by the Executive Directors to the Board of Governors of the International Monetary Fund," December 1958, reprinted in Horsefield, *The International Monetary Fund*, 3:421–441.

124. *La Nación*, November 25, 1959.

125. Ibid., November 27, 1959.

126. For Méndez Delfino's statements at the IMF Board meeting, see EBM/59/49 (December 2, 1959), in IMF Archives.

127. *La Prensa*, December 27, 1959.

128. Ibid., December 28, 1959.

129. *Economic Survey*, December 15, 1959.

130. "Argentina: 1959 Consultation with the IMF and Request for Stand-by Arrangement," memorandum from Frank Southard Jr. to Secretary Robert B. Anderson, December 3, 1959, in box 25, NARA–Anderson.

131. Manzetti, *The International Monetary Fund*, 52.

132. *La Prensa*, December 3, 1960.

133. Ibid., December 7, 1959.

134. Ibid., December 19, 1959.

135. "Argentina: Request for 1960 Financial Assistance," memorandum from Frank Southard Jr. to Secretary Robert B. Anderson, October 1, 1959, in box 25, NARA–Anderson.

136. *La Prensa,* December 23, 1959.

137. *Wall Street Journal,* May 27, 1960.

138. *New York Times,* October 26, 1960. The Development Loan Fund was established in the United States in 1957 as an addition to the Economic Cooperation Act of 1950.

139. Joseph Gold, Legal Department. to Deputy Managing Director, confidential letter, December 11, 1959, box 18, files 1–10, file title 1750-1760, file 6, CFC–Argentina, IMF Archives.

140. Per Jacobsson to Samuel Schweizer, general manager, Swiss Bank Corporation, personal letter, December 22, 1959, box 18, files 1–10, file title 1750-1760, file 6, CFC–Argentina, IMF Archives; Per Jacobsson to G. Guindey, Interbank Basle (Switzerland), personal letter, January 12, 1960, in box 18, files 1–10, file title 1750-1760, file 6, CFC–Argentina, IMF Archives.

141. Eugenio Bertens to H. Merle Cochran, confidential letter no. 13-60, April 1, 1960, in box 18, files 1–10, file title 1750-1760, CFC–Argentina, IMF Archives.

142. Kofas, *The Sword of Damocles,* 6.

143. *La Prensa,* February 1, 1960.

144. "Argentina Developments," letter from Willis to Secretary Anderson, April 28, 1959, box 25, NARA–Anderson. On the World Bank's relations with Frondizi's administration, see García Heras, *El Fondo Monetario y el Banco Mundial en la Argentina,* 81–86.

145. Per Jacobsson to Álvaro Alsogaray, letter, March 15, 1960, box 4, files 1–11, file title 320-420, CFC–Argentina, IMF Archives.

146. Ibid.

147. Álvaro Alsogaray to Per Jacobson, letter, May 4, 1960, box 4, files 1–11, file title 320-420, CFC–Argentina, IMF Archives.

148. Gesualdo Costanzo to Al, confidential letter, February 8, 1960, in box 6, files 1–18, file title 720-810, CFC–Argentina, IMF Archives.

149. Clarence Zuvekas, "Argentine Economic Policy, 1958–1962: The Frondizi Government's Development Plan," *Inter-American Affairs* 22 (Summer 1968): 45–73.

150. Cisneros and Escudé, *Historia general de las relaciones exteriores de la República Argentina,* 11:89–93.

151. Manzetti, *The International Monetary Fund,* 52–55.

152. Gesualdo Costanzo to the Managing Director, "Argentina—Renewal of Stand-by Arrangement," memorandum, September 22, 1960, box 18, files 1–10, file title 1750-1760, file 7, CFC–Argentina, IMF Archives.

153. Quoted in Jorge Marshall, José Luis Mardones and Isabel Marshall, "IMF Conditionality: The Experiences of Argentina, Brazil and Chile", in *IMF Conditionality,* ed. John Williamson (Washington, DC: Institute for International Economics, 1983), 275–346.

154. James R. Vreeland, *The IMF and Economic Development* (New York: Cambridge University Press, 2003), 11.

155. "Argentina—Request for Stand-by Arrangement," prepared by the Western Hemisphere Department (in consultation with the Legal Department and the Office of the Treasury), approved by Jorge del Canto, EBS/60/134 (December 1, 1960), IMF Archives; *El Economista,* January 7, 1961; *New York Times,* December 28, 1960.

156. *El Economista,* January 7, 1961.

157. *La Nación,* December 10, 1960.

158. Gesualdo Costanzo to the Managing Director (September 22, 1960).

159. *Economic Survey,* November 1, 1960.

160. EBS/60/134, supp. 1.

161. Manzetti, *The International Monetary Fund,* 41.

162. Álvaro Alsogaray to Per Jacobsson, letter of intent, November 22, 1960, EBS/60/134, supp. 1.

163. EBS/60/134, pt. 1; *Economic Survey,* December 20, 1960.

164. *El Economista,* July 8, 1961.

165. *New York Times,* May 12, 1961.

166. Ibid., May 25, 1961.

167. Ibid., July 1, 1961.

168. Ibid., July 22, 1961.

169. Ibid., July 17, 1961.

170. Ibid., October 10, 1961.

171. Jorge del Canto to Per Jacobsson, letter, August 23, 1961, box 4, files 1–11, file title 320-420, CFC–Argentina, IMF Archives.

172. Gesualdo Costanzo to the Managing Director, "Argentina—Renewal of Stand-by Arrangement," letter, October 20, 1961, box 19, files 1–10, file title 1760, file 1, CFC–Argentina, IMF Archives.

173. Ibid.

174. Frank Southard Jr. to Douglas Dillon, "Argentina: Stand-by Arrangement with the IMF," letter, November 29, 1961, box 10C-ES, Classified Files of Secretary Douglas Dillon, accumulated by the Executive Secretariat of the Office of the Secretary of the Treasury, 1961–1965, Federal Reserve Bank to International Monetary Fund, 1962, entry 198, RG 56: Miscellaneous Records of the Department of the Treasury, NARA (hereafter, NARA–Dillon).

175. For a discussion of Argentina's international economic relationship during Frondizi's regime, see María de Monserrat Llairó and Rymundo Siepe, *Frondizi. Un nuevo modelo de inserción internacional* (Buenos Aires: Eudeba, 2003), esp. 129–150.

176. EBS/60/134, pt. 1.

177. "Staff Report and Recommendations—1961 Consultation," prepared by staff representatives for the 1961 consultation with Argentina (reviewed by the Committee on Article XIV Consultation), approved by J. del Canto and Irving S. Friedman, November 24, 1961, SM/61/85, pt. 3, IMF Archives.

178. Ibid.

179. Albino Gómez, *Arturo Frondizi. El último estadista,* (Buenos Aires: Lumiere, 2004), 82, 99–100.

180. Haris Jafri to David Finch, "Argentina—Recent Cabinet Reorganization," memorandum, May 18, 1961, box 19, files 1–10, file title 1760, file 1, CFC–Argentina, IMF Archives.

181. Ibid.

182. By April 1961, the IMF had updated U.S. Treasury Secretary Douglas Dillon regarding what it termed the "continued leftist campaign against the IMF": see Frank Southard Jr. to Secretary Douglas Dillon, "Continued Leftist Campaign against the IMF," office memorandum, box 10C-ES, NARA–Dillon.

183. Argentina signed its first loan agreement in 1824, with the British Barings Bank.

184. García Heras, *El Fondo Monetario y el Banco Mundial en la Argentina,* 69–90.

185. On the occasion of Frondizi's visit to Washington, the U.S. press explicitly described the U.S.–Argentine relationship as friendly: see, e.g., *Wall Street Journal*, January 19, 1959.

186. Daniel Muchnik, *La patria financiera. El juego de la especulación* (Buenos Aires: Grupo Editorial Norma, 2005), 148–155.

187. Due to severe restrictions imposed by the World Bank Archives, I am unable at this point to quote explicitly from documents deposited there.

CHAPTER 4

1. James Raymond Vreeland, *The International Monetary Fund: Politics of Conditional Lending* (New York: Cambridge University Press, 2003), 58.

2. Sarah Babb, *Managing Mexico: Economists from Nationalism to Neoliberalism* (Princeton, NJ: Princeton University Press, 2001), esp. chap. 1.

3. Valerie Brender, "Economic Transformations in Chile: The Formation of the Chicago Boys," *American Economist* 55, no. 1 (2010): 111–122.

4. Kenneth Schultz and Barry R. Weingast, "The Democratic Advantage: Institutional Foundations of Financial Power in International Competition," *International Organization* 57 (2003): 3–42.

5. Sebastian Saiegh, "Do Countries Have a 'Democratic Advantage'? Political Institutions, Multilateral Agencies, and Sovereign Borrowing," *Comparative Political Studies* 38, no. 4 (2005): 366–387. For a discussion on the factors that may contribute to a country's decision to repay or reschedule its debts, see, e.g., Allan Drazen, *Political Economy in Macroeconomics*, Princeton, NJ: Princeton University Press, 2000; Jonathan Eaton, "Sovereign Debt: A Primer," *World Bank Economic Review* 7 (1993): 137–172; Jonathan Eaton and Mark Gersovitz, "Debt with Potential Repudiation: Theoretical and Empirical Analysis," *Review of Economic Studies* 48, no. 2 (1981): 289–309; Sebastian Edwards, "LDC Foreign Borrowing and Default Risk: An Empirical Investigation 1976–1980," *American Economic Review* 74 (1984): 726–734; Jeffry A. Frieden, *Debt, Development, and Democracy: Modern Political Economy and Latin America, 1965–1985* (Princeton, NJ: Princeton University Press, 1991).

6. Roberto Alemann to Jorge del Canto, letter, November 2, 1961, box 136, Argentina (1960–1962) file, WHD–Argentina, IMF Archives.

7. Roberto Alemann to Per Jacobsson, "Annex to Stand-by Arrangement," letter of intent, November 2, 1961, EBS/61/154, supp. 1, IMF Archives.

8. *La Nación*, December 3, 1961.

9. Ibid., December 13, 1961.

10. See, e.g., President Arturo Frondizi to President John F. Kennedy, letter, December 7, 1961, box 2, Office of East Coast Affairs, Records Relating to Argentina (1956–1964), lots 62D420–63D44, RG 59: General Records of the Department of State, NARA.

11. Eugenio Kvaternik, "La sucesión presidencial de 1964. El fracaso de la UCRI como partido moderado," *Desarrollo Económico* 35, no. 137 (1995): 127–143.

12. Felix Luna, *Diálogos con Frondizi* (Buenos Aires: Editorial Desarrollo, 1998), esp. 219–237; Catalina Smulovitz, "Crónica de un final anunciado: Las elecciones de marzo de 1962," *Desarrollo Económico* 28, no. 109 (1988): 105–119.

13. *New York Times*, March 20, 1962.

14. Luigi Manzetti, *The International Monetary Fund and Economic Stabilization: The Argentine Case* (New York: Praeger, 1991), 58–59.

15. Jon V. Kofas, *The Sword of Damocles: U.S. Financial Hegemony in Colombia and Chile, 1950–1970* (London: Praeger, 2002), 43–49.

16. Joseph S. Tulchin, *Argentina and the United States: A Conflicted Relationship* (Boston: Twayne, 1990), 120.

17. Vanni Pettinà, "The Shadows of Cold War over Latin America: the U.S. Reaction to Fidel Castro's Nationalism, 1956–59," *Cold War History* 11, no. 3 (2011): 317–339.

18. Eprime Eshag and Rosemary Thorp, "Las políticas económicas ortodoxas de Perón a Guido (1953–1963). Consecuencias económicas y sociales," in *Los planes de estabilización en la Argentina,* ed. Aldo Ferrer, Mario Brodersohn, Eprime Eshag, and Rosemary Thorp (Buenos Aires: Paidós, 1974), 64–132.

19. Raúl García Heras, *Presiones externas y política económica. El Fondo Monetario Internacional y el Banco Mundial en Argentina, 1955–1966* (Bogotá: Universidad de los Andes, Cátedra Corona, 2000), 47.

20. César Tcach, "Radicalismo y fuerzas armadas (1962–1963). Observaciones desde Córdoba," *Desarrollo económico* 40, no. 157 (2000): 73–95.

21. Mario Rapoport, Eduardo Madrid, Andrés Musacchio, and Ricardo Vicente, *Historia económica, política y social de la Argentina (1880–2000)* (Buenos Aires: Ediciones Macchi, 2000), 505–507.

22. Frank Southard Jr. to Douglas Dillon, note, April 11, 1962, box 10C-ES, NARA–Dillon.

23. *New York Times,* April 12, 1962.

24. Jorge del Canto to H. Merle Cochran, letter, April 9, 1962, c/Argentina/810, IMF Archives.

25. Per Jacobsson to Federico Pinedo, letter, April 23, 1962, box 7, files 1–33, file title 810, CFC–Argentina, IMF Archives.

26. Jorge del Canto to Per Jacobsson, "Developments in Argentina," office memorandum, April 30, 1962, box 7, files 1–33, file title 810, CFC–Argentina, IMF Archives.

27. Ibid.

28. Kofas, *The Sword of Damocles,* 28.

29. *New York Times,* June 8, 1962.

30. Ibid., June 9, 1962.

31. Álvaro Alsogaray to Per Jacobsson, letter, July 13, 1962, box 19, files 1–10, file title 1760, file 2, CFC–Argentina, IMF Archives.

32. Ibid.

33. Thomas Scheetz, *Peru and the International Monetary Fund* (Pittsburgh: University of Pittsburgh Press, 1986), 112.

34. Ibid., 113.

35. Juan Carlos de Pablo, "Economic Policy without Political Context: Guido, 1962–3," in *The Political Economy of Argentina, 1946–83,* ed. Guido di Tella and Rudiger Dornbusch (Pittsburgh: University of Pittsburgh Press, 1989), 129–141.

36. Daniel Muchnik, *La patria financiera. El juego de la especulación* (Buenos Aires: Grupo Editorial Norma, 2005), 156–157.

37. García Heras, *Presiones externas y política económica,* 35–36.

38. Cámara Gremial Fabricantes de Maquinaria Agrícola y sus Repuestos to Irving Friedman, David Finch, and Eugenio Bertens, letter, July 4, 1962, box 7, files 1–33, file title 810, file 8, CFC–Argentina, IMF Archives; *Clarín,* November 9, 1962.

39. Irving Friedman and David Finch to Managing Director, "Mission to Argentina," office memorandum, August 29, 1962, box 7, files 1–33, file title 810, file 10, CFC–Argentina, IMF Archives.

40. Ibid.

41. *New York Times,* August 24, 1962.

42. "Argentina—Briefing for Follow-Up Mission under Stand-by Arrangement," confidential briefing prepared by the Western Hemisphere Department (in consultation with the Exchange Restrictions and Legal Departments), approved by Jorge del Canto, October 12, 1962, box 7, files 1–33, file title 810, file 11, CFC–Argentina, IMF Archives.

43. David Finch to Managing Director and Frank Southard Jr., Deputy Managing Director, "Mission to Argentina," office memorandum, November 15, 1962, box 7, files 1–33, file title 810, file 11, CFC–Argentina, IMF Archives.

44. David Finch to Managing Director, "Argentina: Report on Mission, January 7–31," office memorandum, February 6, 1963, box 7, files 1–33, file title 810, file 13, CFC–Argentina, IMF Archives.

45. Ibid.

46. Ibid.

47. Ibid.

48. Raúl García Heras, *El Fondo Monetario y el Banco Mundial en Argentina. Liberalismo, populismo y finanzas internacionales* (Buenos Aires: Lumiere, 2008), 104–107.

49. *Clarín,* February 21, 1963.

50. Eustaquio Méndez Delfino to Per Jacobsson, letter, March 1, 1963, in IMF Archives, Western Hemisphere Department, Immediate Office Sous-fonds, Argentina Country Files, box 5, Argentina (1963–1965) file, folder 1.

51. Confidential letter to Foreign Office Telegram Eager no. 23 of January 31, Washington to Foreign Office, February 1, 1963, FO 371/172351, NAKEW.

52. EBM/63/15 (March 27, 1963), IMF Archives.

53. *Clarín,* February 28, 1963.

54. Ibid.

55. Ibid., March 17, 1963.

56. William B. Dale to Secretary Douglas Dillon, "Argentina: Stand-by Arrangement," note and memorandum, March 28, 1963, box 21C-ES, NARA–Dillon; confidential letter to Foreign Office Telegram Eager no. 53 Saving of March 28, Washington to Foreign Office, March 28, 1963, FO 371/172351, NAKEW.

57. See, e.g., John Mearsheimer, "The False Promise of International Institutions," *International Security* 19, no. 3 (1994): 5–49.

58. Strom Thacker, "The High Politics of IMF Lending," *World Politics* 52, no. 1 (1999): 38–75.

59. For an overview of Illia's political and intellectual background from his entry into politics in 1955 to his election to the presidency of Argentina, see César Tcach and Celso Rodríguez, *Arturo Illia, un sueño breve. El rol del peronismo y de los Estados Unidos en el golpe militar de 1966* (Buenos Aires: Edhasa, 2006), esp. chap. 1.

60. Ben Read, U.S. Department of State, "The President's Meeting with the Argentine Vice President," November 15, 1963, FRUS (1961–1963), 12:417.

61. Gary Wynia, *Argentina in the Postwar Era* (Albuquerque: University of New Mexico Press, 1978), 112–117.

62. Rapoport et al., *Historia económica, política y social de la Argentina,* 566–568.

63. For a discussion of Illia's foreign relations, see Alejandro Siminoff, *Los dilemas de la autonomía. La política exterior de Arturo Illia* (Buenos Aires: Nuevohacer, 2007), esp. chap. 4.

64. García Heras, *El Fondo Monetario y el Banco Mundial en la Argentina,* 121–125.

65. "Mensaje del Excelentísimo Señor Presidente de la Nación, Dr. Arturo Illia, del 12 de Octubre de 1963 al inaugurar su período constitucional," Secretaría de Prensa de la Presidencia de la Nación, Biblioteca Ministerio de Economía, Buenos Aires; *Times* (London), November 12, 1963; R. Radford to David Finch, "Argentina—President Illia's Inaugural Speech," memorandum, October 21, 1963, in box 4, files 1–11, file title 320-420, CFC–Argentina, IMF Archives.

66. García Heras, *El Fondo Monetario y el Banco Mundial en la Argentina,* 122.

67. David Finch to Jack Guenther, letter, September 4, 1963, box 9, files 1–10, file title 810-880, file 5, CFC–Argentina, IMF Archives.

68. Jack Guenther to David Finch, letter, September 20, 1963, box 9, files 1–10, file title 810-880, file 5, CFC–Argentina, IMF Archives.

69. Ibid.

70. Jack Guenther to David Finch, letter, October 9, 1963, box 5, Argentina (1963–1965) file, folder 1, CFC–Argentina, IMF Archives.

71. García Heras, *Presiones externas y política económica,* 45; Muchnik, *La patria financiera,* 157.

72. Guenther to Finch (October 9, 1963).

73. Enrique García Vázquez, "La economía durante la presidencia de Illia," *Desarrollo Económico* 34:134 (1994), 291–295.

74. Ibid.

75. *La Nación,* November 20, 1963.

76. Guillermo Walter Klein to Félix Gilberto Elizalde, letter, October 28, 1964, box 5, Argentina (1963–1965) file, folder 3, WHD–Argentina, IMF Archives.

77. *La Prensa,* January 14, 1964; ibid., January 18, 1964.

78. Kofas, *The Sword of Damocles,* 25–29.

79. *La Prensa,* January 14, 1964.

80. George Woods to Arturo Illia, letter, December 26, 1963, box 5, Argentina (1963–1965) file, folder 1, WHD–Argentina, IMF Archives.

81. *La Prensa,* February 14, 1964.

82. Ibid., December 10, 1963.

83. *La Nación,* April 9, 1965.

84. Jorge del Canto to Pierre-Paul Schweitzer and Frank Southard Jr., "Argentine Views on the International Financial Agencies," confidential memorandum, April 29, 1964, box 19, files 1–10, file title 1760, CFC–Argentina, IMF Archives.

85. Jorge del Canto to Pierre-Paul Schweitzer and Frank Southard Jr., "Report on the Mission to Argentina," confidential memorandum, June 4, 1964, box 7, files 1–33, file title 810, CFC–Argentina, IMF Archives.

86. "Argentina—Recent Economic Developments," memorandum, box 5, files 1–15, file title 420-710, CFC–Argentina, IMF Archives.

87. Jorge del Canto to Managing Director, "Argentina," memorandum, January 27, 1965, box 7, files 1–33, file title 810, CFC–Argentina, IMF Archives.

88. Ibid.

89. Jorge del Canto to Managing Director, "IBRD and Argentina," memorandum, February 26, 1965, box 19, files 1–10, file title 1760, file 5, CFC–Argentina, IMF Archives.

90. Jorge del Canto to Acting Managing Director, "Argentina," confidential letter, March 5, 1965, box 7, files 1–33, file title 810, CFC–Argentina, IMF Archives.

91. Ibid.

92. *New York Times,* April 19, 1965.

93. For urgent IMF correspondence, see Frank Southard Jr. to Managing Director, "Conversation with Mr. Escobar on Argentina," letter, April 1965, and J. Reid to Managing Director, "Argentina," memorandum, April 20, 1965, both in box 19, files 1–10, file title 1760, CFC–Argentina, IMF Archives.

94. Juan Carlos Pugliese, Ministro de Economía, "Mensaje dirigido al país el día 3 de Junio de 1965," August 1965, in Biblioteca Ministerio de Economía, Buenos Aires.

95. *La Nación,* April 28, 1965.

96. Ibid.

97. Ibid., April 13, 1965.

98. *New York Times,* June 26, 1965.

99. Ibid.

100. Secretary to Members of the Executive Board, "Argentina—Request for Technical Assistance," EBD/65/97 (June 3, 1965), and "Argentina—Technical Assistance," EBM/65/31 (June 14, 1965), both in IMF Archives.

101. Carlos García Tudero to Pierre-Paul Schweitzer, letter, June 2, 1965, box 7, files 1–33, file title 810, file 17, CFC–Argentina, IMF Archives.

102. Managing Director to Members of the Executive Board, "Chile—Gold Tranche Purchase Transaction," memorandum, July 28, 1972, box 50, Chile (1972–1973) file, folder 1, Western Hemisphere Department Immediate Office Records, Chile Country Files (hereafter, WHD–Chile), IMF Archives.

103. Pablo Gerchunoff and Lucas Llach, *El ciclo de la ilusión y el desencanto. Un siglo de políticas económicas argentinas* (Buenos Aires: Ariel, 1998), 299–301.

104. Ibid.

105. *New York Times,* February 17, 1966. For the Argentine request and the Fund's decision on this purchase, see "Argentina—Purchase Transaction," decision no. 1998-66/4, EBM/66/4 (January 26, 1966), IMF Archives.

106. See, e.g., IMF Treasurer to Banco Central de Chile, December 10, 1971, box 49, Chile (1968–1971) file, folder 3, WHD–Chile, IMF Archives.

107. Jorge del Canto to Pierre-Paul Schweitzer and Western Hemisphere Department, letter, March 21, 1966, box 6, Argentina (1965–1966) files, WHD–Argentina, IMF Archives.

108. Jorge del Canto to Managing Director, "Argentina," memorandum, March 4, 1966, box 19, files 1–10, file title 1760, CFC–Argentina, IMF Archives.

109. *La Prensa,* December 3, 1963; Banco Central de la República Argentina, *Memoria Anual 1965,* Biblioteca Prebisch, Buenos Aires, 73, 76, 79.

110. For an analysis of the circumstances of Illia's overthrow, see, e.g., Catalina Smulovitz, "La eficacia como crítica y utopia. Notas sobre la caída de Illia," *Desarrollo Económico* 33, no. 131 (1993): 403–423.

111. Tcach and Rodríguez, *Arturo Illia,* esp. chap. 3.

112. Smulovitz, "La eficacia como crítica y utopia," 403–423.

113. F. Solá, Argentine Ministry of the Economy, to Pierre-Paul Schweitzer, letter, October 15, 1965, IMF Archives, Central Files Collection, Country Files series, Argentina subseries, box 15, files 1–24, file title 110-1430, files 12, 15; "Ley 16.901—Aumento de la participación asignada a la República Argentina en el Fondo Monetario Internacional (B.O. 15/VII/66)," *Anales de Legislación Argentina* 26-B, nos. 16.882–16.962 (1966): 778–779.

114. James P. Brennan and Mónica B. Gordillo, "Working Class Protest, Popular Revolt, and Urban Insurrection in Argentina: The 1969 'Cordobazo,'" *Journal of Social*

History 27, no. 3 (1994): 477–498; Mónica B. Gordillo, "Los prolegómenos del Cordobazo. Los sindicatos líderes de Córdoba dentro de la estructura del poder sindical," *Desarrollo Económico* 31, no. 122 (1991): 163–187.

115. For an in-depth discussion of the background for the consolidation of the national security doctrine in the Argentine military, see Guillermo O'Donnell, "Modernización y golpes militares. Teoría, comparación y el caso argentino," *Desarrollo Económico* 12, no. 47 (1972): 519–566.

116. Ibid.

117. For a definition of the term "bureaucratic-authoritarian state," see Guillermo O'Donnell, "Reflecciones sobre las tendencias de cambio del estado burocrático-autoritario," *Revista Mexicana de Sociología* 39, no. 1 (1977): 9–59.

118. Attempts to establish groups of Chicago Boys in other countries on the continent, as well as in Argentina, have all failed. See, among others, Hira Anil, *Ideas and Economic Policy in Latin America: Regional, National, and Organizational Case Studies* (Westport, CT: Praeger, 1998), esp. chaps. 4, 7; Brender, "Economic Transformations in Chile," 111–122; Juan Gabriel Valdés, *Pinochet's Economists. The Chicago School in Chile* (New York: Cambridge University Press, 1995), especially chapters 6 and 8.

119. "Briefing for Mission to Argentina," prepared by the Western Hemisphere Department and the Exchange and Trade Relations Departments, approved by Jorge del Canto and E. Sture, October 12, 1966, box 6, Argentina (1965–1966) file, folder 3, WHD–Argentina, IMF Archives.

120. "Briefing for Mission to Argentina," prepared by the Western Hemisphere Department and the Exchange and Trade Relations Departments, approved by Jorge del Canto and David Finch, January 31, 1967, box 7, Argentina (1967–1968) file, folder 1, WHD–Argentina, IMF Archives.

121. For Krieger Vasena's connections with American interests, see Muchnik, *La patria financiera,* 162–163.

122. This information appears in a World Bank memorandum from January 11, 1967, which I am not yet allowed to quote in full.

123. "Briefing for Mission to Argentina" (January 31, 1967).

124. *Clarin,* January 31, 1967.

125. *La Nación,* March 11, 1967.

126. Ibid., March 9, March 11–15, 1967; *New York Times,* March 14, 1967.

127. For Krieger Vasena's policy, see "The Great Transformation," speech delivered by Minister of Economics and Labor Adalbert Krieger Vasena on radio and television, March 13, 1967, box 7, Argentina (1967–1968) file, folder 1, WHD–Argentina, IMF Archives; Adalbert Krieger Vasena, *El programa económico argentino 1967/1969. Un ataque global y simultáneo a la inflación. Estabilidad y crecimiento* (Buenos Aires: Academia Nacional de Ciencias Económicas, 1998).

128. *La Nación,* March 16, 1967.

129. Ibid., March 21, 1967.

130. *La Prensa,* March 23, 1967.

131. Jorge del Canto to Pierre-Paul Schweitzer, telegram, April 18, 1967, box 7, Argentina (1967–1968) file, folder 1, WHD–Argentina, IMF Archives.

132. *Clarín,* May 2, 1967.

133. *New York Times,* March 29, 1967.

134. Pedro Real, President, Central Bank, to Frank Southard Jr., letter, May 22, 1967, box 7, Argentina (1967–1968) file, folder 1, WHD–Argentina, IMF Archives.

135. Jorge del Canto to Pedro Real, letter, May 17, 1968, box 7, Argentina (1967–1968) file, folder 2, WHD–Argentina, IMF Archives.

136. Decision 2268-67/28, EBM/67/28 (May 1, 1967), IMF Archives; *Clarín,* May 2, 1967.

137. Scheetz, *Peru and the International Monetary Fund,* 113.

138. Jon V. Kofas, "The Politics of Austerity: The IMF and U.S. Foreign Policy in Bolivia, 1956–1964," *Journal of Developing Areas* 29, no. 2 (1995): 213–236.

139. *La Nación,* July 24, 1967.

140. Ibid., September 6, 1967.

141. Adalbert Krieger Vasena and Pedro Real to Pierre-Paul Schweitzer, "Letter of Intent," EBS/67/88 (March 2, 1968), and "Argentina—Request for Stand-by Arrangement," EBS/68/92, March 6, 1968, IMF Archives.

142. Ibid.

143. *Clarín,* June 25, 1968; *La Nación,* July 14, 1968.

144. "Argentina—Request for Stand-by Arrangement," EBS/68/92 (April 15, 1968), supp. 1, IMF Archives.

145. Ibid.

146. Norberto Galasso, *De la Banca Baring al FMI* (Buenos Aires: Colihue, 2002), 200–205.

147. Gerchunoff and Llach, *El ciclo de la illusion y el desencanto,* 326–329.

148. *Clarín,* February 9, 1969.

149. *New York Times,* December 19, 1968, July 1, 1969.

150. "Argentina—Consultation under Stand-by Arrangement," confidential report prepared by the Western Hemisphere Department and approved by Jorge del Canto, EBS/69/46 (March 5, 1969), IMF Archives.

151. *Clarín,* February 8, 1969; *La Prensa,* February 20, 1969.

152. *New York Times,* July 30, 1969.

153. Ibid., December 16, 1969.

154. Ibid., October 9, 1972.

155. Ibid.

156. Ibid., February 26, 1972.

157. Galasso, *De la Banca Baring al FMI,* 202. Many IMF officials hold doctorates in economics from prestigious universities in English-speaking countries, mainly the United States.

158. Jeffrey Chwieroth, *Capital Ideas: The IMF and the Rise of Financial Liberalization* (Princeton, NJ: Princeton University Press), 2009, 48–51.

159. Glen Biglaiser, *Guardians of the Nation? Economists, Generals and Economic Reform in Latin America* (Notre Dame, IN: University of Notre Dame Press, 2002), 31–33.

160. Mensaje del Presidente de la Nación, General de Brigada Roberto M. Levingston, August 21, 1970, in Latin American Network Information Center (LANIK), available online at http://lanic.utexas.edu/larrp/pm/sample2/argentin/levngstn/700001t.html (accessed July 11, 2012).

161. Gerchunoff and Llach, *El ciclo de la ilusión y el desencanto,* 329–331.

162. Biglaiser, *Guardians of the Nation?* 33–34.

163. *Clarín,* July 21, 1969.

164. Sterie T. Beza to Acting Manager, memorandum, August 13, 1969, box 7, files 1–33, file title 810, file 26, CFC–Argentina, IMF Archives; Frank Southard Jr. to Egidio Iannella, president, Argentinean Central Bank, letter, July 7, 1970, and Egidio Iannella to

Frank Southard Jr., letter, July 22, 1970, both in box 9, files 1–10, file title 810-880, file 1, CFC–Argentina, IMF Archives; Sterie T. Beza to Managing Director and Deputy Managing Director, "Mission to Argentina," confidential memorandum, February 9, 1970, box 7, files 1–33, file title 810, file 27, CFC–Argentina, IMF Archives; E. Walter Robichek to Deputy Managing Director, "Informal Staff Visit to Argentina," letter, June 25, 1970, box 8, Argentina (1959–1970) file, folder 4, WHD–Argentina, IMF Archives.

165. The $90 million increase in Argentina's quota was ratified by Law No. 18854 on December 3, 1970. For more on this, see *Memoria Anual 1970*, Banco Central de la República Argentina, pp. 60–61.

166. *Clarín*, September 29, 1971; *La Prensa*, September 17, 1971.

167. *New York Times*, January 30, 1972.

168. E. Walter Robichek to Managing Director, "Argentina—Request for a Mission," memorandum, January 11, 1972, box 7, files 1–33, file title 810, file 30, CFC–Argentina, IMF Archives.

169. Jack Guenther to Jorge del Canto, "Argentina—Stand-by Discussions with Mr. Brignone," memorandum, March 24, 1972, box 9, Argentina (1970–1972) file, folder 30, WHD–Argentina, IMF Archives.

170. Jorge del Canto to Managing Director, "Argentina—Stand-by Negotiations," memorandum, March 28, 1972, box 9, Argentina (1970–1972) file, folder 30, WHD–Argentina, IMF Archives.

171. "Argentina—Purchase Transaction," EBM/72/18 (March 1, 1972), "Argentina—Gold Tranche Purchase Transaction," EBM/72/20 (March 9, 1972), "Argentina—1971 Article VIII Consultation and Purchase Transaction," EBM/72/53 (June 14, 1972), "Argentina—Gold Tranche Purchase Transaction," EBS/72/72 (March 8, 1972), all in IMF Archives. The SDR value is based on a basket of four key international currencies, and SDRs can be exchanged for freely usable currencies.

172. The Grand National Accord was a political plan that Lanusse elaborated in early July 1971. At the core of the plan was an invitation to the main political groups in Argentina to reach an accord on the transition to democracy.

173. The argument about the IMF's failure to distinguish among different regimes and to ask whether the country in question honors human rights has been raised repeatedly in the literature: see, e.g., Thacker, "The High Politics of IMF Lending"; John Williamson, "Reforming the IMF: Different or Better?" in *The Political Morality of the International Monetary Fund: Ethics and Foreign Policy*, vol. 3, ed. Robert J. Myers (New Brunswick, NJ: Transaction, 1987), 1–12.

CHAPTER 5

1. For the negotiations between Perón and Lanusse, with emphasis on Gelbard's mediating role, see María Seoane, *El burgués maldito* (Buenos Aires: Editorial Sudamericana, 1998), esp. chap. 6.

2. Mario Rapoport, Eduardo Madrid, Andrés Musacchio, and Ricardo Vicente, *Historia económica, política y social de la Argentina (1880–2000)* (Buenos Aires: Ediciones Macchi, 2000), 664–670.

3. For an analysis of the election results in terms of socioeconomic and mostly occupational indicators, see Dario Cantón and Jorge Jorrat, "Occupation and Vote in Urban Argentina: The March 1973 Presidential Election," *Latin American Research Review* 13, no. 1 (1978): 146–157.

4. Rapoport et al., *Historia económica, política y social de la Argentina,* 664–670.

5. "'Mensaje de la victoria' desde Madrid, con motivo del aplastante triunfo electoral del 11 de marzo," March 12, 1973, in Juan Domingo Perón, *Todos los mensajes, discursos y conferencias completos, 1973–1974,* vol. 1 (Argentina: Editorial de la Reconstrucción, 1975), in *Presidential Messages,* LARRP, available online at http://lanic.utexas.edu/larrp/pm/sample2, 42–43.

6. "Discussions between Fund Staff and Argentine Delegation to the Committee of Twenty Ministers' Meeting," memorandum for files, August 1, 1973, box 10, Argentina (1972–1975) file, folder 2, WHD–Argentina, IMF Archives.

7. *Clarín,* August 2, 1973.

8. For the CGE's and Gelbard's positions, see James Brennan, "Industrialistas y bolicheros. Business and the Peronist Populist Alliance, 1943–1976," in *Peronism and Argentina,* ed. James Brennan (Wilmington, DE: Rowman and Littlefield, 1998), 79–123.

9. Seoane, *El burgués maldito,* 260–261.

10. Ibid., 254–256.

11. James Brennan, "Prolegomenon to Neoliberalism: The Political Economy of Populist Argentina, 1943–1976," *Latin American Perspectives* 34, no. 3 (May 2007): 49–66; Marcelo Rougier and Martín Fiszbein, *La frustración de un proyecto económico. El gobierno peronista de 1973–1976* (Buenos Aires: Manantial, 2006), 64–65.

12. David Sheinin, *Argentina and the United States: An Alliance Contained* (Athens: University of Georgia Press, 2006), 157–161.

13. Ibid., 160.

14. Marcelo Larraquy, *López Rega. La biografía* (Buenos Aires: Editorial Sudamericana, 2004), 242–245, 268.

15. *La Opinión,* January 30, 1974.

16. Manuel Pastor Jr., "Managing the Latin American Debt Crisis: The International Monetary Fund and Beyond," in *Creating a New World Economy: Forces of Change and Plans for Action,* ed. Gerald Epstein, Julie Graham, and Jessica Nembhard (Philadelphia: Temple University Press, 1993), 289–313.

17. "Minutes of Meeting Held with Argentina Monetary Authorities—IMF," March 28, 1973, box 9, files 1–10, file title 810-880, file 4, CFC–Argentina, IMF Archives.

18. Rougier and Fiszbein, *La frustración de un proyecto económico,* 59.

19. Jorge del Canto to Managing Director, "Argentina—Visit to the Fund by the New Argentine Ambassador to the United States, Hon. Alejandro Orfila," office memorandum, November 26, 1973, box 10, Argentina (1972–1975) files, folder 2, WDH–Argentina, IMF Archives.

20. Ibid.

21. Ibid.

22. Jorge del Canto to Managing Director, "Article VIII—Fund Mission to Argentina, July 9–12, 1974," confidential office memorandum, July 15, 1974, box 7, files 1–33, file title 810, file 31, CFC–Argentina, IMF Archives.

23. Jorge del Canto to Managing Director, "Article VIII Consultation with Argentina," letter, July 1, 1974, box 7, files 1–33, file title 810, file 31, CFC–Argentina, IMF Archives.

24. Del Canto to Managing Director (July 15, 1974).

25. Ibid.

26. Oscar Landi, "La tercera presidencia de Perón. Gobierno de emergencia y crisis política," *Revista Mexicana de Sociología* 40, no. 4 (1978): 1353–1410.

27. Martin Hardy to Jack Guenther, "Argentina—Recent Economic Developments," office memorandum, September 23, 1974, box 10, Argentina (1972–1975) file, folder 2, WHD–Argentina, IMF Archives.

28. Ibid.

29. Rougier and Fiszbein, *La frustración de un proyecto económico,* 89–90.

30. Ibid., 90.

31. See "General Quota Reviews," available online at http://www.imf.org/external/np/exr/facts/quotas.htm (accessed June 7, 2011).

32. Jorge del Canto to Managing Director, "Argentina," office memorandum, May 8, 1975, box 15, files 1–24, file title 1110-1430, file 14, CFC–Argentina, IMF Archives.

33. Alfredo Gómez Morales to Managing Director, cable, May 9, 1975, box 15, files 1–24, file title 1110-1430, file 14, CFC–Argentina, IMF Archives.

34. Johannes Witteveen to Alfredo Gómez Morales, cable, May 22, 1975, box 15, files 1–24, file title 1110-1430, file 14, CFC–Argentina, IMF Archives.

35. "Ley 21.698—Fondo Monetario Internacional—Aporte de la República Argentina—Incremento—Aprobación," in *Anales de Legislación Argentina* 38-A, nos. 21.686–21.757 (1975): 24–25.

36. *La Prensa,* May 10, May 22, 1975.

37. Ibid., May 3, 1975.

38. Ibid.

39. "Argentina—1974 Article VIII Consultation," EBM 74/127 (October 16, 1974), IMF Archives.

40. *La Prensa,* May 5, 1975.

41. Ibid., May 21, 1975.

42. Federico Marongiu, "Políticas de shock en la agonía del estado peronista. El Rodrigazo y el Mondelliazo," July 2006, Munich Personal RePEc Archive, MPRA paper no. 6338, available online at http://mpra.ub.uni-muenchen.de/6338 (accessed July 7, 2011).

43. Ibid.

44. Landi, *La tercera presidencia de Perón,* 1403.

45. Jorge del Canto to Acting Managing Director, "Argentina," confidential office memorandum, June 23, 1975, box 7, files 1–3, file title 810, file 33, CFC–Argentina, IMF Archives.

46. See, e.g., *Última Hora,* March 6, 1972; *El Mercurio,* November 16, 1972; *El Mercurio,* December 10, 1972; Jack Barnouin to Jorge del Canto, "Telephone Conversation with Jorge Marshall," office memorandum, June 30, 1972, box 50, Chile (1972–1973) file, folder 1, WHD–Chile, IMF Archives.

47. "Brazil—Briefing Paper for Article XIV Consultation," approved by Jorge del Canto and Irving S. Friedman, December 28, 1961, box 32, Brazil (1959–1961) file, folder 4, Brazil Country Files, Western Hemisphere Department Immediate Office Records (hereafter, WHD–Brazil), IMF Archives.

48. Managing Director [Witteveen] to Brazilian Working Party, "Discussions with the Brazilian Mission" March 30, 1962, box 33, Brazil (1959–1961) file, folder 2, WHD–Brazil, IMF Archives.

49. Ibid.

50. Ibid., 351–355.

51. "Oil Facility—Argentina—Intention to Request Purchase," EBM/75/170 (October 29, 1975), IMF Archives; *Memoria Anual Banco Central de la República Argentina, 1975,* 85–88.

52. Ibid.

53. Jorge del Canto to Managing Director and Deputy Managing Director, "Argentina," office memorandum, December 17, 1975, box 10, Argentina (1972–1975) file, folder 5, WHD–Argentina, IMF Archives.

54. For a detailed explanation of this instrument, see http://www.imf.org/external/np/ccffbsff/review/index.htm (accessed May 10, 2011).

55. *Memoria Anual Banco Central de la República Argentina, 1975,* 85–88.

56. U.K. Director, IMF/IBRD, to Treasury, confidential cable Eager 389, September 10, 1975, T 354/313, NAKEW.

57. "Briefing for Mission to Chile," February 29, 1972, box 50, Chile (1972–1973) file, folder 1, WHD–Chile, IMF Archives.

58. IMF Treasury to Banco Central de Chile, cable, December 20, 1972, box 50, Chile (1972–1973) file, folder 2, WHD–Chile, IMF Archives.

59. *Memoria Anual Banco Central de la República Argentina,* 1973, 79–82; ibid., 1974, 68–69.

60. *El Economista,* January 30, 1976.

61. María Sáenz Quesada, *Isabel Perón* (Buenos Aires: Editorial Planeta, 2003), 420–422.

62. Ibid.

63. "Argentina—Purchase Transaction—Compensatory Financing," EBM/76/52 (March 26, 1976), IMF Archives.

64. *El Economista,* February 27, 1976.

65. Marongiu, "Políticas de shock en la agonía del estado peronista," 11–12.

66. *El Economista,* February 27, 1976.

67. Ibid.

68. Sáenz Quesada, *Isabel Perón,* 422–423.

69. See, e.g., *New York Times,* February 15, February 18, February 29, 1976.

70. "Argentina—Purchase Transaction—Compensatory Financing."

71. *El Economista,* March 19, 1976.

72. Ibid.

73. Canning House Economic Meeting of March 8, 1976 on Argentina, March 9, 1976, Foreign and Commonwealth Office (hereafter, FCO) 7/3034/090/1, NAKEW.

74. See Daniel James, "The Peronist Left: 1955–1975." *Journal of Latin American Studies,* vol. 8, no. 2 (1976), 273–296.

75. See, e.g., Roberto Frenkel and Guillermo O'Donnell, "The 'Stabilization Programs' of the International Monetary Fund and Their Internal Impacts," in *Capitalism and the State in U.S.–Latin American Relations,* ed. Richard R. Fagen (Stanford, CA: Stanford University Press, 1979), 171–216; Sebastian Saiegh, "Do Countries Have a 'Democratic Advantage'? Political Institutions, Multilateral Agencies, and Sovereign Borrowing," *Comparative Political Studies* 38, no. 4 (2005): 366–387; Thomas E. Skidmore, "The Politics of Economic Stabilization in Postwar Latin America," in *Authoritarianism and Corporatism in Latin America,* ed. James Malloy (Pittsburg: University of Pittsburgh Press, 1977), 149–190.

76. For a comprehensive discussion of the preparations for the coup and the pressure exerted on President Isabel Perón, see María Seoane and Vicente Muleiro, *El dictador. La historia secreta y pública de Jorge Rafael Videla* (Buenos Aires: Editorial Sudamericana, 2001), chap. 2.

77. Ibid., 66–67.

78. Sheinin, *Argentina and the United States,* 161–162.

79. Peter Smith, *Talons of the Eagle: Dynamics of U.S.–Latin American Relations* (New York: Oxford University Press, 2000), 155–163.

80. David Rock, *Argentina, 1516–1987: From Spanish Colonization to Alfonsín* (Berkeley: University of California Press, 1987), 367–369.

81. Adolfo Canitrot, "La disciplina como objetivo de la política económica. Un ensayo sobre el programa del gobierno argentino desde 1976," *Desarrollo Económico,* vol. 19, no. 76 (1980), 453–475.

82. Mario Rapoport, "La saga de los Martínez de Hoz y el banquero arrepentido," *Buenos Aires Económico,* May 5, 2010, available online at http://www.elargentino.com/nota-89533-La-saga-de-los-Martínez-de-Hoz-y-el-banquero-arrepentido.html (accessed June 17, 2011).

83. "Argentina—Purchase Transaction—Compensatory Financing."

84. On Guillermo Klein's connections with Martínez de Hoz, see "Entrevista a Norberto Galasso," *Página 12,* June 21, 2004.

85. Norberto Galasso, *De la Banca Baring al FMI* (Buenos Aires: Colihue, 2002), 211–216.

86. Martin Hardy to Jorge del Canto, "Argentina—New Economic Measures," April 5, 1976, office memorandum, box 8, files 1–24, file title 810-818, file 1, CFC–Argentina, IMF Archives.

87. For a detailed discussion and interpretation of the program's key points, as explained by Martínez de Hoz "15 years later," see José Alfredo Martínez de Hoz, *Quince años después* (Buenos Aires: Emecé, 1991), esp. introduction, chap. 5.

88. Canitrot, "La disciplina como objetivo de la política económica," 483.

89. Interview with Aldo Ferrer, May 17, 2005, Proyecto de Historia Oral, Instituto Gino Germani, Universidad de Buenos Aires.

90. For a detailed discussion of Martínez de Hoz's plan, see Carlos Palacio Deheza, *El plan Martínez de Hoz y la economía argentina* (Buenos Aires: Corregidor, 1981), esp. chaps. 2–3.

91. Naomi Klein, *The Shock Doctrine: The Rise of Disaster Capitalism* (New York: Picador, 2007), 108.

92. Ibid., 94–95.

93. Ibid., 99. On the evolution of the Chicago Boys in Chile, see Juan Gabriel Valdés, *Pinochet's Economists: The Chicago School in Chile* (New York: Cambridge University Press, 1995).

94. Interview with José Alfredo Martínez de Hoz, October 11, 2005, pt. 1, Proyecto de Historia Oral, Instituto Gino Germani, Universidad de Buenos Aires.

95. Ram Hendris to Battler Madden, "Call on Dr. Guillermo Walter Klein," letter, May 26, 1976, FCO 7/3034/ECO90-01, NAKEW.

96. Anglin to Department of Commerce, letter on Enrique J. Loncan's visit to the United Kingdom, May 27, 1976, FCO 7/3034/ALA090/1, NAKEW.

97. Anglin to Treasury, "Argentine Economy," letter, June 2, 1976, FCO 7/3034, NAKEW.

98. Vito Tanzi, *Argentina, an Economic Chronicle: How One of the Richest Countries in the World Lost Its Wealth* (New York: Jorge Pinto, 2007), 19–20.

99. Ibid., 20.

100. Ibid., 21–22.

101. Jack Guenther to Managing Director, "Mission to Argentina," confidential office memorandum, June 15, 1976, box 8, files 1–24, file title 810-818, file 1, CFC–Argentina, IMF Archives.

102. Ibid.

103. Ibid.

104. Jorge del Canto to Managing Director and Deputy Managing Director, "Argentina—Status of Negotiations," confidential office memorandum, June 29, 1976, box 11, Argentina (1976–1981) file, folder 1, WHD–Argentina, IMF Archives.

105. Shakespeare to FCO, restricted telegram, July 29, 1976, FCO 7/3034/090/1, NAKEW.

106. Jorge del Canto to Managing Director and Deputy Managing Director, "Argentina—Status of Negotiations," confidential office memorandum, June 29, 1976, box 11, Argentina (1976–1981) file, folder 1, WHD–Argentina, IMF Archives.

107. José Alfredo Martínez de Hoz and Adolfo Diz to Johannes Witteveen, letter of intent, July 8, 1976, box 19, files 1–10, file title 1760, file 7, CFC–Argentina, IMF Archives.

108. Secretary to Members of Executive Board, "Argentina—Memorandum of Economic Policy," attached to letter of intent dated July 8, 1976, EBS/76/315 (July 14, 1976), IMF Archives.

109. Ibid.

110. Supp. 1, EBS/76/340 (August 9, 1976), annexed to "Argentina—Stand-by Arrangement," IMF Archives.

111. "El Fondo Monetario Internacional otorgó un importante crédito a la Argentina," *Boletín Semanal del Ministerio de Economía,* no. 142, August 13, 1976.

112. "Las gestiones financieras internacionales," *Boletín Semanal del Ministerio de Economía,* no. 150, October 8, 1976.

113. "Argentina—Request for Stand-by Arrangement—Prepared by the Western Hemisphere Department and Approved by J. del Canto," EBS/76/340 (July 27, 1976), IMF Archives.

114. For the full text of the new law of foreign investment ratified on August 13, 1976, see "Ley de inversiones extranjeras," *Boletín Semanal del Ministerio de Economía,* no. 142, August 13, 1976.

115. Interview with José Alfredo Martínez de Hoz, October 18, 2005, pt. 2, Proyecto de Historia Oral, Instituto Gino Germani, University of Buenos Aires.

116. Luigi Manzetti, *The International Monetary Fund and Economic Stabilization: The Argentine Case* (New York: Praeger, 1991), 96–97.

117. Martínez de Hoz interview, pt. 2 (October 18, 2005).

118. David Finch to Deputy Managing Director, "Technical Assistance to Argentina," office memorandum, September 24, 1976, box 11, Argentina (1976–1981) file, folder 2, WHD–Argentina, IMF Archives.

119. Ibid.

120. "Luncheon with Mr. Adolfo Diz, President, Central Bank of Argentina," office memorandum, October 28, 1976, box 11, Argentina (1976–1981) file, folder 2, WHD–Argentina, IMF Archives.

121. "El gobierno hace buenos negocios para el país," *Boletín Semanal del Ministerio de Economía,* no. 151, October 15, 1976.

122. Ibid.

123. "Confidential Briefing to Mission to Argentina," prepared by the Western Hemisphere Department, November 22, 1976, box 11, Argentina (1976–1981) file, folder 2, WHD–Argentina, IMF Archives.

124. Ibid.

125. Marcelo Caiola to Managing Director and Deputy Managing Director, "Argentina—Stand-by Review Mission," confidential office memorandum, December 22, 1976, box 11, Argentina (1976–1981) file, folder 2, WHD–Argentina, IMF Archives.

126. Jorge Schvarzer, *Implantación de un modelo económico. La experiencia argentina entre 1975 y el 2000* (Buenos Aires: A-Z Editora, 1998), 50.

127. Jorge del Canto to Acting Managing Director, "Recent Developments in Argentina," office memorandum, February 17, 1976, box 8, files 1–24, file title 810-818, file 5, CFC–Argentina, IMF Archives.

128. José Alfredo Martínez de Hoz and Adolfo Diz to Johannes Witteveen, letter, April 14, 1977, box 11, folder 3, Argentina (1976–1981) file, WHD–Argentina, IMF Archives.

129. Western Hemisphere Department to Adolfo Diz, July 29, 1977, box 8, files 1–24, file title 810-818, file 6, CFC–Argentina, IMF Archives.

130. "Argentina—Request for Stand-by Arrangement," memorandum, September 19, 1977, box 11, folder 3, Argentina (1976–1981) file, WHD–Argentina, IMF Archives; José Alfredo Martínez de Hoz and Adolfo Diz to Johannes Witteveen, letter of intent, August 22, 1977, box 11, folder 3, Argentina (1976–1981) file, WHD–Argentina, IMF Archives.

131. Supp. 1 confidential, annexed to "Argentina—Stand-by Arrangement," EBS/77/331 (September 19, 1977), IMF Archives.

132. "Argentina—1977 Article VIII Consultation, and Stand-by Arrangement," EBM/77/138 (September 16, 1977), IMF Archives.

133. Manzetti, *The International Monetary Fund and Economic Stabilization*, 111–112.

134. Ibid., 112.

135. Official data published by the Central Bank of Argentina, as quoted in Eric Toussaint, "Crisis financiera en Argentina: El origen de la deuda," January 2002, available at http://www.rcci.net/globalizacion/2002/fg214.htm (accessed June 7, 2011).

136. Schvarzer, *Implantación de un modelo económico*, 53–56.

137. "Argentina—Consultation under Stand-by Arrangement," EBS/78/168 (April 13, 1978), correction 1, IMF Archives.

138. Statement by Mr. Simone on Argentina, Executive Board Meeting, April 24, 1978, box 11, Argentina (1976–1981) file, folder 4, WHD–Argentina, IMF Archives.

139. "Argentina—Request for Technical Assistance," EBD/78/127 (June 1, 1978), IMF Archives.

140. Interview with Martínez de Hoz, pt. 1 (October 11, 2005).

141. Hernán Puentes to Marcelo Caiola, "Argentina—Economic Update," September 29, 1978, box 11, Argentina (1976–1981) file, folder 4, WHD–Argentina, IMF Archives.

142. Daniel Muchnik, *La patria financiera. El juego de la especulación* (Buenos Aires: Grupo Editorial Norma, 2005), 197–200.

143. On the economic plan announced on Christmas Day of 1978, see Marcos Novaro and Vicente Palermo, *La dictadura militar, 1976/1983. Del golpe de estado a la restauración democrática* (Buenos Aires: Editorial Paidós, 2006), 261–278.

144. Glen Biglaiser, *Guardians of the Nation? Economists, Generals, and Economic Reform in Latin America* (Notre Dame, IN: University of Notre Dame Press, 2002), 34–36.

145. Marcelo Caiola to Managing Director, "Mission to Argentina," memorandum, April 9, 1979, box 11, Argentina (1976–1981) file, folder 5, WHD–Argentina, IMF Archives.

146. Ibid.

147. Hernán Puentes to Marcelo Caiola, "Argentina—Economic Update," November 20, 1979, box 11, Argentina (1976–1981) file, folder 5, WHD–Argentina, IMF Archives.

148. "Argentina—Voluntary Repurchase," EBS/78/93 (February 24, 1978), IMF Archives.

149. Klaus F. Veigel, *Dictatorship, Democracy and Globalization: Argentina and the Cost of Paralysis, 1973-2001* (University Park: Pennsylvania State University Press, 2009), 66–70.

150. Law no. 22164 of the National Executive Power, signed by President Videla, Carlos Pastor, and José Alfredo Martínez de Hoz, February 18, 1980, listed in Listado leyes que se dictaron entre el 23 de marzo de 1976 y 10 de diciembre de 1983 que aún siguen vigentes, available online at http://www.perfil.com/docs/leyes_dictadura.pdf (accessed July 5, 2012).

151. Marcelo Caiola to Managing Director, "Mission to Argentina," June 9, 1980, box 11, Argentina (1976–1981) file, folder 5, WHD–Argentina, IMF Archives.

152. Ibid.

153. "Argentina—Request for Technical Assistance," EBD/79/146 (June 6, 1979), IMF Archives; "Visit to Argentina," July 14–19, July 21, 1980, box 11, Argentina (1976–1981) file, folder 5, WHD–Argentina, IMF Archives.

154. "Argentina—Staff Report for the 1981 Article IV Consultation," SM/81/233 (December 2, 1981), IMF Archives.

155. On Galtieri's special relations with the United States, see Richard C. Thornton, *The Reagan Revolution II: Rebuilding the Western Alliance* (Victoria: Trafford, 2005), chaps. 1–2.

156. Biglaiser, *Guardians of the Nation?*, 36–37.

157. Rock, *Argentina, 1516–1987*, 383–386.

158. "Meeting with the Argentine Delegation," May 11, 1982, and "Argentina-Mid Year Review," July 7, 1982, both in box 12, Argentina (1982–1983) file, folder 1, WHD–Argentina, IMF Archives.

159. Ibid.

160. Christian Brachet to Sanson, "Telephone Conversation with Argentina's Central Bank President," September 23, 1982, box 12, Argentina (1982–1983) file, folder 2, WHD–Argentina, IMF Archives.

161. E. Walter Robicheck to Julio González del Solar, telegram, November 5, 1982, box 12, Argentina (1982–1983) file, folder 2, WHD–Argentina, and EBM 83/17 (January 24, 1983), both in IMF Archives.

162. James Boughton, *Silent Revolution: IMF, 1979–1989* (Washington, DC: International Monetary Fund, 2001), 331–336.

163. Sterie Beza to Acting Managing Director, "Staff Visit to Argentina," November 22, 1982, box 12, Argentina (1982–1983) file, folder 2, WHD–Argentina, IMF Archives.

164. Boughton, *Silent Revolution*, 334.

165. "Argentina—Stand-by Arrangement," EBS/83/8, January 24, 1983–January 25, 1983, supp. 1, IMF Archives.

166. "Argentina—Performance under Stand-by Arrangement," March 30, 1983, box 12, Argentina (1982–1983) file, folder 3, WHD–Argentina, IMF Archives.

167. Eduardo Weisner to Managing Director, "Staff Visit to Argentina," April 17–21, April 26, 1983, box 12, Argentina (1982–1983) file, folder 3, WHD–Argentina, IMF Archives.

168. "Briefing for Mission to Argentina," May 3, 1983, box 12, Argentina (1982–1983) file, folder 3, WHD–Argentina, IMF Archives.

169. "Review Mission to Argentina," June 6, 1983, box 12, Argentina (1982–1983) file, folder 3, WHD–Argentina, IMF Archives.

170. Sterie Beza to Managing Director, "Visit of the President of the Central Bank of Argentina," June 23, 1983, box 12, Argentina (1982–1983) file, folder 3, WHD–Argentina, IMF Archives.

171. "Conversation with Citibank in Sequencing of Bank and Fund Operations in Argentina," August 10, 1983, box 12, Argentina (1982–1983) file, folder 3, WHD–Argentina, IMF Archives.

172. Erica Gould, *Money Talks: The International Monetary Fund, Conditionality, and Supplementary Financiers* (Stanford, CA: Stanford University Press, 2006), esp. chap. 6.

173. Pastor, "Managing the Latin American Debt Crisis," 289–313.

174. Victor Bulmer-Thomas, *The Economic History of Latin America since Independence* (New York: Cambridge University Press, 1994), 361–369.

CHAPTER 6

1. Karen L. Remmer, "The Political Impact of Economic Crisis in Latin America in the 1980s," *American Political Science Review* 85, no. 3 (1991): 777–800.

2. Cheryl Payer, *The Debt Trap: The IMF and the Third World* (New York: Monthly Review Press, 1974).

3. Christine Bogdanowicz-Bindert, "The Debt Crisis: The Baker Plan Revisited," *Journal of Interamerican Studies and World Affairs* 28, no. 3 (1986): 33–45.

4. Sarah Babb, *Behind the Development Banks: Washington Politics, World Poverty, and the Wealth of Nations* (Chicago: University of Chicago Press, 2009), chap. 5.

5. See, e.g., Paul Craig Roberts and Karen LaFollette Araujo, *The Capitalist Revolution in Latin America* (New York: Oxford University Press, 1997); Duncan Green, *Silent Revolution. The Rise of Market Economics in Latin America* (London: Cassell, 1995).

6. William Smith, *Authoritarianism and the Crisis of the Argentine Political Economy* (Stanford, CA: Stanford University Press, 1989), 270.

7. Julieta Pesce, "La gestión del ministro Grinspun en un contexto de transición democratic. Errores de diagnostic y subestimación del poder económico local e internacional," *Ciclos* 14, no. 28 (2004), 65–88.

8. David Rock, *Argentina, 1516–1987: From Spanish Colonization to Alfonsín* (Berkeley: University of California Press, 1987), 393–397.

9. Pesce, "La gestión del ministro Grinspun," 65–88.

10. Edgar J. Dosman, *The Life and Times of Raúl Prebisch* (Montreal: McGill–Queens University Press, 2008), 491–492.

11. Ibid.

12. His reputation was based especially on the elaboration of the Singer-Prebisch theory in 1950, a theory that is at the core of dependency theory.

13. Daniel Muchnik, *La patria financiera. El juego de la especulación* (Buenos Aires: Grupo Editorial Norma, 2005), 222–223.

14. Ibid., 223–224.

15. Kendall Stiles, "Argentina's Bargaining with the IMF," *Journal of Interamerican Studies and World Affairs* 29, no. 3 (1987): 55–85.

16. Eduardo Weisner to Acting Managing Director, "Fact Finding Mission to Argentina," December 7, 1983, box 12, Argentina (1982–1983) file, folder 4, WHD–Argentina, IMF Archives.

17. Ibid.

18. Burke Dillon to Managing Director, "Mission to Argentina, December 12–16, 1983," December 19, 1983, box 12, Argentina (1982–1983) file, folder 1, WHD–Argentina, IMF Archives.

19. Ibid.

20. Ibid.

21. Ibid.

22. "Argentina—Cancellation of Stand-by Arrangement," EBS/84/23 (January 31, 1984), IMF Archives.

23. Eduardo Weisner to Managing Director, "Visit of Mr. García Vásquez, President of the Central Bank," December 20, 1983, box 12, Argentina (1982–1983) file, folder 4, WHD–Argentina, IMF Archives.

24. "Argentina—Cancellation of Stand-by Arrangement."

25. "Briefing to Mission to Argentina," prepared by the Western Hemisphere Department, January 30, box 13, Argentina (1984–1985) file, folder 1, WHD–Argentina, IMF Archives.

26. Ibid.

27. "Minutes of Argentine Mission's Report to Management and US Representatives," March 7, 1984, box 13, Argentina (1984–1985) file, folder 1, WHD–Argentina, IMF Archives.

28. Ibid.

29. President Raúl Alfonsín to Raúl Prebisch, letter, March 21, 1984 (Buenos Aires). The original letter is in box 13, Argentina (1984–1985) file, folder 1, WHD–Argentina, IMF Archives.

30. Dosman, *The Life and Times of Raúl Prebisch*, 496.

31. Muchnik, *La patria financiera*, 224.

32. Eduardo Wiesner to Managing Director, "Argentina—Visit by Minister Grinspun and Central Bank President García Vásquez," April 10, 1984, box 13, Argentina (1984–1985) file, folder 1, WHD–Argentina, IMF Archives.

33. Eduardo Wiesner to Managing Director, "Staff Travel to Buenos Aires," May 2, 1984, box 13, Argentina (1984–1985) file, folder 1, WHD–Argentina, IMF Archives.

34. Eduardo Wiesner to Managing Director, "Argentina," May 9, 1984, box 13, Argentina (1984–1985) file, folder 1, WHD–Argentina, IMF Archives.

35. Ibid.

36. Eduardo Wiesner to Managing Director, "Mission to Argentina," May 9, 1984, box 13, Argentina (1984–1985) file, folder 1, WHD–Argentina, IMF Archives.

37. Minister Bernardo Grinspun to Jacques de Larosiere, letter of intent, June 9, 1984, box 13, Argentina (1984–1985) file, folder 1, WHD–Argentina, IMF Archives.

38. Ibid.

39. Grigore Pop-Eleches, *From Economic Crisis to Reform: IMF Programs in Latin America and Eastern Europe* (Princeton, NJ: Princeton University Press, 2009), 118–120.

40. "Argentina," June 13, 1984, Argentina Country Files, box 13, Argentina (1984–1985) file, folder 1, WHD–Argentina, IMF Archives.

41. Ibid.

42. Eduardo Wiesner to Managing Director, "Discussions with Argentine Delegation," June 24, 1984, box 13, Argentina (1984–1985) file, folder 1, WHD–Argentina, IMF Archives.

43. "Staff Visit to Argentina, July 16–24, 1984," July 27, 1984, box 13, Argentina (1984–1985) file, folder 1, WHD–Argentina, IMF Archives.

44. Ibid.

45. Letter of intent, EBS/84/203 (September 18, 1984), IMF Archives.

46. "Argentina—Mr. Grinspun's Visit," November 15, 1984, box 13, Argentina (1984–1985) file, folder 1, WHD–Argentina, IMF Archives.

47. Eduardo Wiesner to Managing Director, "Argentina—Staff Visit," November 30, 1984, box 13, Argentina (1984–1985) file, folder 1, WHD–Argentina, IMF Archives.

48. William C. Hood to Managing Director, "Argentina—Compensatory Financing Facility, November 30, 1984, box 13, Argentina (1984–1985) file, folder 2, WHD–Argentina, IMF Archives.

49. Press Release no. 28, December 28, 1984, box 13, Argentina (1984–1985) file, folder 1, WHD–Argentina, IMF Archives.

50. "Report on Renegotiation of External Foreign Debt," prepared by the Western Hemisphere Department, EBS/85/58 (March 14, 1985), IMF Archives.

51. Ibid.

52. James Boughton, *Silent Revolution: IMF, 1979–1989* (Washington, DC: International Monetary Fund, 2001), 399.

53. Kurt Weyland, *The Politics of Market Reform in Fragile Democracies: Argentina, Brazil, Peru, and Venezuela* (Princeton, NJ: Princeton University Press, 2002), 82–83; José Luis Machinea, "Stabilisation under Alfonsín," in *Argentina in the Crisis Years (1983–1990)*, ed. Colin M. Lewis and Nissa Torrentes (London: Institute of Latin American Studies, 1993), 124–143.

54. Green, *Silent Revolution*, 66–67.

55. Smith, *Authoritarianism*, 281.

56. Ricardo Ortiz and Martín Schorr, "La economía política del gobierno de Alfonsín. Creciente subordinación al poder económico durante la 'década perdida,'" in *Los años de Alfonsín. ¿El poder de la democracia o la democracia del poder?* ed. Alfredo Pucciarelli (Buenos Aires: Siglo Veintiuno Editores Argentina, 2006), 291–334.

57. *Los Angeles Times,* June 7, 1985.

58. Pop-Eleches, *From Economic Crisis to Reform*, 112–116.

59. William, *Authoritarianism*, 281–282.

60. "The Chairman's Summing-Up at the Conclusion of the 1985 Article IV Consultation with Argentina." EBM/86/43 (March 10, 1986), SUR/86/26, IMF Archives.

61. Rock, *Argentina, 1516–1987*, 400–403.

62. "Argentina—Staff Report for the 1985 Article IV Consultation and Review of Stand-by Arrangement," EBS/86/39 (February 21, 1986), IMF Archives.

63. "Argentina—Technical Assistance," EBM/86/58 (March 28, 1986), IMF Archives.

64. "Argentina—Stand-by Arrangement—Extension of Period," EBS/86/39 (May 29, 1986), supp. 1, IMF Archives.

65. Secretary to Members of the Executive Board, "Argentina—Request for Stand-by Arrangement," EBS/87/5 (January 13, 1987), IMF Archive.

66. Ibid.

67. Ibid.

68. Secretary to Members of the Executive Board, "Argentina—Stand-by Arrangement," EBS/87/5 (February 23, 1987), supp. 3, IMF Archives.

69. Machinea, "Stabilization under Alfonsín."

70. Klaus F. Veigel, *Dictatorship, Democracy and Globalization: Argentina and the Cost of Paralysis, 1973–2001* (University Park: Pennsylvania State University Press, 2009), 164–165; Edmar Bacha and Richard Feinberg, "The World Bank and Structural Adjustment in Latin America," paper presented at the Faculty of Economy, University of Rio de Janeiro, July 1985, available online at http://www.econ.puc-rio.br/pdf/td100.pdf (accessed July 10, 2011).

71. Jorge Garfunkel, "Economic Policy and Economic Performance: A Private Sector View of Regime Change," in *Argentina in the Crisis Years (1983–1990),* ed. Colin M. Lewis and Nissa Torrentes (London: Institute of Latin American Studies, 1993), 144–158.

72. "En la memoria, los hechos de 1989," *La Nación,* December 16, 2001.

73. Ernesto Tenembaum, *Enemigos* (Buenos Aires: Norma, 2004), 71–72.

74. Garfunkel, "Economic Policy and Economic Performance," 153–154.

75. Kurt Weyland, "Neopopulism and Neoliberalism in Latin America: Unexpected Affinities," *Studies in Comparative International Development* 31, no. 3 (1996): 3–31. See also Vicente Palermo and John Collins, "Moderate Populism: A Political Approach to Argentina's 1991 Convertibility Plan," *Latin American Perspectives* 25, no. 4 (1998): 36–62; Celia Szusterman, "Carlos Saúl Menem: Variations in the Theme of Populism," *Bulletin of Latin American Research* 19, no. 2 (2000): 193–206.

76. Guillermo Miguel Figari, *De Alfonsín a Menem. Política exterior y globalización* (Buenos Aires: Memphis, 1997), chap. 3.

77. Vicente Palermo and Marcos Novaro, *Política y poder en el gobierno de Menem* (Buenos Aires: Norma, 1996), 15–19.

78. James Brooke, "Peru's Poor Feel Hardship of 'FujiShock' Austerity," *New York Times*, August 12, 1990.

79. Carlos Ares, "Un país en estado de choque. Menem somete el país a una cirugía sin anestecia," *El País,* August 10, 1989.

80. Naomi Klein, *The Shock Doctrine: The Rise of Disaster Capitalism* (New York: Picador, 2007), esp. pts. 1–3.

81. Javier Corrales, "¿Contribuyen las crisis económicas a la implementación de reformas de mercado? La Argentina y Venezuela en los '90," *Desarrollo Económico* 39, no. 153 (1999): 3–29.

82. On the question of whether Menem (and Fujimori) changed their economic plans once in office or not, see Susan Stokes, *Mandates and Democracy: Neoliberalism by Surprise in Latin America* (New York: Cambridge University Press, 2001), chap. 3.

83. Pablo Gerchunoff and Juan Carlos Torre, "La política de liberación económica en la administración de Menem," *Desarrollo Económico* 36, no. 143 (1996): 733–768.

84. William Smith, "State, Market, and Neoliberalism in Post-Transition Argentina: The Menem Experiment," *Journal of Interamerican Studies and World Affairs* 33, no. 4 (1991): 45–82.

85. On the tactics used by Menem to gain wide support for privatizations, see Daniel Triesman, "Cardoso, Menem, and Machiavelli: Political Tactics and Privatization in Latin America," *Studies in Comparative International Development* 38, no. 3 (2003): 93–109.

86. John Williamson, ed., *Latin American Adjustment: How Much Has Happened?* (Washington, DC: Peterson Institute for International Economics, 1990).

87. Carlos Saúl Menem and Roberto Dromi, *Reforma del estado y transformación nacional* (Buenos Aires: Editorial Ciencias de la Administración, 1990), 19–20.

88. Ibid.

89. Ibid., 76–80.

90. Veigel, *Dictatorship, Democracy, and Globalization,* 173–174. The official and full text of Law 23696 of August 17, 1989, is available online at http://mepriv.mecon.gov.ar/Normas/23696.htm.

91. Delia Ferreira Rubio and Matteo Goretti, "Cuando el presidente gobierna solo. Menem y los decretos de seguridad y urgencia hasta la reforma constitucional (Julio 1989–Agosto 1994), *Desarrollo Económico,* 36, no. 141 (1996): 443–474.

92. Smith, "State, Market, and Neoliberalism in Post-Transition Argentina," 55.

93. "Argentina—Staff Report for the 1989 Article IV Consultation and Request for Stand-by Arrangement," EBS/89/199 (October 17, 1989), IMF Archives.

94. Ibid.

95. Ibid.

96. "Argentina—Stand-by Arrangement," EBS/89/199 (November 16, 1989), supp. 1, IMF Archives.

97. "Memorandum on Economic Policy," November 16, 1989, EBS/89/199, IMF Archives, attached to ibid.

98. Ibid.

99. Ibid.

100. "Argentina—Review and Modification of Stand-by Arrangement," EBS/90/90 (May 14, 1990), IMF Archives.

101. Ibid.

102. Veigel, *Dictatorship, Democracy, and Globalization*, 176.

103. "Argentina—Staff Report for the Article IV Consultation and Review and Modification of Stand-by Arrangement," EBS/90/191 (November 12, 1990), IMF Archives.

104. *New York Times*, December 4, 1990.

105. Daniel Azpiazu, "Las privatizaciones en la Argentina. ¿Precariedad regulatoria o regulación funcional a los privilegios empresarios?," *Ciclos* 11, no. 21 (2001): 86–99; Gerchunoff and Torre, "La política de liberación económica," 733–768.

106. Domingo Cavallo and Joaquín Cottani, "Argentina's Convertibility Plan and the IMF," *American Economic Review* 87, no. 2 (1997): 17–22.

107. Domingo Cavallo, "Argentina and the IMF during the two Bush Administrations," *International Finance,* 7:1 (2004), 137–150.

108. Cavallo and Cottani, "Argentina's Convertibility Plan," 18.

109. Ministerio de Economía de la Nación,"Informe Económico 1995," available online at http://www.mecon.gov.ar/informe/infor16/indice.htm (accessed July 29, 2011).

110. Carlos Acuña, Sebastián Galiani and Mario Tommasi, "Understanding Reform: The Case of Argentina," in *Understanding Market Reforms in Latin America*, ed. José María Fanelli (New York: Palgrave, 2007), 31–72.

111. J. Patrice McSherry, "Strategic Alliance: Menem and the Military Security Forces in Argentina," *Latin American Perspectives* 24, no. 6 (1997): 63–92.

112. *Clarín Digital,* July 25, 1995 (http://edant.clarin.com/diario/96/07/25/cavayo.htm).

113. Ibid., July 27, 1995 (http://edant.clarin.com/diario/96/07/27/central.htm).

114. Norberto Galasso, *De la Banca Baring al FMI* (Buenos Aires: Colihue, 2002), 325–328.

115. Marcelo Bonelli, "El FMI quire poner a la Argentina como ejemplo," *Clarín,* October 1, 1989.

116. Ana Baron, "La Asamblea del FMI. Coincidencias con Clinton," *Clarín,* October 7, 1998.

117. Statement by the Hon. Carlos Saúl Menem, President of the Republic of Argentina, at the Annual Meetings of the Board of Governors of the International Monetary Fund and the World Bank Group, October 6–8, 1989, press release no. 5, available online at http://www.imf.org/external/am/1998/speeches/pr05e.pdf (accessed July 25, 2011).

118. Ana María Mustapic, "Inestabilidad sin colapso. La renuncia de los presidents: Argentina en el año 2001," *Desarrollo Económico* 45, no. 178 (2005): 263–280.

119. Ernesto Seman and Mariana García, "De la Rúa present su gabinete y alertó sobre el deficit social y moral," *Clarín,* November 25, 1999.

120. Ernesto Seman, "De la Rúa presidente con cerca del 50%," *Clarín,* October 25, 1999.

121. "De la Rúa dijo que los impuestos son transitorios," *Clarín,* January 15, 2000.

122. "IMF Approves $7.2 Billion Three-Year Stand-by Credit for Argentina," press release no. 00/17, March 10, 2000, available online at http://www.imf.org/external/np/sec/pr/2000/pr0017.htm (accessed July 5, 2011).

123. "Un rojo de $600 millones," *La Nación,* May 6, 2000.

124. Jorge Rosales, "Lanza el gobierno una fuerte reforma del estado," *La Nación,* May 6, 2000.

125. "Apoyo del FMI al plan, en el momento justo," *La Nación,* May 17, 2000.

126. Ibid.

127. Michael Mussa, *Argentina and the Fund: From Triumph to Tragedy* (Washington, DC: Institute for International Economics, 2002), 27.

128. "El FMI apoyó el juste de De la Rúa," *La Nación,* June 14, 2000.

129. "IMF Approves Augmentation of Argentina's Stand-by Credit to $14 billion and Completes Second Review," press release no. 01/3, January 12, 2001, available online at https://www.imf.org/external/pubs/ft/scr/2001/cr0126.pdf (accessed July 5, 2011).

130. Joseph Kahn, "IMF Plans Billions in Aid to Argentina," *New York Times,* December 19, 2000.

131. Mussa, *Argentina and the Fund,* 28.

132. Paul Blustein, *And the Money Kept Rolling In (and Out): Wall Street, the IMF, and the Bankrupting of Argentina* (New York: Public Affairs, 2005), 109–110.

133. Martín Kanenguiser, "López Murphy insiste en privatizar el Banco Nación," *La Nación,* March 12, 2001.

134. Germán Sopeña, "Tras el vértigo, la última carga posible," *La Nación,* March 20, 2001.

135. "Argentina—Third Review under Stand-by Arrangement, Request for Waivers and Modification of the Program," prepared by the Western Hemisphere Department and Policy and Review Departments, May 14, 2001, available online at http://www.imf.org/external/pubs/ft/scr/2001/cr0190.pdf (accessed July 5, 2011).

136. Mussa, *Argentina and the Fund,* 39–40.

137. Ibid.

138. Miguel Ángel Borda, "Déficit cero. La última oportunidad," *La Nación,* July 15, 2001.

139. Blustein, *And the Money Kept Rolling In (and Out),* 150.

140. María Castro, "En agosto se alcnzó el d'eficit cero, dijo Cavallo," *La Nación,* September 4, 2001.

141. "IMF Augments Argentina Stand-by Credit to $21.57 Billion and Completes Fourth Review," press release 01/37, September 7, 2001, available online at http://www.imf.org/external/np/sec/pr/2001/pr0137.htm (accessed July 6, 2011).

142. Mussa, *Argentina and the Fund,* 49–50.

143. "Rige el estado de sitio después de los saqueos; renunció Cavallo," *La Nación,* December 20, 2001.

144. Fernando González, "De la Rúa renunció, cercado por la crisis y sin resplado político," *Clarín,* December 21, 2001.

145. "La Argentina entrará hoy en default," *La Nación,* December 24, 2001.

146. Laura Serra, "Duhalde formará un gobierno de unidad," *La Nación,* January 2, 2002.

147. *Pesification* meant that, except for several transactions that had to be conducted in dollars (such as the import of foreign products), economic transactions would be conducted in pesos. (Even real state prices were denominated in pesos.)

148. "Remes reconoció la economía argentina depende del FMI," *Los Andes,* February 22, 2002.

149. IMF Survey, 23:2, February 3, 2003, available online at (http://www.imf.org/external/pubs/ft/survey/2003/020303.pdf (accessed July 8, 2011).

150. Roberto Cachanosky, "Seis ministros de economía en seis años. ¿Algo más podemos esperar?" *La Nación,* July 8, 2009.

151. Larry Rohter, "Argentina Agrees to Talk Reform with IMF," *New York Times,* June 25, 2003.

152. Roberto Frenkel, "El Fondo se separa de los acreedores," *La Nación,* October 5, 2003; George Trefgane, "IMF Loan to Argentina Sparks Row," *Telegraph,* September 23, 2003.

153. Martín Rodríguez Yebra, "Kirchner busca más aliados frente al FMI," *La Nación,* March 18, 2004.

154. "Kirchner: Error del Fondo costó 15 millones de pobres," *El Universo,* July 31, 2004.

155. Martín Rodríguez Yebra, "Fuertes críticas de Kirchner en la ONU contra el FMI," *La Nación,* September 15, 2005.

156. Cynthia Rush, "Argentina President Kirchner: 'There Is Life after the IMF,'" *Executive Intelligence Review,* April 29, 2005.

157. "Kirchner and Lula: Different Ways to Give the Fund the Kiss-off," *Economist,* December 20, 2005.

CONCLUSIONS

1. Graham Bird, Mumtaz Hussain, and Joseph Joyce, "Many Happy Returns? Recidivism and the IMF," *Journal of International Money and Finance* 23, no. 2 (2004): 231–251.

2. Ernesto Tenembaum, *Enemigos* (Buenos Aires: Norma, 2004), 182.

3. Ibid., 183.

4. Peter Hass, "Introduction: Epistemic Communities and International Policy Coordination." *International Organization* 46, no. 1 (1992): 3.

References

Acuña, Carlos, Sebastián Galiani, and Mario Tommasi. "Understanding Reform: The Case of Argentina." In *Understanding Market Reforms in Latin America,* ed. José María Fanelli, 31–72. New York: Palgrave, 2007.

Adler, Emanuel, and Peter Hass. "Conclusion: Epistemic Communities, World Order, and the Creation of a Reflective Research Program." *International Organization* 46, no. 1 (1992): 367–390.

Amadeo, Eduardo. *La salida del abismo.* Buenos Aires: Editorial Planeta, 2003.

Anil, Hira. *Ideas and Economic Policy in Latin America: Regional, National, and Organizational Case Studies.* Westport, CT: Praeger, 1998.

Asherman, Jane. "The International Monetary Fund: A History of Compromise." *Journal of International Law and Politics* 16 (1984): 235–304.

Azpiazu, Daniel. "Las privatizaciones en la Argentina. ¿Precariedad regulatoria o regulación funcional a los privilegios empresarios?" *Ciclos* 11, no. 21 (2001): 86–99.

Babb, Sarah. *Behind the Development Banks: Washington Politics, World Poverty, and the Wealth of Nations.* Chicago: University of Chicago Press, 2009.

———. *Managing Mexico: Economists from Nationalism to Neoliberalism.* Princeton, NJ: Princeton University Press, 2001.

Bacha, Edmar, and Richard Feinberg. "The World Bank and Structural Adjustment in Latin America." Paper presented to the Faculty of Economy, University of Rio de Janeiro, July 1985. Available online at http://www.econ.puc-rio.br/pdf/td100.pdf (accessed August 2, 2012).

Beckhart, B. H. "The Bretton Woods Proposal for an International Monetary Fund." *Political Science Quarterly* 59 (1944): 489–528.

Behrman, Jack N. "Political Factors in U.S. International Financial Cooperation, 1945–1950." *American Political Science Review* 47 (1953): 431–460.

Belini, Claudio. "D.I.N.I.E. y los límites de la política industrial peronista, 1947–1955." *Desarrollo Económico* 41, no. 161 (2001): 97–119.

Bethell, Leslie. "Britain and Latin America in Historical Perspective." In *Britain and Latin America: A Changing Relationship,* ed. Victor Bulmer-Thomas, 1–26. New York: Cambridge University Press, 1989.

Bethell, Leslie, and Ian Roxborough. "Latin America between the Second World War and the Cold War: Some Reflections of the 1945–8 Conjuncture." *Journal of Latin American Studies* 20 (1988): 167–189.

Biglaiser, Glen. *Guardians of the Nation? Economists, Generals, and Economic Reform in Latin America.* Notre Dame, IN: University of Notre Dame Press, 2002.

Bird, Graham, Mumtaz Hussain, and Joseph Joyce. "Many Happy Returns? Recidivism and the IMF." *Journal of International Money and Finance* 23, no. 2 (2004): 231–251.

Blum, John. *From the Morgenthau Diaries: Years of War, 1941–1945.* Boston: Houghton Mifflin, 1967.

Blustein, Paul. *And the Money Kept Rolling In (and Out): Wall Street, the IMF, and the Bankrupting of Argentina.* New York: Public Affairs, 2005.

Bogdanowicz-Bindert, Christine. "The Debt Crisis: The Baker Plan Revisited." *Journal of Interamerican Studies and World Affairs* 28, no. 3 (1986): 33–45.

Bonelli, Marcelo. *Un país en deuda. La Argentina y su imposible relación con el FMI.* Buenos Aires: Editorial Planeta, 2004.

Boughton, James. *Silent Revolution: IMF, 1979–1989.* Washington, DC: International Monetary Fund, 2001.

Brender, Valerie. "Economic Transformations in Chile: The Formation of the Chicago Boys." *American Economist* 55, no. 1 (2010): 111–122.

Brennan, James. "Industrialistas y Bolicheros: Business and the Peronist Populist Alliance, 1943–1976." In *Peronism and Argentina,* ed. James Brennan, 79–123. Wilmington, DE: Rowman and Littlefield, 1998.

———. "Prolegomenon to Neoliberalism: The Political Economy of Populist Argentina, 1943–1976." *Latin American Perspectives* 34, no. 3 (May 2007): 49–66.

Brennan, James, and Mónica Gordillo. "Working Class Protest, Popular Revolt, and Urban Insurrection in Argentina: The 1969 'Cordobazo.'" *Journal of Social History* 27, no. 3 (1994): 477–498.

Brenta, Noemí. *Argentina atrapada. Historia de las relaciones con el FMI, 1956–2006.* Buenos Aires: Ediciones Cooperativas, 2009.

Brown, Edward E. "The International Monetary Fund: A Consideration of Certain Objection." *Journal of Business of the University of Chicago* 17 (1944): 199–208.

Buira, Ariel, ed. *Challenges to the World Bank and IMF: Developing Country Perspectives.* London: Anthem, 2003.

Bulmer-Thomas, Victor. *The Economic History of Latin America since Independence.* New York: Cambridge University Press, 1994.

Canitrot, Adolfo. "La disciplina como objetivo de la política económica. Un ensayo sobre el programa del gobierno argentino desde 1976." *Desarrollo Económico* 19, no. 76 (1980): 453–475.

Cantón, Dario, and Jorge Jorrat. "Occupation and Vote in Urban Argentina: The March 1973 Presidential Election." *Latin American Research Review* 13, no. 1 (1978): 146–157.

Cavallo, Domingo. "Argentina and the IMF during the two Bush Administrations." *International Finance* 7, no. 1 (2004): 137–150.

Cavallo, Domingo, and Joaquín Cottani. "Argentina's Convertibility Plan and the IMF." *American Economic Review* 87, no. 2 (1997): 17–22.

Cavarozzi, Marcelo. "El 'desarrollismo' y las relaciones entre democracia y capitalismo dependiente en dependencia y desarrollo en América Latina." *Latin American Research Review* 17, no. 1 (1982): 152–165.

Cesarano, Filippo. *Monetary Theory and Bretton Woods: The Construction of an International Monetary Order.* New York: Cambridge University Press, 2006.

Chwieroth, Jeffrey. *Capital Ideas: The IMF and the Rise of Financial Liberalization.* Princeton, NJ: Princeton University Press, 2009.

———. "'The Silent Revolution': Professional Training, Sympathetic Interlocutors, and IMF Lending." Paper presented at the University Seminar on Global Governance and Democracy, Duke University, Durham, NC, April 2008.

Cisneros, Andrés, and Carlos Escudé, eds. *Historia general de las relaciones exteriores de la República Argentinas,* 14 vols. Buenos Aires: Nuevohacer, 1989–1999.

Cohen, Benjamin. "Balance-of-Payments Financing: Evolution of a Regime." *International Organization* 36, no. 2 (1982): 457–478.

Corrales, Javier. "¿Contribuyen las crisis económicas a la implementación de reformas de mercado? La Argentina y Venezuela en los '90." *Desarrollo Económico* 39, no. 153 (1999): 3–29.

Cortés Conde, Roberto. *Progreso y declinación de la economía argentina. Un análisis histórico institucional.* Mexico City: Fondo Cultura Económica, 1998.

———. "Raúl Prebisch: His Years in Government." *CEPAL Review* 75 (2001): 81–86.

de Looper, Johan H. C. "Recent Latin American Experience with Bilateral Trade and Payments Agreements." *IMF Staff Papers* 4 (1954–1955): 85–112.

de Monserrat Llairó, María, and Rymundo Siepe. *Frondizi. Un nuevo modelo de inserción internacional.* Buenos Aires: Eudeba, 2003.

de Pablo, Juan Carlos. "Economic Policy without Political Context: Guido, 1962–3." In *The Political Economy of Argentina, 1946–83,* ed. Guido di Tella and Rudiger Dornbusch, 129–141. Pittsburgh: University of Pittsburgh Press, 1989.

di Tella, Guido, and D. Cameron Watt. *Argentina between the Great Powers, 1939–46.* London: Macmillan, 1989.

Dosman, Edgar. *The Life and Times of Raúl Prebisch, 1901–1986.* Montreal: McGill–Queen's University Press, 2008.

Drazen, Allan. *Political Economy in Macroeconomics.* Princeton, NJ: Princeton University Press, 2000.

Eaton, Jonathan. "Sovereign Debt: A Primer." *World Bank Economic Review* 7 (1993): 137–172.

Eaton, Jonathan, and Mark Gersovitz. "Debt with Potential Repudiation: Theoretical and Empirical Analysis." *Review of Economic Studies* 48, no. 2 (1981): 289–309.

Edwards, Sebastian. "LDC Foreign Borrowing and Default Risk: An Empirical Investigation 1976–1980." *American Economic Review* 74 (1984): 726–734.

Elena, Eduardo. "Peronist Consumer Politics and the Problem of Domesticating Markets in Argentina, 1943–1955." *Hispanic American Historical Review* 87, no. 1 (2007): 111–149.

Epstein, Gerald, Julie Graham, and Jessica Nembhard, eds. *Creating a New World Economy: Forces of Change and Plans for Action.* Philadelphia: Temple University Press, 1993.

Escudé, Carlos. "Un enigma. La 'irracionalidad' Argentina frente a la Segunda Guerra Mundial." *Estudios Interdisciplinarios de América Latina y el Caribe* 6 (1995): 5–35.

———. "The U.S. Destabilization and Economic Boycott of Argentina of the 1940s, Revisited." Universidad del Centro de Estudios Macroeconómicos de Argentina, Serie de Documentos de Trabajo no. 323, Área de Ciencia Política, July 2006.

Eshag, Eprime, and Rosemary Thorp. "Las políticas económicas ortodoxas de Perón a Guido (1953–1963). Consecuencias económicas y sociales." In *Los planes de estabilización en la Argentina,* ed. Aldo Ferrer, Mario Brodersohn, Eprime Eshag, and Rosemary Thorp, 64–132. Buenos Aires: Paidós, 1974.

Ferreira Rubio, Delia, and Matteo Goretti. "Cuando el presidente gobierna solo. Menem y los decretos de seguridad y urgencia hasta la reforma constitucional (Julio 1989–Agosto 1994)." *Desarrollo Económico* 36, no. 141 (1996): 443–474.

Figari, Guillermo Miguel. *De Alfonsín a Menem. Política exterior y globalización.* Buenos Aires: Memphis, 1997.

Francis, Michael J. *The Limits of Hegemony: United States Relations with Argentina and Chile during World War II.* Notre Dame, IN: University of Notre Dame Press, 1977.

Frenkel, Roberto, and José M. Fanelli. "La Argentina y el Fondo en la década pasada." *El Trimestre Económico* 54 (1987): 75–131.

Frenkel, Roberto, and Guillermo O'Donnell. "The 'Stabilization Programs' of the International Monetary Fund and Their Internal Impacts." in *Capitalism and the State in U.S.–Latin American Relations,* ed. Richard R. Fagen, 171–216. Stanford, CA: Stanford University Press, 1979.

Frieden, Jeffry A. *Debt, Development, and Democracy: Modern Political Economy and Latin America, 1965–1985.* Princeton, NJ: Princeton University Press, 1991.

Frigerio, Rogelio. *Las condiciones de la Victoria.* Montevideo: Editoral A. Monteverde y Cia, 1963.

———. *Desarrollo y subdesarrollo económicos.* Buenos Aires: Paidós, 1984.

———. *Estatuto del Subdesarrollo.* Buenos Aires: Librería del Jurista, 1983.

Gambini, Hugo. *Frondizi. El estadista acorralado.* Buenos Aires: Editorial Vergara, 2006.

Galasso, Norberto. *De la Banca Baring al FMI.* Buenos Aires: Colihue, 2002.

García Heras, Raúl. *El Fondo Monetario y el Banco Mundial en la Argentina. Liberalismo, populismo y finanzas internacionales.* Buenos Aires: Lumiere, 2008.

———. "El plan de estabilización económica de 1958 en la Argentina." *Estudios Interdisciplinarios de América Latina y el Caribe* 11, no. 2 (2000): 137–149.

———. *Presiones externas y política económica: El Fondo Monetario Internacional y el Banco Mundial en Argentina, 1955–1966.* Bogotá: Universidad de los Andes, Cátedra Corona, 2000.

García Vázquez, Enrique. "La economía durante la presidencia de Illia." *Desarrollo Económico* 34, no. 134 (1994): 291–295.

Gardner, Richard. *Sterling–Dollar Diplomacy: Anglo-American Collaboration in the Reconstruction of Multilateral Trade.* Oxford: Clarendon, 1956.

Garfunkel, Jorge. "Economic Policy and Economic Performance: A Private Sector View of Regime Change." In *Argentina in the Crisis Years (1983–1990),* ed. Colin M. Lewis and Nissa Torrentes, 144–158. London: Institute of Latin American Studies, 1993.

Garritsen de Vries, Margaret. "The Consultation Process." In *The International Monetary Fund, 1945–1965: Twenty Years of International Monetary Cooperation,* 3 vols., ed. J. Keith Horsefield, 3 vols., 2:229–248. Washington, DC: International Monetary Fund, 1969.

———. *The IMF in a Changing World, 1945–85.* Washington, DC: International Monetary Fund, 1986.

———. "The Retreat of Bilateralism." In *The International Monetary Fund, 1945–1965: Twenty Years of International Monetary Cooperation,* 3 vols., ed. J. Keith Horsefield, 2:297–316. Washington, DC: International Monetary Fund, 1969.

Gerchunoff, Pablo, and Lucas Llach. "Capitalismo industrial, desarrollo asociado y distribución del ingreso entre los dos gobiernos peronistas: 1950–1972." *Desarrollo Económico* 15, no. 57 (1975): 3–54.

———. *El ciclo de la ilusión y el desencanto. Un siglo de políticas económicas argentinas.* Buenos Aires: Ariel, 1998.

Gerchunoff, Pablo, and Juan Carlos Torre. "La política de liberación económica en la administración de Menem." *Desarrollo Económico* 36, no. 143 (1996): 733–768.

Girbal-Blacha, Noemí. *Mitos, paradojas y realidades en la Argentina peronista (1946–1955). Una interpretación histórica de sus decisiones político-económicas.* Buenos Aires: Universidad Nacional de Quilmes, 2003.

Gold, Joseph. *Stand-by Arrangements.* Washington, DC: International Monetary Fund, 1970.

Gómez, Albino. *Arturo Frondizi. El último estadista.* Buenos Aires: Lumiere, 2004.

Gordillo, Mónica. "Los prolegómenos del Cordobazo. Los sindicatos líderes de Córdoba dentro de la estructura del poder sindical." *Desarrollo Económico* 31, no. 122 (1991): 163–187.

Gould, Erica. *Money Talks: The International Monetary Fund, Conditionality, and Supplementary Financiers.* Stanford, CA: Stanford University Press, 2006.

Green, David. *The Containment of Latin America: A History of the Myths and Realities of the Good Neighbor Policy.* Chicago: Quadrangle, 1971.

Green, Duncan. *Silent Revolution: The Rise of Market Economics in Latin America.* London: Cassell, 1995.

Hass, Peter. "Introduction: Epistemic Communities and International Policy Coordination." *International Organization* 46, no. 1 (1992): 1–35.

Helleiner, Eric. "The Development Mandate of International Institutions: Where Did It Come From?" *Studies in Comparative International Development* 44 (2009): 189–211.

———. "Reinterpreting Bretton Woods: International Development and the Neglected Origins of Embedded Liberalism." *Development and Change* 37, no. 5 (2006): 943–967.

Horsefield, J. Keith, ed. *The International Monetary Fund, 1945–1965: Twenty Years of International Monetary Cooperation,* 3 vols. Washington, DC: International Monetary Fund, 1969.

Hull, Cordell. *The Memoirs of Cordell Hull,* vol. 2. New York: Macmillan, 1948.

Ikenberry, G. John. "A World Economy Restored: Expert Consensus and the Anglo-American Postwar Settlement." *International Organization* 46, no. 1 (1992): 289–321.

———. *After Victory: Institutions, Strategic Restraint, and the Rebuilding of Order after Major Words.* Princeton, NJ: Princeton University Press, 2001.

Ikenberry, G. John, and Charles A. Kupchan. "Socialization and Hegemonic Power." *International Organization* 44, no. 3 (1990): 283–315.

James, Daniel. "The Peronist Left: 1955–1975." *Journal of Latin American Studies* 8, no. 2 (1976): 273–296.

James, Harold. *International Monetary Cooperation since Bretton Woods.* New York: Oxford University Press, 1996.

Kapur, Devesh. "The IMF: A Cure or a Curse?" *Foreign Policy* 111 (1998): 114–130.

Kapur, Devesh, John P. Lewis, and Richard Webb, eds. *The World Bank: Its First Half Century.* Washington, DC: Brookings Institution Press, 1997.

Kimball, Warren F. "'The Juggler': Franklin D. Roosevelt and Anglo-American Competition in Latin America." In *Argentina between the Great Powers, 1939–46,* ed. Guido di Tella and D. Cameron Watt, 18–33. London: Macmillan, 1989.

Klein, Naomi. *The Shock Doctrine: The Rise of Disaster Capitalism.* New York: Picador, 2007.

Kofas, Jon V. "The IMF, the World Bank, and U.S. Foreign Policy in Ecuador, 1956–1966." *Latin American Perspectives* 28, no. 5 (2001): 50–83.

———. "The Politics of Austerity: The IMF and U.S. Foreign Policy in Bolivia, 1956–1964." *Journal of Developing Areas* 29, no. 2 (1995): 213–238.

———. "The Politics of Foreign Debt: The IMF, the World Bank, and U.S. Foreign Policy in Chile, 1946–1952." *Journal of Developing Areas* 31, no. 2 (1997): 157–182.

———. "Stabilization and Class Conflict: The State Department, the IMF, and the IBRD in Chile, 1952–1958." *International History Review* 21, no. 2 (1999): 352–385.

———. *The Sword of Damocles: U.S. Financial Hegemony in Colombia and Chile, 1950–1970.* London: Praeger, 2002.

Krieger Vasena, Adalbert. *El programa económico argentino 1967/1969. Un ataque global y simultáneo a la inflación. Estabilidad y crecimiento.* Buenos Aires: Academia Nacional de Ciencias Económicas, 1998.

Kvaternik, Eugenio. "La sucesión presidencial de 1964. El fracaso de la UCRI como partido moderado." *Desarrollo Económico* 35, no. 137 (1995): 127–143.

Landi, Oscar. "La tercera presidencia de Perón. Gobierno de emergencia y crisis política." *Revista Mexicana de Sociología* 40, no. 4 (1978): 1353–1410.

Larraquy, Marcelo. *López Rega. La biografía.* Buenos Aires: Editorial Sudamericana, 2004.

Luna, Felix. *Diálogos con Frondizi.* Buenos Aires: Editorial Desarrollo, 1998.

MacDonald, Callum. "The Politics of Intervention: The United States and Argentina, 1941–1946." *Journal of Latin American Studies* 12 (1980): 365–396.

Machinea, José Luis. "Stabilisation under Alfonsín." In *Argentina in the Crisis Years (1983–1990),* ed. Colin M. Lewis and Nissa Torrentes, 124–143. London: Institute of Latin American Studies, 1993.

Manzetti, Luigi. *The International Monetary Fund and Economic Stabilization: The Argentine Case.* New York: Praeger, 1991.

Marongiu, Federico. "Políticas de shock en la agonía del estado peronista. El Rodrigazo y el Mondelliazo," Munich Personal RePEc Archive, MPRA paper no. 6338. Available online at http://mpra.ub.uni-muenchen.de/6338 (accessed July 7, 2011).

Jorge Marshall, José Luis Mardones, and Isabel Marshall. "IMF Conditionality: The Experiences of Argentina, Brazil and Chile." In *IMF Conditionality,* ed. John Williamson, 275–346. Washington, DC: Institute for International Economics, 1983.

Martínez de Hoz, José Alfredo. *Quince años después.* Buenos Aires: Emecé, 1991.

Mason, Edward, and Robert Asher. *The World Bank since Bretton Woods.* Washington, DC: Brookings Institution Press, 1973.

Mateo, Graciela. "El gobierno de Domingo Mercante. Expresión singular del peronismo clásico." *Estudios Interdisciplinarios de América Latina y el Caribe* 15, no. 2 (2004): 159–191.

McCann, Frank D. "Brazil and World War II: The Forgotten Ally. What Did You Do in the War, Zé Carioca?" *Estudios Interdisciplinarios de América Latina y el Caribe* 6, no. 2 (1995). Available online at http://www.tau.ac.il/eial/VI_2/mccann.htm (accessed August 2, 2012).

McSherry, J. Patripnce. "Strategic Alliance: Menem and the Military Security Forces in Argentina." *Latin American Perspectives* 24, no. 6 (1997): 63–92.

Meier, Gerald M. *Problems of a World Monetary Order,* 2d ed. New York: Oxford University Press, 1982.

Menem, Carlos Saúl, and Roberto Dromi. *Reforma del estado y transformación nacional.* Buenos Aires: Editorial Ciencias de la Administración, 1990.

Minsburg, Naum. *Los guardianes del dinero.* Buenos Aires: Norma, 2003.

Moggridge, Donald, ed. *The Collected Writings of John Maynard Keynes,* vol. 26. London: Macmillan, 1980.

Molineu, Harold. *U.S. Policy toward Latin America: From Regionalism to Globalism.* Boulder, CO: Westview, 1986.

Mount, Graeme S. "Chile: An Effort at Neutrality" in *Latin America during World War II,* ed. Thomas Leonard and John Bratzel, 163–182. Lanham, MD: Rowman and Little-field, 2007.

Muchnik, Daniel. *La patria financiera. El juego de la especulación.* Buenos Aires: Grupo Editorial Norma, 2005.

Mussa, Michael. *Argentina and the Fund: From Triumph to Tragedy.* Washington, DC: Institute for International Economics, 2002.

Mustapic, Ana María. "Inestabilidad sin colapso. La renuncia de los presidents: Argentina en el año 2001." *Desarrollo Económico* 45, no. 178 (2005): 263–280.

Nosiglia, Julio. *El desarrollismo.* Buenos Aires: Centro Editor de América Latina, 1983.

Novaro, Marcos, and Vicente Palermo. *La dictadura militar, 1976/1983. Del golpe de estado a la restauración democrática.* Buenos Aires: Editorial Paidós, 2006.

Ocampo, José. "New Economic Thinking in Latin America." *Journal of Latin American Studies* 22, no. 1 (1990): 169–181.

O'Donnell, Guillermo. "Modernización y golpes militares. Teoría, comparación y el caso argentino." *Desarrollo Económico* 12, no. 47 (1972): 519–566.

———. "Reflecciones sobre las tendencias de cambio del estado burocrático-autoritario." *Revista Mexicana de Sociología* 39, no. 1 (1977): 9–59.

Oliver, Robert W. *George Woods and the World Bank.* Boulder, CO: Lynne Rienner, 1995.

Ortiz, Ricardo, and Martín Schorr. "La economía política del gobierno de Alfonsín. Creciente subordinación al poder económico durante la 'década perdida.'" In *Los años de Alfonsín. ¿El poder de la democracia·o la democracia del poder?* ed. Alfredo Pucciarelli, 291–334. Buenos Aires: Siglo Veintiuno Editores Argentina, 2006.

Palacio Deheza, Carlos. *El plan Martínez de Hoz y la economía argentina.* Buenos Aires: Corregidor, 1981.

Palermo, Vicente, and John Collins. "Moderate Populism: A Political Approach to Argentina's 1991 Convertibility Plan." *Latin American Perspectives* 25, no. 4 (1998): 36–62.

Palermo, Vicente, and Marcos Novaro. *Política y poder en el gobierno de Menem.* Buenos Aires: Norma, 1996.

Pastor, Manuel, Jr. "Managing the Latin American Debt Crisis: The International Monetary Fund and Beyond." In *Creating a New World Economy: Forces of Change and Plans for Action,* ed. Gerald Epstein, Julie Graham, and Jessica Nembhard, 289–313. Philadelphia: Temple University Press, 1993.

Pettinà, Vanni. "The Shadows of Cold War over Latin America: The U.S. Reaction to Fidel Castro's Nationalism, 1956–59." *Cold War History* 11, no. 3 (2011): 317–339.

Payer, Cheryl. *The Debt Trap: The IMF and the Third World.* New York: Monthly Review, 1974.

Payne, Anthony. "After Bananas: The IMF and the Politics of Stabilisation and Diversification in Dominicana." *Bulletin of Latin American Research* 27, no. 3 (2008): 317–332.

Peralta-Ramos, Mónica. *The Political Economy of Argentina: Power and Class since 1930.* Boulder, CO: Westview, 1992.

Perón, Juan D. *Correspondencia,* vol. 1. Buenos Aires: Corregidor, 1983.

———. *La hora de los pueblos.* Buenos Aires: CS Ediciones, 2005.

———. *Todos los mensajes, discursos y conferencias completos, 1973–1974,* vol. 1. Buenos Aires: Editorial de la Reconstrucción, 1975.

Pesce, Julieta. "La gestión del ministro Grinspun en un contexto de transición democrática. Errores de diagnóstico y subestimación del poder económico local e internacional." *Ciclos* 14, no. 28 (2004): 65–88.

Pollock, David, Daniel Kerner, and Joseph Love. "Entrevista inédita a Prebisch. Logros y deficiencias de la CEPAL." *Revista de la CEPAL* 75 (2001): 9–24.

Pop-Eleches, Grigore. *From Economic Crisis to Reform: IMF Programs in Latin America and Eastern Europe.* Princeton, NJ: Princeton University Press, 2009.

Potash, Robert. *The Army and Politics in Argentina, 1945–1962.* Stanford, CA: Stanford University Press, 1980.

Prebisch, Raúl. "Five Stages in My Thinking on Development." In *Pioneers in Development,* ed. Gerald Meier and Dudley Seers, 175–191. Washington, DC: Oxford University Press, 1984.

——. *Informe preliminar acerca de la situación económica.* Buenos Aires: Secretaría de Prensa y Actividades Culturales de la Presidencia de la Nación, 1955.

Proceedings and Documents of the United Nations Monetary and Financial Conference, Department of State, Publication 2866. Washington, DC: U.S. Government Printing Office, 1948.

Ramirez, Miguel. "The Latest IMF-Sponsored Stabilization Program: Does It Represent a Long-Term Solution for Mexico's Economy?" *Journal of Interamerican Studies and World Affairs* 38, no. 4 (1996): 129–156.

Rapoport, Mario. "Argentina y la Segunda Guerra Mundial. Mitos y realidades." *Estudios Interdisciplinarios de América Latina y el Caribe* 6 (1995). Available online at www .tau.ac.il/eial/VI_1/rapoport.htm.

——. "La Argentina y la Guerra Fría. Opciones económicas y estratégicas de la apertura hacia el Este, 1955–1973." *Ciclos* 5, no. 8 (1995): 91–122.

——. *El laberinto argentino. Política internacional en un mundo conflictivo.* Buenos Aires: Eudeba, 1997.

——. "La política británica en la Argentina a comienzos de la década de 1940." *Desarrollo Económico* 16, no. 62 (1976): 203–228.

——. "La saga de los Martínez de Hoz y el banquero arrepentido." *Buenos Aires Económico,* May 5, 2010. Available online at http://www.elargentino.com/nota-89533 -La-saga-de-los-Martinez-de-Hoz-y-el-banquero-arrepentido.html (accessed August 2, 2012).

Rapoport, Mario, Eduardo Madrid, Andrés Musacchio, and Ricardo Vicente. *Historia económica, política y social de la Argentina (1880–2000).* Buenos Aires: Ediciones Macchi, 2003.

Rein, Raanan. *In the Shadow of Perón: Juan Atilio Bramuglia and the Second Line of Argentina's Populist Movement.* Stanford, CA: Stanford University Press, 2008.

Remmer, Karen. "The Political Impact of Economic Crisis in Latin America in the 1980s." *American Political Science Review* 85, no. 3 (1991): 777–800.

——. "The Politics of Economic Stabilization: IMF Standby Programs in Latin America, 1954–1984." *Comparative Politics* 19, no. 1 (1986): 1–24.

Roberts, Paul Craig, and Karen LaFollette Araujo. *The Capitalist Revolution in Latin America.* New York: Oxford University Press, 1997.

Rock, David. *Argentina, 1516–1987: From Spanish Colonization to Alfonsín.* Berkeley: University of California Press, 1987.

Rougier, Marcelo, and Martín Fiszbein. *La frustración de un proyecto económico. El gobierno peronista de 1973–1976.* Buenos Aires: Manantial, 2006.

Roza, Ednei. "The IMF and the Effects of Structural Conditionalities in Brazil: What Is About to Happen?" *Law and Business Review of the Americas* 14, no. 2 (2008): 347–365.

Russell, Roberto, and J. G. Tokatlian. "Los neutrales en la Segunda Guerra Mundial." *Ciclos* 19 (2000): 7–50.

Sachs, Jeffrey. "Social Conflict and Populist Policies in Latin America," National Bureau of Economic Research working paper no. 2897, March 1989. Available online at http://www.nber.org/papers/w2897 (accessed August 2, 2012).

Sáenz Quesada, María. *Isabel Perón*. Buenos Aires: Editorial Planeta, 2003.

Saez, Raúl. "The Nine Wise Men and the Alliance for Progress." *International Organization* 22, no. 1 (1968): 244–269.

Saiegh, Sebastian. "Do Countries Have a 'Democratic Advantage'? Political Institutions, Multilateral Agencies, and Sovereign Borrowing." *Comparative Political Studies* 38, no. 4 (2005): 366–387.

Scheetz, Thomas. *Peru and the International Monetary Fund*. Pittsburgh: University of Pittsburgh Press, 1986.

Schultz, Kenneth, and Barry R. Weingast. "The Democratic Advantage: Institutional Foundations of Financial Power in International Competition." *International Organization* 57 (2003): 3–42.

Schvarzer, Jorge, *Implantación de un modelo económico. La experiencia argentina entre 1975 y el 2000*. Buenos Aires: A-Z Editora, 1998.

Seoane, María. *El burgués maldito*. Buenos Aires: Editorial Sudamericana, 1998.

Seoane, María, and Vicente Muleiro. *El dictador. La historia secreta y pública de Jorge Rafael Videla*. Buenos Aires: Editorial Sudamericana, 2001.

Sheinin, David. *Argentina and the United States: An Alliance Contained*. Athens: University of Georgia Press, 2006.

Sikkink, Katherine. "The Influence of Raúl Prebisch on Economic Policy-Making in Argentina, 1950–1962." *Latin American Research Review* 23, no. 2 (1988): 91–114.

Siminoff, Alejandro. *Los dilemas de la autonomía. La política exterior de Arturo Illia*. Buenos Aires: Nuevohacer, 2007.

Skidmore, Thomas E. "The Politics of Economic Stabilization in Postwar Latin America." In *Authoritarianism and Corporatism in Latin America,* ed. James Malloy, 149–190. Pittsburgh: University of Pittsburgh Press, 1977.

Smith, Joseph. "Brazil: Benefits of Cooperation." In *Latin America during World War II,* ed. Thomas Leonard and John Bratzel, 144–162. Lanham, MD: Rowman and Littlefield, 2007.

Smith, Peter. *Talons of the Eagle: Dynamics of U.S.–Latin American Relations*. New York: Oxford University Press, 2000.

Smith, William. *Authoritarianism and the Crisis of the Argentine Political Economy*. Stanford, CA: Stanford University Press, 1989.

———. "State, Market and Neoliberalism in Post-Transition Argentina: The Menem Experiment." *Journal of Interamerican Studies and World Affairs* 33, no. 4 (1991): 45–82.

Smulovitz, Catalina. "Crónica de un final anunciado. Las elecciones de marzo de 1962." *Desarrollo Económico* 28, no. 109 (1988): 105–119.

———. "La eficacia como crítica y utopía. Notas sobre la caída de Illia." *Desarrollo Económico* 33, no. 131 (1993): 403–423.

Spitzer, Emil. "Factors in Stabilization Programs." In *The International Monetary Fund, 1945–1965: Twenty Years of International Cooperation,* 3 vols., ed. J. Keith Horsefield, 2:492–510. Washington, DC: International Monetary Fund, 1969.

———. "Stand-by Arrangements: Purposes and Forms." In *The International Monetary Fund, 1945–1965: Twenty Years of International Cooperation,* 3 vols., ed. J. Keith Horsefield, 2:468–491. Washington, DC: International Monetary Fund, 1969.

Stiglitz, Joseph. *El malestar en la globalización,* trans. Carlos Rodríguez Braun. Buenos Aires: Taurus, 2002.

Stiles, Kendall. "Argentina's Bargaining with the IMF." *Journal of Interamerican Studies and World Affairs* 29, no. 3 (1987): 55–85.

Stokes, Susan. *Mandates and Democracy: Neoliberalism by Surprise in Latin America.* New York: Cambridge University Press, 2001.

Szusterman, Celia. "Carlos Saúl Menem: Variations in the Theme of Populism." *Bulletin of Latin American Research* 19, no. 2 (2000): 193–206.

———. *Frondizi and the Politics of Developmentalism in Argentina, 1955–62.* London: University of Pittsburgh Press, 1993.

———. "The 'Revolución Libertadora', 1955–8," In *The Political Economy of Argentina, 1946–1983,* ed. Guido di Tella and Rudiger Dornbusch, 89–103. Pittsburgh: University of Pittsburgh Press, 1989.

Tanzi, Vito. *Argentina, an Economic Chronicle: How One of the Richest Countries in the World Lost Its Wealth.* New York: Jorge Pinto, 2007.

Tcach, César. "Radicalismo y fuerzas armadas (1962–1963). Observaciones desde Córdoba." *Desarrollo Económico* 40, no. 157 (2000): 73–95.

Tcach, César, and Celso Rodríguez. *Arturo Illia, un sueño breve. El rol del peronismo y de los Estados Unidos en el golpe militar de 1966.* Buenos Aires: Edhasa, 2006.

Tenembaum, Ernesto. *Enemigos.* Buenos Aires: Norma, 2004.

Thacker, Strom. "The High Politics of IMF Lending." *World Politics* 52, no. 1 (1999): 38–75.

Thornton, Richard C. *The Reagan Revolution II: Rebuilding the Western Alliance.* Victoria: Trafford, 2005.

Thorp, Rosemary. "The Latin American Economies in the 1940s." In *Latin America in the 1940s: War and Postwar Transitions,* ed. David Rock, 41–58. Berkeley: University of California Press, 1994.

Toussaint, Eric. "Crisis financiera en Argentina: el origen de la deuda," January 2002, available online at http://www.rcci.net/globalizacion/2002/fg214.htm (accessed August 2, 2012).

Triesman, Daniel. "Cardoso, Menem, and Machiavelli: Political Tactics and Privatization in Latin America." *Studies in Comparative International Development* 38, no. 3 (2003): 93–109.

Tulchin, Joseph S. *Argentina and the United States: A Conflicted Relationship.* Boston: Twayne, 1990.

———. "The Argentine Proposal for Non-Belligerency, April 1940." *Journal of Inter-American Studies* 11 (1969): 571–604.

———. "The United States and Latin America in the 1960s." *Journal of Interamerican Studies and World Affairs* 30, no. 1 (1988): 1–36.

Valdés, Juan Gabriel. *Pinochet's Economists: The Chicago School in Chile.* New York: Cambridge University Press, 1995.

Veigel, Klaus F. *Dictatorship, Democracy and Globalization: Argentina and the Cost of Paralysis, 1973–2001.* University Park: Pennsylvania State University Press, 2009.

Vreeland, James R. *The IMF and Economic Development.* New York: Cambridge University Press, 2003.

Weyland, Kurt. "Neopopulism and Neoliberalism in Latin America: Unexpected Affinities." *Studies in Comparative International Development* 31, no. 3 (1996): 3–31.

———. *The Politics of Market Reform in Fragile Democracies: Argentina, Brazil, Peru, and Venezuela.* Princeton, NJ: Princeton University Press, 2002.

Williams, John H. "The Postwar Monetary Plans." *American Economic Review* 34 (1944): 372–384.

Williamson, John, ed. *Latin American Adjustment: How Much Has Happened?* Washington, DC: Peterson Institute for International Economics, 1990.

———. "Reforming the IMF: Different or Better?" In *The Political Morality of the International Monetary Fund: Ethics and Foreign Policy,* vol. 3, ed. Robert J. Myers, 1–12. New Brunswick, NJ: Transaction, 1987.

Wood, Bryce. *The Dismantling of the Good Neighbor Policy.* Austin: University of Texas Press, 1985.

———. *The Making of the Good Neighbor Policy.* New York: Columbia University Press, 1961.

Woods, Ngaire. *The Globalizers: The IMF, the World Bank, and Their Borrowers.* Ithaca, NY: Cornell University Press, 2006.

Woods, Randall. "Hull and Argentina: Wilsonian Diplomacy in the Age of Roosevelt." *Journal of Interamerican Studies and World Affairs* 16, no. 3 (1974): 350–371.

Wynia, Gary. *Argentina in the Postwar Era.* Albuquerque: University of New Mexico Press, 1978.

Zuvekas, Clarence. "Argentine Economic Policy, 1958–1962: The Frondizi Government's Development Plan." *Inter-American Affairs* 22 (Summer 1968): 45–73.

Index

0 1341 1501589 0

RECEIVED

MAY 2 9 2013

GUELPH HUMBER LIBRARY
205 Humber College Blvd
Toronto, ON   M9W 5L7

Claudia Kedar is a Lecturer in the Department of Romance and Latin American Studies and in the School of History at the Hebrew University of Jerusalem.